MW00988386

Coleridge's Afterlives

Coleridge's Afterlives

Edited by

James Vigus and Jane Wright

Selection and editorial matter © James Vigus and Jane Wright 2008
Individual chapters © contributors 2008

All rights reserved. No reproduction, copy or transmission of this
publication may be made without written permission.

No paragraph of this publication may be reproduced, copied or transmitted
save with written permission or in accordance with the provisions of the
Copyright, Designs and Patents Act 1988, or under the terms of any licence
permitting limited copying issued by the Copyright Licensing Agency, 90
Tottenham Court Road, London W1T 4LP.

Any person who does any unauthorised act in relation to this publication
may be liable to criminal prosecution and civil claims for damages.

The authors have asserted their rights to be identified as the authors of
this work in accordance with the Copyright, Designs and Patents Act 1988.

First published 2008 by
PALGRAVE MACMILLAN
Houndmills, Basingstoke, Hampshire RG21 6XS and
175 Fifth Avenue, New York, N.Y. 10010
Companies and representatives throughout the world

PALGRAVE MACMILLAN is the global academic imprint of the Palgrave
Macmillan division of St. Martin's Press, LLC and of Palgrave Macmillan Ltd.
Macmillan® is a registered trademark in the United States, United Kingdom
and other countries. Palgrave is a registered trademark in the European
Union and other countries.

ISBN-13: 978-0-230-00828-1   hardback
ISBN-10: 0-230-00828-3   hardback

This book is printed on paper suitable for recycling and made from fully
managed and sustained forest sources. Logging, pulping and manufacturing
processes are expected to conform to the environmental regulations of the
country of origin.

A catalogue record for this book is available from the British Library.

A catalog record for this book is available from the Library of Congress.

10   9   8   7   6   5   4   3   2   1
17 16 15 14 13 12 11 10 09 08

Printed and bound in Great Britain by
CPI Antony Rowe, Chippenham and Eastbourne

Contents

Preface

'I assume a something, the proof of which no man can *give* to another, yet every man may *find* for himself.'[1]

Something of Coleridge's life and work has continued to offer later writers the materials, the methods, the potential to find or to do something for themselves. In this quotation from *Aids to Reflection* (1825), the word 'something' manages to make both a specific reference (to human moral awareness) and a gesture at vaguer possibilities of thought, a poise that is as important as it is apt. Coleridge's afterlives, like his voice on the page, often manifest at once compelling, even rigid, authority and great liberality, offering multiple interpretative avenues that Coleridge himself exploited as he speculated energetically and changed his mind on numerous subjects throughout his life. If, as Seamus Perry has argued, a kind of 'enabling inconsistency' is characteristic of Coleridge's writings, something similar is true of the reactions of his later readers.[2] Echoing Coleridge's own characterisation of Shakespeare, Edgar Allan Poe called Coleridge a 'myriad-minded man'[3]; he has been perceived at once as poet, philosopher, theologian and talker; 'muddle-brained metaphysician'[4]; youthful radical and Sage of Highgate; opium-addict and austere moralist. The present volume presents 14 commissioned contributions to explore roughly a century of Coleridge's afterlives, from his death in 1834 until the year of I. A. Richards's *Coleridge on Imagination* (1934). Richards's intervention, though distinctively a production of Cambridge English, marks the beginning of a new phase in Coleridge's reception history, one based above all on the *Biographia Literaria* and emphasising imagination and practical criticism.[5] At the same time, however, in appropriating Coleridge's thought for his own purposes, Richards's approach typifies much of what had gone before. In 1934, when Eliot asked him whether he had finished his book on Coleridge, Richards replied:

My *Coleridge* – after having turned into a goods train heavily if richly laden – has suddenly turned into a sort of meteor and gone up into the Heavens. It's now a revelation of the essential mythopoeic faculty and settles provisionally all such things as the status of poetic belief (and some others), the co-ordinates of the mind-drift (with some tentative measures of it) and the definition range of Nature. It's all in Coleridge; but it has taken a little interrogation to get it from him.[6]

With that 'settles provisionally' and the phrase 'a little interrogation', Richards acknowledged the fine balancing act required by his task, and the sense that if Coleridge had not quite *given* him all of the proof he wanted, through Coleridge he was still able to '*find* it for himself'.

This essay collection is timely in three senses. First, readers of Coleridge have now had a few years to ruminate upon the completion of the Princeton *Collected Coleridge*, which was some 40 years in the making. The 'new' material that has emerged provides modern readers with a fuller picture of Coleridge than their nineteenth- and early twentieth-century predecessors enjoyed. The appearance of works such as the *Opus Maximum* has also had an important subsidiary effect: to revitalise the speaking voice of Coleridge as he delighted, harangued, and dictated to his contemporaries and younger followers, thus giving us a fresh perception of him. This reminds us of the Coleridge that Arthur Hallam described as a 'good old Man most eloquent, / Who spake of things divine'; the Coleridge that nineteenth-century writers most often encountered and recollected.[7]

Second, this volume of essays contributes to the growing interest in (Romantic) afterlives, recently reflected in publications on (among others) Wordsworth, Byron, Keats and Carlyle. John Beer has subtly explored Coleridge's thinking about the nature of consciousness and its traces in the work of a number of Victorian and later writers.[8] But no study has yet attempted the temporal and interdisciplinary range afforded by our 14 contributions. At a pivotal moment in Modernist thinking, Eliot declared that 'Coleridge was perhaps the greatest of English critics.'[9] He is a figure representative of the contradictory, amalgamated, multiple and ranging needs and practices of our present literary critical work.[10] Now is a good time to highlight this aspect of his heritage explicitly. Coleridge, in other words, lies at the heart of our project, while his own example also calls for acknowledgement of such a project's critical principles.

Third, *Coleridge's Afterlives* supports the current shift away from discussion of Coleridge in terms of a seemingly monolithic and now outdated sense of 'Romantic ideology'. The suspicion that literary research suffers from what Jerome McGann calls an 'uncritical absorption' in the terms and methods of Romanticism has admittedly contributed much to historical precision.[11] In the past few years, however, a welcome reaction has formed against the tendency of ideology-criticism to construct a simplified and deplorable literary 'tradition'. The concept of 'after-lives' accordingly acknowledges the presence of particular but diverse traditions arising from the same writer; traditions at once various and in productive strife with each other. Coleridge has elicited so many con-structions (and deconstructions) that it is impossible for us to read him unmediated. He has been modified by his own afterlives, just as he has modified others. The concept of 'afterlives' describes and allows for process, revision and renewal in the changing responses to texts over time. It recognises that while Coleridge has influenced the fields of poetry, literary criticism, philosophy, theology, social theory and others, these studies have also influenced the Coleridge we read: the process is reciprocal.

Both the concept of literary afterlives and Coleridge's afterlives in par-ticular may never be entirely stable. Literary afterlives might develop from intellectual sympathies that are difficult to document precisely, or they might be formed (as some of Coleridge's were) through considera-tion of sometimes uncomfortably concrete details. William Hazlitt, for example, found Coleridge's genius 'like a spirit [...] eternally floating about in etherealities'[12], and suggested that one 'who has marked the evening clouds uprolled (a world of vapours) has seen the picture of his mind, unearthly, unsubstantial, with gorgeous tints and ever-varying forms'.[13] Leigh Hunt, on the contrary, responded to a 'very corporeal' Coleridge, 'very fond of earth'; one 'reposing with weight enough in his easy chair, [...] a mighty intellect put upon a sensual body'.[14] The first biography, James Gillman's *Life of Coleridge* (1838), may have been (in De Quincey's withering judgement) deader than a doornail;[15] yet a very live biographical focus inflects many subsequent responses to Coleridge, and accordingly appears in several chapters in this volume. It is often implicit in discussions of Coleridge in the period we have selected for study – as indeed in the present day – that his literary and philosophi-cal achievements cannot be considered apart from troublesome ques-tions about his personal conduct. Matthew Arnold declared harshly of Coleridge that 'he had no morals', while Leslie Stephen asked whether a man is to be forgiven for having deserted his family because he has written 'The Ancient Mariner'.[16] Since that time, however, research into the circumstances of Coleridge's life has led to a more explicitly sympa-thetic appraisal from modern biographers than these Victorian writers could have produced.[17]

Though some early responses are ambivalent, many describe absorption in the bewilderment of encountering Coleridge. In *The Life of John Sterling* (1851), Thomas Carlyle describes the experience of listening to Coleridge and sums up the uncertainty the listener may feel with a watery simile that recurs in other such accounts.[18] Carlyle states that Coleridge's

> was talk not flowing anywither like a river, but spreading every-whither in inextricable currents and regurgitations like a lake or sea [...]; *what* you were to believe or do, on any earthly or heavenly thing, obstinately refusing to appear from it. So that, most times, you felt logically lost; swamped near to drowning in this tide of ingenious vocables, spreading out boundless as if to submerge the world.[19]

Other natural similes for describing Coleridge's fertilizing (if not swamping) force were more positive, though still tempered by awareness that the sheer breadth and multiplicity of his influence would probably prove difficult to assess. Wordsworth, for one,

> believed Coleridge's mind to have been a widely fertilizing one, & the seed he had so lavishly sown in his conversational discourses & the Sybilline leaves (not the poem [*sic*] so called by him) which he had scattered abroad so extensively covered with his annotations, had done so much to form the opinions of the highest-educated men of the day; although this might be an influence not likely to meet with adequate recognition.[20]

If he could seem to have no morals, Coleridge's life and work, nevertheless, both demonstrated and demanded a struggle for understanding that for many made his example constructively permissive. The remainder of Arnold's remark makes this clear; he writes:

> that which will stand of Coleridge is this: the stimulus of his continual effort [...] Coleridge's great usefulness lay in his supplying in England, for many years and under critical circumstances, by the spectacle of this effort of his, a stimulus to all minds, in the generation which grew up around him, capable of profiting by it; his action will still be felt as long as the need for it continues; when, with the cessation of the need, the action too has ceased, Coleridge's memory, in spite of the disesteem – nay, repugnance – which his character may and must inspire, will yet forever remain invested with that interest and gratitude which invests the memory of founders.[21]

In this essay, 'Joubert; or a French Coleridge' (1864), Arnold considered Joubert more *'possible'* than Coleridge and suggested that the

Highgate Sage had been unfortunately limited by both his geographical and historical location, as well as by drug addiction.[22] Yet the critical attempt to assess possibility was itself a particularly Coleridgean one. The possibilities for extended sympathy that Coleridge offered, and Henry James noted, also fit the endeavours of the present volume. In a Notebook entry of 1894, James had Coleridge in mind as he began to sketch a challenging new character and the dramatic potential for a story about him; he wrote:

> Would not such a drama necessarily be the question of acceptance by someone – someone with something important at stake – of the general responsibility of rising to the height of accepting him for what he is, recognizing his rare, anomalous, magnificent, interesting, curious tremendously suggestive character, vices and all, with all its imperfections on its head, and not be guilty of pedantry, the stupidity, the want of imagination, of fighting him, deploring him in the details – failing to recognize that one must pay for him and that on the whole he is magnificently worth it.[23]

'Something' of Coleridge gave vitality to this creative testing of 'someone' with 'something' to risk. In the resulting work – *The Coxon Fund* (1895) – James's narrator imagined the Coleridgean character as 'a great suspended, swinging crystal, huge, lucid, lustrous, a block of light, flashing back every impression of life and every possibility of thought'.[24] Some of those possibilities remain for the future; others are elucidated for the first time in the following pages.

*

At this point in a preface to an essay collection it is usual to offer a summary account of the following chapters. Readers looking for an overview are invited, instead, to turn to the end of the book, where John Beer reflects on each of the contributions and gives his own view on the nature of Coleridge's afterlives as here revealed. Chapter 1, 'Coleridge's Textual Afterlives', which charts Coleridge's posthumous publication history, is also designed as an introduction to the themes of the later chapters.

Preparation for this book took longer than planned, partly because, alongside compiling and editing it, we were both writing Ph.D. dissertations and then taking up our first post-doctoral posts. We are grateful to all the contributors of these essays for their interest, support and patience. But there is one we should like to thank in particular: Seamus Perry, who was unfailingly generous with suggestions, guidance and reading. Thanks to all those at Palgrave who have helped us to prepare this volume. We thank Continuum for permission to reprint a slightly revised version of Paul Hamilton's chapter, 'The Consummate Symbol: A Coleridgean Tradition' (chapter 11), which first appeared as 'Reading from the Inside: Coleridge's Contemporary Philosophical Idiom', in *Coleridge and German Philosophy: The Poet in the Land of Logic* (London: Continuum, 2007), pp. 103–120; and the Wordsworth Trust for permission to reprint the cover image. For support of different kinds, we also thank Jeff Barbeau, Stephen Cheeke, Lesel Dawson, Cecilia Muratori, Daniel Neill, Francis O'Gorman, Daren Randell, and our families. A fond acknowledgement, at last, to Chester, a black cat who lives in Cambridge and whose nine lives brighten up the contrastingly singular life of the graduate students he visits.

The Editors

Notes

1. *Aids to Reflection*, ed. John Beer (Princeton, NJ: Bollingen, 1993), p. 136.
2. Seamus Perry, *Coleridge and the Uses of Division* (Oxford: Oxford University Press, 1999), p. 3.
3. *Biographia Literaria*, ed. by James Engell and W. Jackson Bate, 2 vols (1983), II, 19; and Poe, Review of *Letters, Conversations and Recollections of S. T. Coleridge*, in *Essays and Reviews*, ed. G. R. Thompson (New York: Viking, 1984), pp. 181–8, p. 181; first published in the *Southern Literary Messenger*, June 1836.
4. William Morris, quoted in J. W. Mackail, *The Life of William Morris* (London: Longmans, Green, 1899), 2 vols, I, p. 310.
5. See A. C. Goodson, *Verbal Imagination: Coleridge and the Language of Modern Criticism* (New York and Oxford: Oxford University Press, 1988), pp. 3–27.
6. 22 March 1934, Ibid., p. 77.
7. 'Timbuctoo', ll.161–2, *The Writings of Arthur Hallam*, ed. T. H. Vail Motter (London: Oxford University Press, 1943), pp. 42–3.
8. *Romantic Consciousness* and *Post-Romantic Consciousness* (Basingstoke: Palgrave Macmillan, 2003).
9. T. S. Eliot, 'The Perfect Critic' in *The Sacred Wood: Essays on Poetry and Criticism*, 3rd edn (London: Methuen, 1932; first published 1920), p. 1.
10. For recent work to complicate and advance understanding of the many forms that literary influence can take, see Robert Douglas-Fairhurst, *Victorian Afterlives: The Shaping of Influence in Nineteenth-Century Literature* (Oxford: Oxford University Press, 2002).
11. See Jerome McGann, *The Romantic Ideology: A Critical Investigation* (Chicago University Press, 1983), pp. 1, 137.
12. Leigh Hunt summarising Hazlitt's view, cited in Richard W. Armour and Raymond F. Howes, *Coleridge the Talker: A Series of Contemporary Descriptions*

and Comments (New York and London: Johnson Reprint Corp., 1969, first published 1940), p. 266.

13. Hazlitt, 'Mr. Coleridge', in *The Spirit of the Age*, ed. E. D. Mackerness (London and Glasgow: Collins, 1969; first published 1825), pp. 54–67, pp. 54–5.

14. Leigh Hunt (1828), quoted in *Coleridge the Talker*, p. 226.

15. 'Coleridge and Opium Eating', first published in *Blackwood's Magazine* (January 1845), 177–32, reprinted in *The Works of Thomas De Quincey*, 21 vols (London: Pickering & Chatto, 2003), XV, 102–25, p. 104.

16. Matthew Arnold, 'Joubert' (1864) in *The Complete Prose Works of Matthew Arnold*, ed. R. H. Super, 11 vols (Ann Arbor: University of Michigan Press, 1960–77), III, 189 (hereafter cited as 'Joubert'); Leslie Stephen, 'Coleridge' (1888), in *Hours in a Library*, 3 vols (London: Smith, Elder & Co., 1892), III, 341–2.

17. For a sympathetic evaluation of Coleridge's treatment of his family, see Anya Taylor, *The Erotic Coleridge* (Basingstoke and New York: Palgrave, 2005), pp. 125–44.

18. John Beer, *Romantic Influences* (Basingstoke: Macmillan, 1993), pp. 64–5.

19. *The Works of Thomas Carlyle*, 30 vols (London: Chapman and Hall, 1897), XI, 55.

20. Robert Percival Graves to Felicia Hemans, 12 August 1834, quoted in Juliet Barker, *Wordsworth: A Life in Letters* (London, 2002), pp. 227–8.

21. 'Joubert', p. 190.

22. Ibid., p. 193.

23. *The Notebooks of Henry James*, ed. F. O. Matthiessen and Kenneth B. Murdock (New York: Oxford University Press, 1961), p. 152.

24. *The Coxon Fund* (1895), in *The Complete Tales of Henry James*, 12 vols (London: Rupert Hart-Davis, 1964), IX, 133.

List of Contributors

John Beer is Emeritus Professor of English Literature at Cambridge University. Since his first book, *Coleridge the Visionary*, in 1959, he has published numerous articles and books on Coleridge and related writers: *Romantic Influences* (Macmillan, 1993) and *Romantic Consciousness* (Palgrave Macmillan, 2003) are among the most recent, each reaching to the heart of Coleridge's afterlives.

Frederick Burwick is Professor of English at University of California, Los Angeles. He is author of *Thomas De Quincey: Knowledge and Power* (Palgrave Macmillan, 2001) and edited *Coleridge's* Biographia Literaria: *Text and Meaning* (Ohio State University Press, 1989). He is co-editor of the *Works of Thomas De Quincey* (Pickering and Chatto, 2000–2003), and of *Faustus, translated from the German of Goethe by Samuel Taylor Coleridge* (Oxford University Press, 2007).

Paul Hamilton is Professor of English and Drama at Queen Mary, University of London. He is author of several books including *Coleridge's Poetics* (Basil Blackwell, 1983) and *Metaromanticism* (University of Chicago Press, 2003); he contributed the chapter 'The Philosopher' to *The Cambridge Companion to Coleridge* (Cambridge, 2002) and has just published *Coleridge and German Philosophy: The Poet in the Land of Logic* (Continuum, 2007).

Anthony John Harding is Emeritus Professor in the Department of English at the University of Saskatchewan, Canada. He has edited the final volume (V) of Coleridge's *Notebooks* (2002) and is currently working on an online index to the *Notebooks*. Of his many publications those especially oriented to Coleridge's afterlives are *Coleridge and the Inspired Word* (McGill-Queen's University Press, 1985), and 'Coleridge as Mentor and the Origins of Masculinist Modernity' (European Romantic Review, December 2003).

Douglas Hedley is a Fellow of Clare College, Cambridge, and Senior Lecturer in the Philosophy of Religion in the Faculty of Divinity at the University of Cambridge. He is the author of *Coleridge, Philosophy and*

Religion: Aids to Reflection *and the Mirror of the Spirit* (Cambridge, 2000) and *The Living Forms of the Imagination* (T & T Clark, 2008).

Daniel Karlin is Professor of English at the University of Sheffield. He has published extensively on the work of Robert and Elizabeth Barrett Browning and on Rudyard Kipling; he is the editor of the *Penguin Book of Victorian Verse* (1998). He is the author of *Proust's English* (Oxford University Press, 2005) and is writing a book on the figure of the singer in English poetry.

Seamus Perry is a Fellow of Balliol College, Oxford, and Lecturer in English Literature, Oxford. He is the author of *Coleridge and the Uses of Division* (Oxford University Press, 1999), and many critical articles including 'Coleridge the Talker' in *The Cambridge Companion to Coleridge* (Cambridge University Press, 2002), which discusses later writers' responses to Coleridge. He has also published a biography, *Samuel Taylor Coleridge* (British Library, 2003).

Lynda Pratt is Reader in Romanticism at the University of Nottingham. She is general editor of *Robert Southey: Poetical Works, 1793–1810* (Pickering and Chatto, 2004) and co-general editor of *The Collected Letters of Robert Southey* (forthcoming). She has published several Coleridgean articles including 'The "Sad Habits" of Samuel Taylor Coleridge: Unpublished Letters from Joseph Cottle to Robert Southey 1813–17', *Review of English Studies* (2004).

Stephen Prickett is Director of the Armstrong Browning Library and Margaret Root Brown Professor for Browning Studies and Victorian Poetry at Baylor University, Waco, Texas, as well as Regius Professor Emeritus of English Language and Literature at the University of Glasgow, Scotland. His books include the classic study of theological influence *Romanticism and Religion: The Tradition of Wordsworth and Coleridge in the Victorian Church* (Cambridge University Press, 1974), and *Narrative, Science and Religion: Fundamentalism versus Irony 1700–1999* (Cambridge University Press, 2002).

Daniel Sanjiv Roberts is Senior Lecturer in English at Queen's University Belfast. He is the author of *Revisionary Gleam: De Quincey, Coleridge and the High Romantic Argument* (Liverpool University Press, 2000) and has edited De Quincey's *Autobiographic Sketches* and Southey's

The Curse of Kehama for the major collective editions from Pickering and Chatto.

James Vigus is a postdoctoral researcher at the Friedrich-Schiller-University, Jena. Author of *Platonic Coleridge* (Legenda 2008), he is reviews editor for the Coleridge Bulletin, and is currently preparing an edition of Henry Crabb Robinson's essays on German philosophy.

Laura Dassow Walls is John H. Bennett, Jr., Chair of Southern Letters at the University of South Carolina. She has published two books on Thoreau and, most recently, *Emerson's Life in Science: The Culture of Truth* (Cornell University Press, 2003). Currently she is completing her next book project, *The Passage to Cosmos: Alexander von Humboldt and Planet America*, on Humboldt and the concept of Cosmos in nineteenth-century America.

Ross Wilson holds a Leverhulme Trust Early Career Fellowship at Emmanuel College, Cambridge. He is the author of *Subjective Universality in Kant's Aesthetics* (Peter Lang, 2007) and of *Theodor Adorno* for the Routledge Critical Thinkers series (Routledge, 2008). He is also editing a volume on the idea of 'life' in Romantic poetry and poetics. He has recently been awarded a Leverhulme Early Career Fellowship to research '"Immortal Verse" in British Romanticism'.

Jane Wright is Lecturer in English at the University of Bristol. She has published articles on Tennyson and Clough and is currently writing a book on sincerity in Victorian poetry and criticism. Other projects include editing the unpublished letters of the Tennyson family. She is reviews editor for the *Tennyson Research Bulletin*.

1
Coleridge's Textual Afterlives

James Vigus

The modern reader of Coleridge can choose from a range of anthologies, or delve into the *Collected Coleridge*. The earlier readers of Coleridge discussed in this book, however, did not possess these materials, and so their encounters with him necessarily differed from ours. One major difference is quantitative. Coleridge has been posthumously prolific to an extent unique among the Romantics: the rich diversity of his afterlives owes something to the fact that his manuscripts continued to trickle into print throughout the twentieth century, and into the twenty-first. Thus the majority of Coleridge's informal writing – his *Notebooks*, *Marginalia*, and *Letters* – has appeared only during the last half-century or so. Many of the pieces in *Shorter Works and Fragments* (1995) were also new to all but a few specialists. Further, three central texts of Coleridge's later philosophy were unknown except by hearsay until recently: the shorthand manuscript of the *Lectures on the History of Philosophy*, discovered in the 1930s and published in 1949; *Logic*, first published in full in 1984;[1] and most esoteric yet most substantial of all, the *Opus Maximum*, which arose phoenix-like in spite of rumours of its non-existence, in 2002. The fragments comprising the *Logic* and *Opus Maximum* were withheld from publication after Coleridge's death by J. H. Green, to whose scrupulous care Coleridge had entrusted them; while Green's own synthesis, though an interesting complement to Coleridge's later thought, was inadequate as a substitute for it.[2] Twentieth-century editors, however, laboured to present all this material in a readable form, as well as collating the multiple versions of Coleridge's poems. As a result, it is now clear that those Victorian writers who complained of Coleridge's indolent lack of productivity were wrong, though they could not have known.[3]

That is not to claim, however, that the generations following Coleridge's death were deprived of his work. Indeed, many of the afterlives traced in this volume testify to the extent to which the Victorian and later publishing industry busied itself with the enormous task of collecting, selecting, and packaging the philosopher-poet's texts. During his lifetime few of these were widely diffused (he described himself ruefully as 'Author of Tomes whereof, though not in Dutch, the public little knows, the publisher too much'[4]); but this was to change as the nineteenth century wore on. In general the Victorians had more opportunity to read Coleridge's works than his direct contemporaries enjoyed – with the single exception of the political essays. In his time, Coleridge commanded the largest readership with essays in newspapers such as the *Courier* and the *Morning Post*. Although Sara Coleridge, his daughter, assembled a thorough volume of *Essays on His Own Times* in 1850, some half a century later Coleridge's grandson Ernest Hartley Coleridge was to lament that this volume was 'long out of print [... and] scarcely known even to the student of literature.'[5] With this exception, however, the century after Coleridge's death saw an impressive succession of available editions.

The present chapter reviews these editions.[6] It aims both to outline in what textual forms the writers discussed in this book and their readers could have encountered Coleridge; and to highlight certain prefaces and commentaries now largely forgotten, but which remain of intrinsic interest. These two aims are related, in that prefaces both contribute to shape the responses of readers and reflect editors' own expectations as to the prior assumptions of those readers. Coleridge's textual afterlives are of much more than antiquarian interest. Intrinsic to the critical concept of 'afterlife' is that the writer whom we encounter today has been modified by his own after-history: our 'Coleridge' is not static, but evolves perpetually from past constructions of his work. As William St Clair has recently emphasised, for instance, the modern canon of English literature as taught in traditional courses was essentially established in the Victorian period;[7] and this process is nowhere more evident than in the treatment of Coleridge. A few of Coleridge's poems, above all 'The Rime of the Ancient Mariner', 'Christabel', and 'Kubla Khan', were canonised by Victorian poetry anthologies, whereas his prose remained the preserve of a minority, albeit an influential one.[8] Even today, Coleridge is popularly known only for the poems just named, while even undergraduate courses often omit his prose, with the exception of *Biographia Literaria*, a work that became quite central to English literature as a university discipline in the early twentieth century.

The separation of Coleridge's poetry from his prose was accompanied by sharply divergent assessments of the latter. Jackson writes of 'the Victorian enthusiasm for Coleridge's prose', noting that the posthumously published works 'consisted almost entirely of prose, and one of the most striking features of the change that took place in Coleridge's reputation between 1834 and 1900 was the development of the public perception of him as a thinker.'[9] Jane Wright's chapter in this book ('The Sin in Sincerity: ethics, aesthetics, and a critical tradition from Coleridge to Wilde', chapter 9) refines this perspective, suggesting a literary critical afterlife for Coleridge's own emphasis on thinking and taste in Oscar Wilde's defini-tion of the true critic. Devotees of Coleridge's verse, however, frequently *disapproved* of the prose, believing the poet to have wasted his genius by indulging in abstruse metaphysics (as he was supposed to have indulged in opium). Leigh Hunt's statement of the contrast is also typical of its time in contrasting the Englishness of Coleridge's poetry with the foreignness of his philosophy. Hunt introduces a comparison with Eastern thought, which, in the light of Daniel Roberts's chapter ('"The Luther of Brahminism": Coleridge and the Reformation of Hinduism', chapter 6, this volume), may have been truer than he knew:

He was the finest dreamer, the most eloquent talker, and the most orig-inal thinker of his day; but for want of complexional energy, did noth-ing with all the vast *prose* part of his mind but help the Germans to give a subtler tone to criticism, and sow a few valuable seeds of thought in minds worthy to receive them. Nine-tenths of his theology would apply equally well to their own creeds in the mouths of a Brahmin or a Mussulman. His poetry is another matter. It is so beautiful [...].'[10]

Sixty years later Arthur Symons rather similarly summed up the perspec-tive of the partisans of Coleridge's verse, declaring that the prose is

[...] for the most part [...] a kind of thinking aloud, and the form is wholly lost in the pursuit of ideas. With his love for the absolute, why is it that he does not seek after an absolute in words considered as style, as well as in words considered as the expression of thought? In his finest verse Coleridge has the finest style perhaps in English; but his prose is never quite reduced to order from its tumultuous amplitude or its snake-like involution. Is it that he values it only as a medium, not as an art? His art is verse, and this he dreads, because of its too mortal closeness to his heart; the prose is a means to an end, not an end in itself.[11]

Again the notion that Coleridge exhibited a 'love for the absolute' hints at a taint of foreign – in this case German – influence. This influence was often blamed for truncating his artistic achievements as well as introducing a potentially unwholesome element into English thought: 'we owe to Coleridge as much as to anybody', declared T. S. Eliot archly in 1929, 'our enjoyment of the doubtful benefits of German Idealism.'[12] (This topic is unfolded by Ross Wilson, 'Coleridge's German "Absolutism"', chapter 10, this volume.)

Given that most readers would have encountered Coleridge's poetry and prose separately, I accordingly divide the following discussion in two. There was just one notable exception to this division: the *Complete Works of Samuel Taylor Coleridge* edited by W. G. T. Shedd (Philadelphia, 1853, reprinted 1871, 1884), the only edition ever to profess completeness prior to the modern Bollingen collection. However, confirming Coleridge's own recognition that 'I am a poor poet in England, but I am a great philosopher in America', Shedd's real interest is in the prose.[13] Shedd's introduction defends 'Coleridge as a Thinker': he celebrates his 'refutation' of pantheism and his 'general method of Theologizing', though criticises the lack of provision for the doctrine of atonement in his theology. The contents of the edition are *Aids to Reflection* and *Statesman's Manual* (volume one), *The Friend* (two), *Biographia Literaria* (three), notes on Shakespeare, etc. (four), *Literary Remains* (five), *Church and State* (six), and *Poetical and Dramatic Works* (seven). This was a 'complete' Coleridge in the limited sense of incorporating reprints of all the editions edited by Sara Coleridge and/or Henry Nelson Coleridge to date (see below).[14]

J. R. de J. Jackson's chronology of major editions from 1834–1900 lists mainly prose works.[15] I argue, however, that the relative importance of editions of prose and poetry depends on one's criteria. In terms of long-term influence on religious, philosophical, and literary critical thought, the new prose editions indeed stand out. But in terms of acts of reading among the burgeoning Victorian reading classes, editions of the poetry – especially cheap editions and those with prefaces by well-known writers – were more important than bibliographies and critical discussions usually acknowledge.

Part one: Prose

Biographia Literaria

In 1844 Hunt mentioned that a friend had recently shown him a copy of the *Biographia* (first published in 1817), which he had not seen for 22 years.[16] As this anecdotal evidence suggests, the second edition of 1847 re-circulated a rather scarce work. In her fascinating if labyrinthine introduction, Sara Coleridge addresses the issues of the moment, first and foremost defending Coleridge against the charge of plagiarism. (See Frederick Burwick, 'De Quincey on Coleridge', chapter 3, this volume.) Second, she argues for his religious orthodoxy, claiming that he completed the Kantian critical philosophy by harmonising it with Christianity.[17] Third, she rebukes Joseph Cottle for publishing incriminating evidence of Coleridge's opium addiction without the family's consent. (See Lynda Pratt, '"Let not Bristol be ashamed"? Coleridge's Afterlife in the *Early Recollections* of Joseph Cottle', chapter 2, this volume.) A large appendix, containing many marginalia to Schelling, further buttressed Coleridge's position as interpreter of German thought: a deep concern of later nineteenth-century interpreters of Coleridge. These materials were omitted from subsequent editions, however, and by the time of Arthur Symons's edition of 1906, and Shawcross's of 1907, the *Biographia* was valued for a quite different reason: its 'practical criticism' of English poetry. Shawcross's *Biographia*, the standard edition for most of the twentieth century, emphasised the concept of imagination as, above all, a literary critical faculty and correspondingly incorporated the essays 'On Poesy or Art', 'On Taste', 'On Beauty', and 'On the Principles of Genial Criticism' as appendices. Such an emphasis was duly confirmed by I. A. Richards's influential monograph *Coleridge on Imagination* (1934) and shortly afterwards by R. G. Collingwood's *The Principles of Art* (1938), whose argument is rooted in a Coleridgean view of imagination. (See Douglas Hedley, 'Imagination Amended: From Coleridge to Collingwood', chapter 12, this volume.)

Aids to Reflection and *Confessions of an Inquiring Spirit*

The theological work *Aids to Reflection*, though today gradually emerging from a long period of neglect, was immensely popular on both sides of the Atlantic in the nineteenth century. In terms both of its responsiveness to the Higher Criticism of the Bible stemming from Germany and of its aphoristic method, it formed a model for the Hare brothers' comparable work *Guesses at Truth*. (See Stephen Prickett, 'Romantic Fragments and Victorian Pluralisms: From *Lyrical Ballads* to *Guesses at Truth*', chapter 4, this volume.) First published in 1825, it had run to eight editions by 1856. James Marsh's 'Preface' to the 1829 edition, emphasising Coleridge's poeticised concept of Reason, was vital to the new Transcendentalist movement. (See Laura Dassow Walls, 'Ralph Waldo Emerson and Coleridge's American Legacy', chapter 7, this volume.)

However, a major theological controversy ensued in America when the Congregationalist Marsh's interpretation was directly challenged in 1839 by an edition from an Episcopalian, John McVicar.[18] Just how central

Coleridge's theology was to American debates at the time is reflected in a furious tract published anonymously in New York in 1844, entitled *Coleridge and the Moral Tendency of His Writings*. '[T]he theological mists of Coleridgism have been spreading themselves among us', warns the 'Advertisement' to this tract. Attacking Coleridge's opposition to modern Calvinism and his supposed tendency to Pantheism, the writer fumes that the proper title of *Aids to Reflection* should be 'Leighton's Aids to Evangelical Piety, corrupted and perverted by Coleridge'.[19]

The 1840 publication of *Confessions of an Inquiring Spirit*, which Coleridge had originally envisaged as prefatory to *Aids*, occasioned further controversy.[20] The work's denial of the doctrine of literal biblical inspiration further inflamed a debate that had become central to the credibility of the Church of England; so that the second edition of 1849 contained an eruditely defensive introduction by Green, together with a concluding note by Sara Coleridge defending her father against the charge of 'the subversion of faith' levelled in a recent review article.[21] Indeed, the contentious attempt to establish Coleridge's reputation as a '*Christian* philosopher'[22] was key to all these mid-nineteenth-century family editions. Yet just a few years later, the third edition (London: Edward Moxon, 1853) cut most of these editorial materials. Although *Confessions* was printed with *Aids* and the 'Essay on Faith' in 1884 (London: Bell), and Herbert Stewart acclaimed it as 'perhaps [Coleridge's] clearest and most definite service' in theology in 1918, it was sidelined thereafter, and is now buried rather unfortunately in the midst of a volume of *Shorter Works and Fragments*.[23]

A yet more striking instance of a Coleridgean afterlife now buried in an obscure text is Sara Coleridge's 200-page essay *On Rationalism*, which appeared as an appendix to the fifth edition of *Aids to Reflection* (1843) but was reprinted only once (in the sixth edition, 1848). *On Rationalism* is a Coleridgean defence of the Protestant concept of Reason, boldly aimed against John Henry Newman's proto-Catholic 'Tracts for the Times' and (still more) his 'Lectures on Justification'. Despite its theological coherence and pertinence in adapting the arguments of *Aids to Reflection* to the mid-century debate, Sara's essay was not collected in Edith Coleridge's 1873 edition of her letters, and has been rather dismissively treated by biographers and critics of Sara's work.[24]

The Friend, Church and State, Lay Sermons

The 1818 *The Friend* was republished by William Pickering in 1837 in octavo, then again for a wider readership in 12mo (1844) and 16mo (1850). The sixth edition was revised by the author's son Derwent

Coleridge in 1863, by which time the work had evolved considerably from the precarious periodical begun 50 years earlier. Meanwhile the 'Essays on the Principles of Method' in *The Friend* had their own after-life in the form of the *Treatise on Method* that Coleridge contributed to the *Encyclopaedia Metropolitana* in 1818. To Coleridge's fury, the editors considerably altered his text and published it without a proper financial agreement – but the 28-volume encyclopaedia was finally completed in 1845, and enjoyed remarkable success into the twentieth century.[25]

A compound edition of *On the Constitution of The Church and State according to the Idea of Each; Lay Sermons; The Statesman's Manual* was published by H. N. Coleridge (London: William Pickering, 1839), while Derwent Coleridge also edited the *Lay Sermons* in 1852.

New works

Personal and biographical material

Contemporaneously with De Quincey's and Cottle's salacious biographical accounts, there appeared a volume of *Letters, Conversations and Recollections of S. T. Coleridge* (1836, second edition 1858), edited by Thomas Allsop – a work generally felt to portray its subject as bigoted and egotistical.[26] The family editors, on the other hand, laboured to enhance his reputation, not only through the new editions of the *Biographia* and other works noted above, but also through H. N. Coleridge's *Specimens of the Table Talk of S. T. Coleridge* (1835). Despite the acknowledged impossibility of conveying Coleridge's fluid discourse in a series of short summaries, the *Table Talk* proved popular, and a Bohn's Standard Library edition was edited by Thomas Ashe in 1884.

It was not until the 1890s, however, that James Dykes Campbell (with his 1894 biography, see below) and E. H. Coleridge (who edited the *Letters* and *Anima Poetae*, an important selection from Coleridge's notebooks in 1895) presented the life and private thought in a quite new light. Their belief that the more of Coleridge's life was uncovered, the more he would be vindicated from the charge of immoral personal conduct, has persisted among the more sympathetic modern editors and biographers.

Criticism

H. N. Coleridge published four volumes of *Literary Remains* from 1836–9. Derwent Coleridge's edition of *Notes on English Divines* (1853) was mainly drawn from this source, but his *Notes, Theological, Political, and Miscellaneous* (1853) contained about two-thirds new material. Although the editors invariably tidied up the fragments, these works did much to establish Coleridge's reputation as a writer of critical prose. Scattered criticism of Shakespeare was gathered in Sara Coleridge's *Notes and Lectures upon Shakespeare and Some of the Old Poets and Dramatists with other Literary Remains of S. T.* Coleridge, 2 vols (London: Pickering, 1849); while the prolific Shakespeare editor John Payne Collier published a version of his notes on Coleridge's 1811–12 lectures.[27] In a second edition, however, Collier appended to this text a series of emendations of Shakespeare's plays, which he claimed to have discovered in an old book, but had almost certainly forged himself.[28] The resulting controversy deflected attention from the Coleridge material, though Thomas Ashe did collect everything thus far extant in *Lectures and Notes on Shakespeare* (1883). Over a hundred years later, however, R. A. Foakes decoded Collier's original shorthand notes and discovered them to be more reliable than the version he had written up and embellished in 1856. The resulting authoritative texts appeared in the Bollingen *Lectures 1809–1818 on Literature* (2 vols, 1987).

Other works

The collection of *Essays on His Own Times* (1850) and *Confessions of an Inquiring Spirit* (first published 1840) have already been mentioned. A work whose appearance surprised and apparently irritated the family editors was *Hints towards the Formation of a More Comprehensive Theory of Life*, edited by Seth B. Watson (1848). The *Theory of Life* (as it is now titled) reflects Coleridge's most wholehearted period of engagement with German *Naturphilosophie* around 1816. It attracted respectful notice in the few reviews it received,[29] and was reprinted in another of Ashe's collections, *Miscellanies, Aesthetic, and Literary: to which is added The Theory of Life* (London: Bell, 1885). Ashe contributes some speculation about its authorship: whereas Watson believed it to have been co-written by Coleridge and Gillman, Ashe cites a letter by Sara Coleridge referring to 'my father's "Idea of Life"' as evidence that it probably contains little by Gillman. It was later discovered that Coleridge wrote the work, but for Gillman's use;[30] but the authorship debate illustrates how closely Coleridge was believed to have worked with his inner circle.

Part two: Poetry

Many of the prose editions just mentioned were landmarks in Coleridge scholarship. Yet although *The Friend, Aids to Reflection* and, later in the nineteenth century, the *Table Talk* were published in relatively inexpensive editions that would have sold well, the many family editions of

Coleridge's prose were relatively costly and their readership therefore restricted. Editions of the poetry, on the other hand, though not important from a scholarly perspective until the 1890s, proliferated, especially in cheap versions; and I would argue that the increased accessibility of the poetry to all classes of reader was at least as important a later nineteenth-century development as the publication of 'new' prose. This argument owes much to St Clair's pioneering and thorough work *The Reading Nation in the Romantic Period*. If bibliographers heed St Clair's call for print runs, prices, and sales figures to be recorded wherever possible, and for cheap editions to be fully listed, the encounters of ordinary readers with Coleridge (and not only Coleridge) will be greatly illuminated. What follows is no more than a provisional step in this direction.

Coleridge's poetical works, like those of Wordsworth, were relatively expensive during his lifetime: only about 7,000 copies were sold, a paltry figure beside Byron's 200,000 or Thomas Campbell's 45,000.[31] From the late 1820s onwards, however, their accessibility increased vastly. The first cause of this was the cheap reprint (or piracy, from the perspective of the official English publisher) by the Paris publisher Giovanni Antonio Galignani, *The Poetical Works of Coleridge, Shelley and Keats* (Paris, 1829).[32] Galignani's text is taken from *The Poetical Works of S. T. Coleridge* (London: William Pickering, 1828), of which only 300 copies were printed:[33] thus Galignani popularised a very substantial collection. Since this edition drastically undercut the London price, it made reading Coleridge on the continent or in America (it was reprinted in Philadelphia, 1831) easier than in England. Four issues of the Paris edition had appeared by 1835.[34] As St Clair comments, 'The three poets whom it was most difficult to buy from the mainstream bookshops in Britain, Coleridge, Shelley, and Keats, were available to mainstream readers in the United States a generation before they reached such audiences in Britain' (St Clair, 387). The Galignani edition was also prescient in linking Coleridge with those two obscure poets, Shelley and Keats: a link that was to become a Victorian commonplace. The edition duly filtered through to England, and even Wordsworth, though he complained of Galignani's piracy of his own work, acquired a copy of *Coleridge, Shelley and Keats*; while Ruskin recalled the 'large octavo containing the works of Coleridge, Shelley and Keats which so often lay on my niche table' in his boyhood (St Clair, 302).

Between the Galignani edition of 1829 and E. H. Coleridge's monumental *Complete Poetical Works of Samuel Taylor Coleridge* (Oxford, 1912), Coleridge's poetry could be read in four roughly distinct forms: (i) the official *Poetical Works* published by Pickering, then Moxon, then Macmillan; (ii) cheap, rival editions; (iii) books of selected works, often illustrated; and (iv) anthologies. Each of these deserves a separate comment.

Official *Works*

The 1829 edition of the Pickering *Poetical Works* (i.e. the sixth edition) differed quite substantially from that of 1828. It, in turn, was succeeded by a three-volume edition in 1834, the last to appear in the poet's lifetime, edited by H. N. Coleridge. The latter contained 'Juvenile Poems' and 'Sibylline Leaves' (volume one); 'The Ancient Mariner', 'Christabel', 'Miscellaneous Poems', and the dramas *Remorse* and *Zapolya* (two); plus the translations of Schiller's plays, i.e. *The Piccolomini* and *The Death of Wallenstein* (three). It was reprinted five times in the next seven years, then superseded by *The Poems of S. T. Coleridge* (1844 and 1848, though the latter omitted the dramas). The English rediscovery of Schiller warranted a separate publication of Coleridge's translations: in 1846 there appeared a Bohn's Standard Library edition of *The Works of Friedrich Schiller. The Piccolomini. The Death of Wallenstein. Translated by S. T. Coleridge*; then came the family edition, *The Dramatic Works of Samuel Taylor Coleridge*, edited by Derwent Coleridge (London: Edward Moxon, 1852).

Meanwhile Sara Coleridge, with Derwent's help, produced a new, broadly chronological arrangement of the poetry in *The Poems of Samuel Taylor Coleridge* (London: Edward Moxon, 1852). Sara based her arrangement on the texts of 1817 and 1828, for which Coleridge himself had been largely responsible, and split the poems into categories of 'Youth', 'Early Manhood', and 'Declining Age'. This edition was republished in 1863, and again in a new and enlarged form in 1870.

These family efforts laid the foundations for some fine editions thereafter. The four-volume *Poetical and Dramatic Works of Samuel Taylor Coleridge*, edited by Richard Herne Shepherd (London: Pickering, 1877, revised 1880), added 28 'new' poems and a biographical memoir – the latter being a standard feature of editions published after Coleridge's death. Next in the sequence was a two-volume edition by Ashe (London: Bell, 1885). Ashe's extensive introduction celebrates Coleridge as pre-eminently a subtle and imaginative observer of nature: 'Coleridge's imagination—his "shaping spirit of imagination", as he himself puts it—was his fairest possession. The process of its working was methodical as frost-crystals, subtle as odour of flowers'. In this Ashe is following an interpretation by Swinburne (discussed below). Ashe believes that Coleridge was little influenced by other poets, but damaged by the egotistical pursuit of metaphysics. His biographical sketch draws on Cottle's *Early Recollections*, and it comments that 'There is a touch of good-natured humour about the gossiping little publisher, which makes us like him, even when we do not trust him'.[35] (Such supercilious attitudes to Cottle are further discussed by Lynda Pratt in chapter 2.)

A greater milestone in Coleridge editing, however, was James Dykes Campbell's single-volume *Poetical Works* (Macmillan, 1893), based on the 1829 text but adding new poems. Campbell's edition is both comfortably readable and distinguished for its full life of Coleridge. Campbell then extended this life into a separate biography, which inspired Henry James's short story 'The Coxon Fund', and remains a valuable account today.[36] Soon afterwards, Ernest Hartley Coleridge enjoyed Campbell's co-operation for his own project, *The Complete Poetical Works* of 1912. This latter remained the standard edition for the rest of the twentieth century; yet being based on the 1834 text, its editorial principles are diametrically opposed by J. C. C. Mays's Bollingen edition, which contends that there is no reason to print from later collections if a poem is available in an early, authoritative text.[37]

Rival editions

Editions rivalling the official family editions (and selections of Coleridge in general anthologies of poetry – see the Anthologies section, below) became possible as various works published during the poet's lifetime trickled out of copyright. The rival editions tended to be cheaper and more accessible than the official family editions. Derwent Coleridge's 'Preface' to *Poems* (1852) acknowledges the 'competition' of these rival editions, averring '[t]hat the literary productions of S. T. Coleridge should after a given period pass from under the control of his executors is right and fitting. That they should be brought out at the earliest period permitted by law, in various forms, by watchful and expectant publishers, is not a matter of surprise, and will not be alleged by me as a matter of blame.' But predictably enough, this is the prelude to a declaration that his own will for many years be the only complete, or nearly complete, edition. This was true, in the sense that the 1842 Copyright Act extended copyright to a minimum of 42 years from a work's first publication (or the author's lifetime plus seven years):[38] meaning that the family edition was safe until near the end of the nineteenth century. However, Coleridge had died before the 1842 Act, at a time when, under the 1814 Act, the term of copyright was somewhat shorter: 28 years. This meant that certain of his works became generally available much sooner – *Poems* (1796), or the 'Ancient Mariner' of 1798, being clear-cut cases.

Some cheap editions were published in the 1830s and 1840s, therefore, but they did not include all of the most famous works. 'Some contain versions of *The Rime of the Ancient Mariner*, first published in 1798, but the cheap editions mainly consisted of *Poems* (1796), occasional poems which had first appeared in newspapers and whose position under copyright law was uncertain, and some of the plays.'[39] A reader of one of the cheap editions would therefore have encountered a rather eighteenth-century-flavoured Coleridge, sometimes eccentrically presented. For example, the tiny volume *The Ancient Mariner, and other Poems* printed by Scott (London, 184?) reprints the poems of 1796, along with others such as 'Genevieve'; but its centrepiece is the 1834 version of 'The Rime of the Ancient Mariner', with the marginal gloss printed in the form of endnotes to the poem. The copy of this book in the University Library, Cambridge, is bound together with Falconer's 'Shipwreck' and the poems of Bloomfield, so reinforcing the eighteenth-century presentation of Coleridge. The frontispiece depicts an albatross above a crossbow, around which is coiled a winged serpent with a human skull.

Despite such irregularities of text and content, however, it is true that as the nineteenth century wore on, ever more presentations of Coleridge became available, many of great interest. When David Scott published his illustrations of the 'Ancient Mariner' in 1837, he set a trend: notable followers were J. Noel Paton followed in 1863 and, most famously, Gustav Doré in 1875.[40] The number and variety of such illustrated editions is testimony to the extent to which the 'Ancient Mariner' gripped the collective imagination until well into the twentieth century, a compulsion which Daniel Karlin traces in narratorial figures in fiction. (See Daniel Karlin, '"I Have Strange Powers of Speech": Narrative Compulsion After Coleridge', chapter 8, this volume.)

Selections

Countless volumes of selections, often with celebrity prefaces, appeared from the late 1850s, once most of Coleridge and other Romantic poets had reached the public domain.[41] Series of cheap reprints of the 'English Classics' became very popular,[42] and their prefaces influential. The idea of Coleridge as inspired author of a few poems of genius but nothing else of worth was established by Swinburne's selection,[43] and other editors followed him. Of 'Kubla Khan' and 'Christabel' Swinburne declares, 'There is a charm upon these poems which can only be felt in silent submission of wonder', celebrating the 'melody and splendour' of the one, and the surpassing 'sweetness' of the other, and summing up: 'for height and perfection of imaginative quality he is the greatest of lyric poets. This was his special power, and this is his special praise.' Regarding his later work, 'The rare fragments of work done or speech spoken in his latter years are often fragments of gold beyond price', but due to lack of self-command, he emerged all too rarely from the 'holy and pestilential jungle' of transcendental metaphysics.[44] As Anthony Harding observes in chapter 5, Swinburne constructs the poet in gendered terms, as femininely sensitive to beauty, but too weak to sustain his unparalleled achievements for long. Swinburne is quoted and echoed in a selection of Coleridge by William Michael Rossetti. The latter adds the view that Coleridge's achievement was hampered by 'tenuity of *character*, a want of grasp of realities in life as realities'; Rossetti very unusually finds even the 'Ancient Mariner' 'essentially meagre—defective in the core of common sense'.[45]

Echoes both of Swinburne's lyrical manner and his interpretation appear in Stopford Brooke's *Golden Book of Coleridge* (London: J. M. Dent, 1895), a selection of the few 'very best' poems together with a number of others supposedly inferior. Celebrating Coleridge's 'Preface' to *Poems* (1796) Brooke writes:

> The languid meditativeness of his character, combined with hours of ardent delight in all things; his child-like pity for himself; the imaginative dreaminess, which he had not enough physical animation to continuously meet in battle, to which we owe part of his special charm, and which was never ungraceful, for it was mixed with so much love; the self-thinking, in which he was more pleased with the thinking than with the self—are already contained in this preface, and are still more vividly present in the poems that follow it.
>
> (8)

Love, glossed as 'love for mankind' in general, is, for Brooke, the leading quality of Coleridge's life, redeeming him from the 'brutal' moral charges levelled by critics such as Carlyle; while the juvenile poems are significant in embodying the transition between 'the reticent grace' of Gray and Collins and the new energy of *Lyrical Ballads*.

Richard Garnett's once-famous 'Preface' to *The Muses' Library* edition of Coleridge's poetry likewise responds to Swinburne, agreeing that 'our estimate of him is formed entirely by a consideration of a phial of some of the most quintessential poetry in the world' – the 'Ancient Mariner',

'Christabel', 'Kubla Khan', 'Genevieve', and 'The Nightingale'.[46] In asserting that Coleridge's 'was one of the class of minds which require to be impregnated' (xxvi), Garnett adopts Swinburne's feminisation of the poet. However, he follows Brooke in printing a larger selection than Swinburne supplies, on the basis that Coleridge's minor work is significant in being obviously transitional between eighteenth-century (intellectual) and nineteenth-century (imaginative) modes. According to Garnett the superiority of the latter is now 'undisputed', and this can be intuitively sensed by comparing 'Frost at Midnight' with any usual eighteenth-century descriptive poetry (even Coleridge's own): 'we are conscious of a great deliverance, an emergence into a higher and purer region.'[47]

Later accounts of Coleridge's lyric genius likewise emphasised its subtle and ethereal beauty. Arthur Symons wrote that 'Rossetti called Coleridge the Turner of poets, and indeed there is in Coleridge an aerial glitter which we find in no other poet, and in Turner only among painters. With him colour is always melted in atmosphere, which it shines through like fire within a crystal. It is liquid colour, the dew on flowers, or a mist of rain in bright sunshine.'[48] The persistence of this comparison between Coleridge and Turner is illuminated by Paul Hamilton's investigation of the Coleridgean roots of Ruskin's famous image of Turner as 'the master of the science of *Essence*'. (Paul Hamilton, 'The Consummate Symbol: A Coleridgean Tradition', chapter 11, this volume.)

It is ironic that Swinburne, the notorious transgressor, had thus established a new orthodoxy regarding Coleridge's poems. Yet even the criteria themselves by which he judged a few of Coleridge's poems surpassingly beautiful constitute, in a way, a Coleridgean afterlife. Not only is this choice responsive to the personal mythology of 'Kubla Khan', according to which the briefly inspired poet might never remember the symphony and song once 'given' to him; but also, in his criticism, Swinburne frequently echoed Coleridge's distinction between primary and secondary imagination.[49]

Anthologies

If the effect of the selections with prefaces was to canonise a few of Coleridge's poems as representing the essence of his genius, general anthologies of poetry carried this process even further. Once again it was from the late 1850s, once most copyrights on their work had trickled away, that Romantic period works could begin to appear in anthologies (St Clair, 224). Since they were so commercially successful, Victorian poetry anthologies were therefore responsible for diffusing Coleridge, along with other Romantics, to a wider audience than ever before.[50] However, this diffusion was in another sense limited. In Robert Aris Willmott's deluxe *The Poets of the Nineteenth Century* (London: Routledge, 1857), Coleridge is represented only by 'Love'. At the other end of the market, Palgrave's *Golden Treasury* of 1861 (which cost just 4s 6d, later reduced to 3s 6d) prints only 'Love' and 'Youth and Age', compared with 41 specimens of Wordsworth, and 11 of Campbell.[51] Another popular collection, Robert Inglis's edition of *Gleanings from the English Poets. Chaucer to Tennyson* (Edinburgh: Gall and Inglis, 1862, 1881), prints the Mariner's concluding moral to the Wedding Guest, together with brief extracts from 'Ode to the Departing Year', the 'Hymn Before Sunrise', and *Christabel*. Although the readership for such books may have been extensive, then, the selections themselves were not.

Conclusion

The magnificent Bollingen *Collected Coleridge* now overshadows the majority of the texts discussed in this chapter. Yet without awareness of these past editions, we can never fully appreciate the diversity of ways in which Coleridge lived on through successive generations of readers. Editions from 1834 to the early twentieth century are usually valued chiefly insofar as they discovered 'new' material, unpublished during the writer's lifetime; and this was indeed a major achievement of the family editors. Prefaces and appendices such as those by Sara Coleridge ('Preface' to the *Biographia*, 1847; *On Rationalism*, Appendix to *Aids*, 1843) deserve continued attention, but are very inaccessible today. However, given that traditional 'parade models' of landmark texts fail to correspond to the experiences of the majority of actual readers (as St Clair has so well demonstrated), the proliferation of cheap editions of Coleridge selections and their prefaces, and the rise of general anthologies, must be considered at least as significant as the 'new' prose works. If Swinburne's was the most influential of the prefaces, those by Brooke and Garnett should not be forgotten; while all kinds of earlier Coleridgean curiosities are probably still languishing on dusty shelves, awaiting the attention of a library cormorant.

Many of these works could be recovered for modern readers through electronic publication. Indeed, if the present book runs to a second edition in the future, I hope that 'Coleridge's electronic afterlives' might form a substantial chapter. In the meantime, his textual afterlives alone seem sufficient to justify Goethe's maxim, aptly quoted by Holmes at the conclusion of his biography of Coleridge, that the one proof of genius is posthumous productivity.[52]

Notes

1. *Logic*, ed. J. R. de J. Jackson (Princeton, NJ: Bollingen, 1984). Alice D. Snyder, *Coleridge on Logic and Learning* (New Haven: Yale University Press, 1929), published selections from *Logic* with an excellent introduction.
2. On Green's reasons and the resulting controversy, see Thomas McFarland's introduction to *Opus* (pp. cxliii–clvii) and Snyder, *Coleridge on Logic*, pp. 66–74. For a full discussion of the genesis of the *Opus Maximum*, see Jeffrey W. Barbeau, 'The Quest for System: An Introduction to Coleridge's Lifelong Project', in *Coleridge's Assertion of Religion: Essays on the Opus Maximum*, ed. by Jeffrey W. Barbeau (Leuven: Peeters, 2006), pp. 1–32. J. H. Green, *Spiritual Philosophy: Founded on the Teaching of the Late Samuel Taylor Coleridge*, ed. John Simon, 2 vols (London: Macmillan, 1865); see further John Beer, *Romantic Influences* (Basingstoke: Palgrave Macmillan, 1993), p. 149.
3. For one such accusation, see De Quincey's article on Coleridge in the 8th edition of the *Encyclopaedia Britannica*; cf. Alan Gregory, 'Putting Him in His Place: Coleridge in the *Encyclopaedia Britannica*', *Coleridge Bulletin*, n.s. 20 (Winter 2002), pp. 137–40.
4. *The Notebooks of Samuel Taylor Coleridge*, ed. Kathleen Coburn, Merton Christensen and Anthony Harding, 5 vols in 10 (New York, London, and Princeton, New Jersey: Routledge and Kegan Paul, 1957–2002), V, 5868; cf. *The Collected Letters of Samuel Taylor Coleridge*, ed. Earl Leslie Griggs, 6 vols (Oxford: Oxford University Press, 1956–71), V, lix.
5. In G. H. B. Coleridge, 'Biographical Notes, Being Chapters of Ernest Hartley Coleridge's Fragmentary and Unpublished Life of Coleridge', in *Coleridge: Studies by Several Hands on the Hundredth Anniversary of His Death* ed. Edmund Blunden and Earl Leslie Griggs (London: Constable, 1934), p. 42.
6. No full bibliography of editions of Coleridge has yet been compiled. I have referred to Richard Herne Shepherd, *The Bibliography of Coleridge [...] Revised, Corrected and Enlarged by Colonel W. F. Prideaux* (London: Frank Hollings, 1890); John Louis Haney, *A Bibliography of Samuel Taylor Coleridge* (Philadelphia, printed for private circulation, 1903); and Thomas J. Wise, *A Bibliography of the Writings in Prose and Verse of Samuel Taylor Coleridge* (London: Richard Clay & Sons, 1913). Haney's bibliography was reprinted together with his *Coleridgeiana* (London, 1919) in a single volume (London, 1970). Haney is fullest and most reliable; but still omits many of the cheaper editions. For secondary literature, invaluable is the following three-volume bibliography: vol. I: *Samuel Taylor Coleridge: A Bibliography of Criticism and Scholarship [1793–1899]*, ed. Richard Haven, Josephine Haven, and Maurianne S. Adams (Boston: G. K. Hall & Co., 1976); vol. II: *Samuel Taylor Coleridge: A Bibliography of Criticism and Scholarship [1900–39]*, ed. Walter B. Crawford and Edward S. Lauterbach, assisted by Ann M. Crawford (Boston: G. K. Hall & Co., 1983); vol. III: *Part I, 1793–1994, including Supplement to Volume I, 1793–1939; Comprehensive Bibliography, 1940–1965; Selective Bibliography, 1966–1994; and Part II, 1791–1993*, ed. Walter B. Crawford, assisted by Ann M. Crawford, New York: G. K. Hall & Co., 1996). For further

information and updates on the Crawford bibliography, see: http://www. csulb.edu/library/donors/Crawford/Supplement2003.html.

7. *The Reading Nation in the Romantic Period* (Cambridge: Cambridge University Press, 2004). Henceforth: St Clair.

8. See e.g. John Beer, 'Coleridge's Elusive Presence among the Victorians', *Romantic Influences* (Basingstoke: Macmillan, 1993), pp. 147–68.

9. *Coleridge: The Critical Heritage* (London: Routledge and Kegan Paul, 1970), ed. J. R. de J. Jackson, p. 1.

10. *Imagination and Fancy*, ed. Edmund Gosse (London: Gresham, n.d.; first published 1844), pp. 263–4. Hunt's view is, of course, one-sided: the English heritage of Coleridge's theological prose is highlighted throughout Douglas Hedley, *Coleridge, Philosophy and Religion: Aids to Reflection and the Mirror of the Spirit* (Cambridge: Cambridge University Press, 2000).

11. Arthur Symons, *The Romantic Movement in English Poetry* (London: Archibald Constable, 1909), p. 136.

12. 'Experiment in Criticism'; in *Tradition and Experiment in Present-Day Literature: Addresses Delivered at the City Institute* (London: Oxford University Press, 1929), 198–215, p. 202.

13. T. W. Reid, *The Life, Letters and Friendships of Richard Monckton Milnes* (Place unspecified: Cassell, 1890), II, 432, quoted in *Aids to Reflection*, ed. John Beer (Princeton, NJ: Bollingen, 1993), p. cxxviii.

14. There was considerable overlap between English and American editions from around the time of Coleridge's death: the official 'family' editions were invariably reprinted in America shortly after their first appearance in England.

15. *Critical Heritage*, II, 24–6.

16. Hunt, p. 4 (n.)

17. For a similar perspective, compare F. J. A. Hort's well-informed essay, 'Coleridge', in *Cambridge Essays, contributed by members of the University* (Cambridge: Cambridge University Press, 1856), pp. 292–351.

18. See Alice D. Snyder, 'American Comments on Coleridge a Century Ago', in *Coleridge: Studies by Several Hands*, 201–21, pp. 214–21; *Aids*, cxx–cxxii.

19. Pp. 5, 10. (*Aids* quotes and discusses many aphorisms by the seventeenth-century archbishop Robert Leighton.)

20. Ed. H. N. Coleridge (London: William Pickering, 1840; facsimile reprint Menston: Scolar Press, 1971).

21. William Palmer, 'Tendencies toward the Subversion of Faith', *English Review* X (December 1848), 399–444. For the attribution to Palmer, see C. R. Sanders, *Coleridge and the Broad Church Movement* (Durham, North Carolina: Duke University Press, 1942), p. 239.

22. J. C. Hare, 'Samuel Taylor Coleridge and the English Opium-Eater', *British Magazine and Monthly Register of Religion and Ecclesiastical Information*, 1 January 1835, 7 (1), 15–27, p. 15.

23. Herbert L. Stewart, 'The Place of Coleridge in English Theology', *Harvard Theological Review* 11 (1918), 1–31, p. 19. On the reception history of *Confessions of an Inquiring Spirit*, see Jeffrey W. Barbeau, *Coleridge, the Bible, and Religion* (New York: Palgrave Macmillan, 2007), chapter 9.

24. See Jeffrey W. Barbeau, 'Sara Coleridge the Victorian Theologian: Between Newman's Tractarianism and Wesley's Methodism', *Coleridge Bulletin* n.s. 28 (Winter 2006), 29–36.

25. *S. T. Coleridge's Treatise on Method, as published in The Encyclopaedia Metropolitana*, ed. Alice D. Snyder (London: Constable, 1934).
26. *Critical Heritage*, II, 5.
27. *Seven Lectures on Shakespeare and Milton* (London: Chapman and Hall, 1856).
28. See Arthur Freeman and Janet Ing Freeman, *John Payne Collier: Scholarship and Forgery in the Nineteenth Century*, 2 vols (New Haven and London: Yale University Press, 2004), I, 670–91; II, 1230–2.
29. *Critical Heritage* II, 13; 134–40.
30. Coleridge, *Shorter Works and Fragments*, ed. by H. J. Jackson and J. R. de J. Jackson, 2 vols (Princeton, NJ: Princeton University Press, 1995), I, 481–557, p. 481.
31. St Clair, p. 217; for prices and print-runs of each edition, see pp. 594–5.
32. Edited with introductory lives of the poets by Cyrus Redding. Reprinted in facsimile with an introduction by Jonathan Wordsworth (Othey and Herndon: Woodstock, 2002).
33. Figure from Haney.
34. All had 1829 on the title page. Noted by Mays in *PW* I, cxxiv.
35. Pp. cxxviii, xix–xx.
36. *Samuel Taylor Coleridge* (London and New York: Macmillan, 1894, 1896). A hundred years on, Campbell's work was warmly appreciated by the biographer Richard Holmes: see *Coleridge: Early Visions* (London: Hodder & Stoughton, 1989), p. xiii.
37. I, cxlvii. For criticism of E. H. Coleridge's texts and collation of variants, see David V. Erdman, 'Unrecorded Coleridge Variants', *Studies in Bibliography* 11 (1958), 143–62.
38. See Catherine Seville, *Literary Copyright Reform in Early Victorian England: The Framing of the 1842 Copyright Act* (Cambridge: Cambridge University Press, 1999).
39. St Clair (p. 208n.), who cites *The Poetical and Dramatic Works of Samuel Taylor Coleridge, With a Life of the Author* (John Thomas Cox, 1836); *The Poetical and Dramatic Works of Samuel Taylor Coleridge, With a Life of the Author* (Allman, 1837); *The Poetical Works of Samuel Taylor Coleridge, With Life of the Author* (Daly, n.d., c. 1839); *The Poetical and Dramatic Works of Samuel Taylor Coleridge* (John James Chidley, 1847); and *The Poetical and Dramatic Works of Samuel Taylor Coleridge, New Edition* (Daly, n.d.).
40. Robert Woof and Stephen Hebron, *The Rime of the Ancient Mariner* (Grasmere: Wordsworth Trust, 1997) is a beautiful collection of illustrations to the 'Ancient Mariner' with commentary. See further Antje Klesse, *Illustrationen zu S. T. Coleridges 'Rime of the Ancient Mariner'* (Memmingen: Curt Visel, 2001).
41. See St Clair, p. 420, and Appendix 13 (pp. 715–23).
42. Richard D. Altick, 'From Aldine to Everyman: Cheap Reprint Series of the English Classics 1830–1906', *Studies in Bibliography* 11 (1958), 3–25.
43. *Christabel, and the Lyrical and Imaginative Poems of S. T. Coleridge* arranged and introduced by Algernon Charles Swinburne (London: Sampson Low, and New York: Scribner & Welford, 1869) 16mo [Bayard Series], reprinted 1875. Swinburne's introduction is reprinted in *Critical Heritage*, II, 145–56.
44. Ibid., pp. 263, 275, 271.
45. *The Poetical Works of Samuel Taylor Coleridge*, edited with a Critical Memoir by William Michael Rossetti (London: E. Moxon, 1872), pp. xxv, xxvi.

46. *The Poetry of Samuel Taylor Coleridge* (London and New York, 1898), p. xxii. Garnett's introduction was reprinted in *Essays of an Ex-Librarian* (London and New York, 1901), pp. 55–97.
47. Pp. xxx–xxxi.
48. *Romantic Movement*, p. 142.
49. Thomas E. Connolly, *Swinburne's Theory of Poetry* (New York: State University of New York, 1964), pp. 53–63.
50. Sabine Haas, 'Victorian Poetry Anthologies: Their Role and Success in the Nineteenth-Century Book Market', *Publishing History* 17 (1985), 51–64.
51. *The Golden Treasury*, ed. Francis Turner Palgrave (Cambridge and London: Macmillan, 1861); facsimile reprint with an introduction by Andrew Motion (Basingstoke: Palgrave Macmillan, 2000).
52. Richard Holmes, *Coleridge: Darker Reflections* (London: HarperCollins, 1998), p. 561.

2
'Let not Bristol be ashamed'?: Coleridge's Afterlife in the *Early Recollections* of Joseph Cottle

Lynda Pratt

> The refuse of advertisements and handbills, the sweepings of a shop, the shreds of a ledger, the rank residuum of a life of gossip,—this forty-years' deposit of Bristol garbage, smeared in the very idiocy of anecdote-mongering on a shapeless fragment, and a false name scratched in the filth [...] Unable, or unwilling, to distinguish between the statement and censure of a vice or a weakness, and a pandering to the vilest curiosity by a narrative of the loathsome minutiæ of either, this respectable writer of biography, 'as it ought to be,' in performance, as he says, of a solemn duty, prints and publishes a mass of wretched reminiscences, which, unless sick rooms are to be invaded, and the symptoms and phases of bodily disease recorded for the delectation of the crowd, the least supposable attention to the decencies of life, the most ordinary regard for the awfulness of our common humanity, would have left, where they were found, in the shade.[1]

Thus – for just under eight pages – fulminated the *Quarterly Review* in July 1837 about one of the earliest attempts to construct Samuel Taylor Coleridge's afterlife. Joseph Cottle's two-volume *Early Recollections* (1837), the subject of this critical rubbishing, was – and has remained – one of the most controversial accounts of its subject, attacked by nineteenth-century, and more recent, critics for both its cavalier handling of original documents and its queasy mix of gossip and Christian morality.[2] Even the climate of canonical revisionism that has dominated recent studies of the romantic period has – as yet – had little impact on

Cottle's reputation.[3] Although the importance of his narrative of the time Coleridge spent in Bristol is now acknowledged, it is still viewed as untrustworthy. As Rosemary Ashton, one of Coleridge's most recent biographers, notes, Cottle is an unfortunate and unreliable necessity: 'We must treat his account with caution, but we cannot do without it.'[4]

The *Early Recollections* appeared at a potentially crucial time for Coleridge's posthumous life, during a period when competing claims for and about him were being made by his family, friends and critics.[5] The instability and incoherence of his reputation were, indeed, manifested in the pages of the *Quarterly Review*, which noticed the *Early Recollections* after, and against, a detailed and laudatory appraisal of Coleridge's two-volume *Literary Remains* (1836), edited by his nephew and son-in-law Henry Nelson Coleridge.[6] This juxtaposition of very different, conflicting, views of Coleridge presented readers with the potential – and radically alternative – afterlives that awaited him. Was Coleridge, as the *Quarterly* notice of the *Literary Remains* claimed, 'one of the most brilliant and pro-found of English writers, in the higher and more generally interesting departments of criticism'?[7] Or was he, as Cottle's memoir implied, a sad addict, financially and morally indebted to others: would his moral example as someone who had wasted prodigious talents be, as the *Edinburgh Review* suggested, 'more extensively and practically useful than all [...] he ever wrote'?[8] Was Coleridge a success or a failure? Was he a man who had laboured for the benefit of society and the nation, or had he been irretrievably mired in self-abuse and selfishness?

The *Quarterly*'s attack on Cottle (which he responded to in early 1839 in a second preface to the *Early Recollections*) was a direct result of these ambivalences and uncertainties.[9] Indeed its author was none other than Henry Nelson Coleridge, one of the chief promoters of Coleridge as con-temporary prophet and sage. Yet even given the context in which it appears, the review does seem particularly vicious and personal. Undoubtedly, the *Quarterly Review* and the Coleridge family's fury at Cottle's book were shaped by private knowledge of what lay behind its production.[10] Since shortly after Coleridge's death in 1834, Henry Nelson and Sara Coleridge and their representatives had become involved in a series of increasingly tense and acrimonious negotiations with Cottle. The subject of these had been the letters written by Coleridge to his publisher and friend between the mid 1790s (when the two had first met) and c. 1815 (the date of the last surviving letter in their correspondence).[11] The Coleridge family wished Cottle to hand these manuscripts over so that they could be used in an 'official' life – probably one written by Joseph Henry Green, Coleridge's literary executor and the family-designated

biographer. However, Cottle, concerned that any 'official' life would sani-
tise the life actually lived by Coleridge, was unwilling to do so and moved
increasingly to the idea of producing his own, as he saw it, unvarnished
memoir based upon these and other documentary sources. The end results
were both the opening up of an unbridgeable gulf between himself and
the Coleridge estate, and the composition and publication of the *Early
Recollections*.[12]

As if these personal tensions were not enough, another potent factor in
the hostility Cottle's memoir encountered from the *Quarterly* (and
Coleridge's family) centred on the subject of what he had chosen to reveal:
in particular, Coleridge's addiction to opium and his financial indebted-
ness to Thomas De Quincey. Annoyance at the publication of such
intimate – and potentially damaging – information, especially when given
the 'authority' of primary sources (in particular, Coleridge's own letters,
which Cottle quoted at length), long-standing friendship and first-hand
observation was understandable. It explains the *Quarterly*'s efforts to
undermine the *Early Recollections* by citing inaccuracies in Cottle's use of
sources, and indeed even by quoting Coleridge against him.[13] Yet it is
important to remember that at least some of what Cottle had to say was
not new: Coleridge's drug dependency had already been made public
knowledge by De Quincey.[14] (Though, of course, the confirmation of this
by a second, independent source – Cottle – undoubtedly gave added currency to the story and made it much harder to dismiss.) Moreover, Cottle
did not (as De Quincey had done) level against Coleridge the potentially
much more serious accusation of plagiarism.[15] So why, then, did his book
attract such critical ire?

I will argue that the reasons go beyond issues connected to Cottle's
handling of his primary source materials and public revelation of
embarrassing information. The vitriol reserved for Cottle by some
Coleridgeans is a response to the fact that the *Early Recollections* is a
deeply subversive text – that its attempts to invest in Coleridge's afterlife undermined more 'official' constructions of that posthumous reputation in crucial ways. This subversiveness is concentrated in three main
areas: class, geography and the cult of the individual.

Class

The *Quarterly*'s review of the *Early Recollections* made it clear that class was
an issue: Cottle's book was a product of his relatively lowly origins in
trade and, as such, deserved to be disregarded. The review criticised his
lack of 'taste' and education, peppering its attacks with the vocabulary of

commerce – shops, guineas, shillings, account books and reckonings – in order to portray Cottle as a literary tradesman, someone selling his old associate for financial gain. It also flagged up Cottle's use of inappropriate or nonsensical vocabulary with question marks, literally using his own words to expose him as uneducated and therefore vulgar: '"a period in which, as a nucleus," (? so Mr. Cottle writes)'.[16]

The *Quarterly*'s suggestion that Cottle should have known his place, stuck to his account books and not ventured into the realm of letters is an important reminder of the class dynamics present in early nineteenth-century literary culture and cultural politics. It was a society in which John Keats could be ridiculed as a 'Cockney' rhymester and John Murray dismissed as just a 'bookseller'.[17] Yet class not only impacted on the interactions between the reviewer Henry Nelson Coleridge (product of an elite education, London-based barrister and member of an upwardly mobile, increasingly establishment family) and Joseph Cottle (product of the Bristol lower-middle class, Baptist and failed tradesman who by the mid-late 1830s was living in reduced circumstances in Bedminster, working as an odd-job man in a school run by his sisters).[18] It had also fundamentally shaped the interactions Cottle had with the writers he liked to think of as *his* 'poets': Coleridge, Southey and Wordsworth. During their association, all three were engaged in professional negotiations with Cottle, writing to him in detail about the production and distribution of their respective works.[19] In addition, all three were anxious to ensure that Cottle knew his place, mocking his lack of a classical education and his attempts to write and publish his own poetry (for example, *CL* I, 645 and 746).[20] Cottle was, therefore, acceptable as a generous publisher and willing factotum (he famously supplied furnishings and food for Coleridge's honeymoon retreat) but much less so when he tried to put himself on the same level as his protégés.[21] Keen to negotiate and preserve their own professional (and class) boundaries, Coleridge, Southey and Wordsworth assumed that the roles of 'poet' and 'bookseller/publisher' were mutually incompatible.

Cottle's *Early Recollections* was an attempt to demonstrate that this was not so: that bookseller and poet were more intimately linked – and involved in kindred cultural and commercial transactions – than his 'poets' liked to admit. Although it was partly motivated by what Cottle saw as Coleridge's ingratitude (his complete omission of Cottle from the *Biographia Literaria* (1817)),[22] the *Early Recollections* was also an assertion of the right of a poet–bookseller from Cottle's social and educational background both to write about those who might be considered his superiors and to demonstrate that without him they would not have got very far. (Cottle's insistence that he was essential to their careers was also, of course, a claim that he should be involved in the construction of their posthumous lives.) The controversial nature of this endeavour was picked up on by the *Quarterly*, which implied that Cottle was taking liberties that should not be accorded to men of his social standing:

> [...] to rake up receipts, and to schedule every guinea for the wretched guinea's sake! [...] it is matter of taste; and certainly Mr. Cottle has done no disservice in this to any one but himself.[23]

The *Quarterly* was, however, not just concerned that the lowly Cottle was writing potentially scandalous and damaging things about Coleridge. It also disliked his attempts to place Coleridge in a different sphere: a world of business and commerce.[24]

Cottle claimed in the *Early Recollections* that he was gratified to be 'the publisher of the first volumes of three such Poets, as Southey, Coleridge, and Wordsworth; a distinction that might never again occur to a Provincial bookseller'.[25] However, the exchanges involved between him and his protégés – and the ways in which Cottle wrote about those exchanges – were more complex. The *Early Recollections* is marked by Cottle's ability to portray his subjects in an ironic, deflatory fashion. In describing episodes such as a disastrous outing to Tintern Abbey in 1795, he exposes the human flaws of his poets, their potential for vanity and habit of indulging in petty squabbles and feuds.[26] Their more grandiose schemes are similarly brought down to earth by Cottle's narrative. Coleridge's plan to settle on the banks of the Susquehannah is attributed – much to the puzzlement of his 'cooler friends' – to his love of the river's 'imposing name, which, if not classical, was at least, poetical'.[27] In turn, Cottle's account of the much-anticipated arrival of Coleridge and his fellow Pantisocrats in Bristol concludes not with praise of their visionary radicalism but with a reminder of their financial circumstances, a begging letter from Coleridge asking the bookseller

> [...] for the loan of a little cash,—to pay the voyagers' freight? or passage?
> No,—LODGINGS. They all lodged, at this time, at No. 48, College-Street.[28]

As Cottle explains, even radical, visionary, would-be emigrants need a place to live and money to pay for it.

Some contemporary reviewers of the *Early Recollections* found the inclusion of this kind of detail inappropriate. The *Athenaeum* (which quoted the arrival of the Pantisocrats section in detail) described the information it provided as 'fragmentary rubbish', adding

> [...] it is but too evident that [Cottle] might have lived with Coleridge till doomsday without acquiring a thorough knowledge of his subject—without being able to give us what alone is wanting, and what alone the public have a right to require, a clear and philosophic estimate of Coleridge's character.[29]

In the (almost-Coleridgean) view of the *Athenaeum*, the *Early Recollections* had its priorities wrong: in it 'the subordinate becomes the predominant [...] the great is overshadowed by the little—and the permanent gives place and precedence to the temporary and accidental'.[30] Whether the *Athenaeum* was right in its claims about what the reading public expected a biography of Coleridge to provide is debatable. Certainly, its hostility to the very different (it thought, trivialising) account offered by Cottle picks up on an important, and potentially very subversive, feature of the latter's book.

The family-edited collections of Coleridge's writings that were appearing at the same time as the *Early Recollections* tried to make the case for him as a leading critic of society – a philosopher-poet whose work tended towards the good of all. Henry Nelson Coleridge's preface to the first volume of the *Literary Remains* (1836) offered its contents as 'the reliques of a great man to the indulgent consideration of the Public.'[31] In turn, his introduction to the fourth, revised edition of the *Aids to Reflection* (1839) commended the work to the reader

> [...] in the hope and trust that the power which the book has already exercised over hundreds, it may, by God's furtherance, hereafter exercise over thousands. No age, since Christianity had a name, has more pointedly needed the mental discipline taught in this work than that in which we now live; when, in the Author's own words, all the great ideas or verities of religion seem in danger of being condensed into idols, or evaporated into metaphors [...] Coleridge—in all his works, but pre-eminently in this—has kindled an inextinguishable beacon of warning and of guidance. In so doing, he has taken his stand on the sure word of Scripture, and is supported by the authority of almost every one of our great divines [...][32]

If Henry Nelson Coleridge was promoting an image of Coleridge as a labourer 'in this mighty cause of Christian philosophy', the saviour of a troubled age and a guide for the human spirit, Cottle's book offered something very different.[33] Cottle believed that it was what Coleridge had done (i.e. his opium taking) – rather than what he had thought and written – that should provide 'contemporaries and successors' with 'a loud and salutary warning'.[34] Cottle's Coleridge, and his Southey and Wordsworth, therefore exist in a vividly and often comically realised material rather than spiritual world. They eat and drink: most notably bread, lettuce and water at Alfoxden. They are also – and crucially – professional writers, engaged in the business and commerce of literature in order to make both their living and their reputations. For example, when Coleridge is depressed over the practicability of Pantisocracy, Cottle notes that

> [...] finding Mr. Coleridge in rather a desponding mood, I urged him to keep up his spirits, and recommended him to publish a volume of his poems. 'Oh,' he replied, 'that is a useless expedient.' He continued: 'I offered a volume of my poems to different booksellers in London, who would not even look at them! [...] At length, one, more accommodating than the rest, condescended to receive my MS. poems, and ... offered me, for the copy-right, six guineas, which sum, poor as I was, I refused to accept.' 'Well,' said I, 'to encourage you, I will give you twenty guineas.' [...] 'Nay,' I continued, 'others publish for themselves, I will chiefly remember you. Instead of giving you twenty guineas, I will extend it to thirty, and without waiting for the completion of the work, to make you easy, you may have the money, as your occasions require.'[35]

Cottle presents Coleridge as well-versed in the idea of publishing as a form of economic bargaining and exchange and conscious of the monetary value of his writing. Even at the beginning of his literary career, he knows his own worth (literary and commercial) and is not prepared to undersell his work. Coleridge is not unique. Immediately after this incident, Southey is implicated in the same cash-nexus, as Cottle details how he offered him identical terms for a volume of poems and also agreed to publish *Joan of Arc* in exchange for 50 guineas and 50 free copies.[36] Wordsworth – a later recruit to Cottle's 'poets' – is, in turn, drawn into this literary economy. Further on in his memoir, Cottle moves swiftly from a letter in which Coleridge details (once more) the parlous state of his finances ('my money is utterly expended'), to an account of how he offered Wordsworth 'the same sum which I have given Mr. Coleridge and Mr. Southey'.[37] Cottle's retelling of these financial transactions may, as the *Quarterly* noted, be self-serving, in that he is keen to suggest his continued generosity. Yet it also establishes the commercial nature of the literary enterprises Coleridge and his friends were involved in: they were all selling their poems and other writings for hard cash. In spite of the efforts of the writers and their posthumous propagandists to disguise it, Cottle's narrative affirms that the poet was also – of necessity – a tradesman.

Geography

If the *Early Recollections* placed Coleridge in a literary economy that his defenders found unappealing (and too involved in trade), it also engaged in another equally radical act of displacement – this time relating to geography. Coleridge was born in Devon and educated in London and Cambridge, and had spent most of his later years living in London. The *Early Recollections* reclaimed him for the city of Bristol, where he had lived and worked for part of the 1790s, 1800s and 1810s.

Cottle was a provincial patriot – a Bristolian born and bred, proud of his city and of its (and by extension his own) role in what was by the 1830s becoming seen as a cultural golden age.[38] His civic pride and determination to celebrate Bristol as a cultural centre saw his involvement (in the 1790s and 1800s) in a subscription edition of the works of Thomas Chatterton and (in the 1840s) a campaign to erect a statue to the memory of Southey.[39] The *Early Recollections*, too, was the product of his provincial pride. On the first page, Cottle introduced himself as 'having been a bookseller in Bristol, from the year 1791, to 1798'.[40] His sense of the importance of geography – of the intimate, indissoluble connections between writers, their associates, and the places where they had flourished – was given added piquancy by Coleridge's failure in the *Biographia Literaria* to mention his Bristolian connections in any detail. Coleridge's account of *The Watchman*, for example, skates over the 'year' between his final departure from 'the friendly cloysters, and the happy grove of quiet, ever honored Jesus College, Cambridge' and his decision 'to set on foot a periodical work, entitled THE WATCHMAN' (*BL* I, 179). It was, of course, a period (late 1794 to late 1795) when he had spent a substantial amount of time in Bristol and when his professional and personal association with Cottle had largely been forged. Cottle was not prepared to let this pass. The opening of the 'Preface' to the *Early Recollections* tackled this Coleridgean omission head on:

> It must be regarded as an extraordinary circumstance, that Mr. Coleridge, in his 'Biographia Literaria,' should have passed over, in silence, all distinct reference to BRISTOL, the cradle of his litera- ture, and for many years his favourite abode; the enlightened inhab- itants of which city ever warmly patronized him, and whom he thus addressed, at one of his public lectures, 1814: 'You took me up in younger life, and I could wish to live and die amongst you:' so that but for these reminiscences, no memorial would be preserved of the eventful portion of Mr. Coleridge's days, here detailed; and conse- quently all that follows is so much snatched from oblivion.[41]

The *Early Recollections* acts, then, as a corrective to the *Biographia*. It emphasises the centrality of Bristol in Coleridge's career, particularly because the time he spent there was at a period 'in which, as a nucleus, so many men of genius were [...] congregated' in the city.[42] As well as making the case for Bristol as the centre of a thriving literary culture (one that includes Hannah More, Ann Yearsley, William Gilbert and numerous other writers), Cottle also highlights its importance as a place of cutting-edge scientific experimentation (centred on the work of Thomas Beddoes and Humphry Davy at the Pneumatic Institution).[43] Bristol is removed from its associations with the slave trade and is reconfigured as a centre of modernity and progress. Cottle's emphasis on the south western provincial context for Coleridge – and for what might be called early Romanticism – gains importance because of the later migration of Coleridge and his peers from Bristol and their emergence in early nineteenth-century critical vocabulary (and demonology) as the 'Lake' school. The *Early Recollections* thus provides a salutary and much-needed reminder of the provincial – but non-Lake District – contexts for Coleridge, Southey and Wordsworth.

Moreover, in reaction to the *Biographia Literaria* with its parade of Coleridge's (ambiguous) engagement with German philosophy, Cottle's account is geographically concentrated: it is simultaneously both more local and more English than Coleridge's. Throughout his narrative, Cottle focuses on native-born (i.e. Bristolian and English) individuals. Concerned in his own epic poetry to reclaim the vernacular from degraded classical (i.e. non-native) traditions, he uses his memoir to illustrate that a national (not merely a provincial) cultural renaissance had occurred in his own locality – and that he had played his part in bringing it about.[44]

The highly controversial nature of Cottle's provincial realignments was indicated by the *Quarterly*'s dismissal of it as 'Bristol garbage'.[45] However, other writers without Coleridgean axes to grind shared his perception of Bristol as the birthplace of a 'native', national cultural movement. In 1838 the poet James Montgomery (himself the product of the vigorous literary culture in Sheffield) delivered a lecture in Bristol. He claimed:

> [O]ur native country and our native poetry [...] are more indebted to Bristol than to any other city in the realm, except London and Edinburgh (if even they may be excepted), for poets who raised poetry from the dust at the latter end of the last century, and who, after Cowper, mainly exalted her to that glorious eminence on which she held supreme dominion in literature between the years 1796 and 1825 [...] *Bristol* has thus laid not *England* only, but all lands where British poetry is relished and read, under obligation, as having been the place and the scene where Southey, Coleridge, and Wordsworth, first tried their prowess and achieved their first triumphs in song [...][46]

Montgomery's lecture, delivered within a year of the publication of the *Early Recollections*, helps validate one of Cottle's key arguments. It is also an important reminder of the contributions of the provinces to what we now think of as romantic period culture. Moreover, after praising Coleridge, Southey and Wordsworth, Montgomery went on to draw attention to the contributions of a fourth figure:

> Bristol is under proportionate obligation to one of her most amiable and accomplished citizens, himself a poet of no mean rank, and whose merits have never been duly appreciated for having been the first patron of the youthful triumvirate, by such aid as a bookseller of taste, liberality, and enterprise alone could lend. Joseph Cottle,— and I pronounce his name with affection as well as veneration,— Joseph Cottle at that time did more to foster, encourage, and compensate rising talent (poetic talents I mean) than has been done (so far as I know) to help or reward its possessors by any one or by all its noble and wealthy patrons from one end of the kingdom to the other. And so long as Bristol shall have cause to be proud of Wordsworth, Coleridge, and Southey, let not Bristol be ashamed of Joseph Cottle.[47]

The fact that what to the *Quarterly* was provincial, specifically Bristolian, garbage could be perceived differently by Montgomery is a crucial reminder of the conflicted nature of culture and cultural identities in early- and mid-nineteenth-century Britain. Fiercely fought contests over the posthumous reputations of individual authors – the need to place a writer such as Coleridge critically, historically and geographically – were all part of this. The *Quarterly Review* was anxious to move Coleridge away from a rubbishy provincial context and from trashy provincial associations (in the form of his connection with Cottle). It pointed out, for example, that Coleridge lived 20 years more after his last visit to Bristol and that Cottle's account of him was therefore not up-to-date.[48] It was also keen to stake a claim for Coleridge's place in national literary history – and thus for the national and international significance of his writings. This was, of course, not the only point of view. Cottle and Montgomery (both products of a dynamic, urbanised, provincial culture) were equally keen to demonstrate that this removal of Coleridge from his provincial context (i.e. Bristol) was not needed: that it was possible to have strong localised roots and to write for the benefit of all. In other words, they show that the localised and the provincial could shape national identity.

Collective biography

The *Early Recollections* is subversive in both its assertion of Cottle's right (as a tradesman-poet) to write about his more eminent contemporaries and its affirmation of the centrality of Bristol in Coleridge's literary history. It rewrites *Biographia Literaria* in other ways too – its emphasis on Coleridge's human flaws and needs (for opium and cash) shows that there was more to him than the life of the mind, that Coleridge's account of his 'Literary Life and Opinions' was not the only one possible. Cottle's memoir is, however, subversive in one other crucial respect. Its refusal to propagate the image of an isolated genius strikes a central blow against the idea of Coleridge as an autonomous great thinker and (in a longer term critical perspective) against what was to become one of the central tenets of Romanticism. In the *Biographia Literaria*, Coleridge had claimed that with the exception of Wordsworth and Southey, 'my acquaintance with literary men has been limited and distant' (*BL* I, 53). Cottle's book was to reveal the disingenuousness of this statement.

Although Coleridge is the only individual named in the full title of the *Early Recollections*, Cottle's memoir is not just an account of him. It is in fact a collective biography, an extraordinarily digressive narrative that encompasses the lives and writings of a large number of individuals, all connected to the Bristolian culture of which Coleridge was – in the 1790s, 1800s and early 1810s – part. The book's title does in fact make this clear: Cottle's 'Early Recollections' relate 'Chiefly to the late Samuel Taylor Coleridge, during his long residence in Bristol' but not *exclusively* to him. The 'Preface' to the first edition of 1837 further develops this idea of the significance of a grouping of writers, reminding readers that Cottle is recalling a time when 'so many men of genius were there congregated as to justify the designation, "The Augustan Age of Bristol"'.[49] This idea of a collective (Bristolian) identity – or rather of an individual (Coleridgean) identity being forged within the context of a collective one – is demonstrated in the contents pages of the two volumes. The 'List of Portraits' announces that the reader will be presented with images of Southey, Lamb, Wordsworth and Amos Cottle, as well as of Coleridge.[50] The table of 'Contents' for the first volume introduces the reader to 'Robert Lovell, and Pantisocracy' and 'Mr. Southey and Mr. Burnet['s]' arrival 'in Bristol from Oxford' before they eventually turn to 'Mr. Coleridge's' arrival in the city from Cambridge.[51] This growing sense of Coleridge's life being inextricably tied up in the lives and activities of others is reiterated throughout the narrative. Indeed Cottle insisted that this was an integral part of his account, that it was impossible to elucidate 'a few years of the life of Mr. Coleridge' without 'references to other men of genius, living and dead, with whom he was intimately associated'.[52] In other words, it was impossible to think of Coleridge by himself or to write a biography of him that did not encompass the lives of others.

Cottle promised to keep these other lives as short as possible and to include 'Brief notices' of only 'two or three other eminent individuals'.[53] In fact, the *Early Recollections* actually encompassed potted accounts and mini-biographies of several more: including Robert Lovell, Robert Southey, William Gilbert, Ann Yearsley, Hannah More, More's servants, Robert Hall, Amos Cottle, John Henderson, Thomas Chatterton, some Bristol merchants and Lord Byron. A digressive style allowed Cottle to move seamlessly from one to the next, at one point interrupting his account of Coleridge's connubial bliss at Clevedon with a 73-page 'almost [...] digression' on other notable individuals, concluding with his older brother Amos Cottle.[54] Although Cottle's avowed overall aim in these potted biographies was to 'furnish a view of the Literature of Bristol, during a particular portion of time', his digressions (though he did not like to call them such) have another cumulative and significant effect.[55] They draw attention to Coleridge's place within a literary community – to his writings as the product of a rich network of affiliations and influences. In turn, the digressions are also evidence of Cottle's cultural promiscuity – his willingness to include many different sorts of writers and to assign the label 'poet' to figures excluded (as he had been) from the narrower definitions of the word propagated by his protégés such as Coleridge.[56] The end result is a narrative that is more inclusive and democratic in its realisation of a literary community than many of its high Romantic counterparts.

Conclusion

Cottle's construction of an afterlife for Coleridge was in direct opposition to that which his family were attempting to build, and this (as much as Cottle's handling of his sources) explains the ferocity of the attacks it generated. Coleridge as tradesman-poet, Bristolian and member of an extraordinarily talented group of individuals did not sit well with the image of him as a lone national sage so sedulously cultivated by his family. It was, of course, Coleridge (the events of his life and the ambiguities of his character) who allowed such vastly differing assessments of his achievements to exist. Cottle's *Early Recollections* and the controversy it generated are, then, ultimately indicative of the problematic birth of Coleridge's literary posterity. They are compelling evidence that from the very outset his afterlife/s was/were to as be varied, complex and contested as the man himself. They demonstrate that in the crucial post-Romantic decade of the 1830s, Coleridge was a problematical figure – a poet-sage of whom the nation (let alone Bristol) could be simultaneously ashamed, not ashamed, or perhaps somewhere between the two.

Notes

1. *Quarterly Review*, 59 (July–October, 1837), 25, 30.
2. Joseph Cottle, *Early Recollections: Chiefly Relating to the Late Samuel Taylor Coleridge*, 2 vols (London: Longman, Rees and Co., Hamilton, Adams and Co., 1837). This text has been chosen in favour of Cottle's later revised version, *Reminiscences of Samuel Taylor Coleridge and Robert Southey* (London: Houlston and Stoneman, 1847), because of the immediate and extreme controversy it generated. The extent of Cottle's treatment of letters by Coleridge and Southey is illustrated in a copy of Joseph Cottle, *Reminiscences of Samuel Taylor Coleridge and Robert Southey*, 2nd edn (London: Houlston and Stoneman, 1848), Huntington Library, San Marino. This was marked up by Ernest Hartley Coleridge, who compared the published text of letters by Coleridge and Southey with the manuscript originals. A note in E. H. Coleridge's hand on a letter from Southey to Cottle, 17 August 1814 observes, 'There is hardly a sentence in this letter which is not garbled in the printing', Cottle, *Reminiscences* (1848), p. 378.

3. This neglect is indicated by the scarcity of studies of Cottle's life and works. Exceptions include Timothy Whelan, 'Joseph Cottle the Baptist', *Charles Lamb Bulletin*, 111 (2000), 96–108 and Lynda Pratt, 'Anglo-Saxon attitudes? Alfred the Great and the Romantic national epic', in *Literary Appropriations of the Anglo-Saxons from the Thirteenth to the Twentieth Century*, eds Donald Scragg, and Carole Weinberg (Cambridge: Cambridge University Press, 2000), 138–56.

4. Rosemary Ashton, *The Life of Samuel Taylor Coleridge. A Critical Biography* (Oxford: Blackwell, 1996), p. 63.

5. Accounts of Coleridge's life included Thomas Allsop, *Letters, Conversations and Recollections* (1836) and James Gillman's *Life of Samuel Taylor Coleridge* (1838). Editions of Coleridge's works included *Specimens of the Table Talk* (1835), *The Friend* (1836, 1837), *Aids to Reflection* (1837), and *Poetical Works* (1837).

6. *Quarterly Review*, 59 (1837), [1]–25.

7. *Quarterly Review*, 59 (1837), 2.

8. *Edinburgh Review*, 66 (October 1837–January 1838), 32.

9. Joseph Cottle, *Mr. Cottle and the 'Quarterly Review'*, a 'Second Preface to the 2nd 500 of J. Cottle's *Early Recollections of Coleridge*' ([Bristol?]: n.p., [c. 1839]).

10. For detailed accounts of this see W. E. Gibbs, 'Unpublished Letters concerning Cottle's Coleridge', *PMLA*, 49 (1934), 208–28 and Lynda Pratt, 'The media of friends or foes? Unpublished letters from Joseph Cottle to Robert Southey, 1834–1837', *Modern Language Review*, 98 (2003), 545–62.

11. Coleridge's last surviving letter to Cottle dates from March 1815, *CL* IV, 551–2.

12. See Gibbs, 'Unpublished Letters', passim and Pratt, 'Media of friends or foes', passim.

13. *Quarterly Review*, 59 (1837), 28–9 [Cottle's omissions], 26–7 [citing Coleridge's views on what biography should be, cf. *Friend* I, 357–8].

14. See the four biographical essays on 'Samuel Taylor Coleridge', published by De Quincey in *Tait's Edinburgh Magazine* (September 1834–January 1835), and Grevel Lindop, *The Opium-Eater: A Life of Thomas De Quincey* (London: J. M. Dent and Sons, 1981), pp. 314–15.

15. See also, J. R. de J. Jackson (ed.), *Coleridge. The Critical Heritage. Volume 2: 1834–1900* (London and New York: Routledge, 1991), pp. 10–11.

16. *Quarterly Review*, 59 (1837), 27.

17. For Keats, see Nicholas Roe, *John Keats and the Culture of Dissent* (Oxford: Clarendon Press, 1997), Martin Aske, 'Keats, the critics and the politics of envy', in *Keats and History*, ed. Nicholas Roe (Cambridge: Cambridge University Press, 1995), 46–64 and 'Daniel P. Watkins, 'History, self and gender in the *Ode to Psyche*', in Ibid., 88–106 (esp. p. 101). For Murray, see Robert Southey to Margaret Holford Hodson, 26 June 1829, Huntington Library, San Marino, HM 2874: 'The said Murray has delivered unto me a very bookseller-like opinion upon my Colloquies: – to wit, that "if religion & politics had been excluded from them" – the sale would have been tenfold of what it now can be.'

18. The most detailed accounts of Cottle's life are Basil Cottle's 'The Life (1770–1853), writings and literary relationships of Joseph Cottle of Bristol' (unpublished Ph.D. thesis, University of Bristol, 1958) and *Joseph Cottle of Bristol*, Bristol Branch of the Historical Association Pamphlet no. 64 (Bristol: Historical Association, 1987). Cottle's religious affiliation is discussed in Whelan, 'Joseph Cottle the Baptist', 96–108.

19. See, for example, *The Collected Letters of Samuel Taylor Coleridge*, 6 vols, ed. Earl Leslie Griggs (Oxford: Clarendon Press, 1956–71), I, 297–300, 315–16, 325, 329–32. Hereafter cited as *CL*. For examples of Southey's professional relationship with Cottle see his letters to the publisher of [c. December 1796], Kenneth Spencer Research Library, University of Kansas, and [c. 18 May 1797], Morgan Library, New York. For Wordsworth, see *The Letters of William and Dorothy Wordsworth*, ed., E. de Selincourt, *The Early Years*, 2nd edn rev. C. Shaver (Oxford: Clarendon Press, 1965), pp. 198, 259, 262–6.

20. See, for example, Robert Southey, *Journals of a Residence in Portugal 1800–1801 and a Visit to France 1838*, ed. Adolfo Cabral (Oxford: Clarendon Press, 1960), p. 109 and *Life and Correspondence of Robert Southey*, ed. C. C. Southey, 6 vols (London: Longman, Brown, Green, and Longmans, 1849–50), I, 267. Cottle's *Alfred: an Epic Poem, in twenty-four books* (1800) led to him acquiring the nickname of the 'Regicide' in the Wordsworth circle. See *The Letters of William and Dorothy Wordsworth*, ed. E. de Selincourt, *The Later Years: Part III: 1835–1839*, 2nd edn rev. A. G. Hill (Oxford: Clarendon Press, 1982), pp. 312–13 and n. 1.

21. For example, Coleridge, in a letter to Cottle of 6 January 1797, made the distinction between poet and those involved in the mechanics of book production (silently) clear: giving instructions on how his own forthcoming collection (*Poems* (1797)) should look. Coleridge noted that he wished Cottle to follow these directions 'for my sake as a poet & for Biggs sake as a printer', *CL* I, 297. Presumably Cottle – given no title at all – was somewhere between the two.

22. Coleridge did however mention the generosity of Thomas Poole, 'a dear friend who attached himself to me from my first arrival at Bristol, who has continued my friend with a fidelity unconquered by time or even by my own apparent neglect; a friend from whom I never received an advice that was not wise, or a remonstrance that was not gentle and affectionate', *BL* I, 186. The implicit comparison was, perhaps, with two other friendships formed at about the same time – those with Cottle and Southey.

23. *Quarterly Review*, 59 (1837), 28. Even Cottle's supporters, such as the Bristol evangelical John Foster, cautioned him, warning that if the Coleridge family took any legal action against him, Cottle's non-establishment status would make him an easy target: 'There is a *Judge* Coleridge, a *Bishop* C. and several other interested persons, who would be in great wrath at your disclosures', John Foster to Joseph Cottle, [undated, c. mid 1830s], Bristol Reference Library, B20878.

24. For an example of Coleridge's dislike of the world of Bristolian trade see his distancing of himself from the 'wealthy son of Commerce ... Bristowa's citizen' in 'Reflections on Having Left a Place of Retirement', lines 11–12.

25. *Early Recollections*, I, 309. For another version of this see Cottle's undated fragmentary autobiographical memoirs, John Rylands Library, University of Manchester Eng MS 351/50.

26. *Early Recollections*, I, 40–51.

27. *Early Recollections*, I, 31–2.

28. *Early Recollections*, I, 15.

29. *The Athenaeum*, 498 (13 May 1837), 343; the review quotes in part, *Early Recollections*, I, 2–16. Hereafter cited as *Athenaeum*.

30. *Athenaeum*, 343. Compare with Coleridge's observation 'all parts are *little* – ! – My mind feels as if it ached to behold & know something *great*', *CL* I, 349.

31. S. T. Coleridge, *Literary Remains*, ed. H. N. Coleridge, 4 vols (London: William Pickering, 1836–9), I, xii.
32. S. T. Coleridge, *Aids to Reflection*, 4th edn, ed. H. N. Coleridge (London: William Pickering, 1839), pp. vii–viii.
33. Coleridge, *Literary Remains*, III, xiii.
34. *Early Recollections*, I, xxv.
35. *Early Recollections*, I, 17.
36. *Early Recollections*, I, 18.
37. *Early Recollections*, I, 308–9. In a footnote, Cottle announces that on this occasion he settled Coleridge's debt, *Early Recollections*, I, 309n.
38. Cottle's opinion that his city had experienced a golden age – which had now passed – was echoed in Joseph James, *Bristol; a Poem* (Bristol: printed by W. Angleis, 1848), p. 6. A more optimistic view of Bristol's continued economic and cultural prosperity was expressed in John Crudge, *Poems, partly descriptive of Bristol and its environs* (Bristol: printed by John Wright for the author, 1836), 'The Chronicle', pp. 9–10.
39. For the Chatterton edition (which was co-edited with Southey) see Nick Groom, 'Love and Madness: Southey editing Chatterton', in *Robert Southey and the Contexts of English Romanticism*, ed. Lynda Pratt (Aldershot: Ashgate, 2006), 19–35. For Cottle's plan for a statue to Southey see Lynda Pratt, 'Southey in Wales: Inscriptions, monuments and Romantic Posterity', in *Wales and the Romantic Imagination*, ed. Damian Walford Davies, and Lynda Pratt (Cardiff: University of Wales Press, 2007), pp. 86–103. Cottle's other monument to Southey was, of course, the *Reminiscences of Samuel Taylor Coleridge and Robert Southey* (1847).
40. *Early Recollections*, I, [1].
41. *Early Recollections*, I, [vii]. Cottle also attempted to correct what he perceived as Coleridge's unjust account of the printer Nathaniel Biggs, compare *BL* I, 186 and n. with *Early Recollections*, I, 161–3.
42. *Early Recollections*, I, ix.
43. *Early Recollections*, II, 28–42.
44. For Cottle's preference for vernacular over classical epic see Pratt, 'Anglo-Saxon Attitudes?', 138–56.
45. *Quarterly Review*, 59 (1837), 25.
46. *Memoirs of the Life and Writings of James Montgomery*, ed. J. Holland, and J. Everett, 7 vols (London: Longman, Brown, Green and Longmans, 1854–6), V, 438.
47. Ibid., V, 438–9.
48. *Quarterly Review*, 59 (1837), 31.
49. *Early Recollections*, I, xi–xii.
50. *Early Recollections*, I, [v].
51. *Early Recollections*, I, [xxxv].
52. *Early Recollections*, I, [1]–2.
53. *Early Recollections*, I, 2.
54. *Early Recollections*, I, 62–134.
55. *Early Recollections*, I, 69.
56. For Coleridge's description of Cottle as a 'ψευδο-poet' rather than a 'true Poet', see *The Notebooks of Samuel Taylor Coleridge*, 5 vols, ed. Kathleen Coburn, Merton Christenson, and Anthony John Harding (Princeton, NJ: Princeton University Press, 1957–2002), II, 2601.

3
De Quincey on Coleridge
Frederick Burwick

Traditionally Thomas De Quincey has been seen as an initiator of the accusations of plagiarism against Coleridge and as a resentful commentator on his opium addiction. This chapter argues, however, that these emphases were produced by De Quincey's own later revisions of his first articles: and they tend to obscure the complex engagement with Coleridge in De Quincey's major creative writing, in which the experiences of his alter ego Coleridge at times become more real than those of De Quincey's own authorial persona.

Although De Quincey wrote a brief commentary in 1828,[1] the essays in which he described his acquaintance with Coleridge were all written after Coleridge's death. The articles published in *Tait's Magazine* between 1834 and 1839 were, however, subsequently revised to form part of the two volumes of *Autobiographic Sketches* (1853–54): and this revised version is the one from which most readers throughout the past 150 years have drawn their understanding of De Quincey's appraisal of Coleridge.[2]

Ferrier and 'The Plagiarisms of Coleridge'

As central as they have been to the historical reception of Coleridge, however, the *Autobiographic Sketches* are inadequate as a source for De Quincey's understanding of Coleridge. The problem is not simply that he alters what he says about Coleridge. He also exercises a different set of criteria which recontextualizes the earlier accounts. It is, for example, significant that in 1854 he added a lengthy note on Coleridge's plagiarism as a belated response to James Frederick Ferrier's attack on Coleridge 14 years earlier, an attack to which he did not respond in his own somewhat scurrilous survey of strengths and weaknesses in 'Coleridge and Opium-Eating' (*Blackwood's Magazine*, January 1845). De Quincey's silence on Ferrier's 'The Plagiarisms of Coleridge' (*Blackwood's Magazine*, March 1840, 287–99) had much to do with De Quincey's precarious status with Alexander and Robert Blackwood, who had taken over publication of *Blackwood's Magazine* upon the death of their father, William Blackwood, in 1834.[3] Ferrier was on much firmer ground when he began writing for *Blackwood's* in 1838. Ferrier's philosophical interests had been nurtured by Sir William Hamilton, who prompted him to spend some months at Heidelberg in 1834 to study German philosophy. In 1837 he married his cousin, Margaret Anne, daughter of the novelist Susan Ferrier and John Wilson. His uncle and father-in-law had a lifelong association with *Blackwood's*, for whom he published the *Noctes Ambrosianæ* under the *nom de plum* Christopher North. Wilson was also professor of moral philosophy in the University of Edinburgh. Just as Wilson had supported De Quincey's first contribution to *Blackwood's* in 1820, he similarly recommended his son-in-law. Ferrier's first publication was the series entitled 'An Introduction to the Philosophy of Consciousness.'[4]

With a De Quinceyan gambit, Ferrier opens his account of 'Consciousness' with a tale in the manner of the *Arabian Nights*: a boy possesses a magic lamp with 12 branches. As each branch is lit a dervish appears and gives the boy a piece of gold. The boy becomes greedy and wants more. A magician instructs the boy on how to increase the gifts by striking the genii with a rod held in his left hand. When the dervishes again appear, the boy mistakenly strikes them with a rod held in his right hand, whereupon the dervishes are transformed into demons. The boy is beaten, the lamp shattered. So it is with 'natural understanding,' Ferrier declares. As 'a sacred thing,' it is wise 'to let it shine unquestioned.' Or, if you must question, Ferrier advises that you question only after careful observation: 'Think of the fate of the young man who observed imperfectly, [...] pass over no fact which philosophy may set before thee, however insignificant it may at first sight appear. Do thou note well and remember *in which hand* the magician holds his staff' (187–9). For Ferrier, the left-handed philosopher holds onto idealism. Like Hamilton, he was suspicious of the German idealists, but after a quick summary of Locke and Hume (190–1), he is ready to begin quoting Schelling. He presents the problem of consciousness much as did Kant and Fichte: how does perception lead to apperception? How, that is, does the mind reflect upon itself as having, organizing, and recalling perceptions?[5] Henrik Steffens famously recalled the thought-experiment that Fichte introduced into his lectures at Jena: 'Gentlemen,' he instructed them, 'think the wall.' Then, while they were all engaged in thinking the wall, he complicated the matter: 'Now gentlemen, think him who is thinking the wall.'[6] From

Schelling he quotes the postulate that longing for more is coincident with the moment of consciousness: 'Arouse man,' Schelling says, 'to the consciousness of what he *is*, and he will soon learn to be what he *ought*.'[7] This longing, of course, is analogous to the predicament of the boy with the magic lantern. In a later essay, De Quincey repeats Ferrier's appropriation from Schelling the argument on how the reflecting consciousness enables a person to alter a strongly held conviction when exposed to opposing convictions.[8] Ferrier's sources in Schelling are the same sources from which Coleridge drew in *Biographia Literaria*.[9]

Although Ferrier cites at the opening of 'The Plagiarisms of S. T. Coleridge' both De Quincey's accusations and Hare's defense,[10] Ferrier became aware of Coleridge's plagiarism from Schelling in the course of writing 'An Introduction to the Philosophy of Consciousness.' The complex intertextuality of Ferrier's commentary involves his own borrowing from the same sources as Coleridge. As in Coleridge's *Biographia Literaria*, Ferrier's references are unburdened by footnotes, or titles, or often even explicit mention of the philosopher's name. Ferrier's accusations of plagiarism cannot be reduced to a case of 'the pot calling the kettle black,' but it is certainly true that Ferrier conducts his historical survey more with a popularizer's ease than with a scholar's punctilious documentation. In his comments on Ferrier, De Quincey seems to have realized what Ferrier had been up to, but he clearly considered it more politic to support rather than to expose Ferrier.

De Quincey's review of Ferrier's 'Philosophy of Consciousness,' apparently written for *Blackwood's* but not published, is circumspect in defining Ferrier's merit: 'in him beyond all other philosophers of his own generation existed the synthesis of redundant philosophic possibility in combination with the most rigorous limitation reshaping of vital ideas, recombination, and power to create anew and remould the chaos of seething ideas' (20:295). Ferrier's gift in reshaping, recombining, and remoulding, De Quincey observes, has largely been ignored because the 'unpopularity' of metaphysical speculations renders them ill-suited to publication in a popular periodical such as *Blackwood's*: 'The "gross" public [...] has neither leisure nor interest to spare for subjects so subtle: and this public passes on for ever "oculo irretorto": what it fails to see in the month of publication, it *never* sees' (20:292–3). Ferrier's career, nevertheless, advanced. In 1842 he was appointed professor of civil history in the University of Edinburgh; in 1844–5 he lectured as William Hamilton's substitute. In 1845 he was elected professor of moral philosophy and political economy at St. Andrews. De Quincey wrote in Ferrier's behalf when he applied as a candidate for the professorship of moral philosophy, which

Wilson resigned in 1852 (17:250–62). Ferrier was again unsuccessful when he applied for the professorship of logic and metaphysics vacated by Hamilton's death in 1856. He continued at St. Andrews until his death.

Two years after the appearance of this essay, Sara Coleridge brought out a second edition of *Biographia Literaria* (1847) in which she documented all the passages Coleridge appropriated from J. G. E. Maass and Friedrich Schelling. In her 180-page 'Introduction,' Sara Coleridge took Ferrier to task for misrepresenting her father's use of his sources; and to some degree, she excused De Quincey as one who did not insist the lapse was evidence of Coleridge's intellectual inadequacy.[11] De Quincey had been more harshly scolded by Julius Hare in the *British Magazine* (January 1835); Hare denied that the instances cited by De Quincey, in the first of his essays on Coleridge in *Blackwood's Magazine* (September 1834; 10:290–3), ought to be construed as plagiarism. Had Sara Coleridge not died in 1852, she would have recognized an echo of her defence in De Quincey's explanatory note of 1854: 'Many of his plagiarisms were probably unintentional,' De Quincey wrote, 'and arose from that confusion between things floating in the memory and things self-derived.' But that excuse, De Quincey was quick to add, cannot be applied to passages 'literally translated from the German, and stretching over some pages' (19:420–1). He concludes with acknowledgement of Sara's edition:

> The notes contributed to the Aldine edition of the 'Biographia Literaria', by Coleridge's admirable daughter, have placed this whole subject in a new light; and, in doing this, have unavoidably reflected some degree of justification on myself. Too much so, I understand to be the feeling in some quarters. This lamented lady is thought to have shown partialities in her distributions of praise and blame upon this subject. I will not here enter into that discussion. But, as respects the justification of her father, I regard her mode of argument as unassailable. [...] Wherever the plagiarism was undeniable, she has allowed it; whilst palliating its faultiness by showing the circumstances under which it arose. She has also opened a new view of other circumstances under which an apparent plagiarism arose that was not real.
>
> (19:422)

De Quincey revises 'Coleridge and Opium-Eating'

There are two major disadvantages in building the case for De Quincey's reception of Coleridge on the 1853–4 texts: (1) the chronology and context of those seven years immediately following Coleridge's death is obscured in the later reprisal; (2) the *Autobiographic Sketches* detract attention from the much more extensive dimensions of De Quincey's reception of Coleridge as manifest persistently throughout his career. Beyond the mere circumstance of personal acquaintance, De Quincey had peculiar advantages as a commentator on Coleridge. He had, after all, first-hand insight into the composition of *The Friend* as it was being prepared in 1809 and 1810. Throughout his career as a journalist, De Quincey introduced Coleridgean themes and concepts in his essays. Also, he had access to entries of marginalia, for Coleridge frequently borrowed from De Quincey's vast library at Dove Cottage. Little of that insight into Coleridge's mind and character appears in De Quincey's later writings.

Prominent in De Quincey's account of 'Coleridge and Opium-Eating' are precisely those factors in which he considered himself an experienced rival. He, after all, had openly confessed his use of opium, whereas Coleridge attempted to conceal his addiction. The rivalry, of course, was neither their consumption of opium nor their experience as opium-dreamers, but rather their respective expertise in classical scholarship, German literature, and philosophy. 'Coleridge and Opium-Eating' was another of those essays to which De Quincey added a revisionary note when he prepared it for inclusion in *Selections Grave and Gay* in 1859. The addendum of 1859 insists that the article as published in 1845 was, in fact, incomplete and 'wanting its more interesting half.' The missing part of the essay would have been a corrective

> to a very inaccurate report characterizing Coleridge's person and conversation by an American traveller, who had, however, the excuse that his visit was a hasty one, and that Coleridge had then become corpulent and heavy – wearing some indications that already (though, according to my present remembrance, not much more than forty-eight at that time) he had entered within shadows of premature old age.
> (20:123–7)

The 'American traveller' was Louis Simond, whose account of his meeting with Coleridge in October 1810, is given in his *Journal of a Tour and Residence in Great Britain*.[12] Although De Quincey may not be disingenuous in claiming that he had intended to counter Simond's description, there is no hint of refuting the account in 'Sketches of Life and Manners: from the Autobiography of an English-Opium Eater,' *Tait's Magazine* (January 1840) when De Quincey had earlier reported on Simond's visits to Allan Bank and Greta Hall.[13]

Although De Quincey claims in 1859 that he intended to counter what he had already written in 1840 and 1845, he instead reconfirms the description of a Coleridge in 1810 grown languid and corpulent under the influence of his addiction. To be sure, he does go on to explain how he might have, in the supposedly missing half of the 1845 essay, presented an image of Coleridge as the lively and slender young man whom Wordsworth had met in 1795. But this, of course, would have been 12 years before De Quincey himself first met Coleridge; and to guide his way into this retrospect, he uses Wordsworth's 'Stanzas written in my Pocket-Copy of Thomson's *Castle of Indolence.*' Wordsworth penned this description of Coleridge in 1802, but De Quincey interprets it as having been written in 1807, after Coleridge's return from Malta. It is worth noting that De Quincey, as he most often does when giving lines from Wordsworth or Coleridge, quotes these lines (19–20) from memory – 'Ah! piteous sight it was when he / This Man, came back to us a withered flower.'[14] According to the scenario that De Quincey has imagined for the composition of these lines, Wordsworth is shocked by what had happened to Coleridge during his stay in Malta, 'where it was that, from solitude too intense, he first took opium in excess' (20:124). Continuing with this interpretation, De Quincey sees lines 47–8 as harkening back to a happier time in 1796, 'whilst [Coleridge was] yet apparently unacquainted with opium':

> Noisy he was, and gamesome as a boy,
> Tossing his limbs about in delight.

The problem here is not that De Quincey has made slight changes in remembering the lines, but rather that he has the context wrong and the dates wrong: Coleridge returned from Malta in 1806 not 1807, and Wordsworth's poem was written in 1802 not 1807. Nevertheless, it is remarkable that Wordsworth's poem on Coleridge remains still fairly intact in his memory. Also, De Quincey's attributing Coleridge's taking 'opium in excess' to his isolation on Malta reveals how well the Wordsworths had kept that secret. When quoting from 'Kubla Khan' the lines about 'ancestral voices prophesying war,' De Quincey associates the ominous vision of the 'sunless sea' with the maritime misadventure of his brother Pink, and not with the opium-haunted imagination (10:223). But De Quincey was not inattentive to the influences of opium on Coleridge's writing.

De Quincey's Coleridgean opium addiction

It is not just the 1859 note that is belated; the 1845 essay on 'Coleridge and Opium-Eating' was itself belated. It was written, as De Quincey announced in the opening paragraph, as a response to the biography of Coleridge which James Gillman had published seven years earlier.[15] De Quincey claims that Gillman's biography was not known to him 'until late in this summer, *Anno Domini* 1844.' This statement is (to a degree) corroborated by a letter to Robert Blackwood (15 August 1844): 'The Gilman's Life of Coleridge, which you were to have got for me, I have been waiting for with anxiety.'[16] Published in January, 1845, the essay on 'Coleridge and Opium-Eating' had a Janus-faced doubleness: it immediately preceded the serial publication of the continuation of his own opium confessions, the *Suspiria de Profundis*; it also emerged from De Quincey's most painful period of withdrawal in 1844, when he frequently thought of Coleridge's opium addiction. During the previous year, De Quincey had increased his dosage to 10,000 drops a day, sometimes even more. Struggling against the debilitating effects, he began to lower his daily dosage. In the very midst of his withdrawal pains, he confided to Edmund Law Lushington that in his own writings he recognized 'the mind affected by my morbid condition.' He went on to compare his addiction to Coleridge's: 'Through that ruin, and by help of that ruin, I looked into and read the latter states of Coleridge. His chaos I comprehended by the darkness of my own, and both were the work of laudanum' (March–April 1844, 15:102). If De Quincey knew nothing of the existence of Gillman's biography until August 1844, what source did he consult to 'read the latter states of Coleridge?' He may have read of the earlier years in Joseph Cottle's 1837 reminiscence.[17] Yet unless he meant that he could detect indications of the 'latter states' of Coleridge's addiction in such late poems as 'Work without Hope' (1825, published 1828), or, as seems less likely, such late prose works as *Aids to Reflection* (1825) or *On the Constitution of the Church and State* (1829), De Quincey may have turned to Gillman earlier than he acknowledged.

In this letter to Prof. Lushington, De Quincey explained that his own struggle had enabled him to understand Coleridge's opium entrapment:

> Coleridge had often spoken to me of the dying away from him of all hope; not meaning, as I rightly understood him, the hope that forms itself as a distant look out into the future, but of the gladsome vital feelings that are born of the blood, and make the goings-on of

life pleasurable. Then I partly understood him, now perfectly; and laying all things together, I returned obstinately to the belief that laudanum was at the root of all this unimaginable hell. Why then not, if only by way of experiment, leave off? Alas! that had become impossible.

Gradually reducing his dosage, De Quincey 'descended to a hundred drops,' with each diminution bringing renewed agonies of withdrawal. De Quincey closed his letter with an insight that anticipates the theme of *Suspiria de Profundis*: 'This long story I have told you, because nothing short of this could explain my conduct, past, present, and future. And thus far there is an interest for all the world that I am certain of this, viz., that misery is the talisman by which man communicates with the world outside our fleshly world' (March–April 1844, 15:103).

In comparison to the revelations about addiction in the letter to Lushington, the published essay on 'Coleridge and Opium-Eating' has little to say about the topic promised in its title. De Quincey commences with ridicule of Gillman's inability to give vitality to his subject, to examine the 'real merits' of Coleridge as poet, philosopher, scholar, and Gillman's reliance, instead, on anecdotes that seem insipid or fabricated (15:105–7). De Quincey then examines Coleridge's weaknesses (which, although he does not announce it, happen to be precisely what De Quincey considered his own strengths), such as mastery of political economy, of German, of Greek. He surveys those persons whom 'Coleridge detested, or seemed to detest.' He provides a brief critique of Coleridge as conversationalist, a topic which De Quincey was to take up again in 'Conversation and S. T. Coleridge' (1850; 21:42–70). Having expended four-fifths of his article on these topics, he finally turns to the subject of 'Coleridge as an opium-eater.' In these final paragraphs, De Quincey addresses Coleridge's misconceptions about addiction and withdrawal, the effects of opium on Coleridge's creativity, citing 'Dejection: An Ode,' and the effects on Coleridge's temperament. With the intent of curing his addiction, Coleridge became Gillman's house-guest from 1816 until his death in 1834. Rather than curing Coleridge, Gillman himself began to use the drug. In this context, too, De Quincey misquotes 'Stanzas written in my Pocket copy of the *Castle of Indolence*,' making it seem as if, in saying that Coleridge 'did that other man entice,' Wordsworth referred to Gillman's acquiescence to opium.[18]

De Quincey denounced the report which Gillman gave of Coleridge's distinction 'between himself and the author of *Opium Confessions*.'

Gillman quoted Coleridge denouncing the *Confessions* for seducing others to repeat the dangerous experiments with the drug:

> oh! With what unutterable sorrow did I read the 'Confessions of an English Opium-Eater,' in which the writer with morbid vanity, makes a boast of what was my misfortune [...] Heaven be merciful to him![19]

De Quincey insisted that, like Coleridge, he too sought relief from pain, and he too discovered that in the 'ruby-coloured elixir, there lurked a divine power' ('Coleridge and Opium-Eating,' 15:124). The record shall be set straight, De Quincey declared in his final paragraph, for in the next issue of *Blackwood's*, he would commence 'a sequel or *finale* to those *Confessions*.'

Opium-eating and plagiarism, the two monstrous monuments erected by De Quincey in the field of his commentary, have overshadowed much else that he wrote about Coleridge. The fault is entirely De Quincey's because he built them even higher in his revisions. Absent entirely from the early versions of the *Confessions* in 1821, they loom large in the late revision of 1856, where De Quincey must once again answer Coleridge's indictment of the *Confessions* as reported in Gillman's biography: 'Coleridge, therefore, and myself, as regards our baptismal initiation into the use of that mighty drug, occupy the very same position. We are embarked in the self-same boat' (2:105–6). De Quincey repeatedly cited lines from 'Stanzas written in my Pocket copy of the *Castle of Indolence*' as an apt source for conjuring Coleridge's character.[20] According to the note that Wordsworth dictated to Isabella Fenwick, even Coleridge's 'son Hartley has said that his father's character & habits are here preserved in a livelier way than in anything else that has been written about him.'[21] De Quincey, professing that his 'enthusiastic admiration' of Coleridge has been answered by 'wanton injustice,' imagines his accuser, just as depicted in that 'exquisite picture' in Wordsworth's 'Stanzas,'

> rushing forward with a public denunciation of my fault:—'Know all men by these presents, that I, S.T.C., *a noticeable man with large grey eyes*,[22] am a licensed opium-eater, whereas this other man is a buccaneer, a pirate, a filibuster, and can have none but forged license in his disreputable pocket. In the name of Virtue, arrest him!'
>
> (2:106)

Casting himself in the role of the unjustly accused, De Quincey deftly turns the accusation back upon the accuser. He links together, as cause and effect, Coleridge's opium-addiction and his plagiarism: 'the truth is, that inaccuracy as to facts and citations from books was in Coleridge a mere necessity of nature' (2:106).

Coleridge in De Quincey's dream-visions

Yet there is much more to De Quincey's reception of Coleridge than the charges of opium-addiction and plagiarism which overwhelm the later accounts. From the time that the 17-year-old De Quincey recorded in his diary his enthusiasm for the *Lyrical Ballads*,[23] both Wordsworth and Coleridge remain central to his interests. Acknowledging his debt to Coleridge's principles of theology and literary criticism, De Quincey delves repeatedly into the *Biographia Literaria*.[24] *The Friend* is also frequently cited.[25] Living with the Wordsworths at Allan Bank from November through February of 1809, then at Dove Cottage, which he leased in 1809, De Quincey was on hand during the time that Coleridge was editing the 27 issues of *The Friend*, June 1809 to March 1810.

Throughout De Quincey's career, Coleridgean ideas inform his critical vocabulary, his choice of themes and topics, and – most integrally – even the imagery of his dream-visions and imaginative prose. A notable example of De Quincey's many appropriations of Coleridge's critical vocabulary is the word 'subconscious,' coined by Coleridge in a notebook but first used in print by De Quincey. Here I analyze Coleridge's thoroughly integrated presence in De Quincey's dream-visions, which constitute a richer, more positive (and to some extent itself 'subconscious') response to Coleridge than the writings on opium.[26] This response begins with the use of Coleridge's description of Piranesi's *Le Carceri* in De Quincey's *Confessions*; it continues with the echoes from *Christabel* in the pseudo-Scott novel *Walladmor*, and the echoes from *Wallenstein* in *Klosterheim*; through the re-enactment of Coleridge's ascent of the Brocken in *Suspiria de Profundis*; and culminates with Coleridge's account of the Campo Santo in Pisa revisited as the finale to the Dream Fugue in *The English Mail Coach*.

In the opening of his *Confessions of an English Opium Eater* (1821), De Quincey names Coleridge as foremost among those who might be 'styled emphatically *a subtle thinker*' (2:13). The first example of that subtlety in the *Confessions* occurs when De Quincey 'was looking over Piranesi's *Antiquities of Rome.*'[27] Coleridge, who has apparently been looking over his shoulder, described to him a completely different 'set of plates by that artist, called his *Dreams*' (*Invenzioni capricci di carceri*, 1745), 'and which record the scenery of his own visions during the delirium of a fever.'

Although he had never seen these engravings by Piranesi, neither then nor since, and more than ten years have passed, De Quincey retrieves from memory the scenes as Coleridge described them to him:

> Some [...] represented vast Gothic halls: on the floor of which stood all sorts of engines and machinery, wheels, cables, pulleys, levers, Catapults, &c. &c. expressive of enormous power put forth, and resistance overcome. Creeping along the sides of the walls, you perceived a staircase; and upon this, groping his way upwards, was Piranesi himself: follow the stairs a little farther, and you perceive them reaching an abrupt termination, without any balustrade, and allowing no step onwards to him who should reach the extremity, except into the depths below. Whatever is to become of poor Piranesi, you suppose, at least, that his labours must now in some way terminate here. But raise your eyes, and behold a second flight of stairs still higher: on which again Piranesi is perceived, by this time standing on the very brink of the abyss. Again elevate your eye, and a still more aerial flight of stairs is beheld; and again is poor Piranesi busy on his aspiring labours: and so on, until the unfinished stairs and Piranesi both are lost in the upper gloom of the hall.
>
> (2:68)

What is remarkable in this ekphrasis of visual conjuring is the apparent ease of the imagistic transference from the mind of Piranesi, through the mind of Coleridge, into the mind of De Quincey. Nor does the imagistic frisson cease with this one act of communication. It continues to reverberate with 'endless growth and self-reproduction.' The images of Piranesi's delirium become the defining reference for the 'architecture' of De Quincey's opium-dreams.

In his translation-adaptation of *Walladmor* (1825), a forgery of a Sir Walter Scott novel by the German Willibald Alexis, De Quincey was determined to 'out-hoax the hoaxer' (4:263) by producing a better Waverley novel than the German version. Among the many changes, De Quincey introduced a dream-vision at the end of chapter fifteen and the beginning of chapter sixteen. Twin boys, heirs to the Walladmor estate, were abducted as children. Although both are presumed to have perished, one has been reared by pirates, the other brought up in Germany. The German twin appears as a tourist on the coast of Wales, is mistaken for his brother, is arrested, and is to be imprisoned in castle Walladmor to await sentencing. As he is being delivered to prison, exhausted and hungry, Betram falls into tormented slumbers. The dream sequence is introduced by the lines from *Christabel* that describe the castle gates 'Whence an army in battle array had marched out' (Part 1, 127–8). To dramatize Bertram's nightmare visions of 'many a secret crime,' De Quincey quotes, not quite accurately, from Coleridge's 'The Pains of Sleep':

> Confusion, struggle, shame, and woe:
> Things to be hid that were not hid;
> Which all confus'd he could not know,
> Whether he suffer'd or he did:[28]

Again, as so often for De Quincey, the words and images of nightmare were to be found in the works of Coleridge.

In his headnote to the novel, Rob Morrison observes that 'De Quincey's *Klosterheim* inhabits the same political world as Friedrich Schiller's tragedy Wallenstein (much admired by De Quincey in Coleridge's translation)' (8:225). Both are set in midst of the Thirty Years War. Indeed, the historical Wallenstein is among the military leaders and is identified as 'the magnificent and the imaginative, with Hamlet's infirmity of purpose' (8:251). De Quincey recognizes the similarity between Schiller's Wallenstein and Shakespeare's Hamlet – both being psychological victims to their own indecision. Coleridge, in a note to his 1800 translation, observed that Schiller's character sought to pass off 'real irresolution and fancy-dalliance for depth of Reserve and for Plan.'[29] The action of De Quincey's novel resides in the mysterious appearances of The Masque, a 'criminal disturber of the public peace,' and that action comes to a head when a message from The Masque promises that he will appear at the planned celebration in the castle of Klosterheim. The description of the guards assembled 'in long and gorgeous files along the sides of the vast gothic halls' (8:289–90), as Morrison notes, resembles the dream finale of *Confessions*, 'when I lay awake in bed, vast processions passed along in mournful pomp' and Coleridge's account of the plates of Piranesi which 'represented vast Gothic halls' (2:66, 68). Castle Klosterheim is depicted as no longer a powerful fortress, but beginning to crumble in decay. The music within its vast halls echoes more like a storm. The dancers seem to be whirled about in dizzying mazes. Into their midst steps The Masque – the disguised, uninvited guest at a ball, more ominous and threatening than Romeo intruding upon the ball of the Capulets, or the masque in De Quincey's earlier tale 'The King of Hayti' (3:263–83). The Masque of De Quincey's *Klosterheim* anticipates Poe's 'The Masque of the Red Death.' When he appears within the castle walls of Klosterheim, he stands in an uncannily familiar pose: 'He had been leaning against a marble column, as if wrapped up in a reverie, and careless of everything about him' (8:296). Yes, it is Coleridge's pose when De Quincey first beheld him: 'I noticed a gateway [...] Under this was standing [...] a man. [...] He was in a deep reverie (10:295).[30] The implication, of course, is that Coleridge, as the Masque, or as the lost Piranesi, joins rank with other personae of guilty self-persecution – the Malay, the Dark Interpreter – who haunt De Quincey's dreams.

Coleridge, Ferrier, and De Quincey, all affirmed Schelling's argument that ideas are altered even as they are reflected upon in consciousness. To think is to change: identity is ever being transformed by alterity. 'The great catholic principle the *Idem in alio*' (19:18–19; also 15:318; 16:382), is not a principle superimposed upon the work of art, but one that is inseparable from its very birth. To describe the mimetic process whereby the author attempts to represent the images of childhood, De Quincey invites the reader to ascend with him the Brocken, one of the Hartz Mountains in North Germany. The Brocken Spectre is caused by the sun's rays at dawn throwing the viewer's shadow horizontally across the valley onto the cloud bank of the adjacent mountain. Because the appearance and move-ment of the giant shadow is affected by winds disturbing the clouds, by temperature inversion, and by refraction, it is distorted and does not move in obedience to the person who casts it. Of all the Coleridgean moments that De Quincey has appropriated into his own prose, this one is the most hauntingly complex. Its Coleridgean character is doubly marked: in recounting the ascent that Coleridge once made; but also in interpreting the symbol as *Idem in alio*. The relation of the self and the spectre, iden-tity, and alterity, is at once the present consciousness and the phantom of the mind (be it memory or imagination), but also the encounter between De Quincey's self and his mental construction of Coleridge.

De Quincey had never climbed the Brocken, but Coleridge had. The situation, then, is similar to the visual conjuring by which Coleridge guided De Quincey through an absent book of Piransi's engravings. Here De Quincey ascends the mountain that he might have hoped to ascend, but did not. He then tells of the famous Spectre of the Brocken, the illu-sion that Coleridge had hoped to see, but did not. To conjure the image of the absent phantom, De Quincey relies on the account in Sir David Brewster's *Natural Magic*.[31] This recollection of someone else's experience, supplemented by still another person's experience, is not inappropriate to the case that De Quincey wants to make about the otherness of one's own experiences. To introduce 'Dream-Echoes' of remote childhood, he pres-ents this narration as 'a *real* ascent of the Brocken' to be distinguished from the 'spiritualizing haze which belongs [...] to the action of dreams, and to the transfigurings worked upon troubled remembrances by retrospects so vast as fifty years.' Coleridge's experience is more '*real*,' and perhaps less 'other,' than his own 'troubled remembrances' (19:18).

De Quincey records the date of Coleridge's ascent, Whitsunday 1799.[32] Coleridge might well have made some connection between the Spectre, had he but seen it, and the special observance of the Trinity on that particular day. De Quincey, for his part, did not neglect due reverence. When he makes the sign of the cross, the phantom repeats the gesture, not spontaneously but with 'the air of one who acts reluctantly or evasively' (19:20). Cast by the rising sun onto the clouds on the opposite peak, the illusion is no more obedient than the images in De Quincey's 'spiritualizing haze.' As Brewster explains, its appearance and movement is also affected by atmospheric refraction. Thus De Quincey blames the reluctance of his giant alterego on 'driving April showers' which 'perplex the images.' His prayer, true to his formulation of the *Idem in alio*, describes the phantom, not as external apparition but as engendered in his own perception:

> lo! I thy servant, with this dark phantom, whom for one hour on this thy festival of Pentecost I make *my* servant, render thee united worship in this thy recovered temple.
>
> (15:184)

The imaginary servant then plucks a blossom, kneels before the altar, and raises his right hand to God. 'Dumb he is,' De Quincey concludes, 'but sometimes the dumb serve God acceptably.'

This *'real* ascent of the Brocken,' composed of borrowed details about an optical phenomenon, is the symbol De Quincey chooses to depict how his present mind beholds 'the solemn remembrances that lie hidden below.' It is a symbol both *of* and *about* sameness in difference:

> The half-sportive interlusory revealings of the symbolic tend to the same effect. One part of the effect from the symbolic is dependent on the great catholic principle of the *Idem in alio*. The symbol restores the theme, but under new combinations of form or colouring; gives back, but changes; restores, but idealises.
>
> (19:18–19)

The image of the self is no less elusive an apparition: a shadow engulfed in shadows, a self transformed by otherness. Art can do no more than retrieve, *Idem in alio*, the phantom images of perception, memory, and imagination. For De Quincey, as for Coleridge, this is the only valid claim to be made for artistic imitation.

Finally, De Quincey may well have absorbed images of the Campo Santo from conversations with Coleridge. Similar to that occasion when Coleridge described for him the vast architecture of Piranesi's *Carceri*,

Coleridge also told him of his tour through Italy in 1805–6. Twice Coleridge had visited the Campo Santo of Pisa, where the fresco depicting *The Triumph of Death* impressed him with its stark and powerful images. Describing the fresco in one of his lectures, Coleridge emphasized how it visually dramatized

> the effect of the appearance of Death on all men—different groups of men—men of business—men of pleasure—huntsmen—all flying in different directions while the dreadful Goddess descending with a kind of air-chilling white with her wings expanded and the extremities of the wings compressed into talons and the only group in which there appeared anything like welcoming her was a group of beggars.[33]

Although the power he attributes to the fresco may well reside in its invitation to the beholder to stand among the 'different groups of men' who witness the descent of 'the dreadful Goddess,' Coleridge here avoids the implication of ekphrastic entrapment and maintains a position safely out of the reach of the deadly talons. But he has clearly recognized the threat of entrapment, if we trust De Quincey's 'memory of Coleridge's account,' in his description of Piranesi imprisoned in his own nightmare dungeons (2:68). Not only the same vast architecture, De Quincey says, but the same 'endless growth and self-reproduction' were experienced in his own opium-dreams. Unlike Coleridge's aloof description of the fresco at Campo Santo, De Quincey reproduces its imagery with himself caught in the very midst. Indeed, entrapment is the explicit and characteristic feature of his ekphrasis: like Piranesi clambering the dungeon walls, De Quincey has entombed himself upon the sculptured sundial, among the heraldic emblems of the shield, and in the final confrontation with the statue of the Dying Trumpeter.

Conclusion

As biographer, De Quincey preserved the stories of his relationship with Coleridge from 1807 to 1810, yet he also turned some of that narrative into accusations of plagiarism and opium-addiction. As literary critic, De Quincey appropriated from Coleridge such key terms as 'subconscious' and 'idem in alio.' As journalist, he included among his essay topics many adumbrations on Coleridgean themes. Finally, as specialist in the genre of dream-visions, De Quincey absorbed Coleridge's imagery into the very process of dreaming. Indeed, Coleridge himself seemed to be assimilated into the dreams as an alter ego when De Quincey reenacted the ascent of the Brocken in *Suspiria de Profundis* and concluded the Dream Fugue in *The English Mail Coach* by galloping into the Campo Santo.

Notes

1. 'On Coleridge, Southey, and "The Devil's Walk"' (*Edinburgh Evening Post*, 1828). In this chapter, reference to both the original and revised versions will be cited parenthetically (volume: page) in the text from *The Works of Thomas De Quincey*, 21 vols, ed. Grevel Lindop, Edmund Baxter, Frederick Burwick, Alina Clej, Robert Morrison, Julian North, Daniel Sanjiv Roberts, Laura Roman, Barry Symonds, and John Whale (London: Pickering & Chatto, 2000–3).

2. The initial texts were the four installments on 'Samuel Taylor Coleridge' (*Tait's Magazine*, September, October, November 1834; January 1835) and the concluding fifth section of the 'Lake Reminiscences' (*Tait's Magazine*, Aug. 1839). The 34 installments, originally announced as 'Sketches of Life and Manners; from the Autobiography of an English Opium-Eater' and 'Lake Reminiscences' (*Tait's Magazine*, February 1834–February 1841), were subsequently revised as part of the two volumes of *Autobiographic Sketches* (1853–4) in De Quincey's *Selections Grave and Gay* (14 vols; Edinburgh: James Hogg, 1853–60). The American edition of *De Quincey's Writings* (24 volumes; Boston: Ticknor and Fields, 1851–9) initially printed the earlier version from *Tait's Magazine* as *Life and Manners* (1851) and *Literary Reminiscences* (2 vols; 1852), but then substituted the revised version, *Autobiographic Sketches* (1853), published with a note explaining that 'This volume takes the place in this Series of 'Life and Manners.' It is a reproduction of that volume, with additional matter, and is printed from Mr. De Quincey's own revision.' Reprintings of the Ticknor and Fields edition, later reissued by Houghton and Mifflin, included only the revised *Autobiographical Sketches*.

3. Margaret Oliphant, *William Blackwood and his Sons, their Magazine and their Friends*, vols. 1 and 2; the third volume dealing with John Blackwood, was written by his daughter, Mrs Gerald Potter (Edinburgh: William Blackwood and Sons, 1897–8), 2:138–375; *Works of Thomas De Quincey*, 3:3.

4. *Blackwood's Magazine*, February, April, June, August, October, 1838: 13:187–201, 437–52, 784–91; 14:234–44, 539–52; February, March, April 1839: 15:201–11, 419–430.

5. Immanuel Kant, *Kritik der reinen Vernunft* (2nd edn 1787), *Werke*, 6 vols, ed. Wilhelm Weischedel (Wiesbaden: Insel, 1960–4), 2:B 130–2.

6. Heinrich Steffens, *Was ich erlebte. Aus der Erinnerung niedergeschrieben*, 10 vols (Breslau: Josef Max, 1840–4), 2:112.

7. Friedrich Schelling, *Vom Ich als Prinzip der Philosophie* (1795), *Sämtlichen Werken*, 12 vols, ed. K. F. A. Schelling (Stuttgart: Cotta, 1856–61), 1:19, 51; Ferrier, 'An Introduction to the Philosophy of Consciousness,' *Blackwood's Magazine* (February 1838), 13:191.

8. Schelling, *System des transzendentalen Idealismus* (1800), *Sämtlichen Werken*, 147–9; De Quincey, 'Professor Ferrier,' 17:258–9.

9. Coleridge, *Biographia Literaria. The Collected Works of Samuel Taylor Coleridge*, 7 (in 2 vols), ed. W. J. Bate, and James Engell (London: Routledge & Kegan Paul; Princeton, NJ: Bollingen, 1983), 1:132–6, 153, 252–60, 264–77, 281–5.

10. De Quincey, *Tait's Magazine* (September 1834); Hare, *British Magazine* (January 1835); see *Works of Thomas De Quincey*, 10:287–308, 15:102–4; 19:302–50. Ross Wilson discusses Ferrier's critique of Coleridge further in 'Coleridge's German Idealism', chapter 10, this volume.
11. Coleridge, *Biographia Literaria*, 3 vols, ed. Henry Nelson Coleridge, and Sara Coleridge (London: William Pickering, 1847); see esp. pp. v–xvi.
12. Louis Simond (1767–1831), French traveller who married the niece of John Wilkes (1727–97) and settled in the Carolinas; *Journal of a Tour and Residence in Great Britain, during the years 1810–1811, by a French Traveller. With remarks on the country, its arts, literature, and politics, and on the manners and customs of its inhabitants*, 2 vols (Edinburgh: Archibald Constable and Company; London: Longman, Hust, Rees, Orme, and Brown, 1815) 2:338–44. That the identity of the 'American traveller' is marked 'untraced' in this reference (2:460) is an oversight; he is identified in 11:187–90, 628; 3:166n, 441; and 20:329, 489. I discuss Louis Simond's account of his meeting with Wordsworth, Coleridge, and Southey in *Thomas De Quincey: Knowledge and Power* (Basingstoke: Palgrave Macmillan, 2001), pp. 35–40.
13. The account of Simond's visit to Grasmere and Keswick is in 'Sketches of Life and Manners: from the Autobiography of an English-Opium Eater,' *Tait's Magazine* (January 1840; 11:186–90). De Quincey also refers to Simond in 'On Suicide,' *London Magazine* (November 1823; 3:116).
14. *Poems in Two Volumes, and Other Poems, 1800–1807*, ed. Jared Curtis, *The Cornell Wordsworth*, vol. 7 (Ithaca: Cornell University Press, 1983), pp. 581–3. Wordsworth's actual lines run: 'Ah! piteous sight it was to see this man | When he came back to us, a withered flower, –.'
15. *The Life of Samuel Taylor Coleridge*, Vol. I (London: W. Pickering, 1838). Because Gillman died in 1839, Vol. I was never followed by a Vol. II.
16. National Library of Scotland MS, 4070, ff215/16.
17. Joseph Cottle (1770–1853), *Early recollections; chiefly relating to the late Samuel Taylor Coleridge, during his long residence in Bristol*, 2 vols (London: Longman, Rees & Co.; and Hamilton, Adams & Co., 1837). See Lynda Pratt, '"Let not Bristol be ashamed"? Coleridge's Afterlife in the *Early Recollections* of Joseph Cottle' (chapter two, in this volume).
18. 'Stanzas written in my Pocket copy of the *Castle of Indolence*,' *Poems in Two Volumes, and Other Poems, 1800–1807*, p. 583. De Quincey has substituted 'opium' for 'music' in ll. 64–5: 'He would entice that other man to hear / His music, and to view his imagery.' Wordsworth refers to 'Kubla Khan,' ll.46–8: 'I would build that dome in air, / That sunny dome! those caves of ice! / And all who heard should see them there.'
19. Gillman, op. cit., pp. 247–8.
20. For De Quincey's references to 'Stanzas written in my Pocket copy of the *Castle of Indolence*,' see *Works*, 2:106, 341; 10:303, 427; 15:123, 656; 20:123–4, 460; 21:62n, 162.
21. Isabella Fenwick note, quoted in *Poems in Two Volumes, and Other Poems, 1800–1807*, p. 678.
22. 'Stanzas written in my Pocket copy of the *Castle of Indolence*,' lines 39–41: 'A noticeable Man, with large dark eyes, / And a pale face, that seem'd undoubtedly / As if a *blooming* face it *ought* to be.'
23. See *Works*, 1:13, 26, 29–30, 44–5, for references to Coleridge and the *Lyrical Ballads* in De Quincey's Diary, 1803. See also: Daniel Sanjiv Roberts,

'De Quincey's Discovery of *Lyrical Ballads*: The Politics of Reading,' *Studies in Romanticism* 36 (1997): 511–40.

24. For his references to *Biographia Literaria*, see De Quincey, *Works*, 2:33, 67, 332, 337; 3:40, 42–4, 47–9, 120n, 421–2, 434, 440, 442; 5:937:49, 106, 303, 323–4, 351; 10:152, 155, 167, 291–2, 323, 403; 14:321, 342; 17:166, 354; 20:76, 453; 21:90, 161.

25. For his references to *The Friend*, see De Quincey, *Works*, 3:48, 131, 148, 155, 195, 422, 433, 436, 439, 445; 5:20, 21, 332, 362, 370; 6:203, 369; 7:3, 295, 309, 349, 351; 10:253; 264, 310, 321, 322–3; 14:321; 20:462.

26. On a related topic, see Burwick, 'The Dream-Visions of Jean Paul and Thomas De Quincey,' *Comparative Literature* 20, no. 1 (Winter, 1968): 1–26.

27. *Le Antichità Romane*, 3 vols (Rome, 1756).

28. De Quincey notes that he renders this passage 'from imperfect recollection.' The lines are:

> Fantastic passions! Mad'ning brawl!
> And shame and terror over all!
> Deeds to be hid which were not hid,
> Which all confused I could not know,
> Whether I suffered, or I did:
> For all seemed guilt, remorse or woe,
> My own or others still the same
> Life-stifling fear, soul-stifling shame.

Coleridge, 'The Pains of Sleep,' lines 25–32, *Poetical Works, The Collected Works of Samuel Taylor Coleridge*, 16 (3 vols in 6) ed. J. C. C. Mays, (Princeton, NJ: Bollingen, 2001) 1 Part 2:754.

29. Coleridge, *Poetical Works*, 3 Part 1:620.

30. Rob Morrison, in his explanatory note (8:290), draws attention to the similarities of these two passages.

31. Sir David Brewster, *Letters on Natural Magic* (London: John Murray, 1832), pp. 128–30.

32. Coleridge made the trip twice: first on Monday, 13 May 1799; second ascent on Sunday, 24 June 1799. On the first occasion, he and his friend left Göttingen on Saturday, 11 May, and arrived on top of the Brocken on 13 May, missing by one day the planned arrival on Whitsunday. For Coleridge's account of the first and second ascent, see *The Notebooks of Samuel Taylor Coleridge*, ed. by Kathleen Coburn, Merton Christensen and Anthony Harding, 5 vols in 10 (New York, London, and Princeton, New Jersey: Routledge and Kegan Paul, 1957–2002), 1:412, 447; see also his letter to Sara Coleridge, Friday, 17 May 1799; *The Collected Letters of Samuel Taylor Coleridge*, ed. by Earl Leslie Griggs, 6 vols (Oxford: Oxford University Press, 1956–71), 1:504. Compare Coleridge's poem 'Lines Written in the Album at Elbingerode, in the Hartz Forest' (1799), *Poetical Works*, 1 Part 1:200; and the account in *Aids to Reflection, The Collected Works of Samuel Taylor Coleridge*, 9, ed. John Beer (Princeton, NJ: Bollingen, 1993), p. 227: 'The beholder either recognizes it as a projected form of his own Being, that moves before him with a Glory round its head, or recoils from it as a Spectre.'

33. Coleridge, *Lectures 1818–1819: On the History of Philosophy. The Collected Works of Samuel Taylor Coleridge*, 8 (in 2 vols), ed. J. R. de J. Jackson, (Princeton, NJ: Bollingen, 2000), 1:195.

4
Romantic Fragments and Victorian Pluralisms: From *Lyrical Ballads* to *Guesses at Truth*

Stephen Prickett

'Fragment' is not a word we tend immediately to associate with the *Lyrical Ballads*. Their subjects and themes may be diverse and wide-ranging enough to embrace ancient mariners, old huntsmen, mothers (both of the mad and foster varieties), idiot boys, lost sheep, convicts, tables turned and abbeys revisited, old men travelling, and Indian women complaining, but the accompanying theory in the form of the 'Prefaces', Coleridge's recapitulation of the debate in *Biographia Literaria*, and much reminiscence by both parties afterwards, has always stressed the unity rather than the fragmentary nature of the original project. Unity with diversity perhaps; a reconciling of opposite and discordant qualities, maybe; a bringing together of the mundane and the supernatural – well, yes, of course ... but a *unity*, nonetheless.

Yet the more one considers the success of Wordsworth and Coleridge in putting across a vision of overriding unity to their work the more impressive, and indeed, unlikely, seems their thesis. All the textual evidence we have suggests that theory *followed* rather than preceded the collection of the particular poems assembled for the 1798 edition. If ever there was an aesthetic revolution led from behind, that of the *Lyrical Ballads* was surely it.

But before we dismiss its authors' dubious attempts to defend the patently indefensible, it is perhaps worth asking *why* so doggedly, and against all the odds, they attempted to claim a unity for their collection at all. After all, the fragment was not merely the endemic form of English as much as German Romanticism, but it had by 1798 acquired both respectability and widespread acceptance as an aesthetic form in itself.

One answer may lie with another key word that is often overlooked in discussions of Wordsworth and Coleridge's 1798 poetic theory. That word is the innocent-seeming term, 'experiment'. It is, you will recall, the key word in the original 'Advertisement' to the 1798 first edition of the *Ballads*: all too often passed over in any theoretical discussion of the poems in favour of the more famous 'Prefaces' of 1800, and 1802. Let me remind you of Wordsworth's actual words:

> It is the honourable characteristic of Poetry that its materials are to be found in every subject which can interest the human mind. The evidence of this fact is to be sought, not in the writings of Critics, but in those of Poets themselves.
>
> The majority of the following poems are to be considered as experiments. They were written chiefly with a view to ascertain how far the language of conversation in the middle and lower classes of society is adapted to the purposes of poetic pleasure. Readers accustomed to the gaudiness and inane phraseology of many modern writers, if they persist in reading this book to its conclusion, will perhaps frequently have to struggle with feelings of strangeness and aukwardness [*sic*]: they will look round for poetry, and will be induced to enquire by what species of courtesy these attempts can be permitted to assume that title. It is desirable that such readers, for their own sakes, should not suffer the solitary word Poetry, a word of very disputed meaning, to stand in the way of their gratification; but that, while they are perusing this book, they should ask themselves if it contains a natural delineation of human passions, human characters, and human incidents; and if the answer be favourable to the author's wishes, that they should be content to be pleased in spite of that most dreadful enemy to our pleasures, our own pre-established codes of decision.[1]

One can see why for most sophisticated readers the word 'experiment', having once been introduced, rapidly drops out of sight again. Here in embryo, in the rest of that paragraph, is the famous theory of poetic diction which was vastly elaborated by the two subsequent 'Prefaces' of 1800 and 1802, and finally challenged by Coleridge in his *Biographia Literaria* of 1817. Together with pregnant hints of the polemical redefinition of poetry, and of the poet as 'a man speaking to men' etc., we have ample evidence of the continuity of these lightly sketched ideas with the more highly developed theory of the later 'Prefaces'. What is not developed in any way is that odd and interesting word 'experiment', and it is quoted, if at all, by literary historians to show how as the sales and confidence of the two poets increased with the following editions of the Ballads, their somewhat defensive opening stance was found to be unnecessary, and so discarded.

But is this really all there is to that word 'experiment'? The *OED* suggests that in addition to the obvious modern meaning of something that is tried in order to see if it works, there were other, now obsolete meanings to both noun and verb still current at this period. The most striking is the oldest meaning of all, that of 'experience'. Hammond's 1659 paraphrase of the Twenty Third Psalm, for instance, praises God's fatherly mercy 'so often experimented by me'. Clearly this is not the *primary* meaning of Wordsworth's description of his poems here, but nor, I think, is it totally absent from his mind. These poems are not merely 'trials', they are also 'experiences' intended to be *participated in* by the attentive reader. Poets are still poets even when they are writing prose, and I suggest that incipient and understated puns and double-meanings of this kind should be given careful attention. They can betray not merely compression of thought, but sometimes even the birth of new ways of thinking.

At a most obvious level I believe that we are being urged to try and enter into these poems, and, as it were to experience them from the inside. In Keble's words, Wordsworth was for most of the following century 'the poet of the poor', and even his contributions to that first 1798 volume tells us why. 'The Female Vagrant', 'The Last of the Flock', 'Simon Lee', 'The Convict', and 'The Idiot Boy' all focus on the poor, the dispossessed, and the marginalized in a way that few poets have done before or since. But Wordsworth's concentration on the poor and marginalized, is nevertheless far from an economic analysis of the ills of society. How do the supernatural adventures of ancient mariners or the sorrows of forsaken Indian women fit in?

I want to suggest that behind those twin concepts of the 'fragment' and the 'experiment' is another for which neither Wordsworth nor Coleridge yet has a word. Indeed, if I am right, the word eventually chosen still had some way to go after its coinage in the early nineteenth century before it acquired the meaning for which the *Lyrical Ballads* were striving. That word is 'pluralism'. What makes this collection of lyrics unique, it seems to me, is not their reference to the economic distress of the poor so beloved by social historians, but their sense of the sheer diversity and complexity of the society they portray. Alongside poems of the poor, are tales of children ('We are Seven', 'Anecdote for Fathers'), tales of the supernatural – not just Coleridge's 'Ancient Mariner', but also, remember, Wordsworth's 'Goody Blake and Harry Gill' – the mystery of a dead child ('The Thorn'), and a quite different kind of poem celebrating a new kind of aesthetic sensibility ('Expostulation and Reply', 'The Tables Turned', and – supremely – 'Tintern Abbey').

'Pluralism' is a relatively new word for a relatively new way of looking at society. It was first used in the early nineteenth century in a
strictly material sense to describe the practice of well-placed clergy
drawing salaries from several churches at the same time – often without
residing at any of them. It was only in 1887, that it was first applied,
presumably as a metaphor from the corruptions of Anglicanism, to the
holding of fundamentally different and incompatible ideas – perhaps
originally with the implication that, like the *rentier* clergy, any such
mental 'pluralist' would in the end 'reside' in none of them. In practice,
however, it quickly came to refer less to individual people than to the
kind of society whose inhabitants held widely differing views about
themselves and about how that society should operate.

Nevertheless, what is important about pluralism is not the fact of
social fragmentation, but the *recognition* of that fact. Most eighteenth-
century thought still assumed that it could call upon an agreed common basis, whether governed by a religious, social, aesthetic, or a
scientific hierarchy of values. Burke was as certain as Locke or Hobbes
that there had to be a single civil power. Catholics were as certain as
Protestants of the universality of their claims. The canons of neo-classical
taste assumed general validity. That the world might be composed not
of conflicting values, but values that were fundamentally *incommensu-
rable* with one another does not really begin to appear before the very
end of the century. In this light, the very heterogeneity of the *Lyrical
Ballads* can be seen as part of their principal of construction.

The problem is, of course, that neither the authors nor the first readers
of the volume had either words or concepts to describe this complex mental readjustment of perspective. Indeed, it has been convincingly argued
that Wordsworth never shook himself free from eighteenth-century
uniformitarianism: the belief that all people, everywhere, are really very
much the same if we were once to strip away the accidents of colour,
creed, and social hierarchy. It may be so. Yet poets may write better than
they know, and whatever the theory, what comes across to the reader is
not the sameness that underlies the differences between Wordsworth's
characters, but the sheer variety of their differences. Moreover, the open
scorn for 'pre-established codes of decision' and stress on personal
'experiment' of Wordsworth's first advertisement reinforces the studied
lack of a polemical centre to the *Lyrical Ballads*. Instead we are urged to see
poetry as 'the spontaneous overflow of powerful feelings' put into the
language of ordinary people. The sixty-four-thousand-dollar question,
What is a poem?, is notoriously answered not by a theoretical account of
poetry, but a description of the qualities that go to make up a *poet*. We are

constantly referred back not to the canons of an aesthetic discipline, but to the endless *variety* of the human spirit.

But if the nascent pluralism of Wordsworth and Coleridge is still implicit rather than explicit in 1798, the same cannot be said of the work of one of their most devoted followers who, in the 1820s, brings out some of these still inarticulate implications of the *Lyrical Ballads*. Julius Hare was not merely the most avowed and articulate Coleridgean of his generation, he was also one of the finest German scholars in England. His Rectory at Hurstmonceux was said to contain more than 2,000 books in German alone.[2] It was he, if anyone, who finally Anglicised the Schlegelian fragment, and brought together the German and English romantic aesthetic traditions.

In this he was exceptional. The Germanophilia of Carlyle and De Quincey was still unusual rather than the beginning of a new trend. When, for instance, in 1823 E. B. Pusey decided to find out more about recent developments in Lutheran theology he could find only two men in the whole University of Oxford who knew any German at all.[3] Cambridge was only slightly better off. Herbert Marsh, the translator of Michaelis's *Introduction to the New Testament* (1793–1801) had become Lady Margaret Professor of Divinity there in 1807, and had introduced some knowledge of German scholarship. Hare was lucky in that had been introduced to German at the age of ten, when his parents spent the winter of 1804–5 in Weimar. Though, like most of his fellow-students (including Wordsworth and Coleridge a generation earlier) he started by reading mathematics at Cambridge, he switched to classics, and in 1818 he was elected to a Fellowship in classics at Trinity College. By the 1820s, he had come to know most of the leading English Romantics personally, including both Coleridge and Wordsworth, and he made himself responsible for overseeing the publication of Walter Savage Landor's *Imaginary Conversations* while the latter was convalescent in Italy. At the same time, he produced a series of translations from German, including Fouqué's novel, *Sintram*, some of Tieck's poems, and most important of all, with Connop Thirlwall, Niebuhr's massive *History of Rome* (1827). He was also reading German theology with the same enthusiasm as the literature and history, and a visit to Bonn at the end of the decade brought meetings with Tieck, A.W. Schlegel, and Schleiermacher. In 1827 he was ordained as an Anglican clergyman, and in 1832 became rector of Hurstmonceux, the family home in Sussex. In 1840 he became Archdeacon of Lewes.[4]

Though he was the author of a number of distinguished theological works, the book that was to have the widest literary and aesthetic influence was *Guesses at Truth*, a collection of literary, philosophic, and religious fragments, jointly composed with his brother, Augustus, and published anonymously in 1827. In spite of its seemingly bland title it was to show astonishing durability, going through a second, much enlarged edition, in 1838, a third in 1847, and thereafter being reprinted in 1867, 1871, and 1884. Charlotte Bronte ordered herself a copy in 1849.[5] Though English contemporaries, more familiar with French than German models, usually invoked the familiar *Pensées* of Pascal, or La Bruyère's *Charactères*, to anyone familiar with the *Athenaeum* Hare's much greater debt to the Schlegels and the Jena circle is obvious. In fact, there is circumstantial evidence of his knowledge of the *Athenaeum* as early as 1816. To Whewell's comment that Hare was ready to adopt the philosophy of 'certain writers' (from the context, one suspects Wordsworth and Coleridge) because he admired their poetry, Hare is reported to have replied, 'But poetry is philosophy, and philosophy is poetry.'[6]

Though it seems clear that Julius and Augustus Hare (together with a third brother, Marcus) saw themselves as in some way the English counterpart of the Schlegel brothers, there is no slavish imitation of the Jena model. Indeed, it would be much better to describe the various editions of *Guesses at Truth* as an extended critical dialogue with both the fragments of the *Athenaeum* (and therefore with Friedrich Schlegel) and with Coleridge – not just the Coleridge of the *Lyrical Ballads*, but also of *Church and State* and *Aids to Reflection*. From contemporary accounts of his long and boring sermons, both at Hurstmonceux and Cambridge, it may be that fragments were peculiarly well suited to Hare's particular gifts. Interspersed with one-liners on religious and aesthetic topics are much longer essays on specific points of history, philology, and literary criticism. These essays are augmented and increased in number in later editions, constituting perhaps the best source of second-generation romantic critical theory in the English language, and developing ideas that are only latent or embryonic in Peacock's *Four Ages of Poetry* or Shelley's more famous reply, the *Defence of Poetry*. Though Hare shows himself better aware of current German theory than any of his contemporaries, with explicit references to and quotations from Goethe, Novalis, Schiller, the Schlegels, Schleiermacher, and Tieck, the theoretical emphasis is subtly different.

In keeping with his specifically Coleridgean English – and, indeed, Anglican – theme, Hare's tone in *Guesses at Truth* is at once more practical and specific and, above all, more explicitly religious than anything produced by the Jena circle. Though it is no less theoretical in its own way, the result is less idealistic, less generalised, and more religious, more historical, more engaged with actual literature and society, and more pietistic than its German models. Thus the future rector and magistrate can never forget his social responsibilities. 'It is an odd device', writes Hare at one point, 'when a fellow commits a crime, to send him to the antipodes for it'.[7]

If the pluralism of the *Lyrical Ballads* is still inarticulate and embryonic, even that odd title, *Guesses at Truth*, indicates a much more explicit sense of a world so fragmented and undergoing such complex transformations, that no single account of it is adequate. Moreover Hare is part of a much more powerful existing and socially engaged literary tradition. Whereas Friedrich Schlegel's views on the novel are derived from only a handful of examples, Hare has a sense not merely of the enormous range and diversity of his own literary heritage, but also of how far it had developed and changed over the years. This shift in perspective is very clear in a lengthy piece devoted to a comparison between ancient and modern poetry:

> Goethe in 1800 does not write just as Shakespeare wrote in 1600: but neither would Shakespeare in 1800 have written just as he wrote in 1600. For the frame and aspect of society are different; the world which would act on him, and on which he would have to act, is another world. True poetical genius lives in communion with the world, in a perpetual reciprocation of influences, inbibing feeling and knowledge, and pouring out what it has inbibed in words of power and gladness and wisdom. It is not, at least when highest it is not, as Wordsworth describes Milton to have been 'like a star dwelling apart'. Solitude may comfort weakness, it will not be the home of strength [...]. In short, Genius is not an independent and insulated, but a social and continental, or at all events a peninsular power [...]. Now without entering into a comparison of Shakespeare's age with our own, one thing at least is evident, that, considered generally and as a nation, we are more bookish than our ancestors ... While the conflict and tug of passions supplied in Shakespeare's days the chief materials for poetry, in our days it is rather the conflict of principles [...]. This appears not only from the works of Goethe and others of his countrymen, but from the course taken by our own greatest poets, by Wordsworth, Coleridge, and Landor. They have been rebuked indeed for not writing otherwise: but they have done rightly; for they have obeyed the impulse of their nature, and the voice of their age has been heard speaking through their lips.[8]

Hare's is a progressive and historical rather than an idealist aesthetic. His strong historical sense is impelled by a thoroughly English pragmatism. The development of human sensibility is indeed closely enmeshed with the particular conditions of time and place, rather than with any abstract Hegelian outworking of the spirit of the age. Wordsworth, Coleridge, and Landor are not products of the prevailing *Geist,* but of specific and concrete historical and cultural conditions – and none the less great for that.

Yet the comparison between Shakespeare and Goethe is revealing. For Hare, not merely does each represent the greatest of their respective ages, but the comparison also reminds us that no country (not even England) is a cultural island in itself. Though Coleridge's lectures on Shakespeare are rightly seen as a milestone in the British appreciation of Shakespeare, the fact is, of course, that they follow A. W. Schlegel's in Germany. But as Germany has learned to appreciate Shakespeare's genius – and, incidentally, taught the British to do so – so Britain must learn to respond to the genius of Goethe. 'True genius lives in communion with the world' – or, as Eliot was a say a hundred years later, in relation to that reformulated collective cultural entity, 'the mind of Europe'.[9]

But 'genius' we note is singular. Despite superficial appearances of multiplicity and confusion, for Coleridge and Hare alike, once again unity overrides plurality. Here is Coleridge:

> And still mounting the intellectual ladder, he [Shakespeare] had as unequivocally proved the indwelling in his mind of imagination, or the power by which one image or feeling is made to modify many others, and by a sort of *fusion to force many into one* [...] which, combining many circumstances into one moment of consciousness, tends to produce that ultimate end of human thought and feeling, unity, and thereby the reduction of the spirit to its principle and fountain, who is alone truly one.[10]

Hare's version of this idea is typically a more punchy fragment, but the overall theme of unity from diversity is essentially similar.

> A man may have a talent of a particular kind; he may have several talents of particular kinds [...] but he can no more have talent or be a man of talent, than he can have a pound or be a man of pound, than he can have a letter or be a man of letter.
>
> Genius on the other hand is whole and indivisible. We cannot say that a man has geniuses, as we ought not to say that he has talent. Shakespeare was a man of genius; but even Shakespeare was not a man

of geniuses. Genius is the excellence of the soul itself as an intelligence. It is that central pervading essence which modifies and regulates and determines all the particular faculties; it is above the soul and one with it; as the talents are its executive ministry and may be many, so genius being its legislative principle can only be one [...].[11]

Yet the unity of genius is not to be confused with completeness. A thing may be complete and yet unfinished, finished and yet incomplete. This distinction serves as the basis for a further distinction, that between the classic and gothic spirit:

Is not every Grecian temple complete even though it be in ruins? just as the very fragments of their poems are like the scattered leaves of some unfading flower. Is not every Gothic minster unfinished? and for the best of reasons, because it is infinite [...].[12]

Certainly, however random as the actual juxtaposition of pieces often appears to be, *Guesses at Truth* is permeated by an insistence on an overriding organic unity. The same organic unity provides, too, the theoretical underpinning for the mixture of literary theory and natural observation that make up so much of the content:

The difference between desultory reading and a course of study may be well illustrated, by comparing the former to a number of mirrors placed in a straight line so that each of them reflects a different object, the latter to the same number so artfully arranged as to perpetuate one set of objects in an endless succession of reflexions.

If we read two books on the same subject, the contents of the second bring under review the statements and arguments of the first; the errors of which are little likely to escape this kind of *proving*, if I may so call it; while the truths are more strongly imprinted on the memory.[13]

The juxtaposition of ideas is important here. For Hare, books *themselves* constitute, as it were, an organic unity: such is their relationship to one another, their intertextuality, that their collective power is far greater than the sum of their parts. Meaning is enhanced by context. In a move that anticipates T. S. Eliot's thesis in *Tradition and the Individual Talent* by almost exactly a century, Hare argues that the poet is the rightful interpreter to his own age of this written tradition. This is a point he repeats in a more general context a few pages further on:

Every age has a language of its own; and the difference in words is oftentimes far greater than the difference in the thoughts. The main employment of authors, in their collective capacity, is to translate the discoveries of other ages into the language of their own: nor is it an useless or unimportant task; for this is the only way of making knowledge either fruitful or influential.[14]

More than this, however, the artist is the representative consciousness of the time. Just as he possesses a greater than usual individual self-consciousness, so he will also have also a greater sense of what is common to humanity. It is this tension between what is common and what is individual that gives the artist his unique balance and insight into his own times.

Yet such insight can never be more than at best partial or incomplete. [...] from the nature of man, no age has ever been able to comprehend itself: a Thucydides or a Burke may discern some of the principles which are working, and may guess the consequences they are bringing on: but they who draw the car of Destiny cannot look back upon her: they are impelled onward and ever blindly onward by the throng pressing at their heels. Far less then can any age comprehend what is beyond it and above it [...].[15]

Aware of the wider world of European thought as almost none of his contemporaries were, Hare's idea of unity is neither a matter of a coherent system, nor even of consistency, but part of a far wider coherence comparable with that of Nature itself. It is by no means the only answer to the problems presented by pluralism, but by developing the contradictions of the first Romantics into an aesthetic, Hare's was one of the first, and one of the most enduring.

Notes

1. *The Prose Works of William Wordsworth*, ed. W. J. B. Owen and Jane Worthington Smyser, 3 vols (Oxford: Clarendon, 1974), I, 116.
2. 'You entered and found the whole house one huge library,—books overflowing in all corners, into hall, on landing-places, in bedrooms, and in dressing-rooms. Their number was roughly estimated at 14,000 volumes, and, though it would be too much to say that their owner had read them all, yet he had at least bought them all with a special purpose, knew where they were, and what to find in them, and often, in the midst of discussion, he would dart off to some remote corner, and return in a few minutes with the

passage which was wanted as an authority or illustration. Each group of books (and a traceable classification prevailed throughout the house) represented some stage in the formation of his mind,—the earlier scholarship, the subsequent studies in European literature and philosophy, the later in patristic and foreign theology.' 'Memoir of Julius Hare', *Guesses at Truth*, (London: Macmillan, 1871), p. xlv.

3. David Newsome, *The Parting of Friends* (London: Murray, 1966), p. 78.
4. See the unusually perceptive and frank 'Memoir' attached to the 1871 edition of *Guesses at Truth*. The author, who merely signs himself 'E.H.P.', was in fact Edward Henry Palmer (1840–82) whose own life was as dramatic as any Victorian adventure story. Coming from a humble background, he was a self-taught linguist who started by learning the Romany language of the local gypsies and eventually became Professor of Arabic, Hindustani, and Persian at Cambridge. He was shot by Arab brigands in Egypt while on a secret service mission for the British Government.
5. It was one of a parcel of books ordered by Charlotte Brontë from her publishers in November 1849, along with a translation of Goethe's Conversations with Eckermann and Soret.
6. *Guesses at Truth* (London: Macmillan, 1871), p. xxii.
7. *Guesses at Truth*, 2 vols (London: J. Taylor, 1827), I, 98.
8. Ibid., II, 136–40.
9. T. S. Eliot, 'Tradition and the Individual Talent', *The Sacred Wood* (London: Faber, 1922), 47–59, p. 51.
10. Coleridge's Shakespeare lectures are all reconstructed from notes of those present, and therefore differ considerably in detail. Here I have used that of the *Literary Remains*, ed. H. N. Coleridge, 4 vols (London: Pickering, 1836; reprinted (ed. Rhys) Everyman, 1907), p. 39. For a somewhat different version, see also S. T. Coleridge, *Shakespearean Criticism*, ed. T. M. Raysor (London: Dent: Everyman, second edn, 1960), I, 188.
11. *Guesses at Truth* (1827), II, 160.
12. Ibid., p. 250.
13. Ibid., pp. 93–4.
14. Ibid., p. 134.
15. Ibid., p. 262.

5
Gendering the Poet-Philosopher: Victorian 'Manliness' and Coleridgean 'Androgyny'

Anthony John Harding

Victorian representations of Coleridge show that he was as troubling a figure for nineteenth-century ideas about gender as he remains in our own time. If on the one hand he left the Victorians an influential legacy as the teacher of a reflective, personal, yet philosophically mature system of religious discipline, which contributed to the Broad Church idea of the Christian gentleman, on the other hand, he was the poet of 'Love', 'Lewti', 'Kubla Khan', and the even more dubious, sexually suggestive 'Christabel'. Biographers frequently found it necessary to censure Coleridge for weaknesses of various kinds, and alluded to a certain effeminacy in his appearance and behaviour. Even those who made claims for his significance as a thinker were often forced to concede that in private life his behaviour was not what should be expected of a man of the nineteenth century, and these criticisms were often couched in terms of gender, referring, that is, to his alleged lack of 'manliness'.

It would be wrong, of course, to assume that Victorian concepts of gender were stable and unambiguous. Then as now, gender was a contested field, and behaviour – or literary work – that some would view as embarrassing or unmanly might well be hailed by others as attractively open, artless, and refreshing. Moreover, as a new generation of poets came to prominence, and Coleridge's religious and philosophical writings lost the hold they had once exerted on the minds of earnest seekers after truth, his poetic achievement came to be more closely associated with that of the younger Romantics rather than with that of Wordsworth and Southey, and his propensity for erotic subjects and magical imagery could be forgiven. By the 1870s, critics were comparing Coleridge with Shelley as much as with male poets of his own generation. As a poet, he was thought to inhabit a more ethereal and exotic realm than his immediate contemporaries, and to express with something like Shelleyan grace the gentler feelings of affection and love. 'His muse', one critic observed, was 'rather tender and sweet than pathetic and grand'.[1] Such judgments tended to place Coleridge beyond gender categories, though equally reflecting the late-nineteenth-century interest in the androgyne as a sexual possibility. Nevertheless, the very frequency with which biographers and critics of Coleridge kept returning to the topic of gender identity seems to show that his chameleon nature, where gender and sexuality were concerned, intrigued many Victorian writers.

This Victorian ambivalence about the gender identity of the poet-philosopher has been repeated in our own time in a vigorous debate about whether Coleridge was exceptionally sympathetic to, and insightful about, women – even, perhaps, a kind of feminist – or was to a greater or lesser degree masculinist or misogynist, both in his emotional-psychological makeup and in his moral outlook. Looking at the contradictory ways in which Coleridge was represented by nineteenth-century writers will not of itself resolve the question, of course, but it may suggest that there is something in the nature of Coleridge, both as man and as literary eminence, that is refreshingly unsettling to our received notions about gender. At the end of this essay, therefore, I will return to the recent debate. Julie Carlson has already made the perceptive suggestion that Coleridge is a particularly 'useful' literary figure for 'thinking about gender and its articulation in the early nineteenth century'.[2] Indeed, by 1850 he had been singled out by some critics as an object-lesson in how a man may fail most of the tests of manliness, yet still salvage some measure of credibility as a teacher of younger men; and by 1890, in a near-reverse of earlier portrayals, he had undergone reincarnation as an androgynous poet of the softer feelings, either beyond gender altogether or subsuming both genders in a new creative synthesis.

It is now well recognized that the first half of the nineteenth century, the period during which Coleridge's legacy was first defined and the outline of his character as man and writer first sketched out, was a time when the behaviour and tastes appropriate to a modern middle-class man were being more explicitly pronounced upon than ever before. Coleridge himself was drawn into these debates, partly by the emergence of an influential periodical press between 1802, when the *Edinburgh Review* was founded, and 1824, when the *Westminster Review* first appeared. These periodicals provided a new forum for discussion of moral and social values and their connection to literary taste, and one of the issues debated was the literary and cultural aspirations of women, and whether women's natures fitted them for participation in public life. The men who contributed to the *Edinburgh Review*, one historian has recently argued, were 'deliberately and quite self-consciously, redefining the republic of letters as a space for gentlemen, and constructing, shaping, and identifying with a mainly though not entirely upper-middle-class reading public'.[3] The other side of this story is the level of criticism directed by the *Edinburgh* and some other periodicals against 'bluestockingism' and the published work of female writers.

Already in Coleridge's lifetime, then, new lines of demarcation were being drawn, and in the realm of letters a certain separation between the sexes was being established. As a result of this trend, judgments about literary reputation and even about the worth of an individual literary work were more likely to involve consideration of an author's gender identity, or what might now be called his 'performance' of gender. And, as Tim Fulford has argued, it was partly Coleridge's own anxiety about his own lack of 'manly self-command' that drove him to emphasize the 'formation of a manly character' in *Aids to Reflection* and other writings of the 1820s.[4]

After Coleridge's death, his reputation continued to be entangled with conflicts around gender; in particular, mid-century evaluations of his prose works rarely lack at least indirect reference to his supposed failure of 'manliness'. One commentator, John Campbell Colquhoun, suggested that in contrast to Wordsworth, Coleridge suffered from an inability to emerge from the 'trance' of youth. A reviewer for the *London and Westminster Review* used subtly gendered language to question the value of a thinker whose 'reasoning powers, strong as they were, lay too much under the influence of his feelings to be adapted to the calm as well as severe toils of philosophy': philosophy, clearly, demands a manly severity.[5] Victorian manliness, as has been thoroughly demonstrated in recent studies by David Alderson, Andrew Dowling, Jonathan Rutherford, J. A. Mangan, James Walvin, and others, was more than just a code of behaviour for the boys of Rugby and other schools that took Rugby as a model. The hold which it exercised over the English middle class derived from its connection with a counter-revolutionary, post-Waterloo notion of Englishness: plain-speaking, Protestant, patriotic, insular, and (especially) loyal to constitutional monarchy. David Alderson indicates its ideological importance: 'the privileged access to "truth" which manliness claimed in England over the course of the nineteenth century acquired particular inflections [...] but, in so far as a stable society was believed to be founded on reasonable and natural – and therefore ineluctable – laws, it will be immediately obvious that manliness could acquire a conservative force predicated on the sure grasp of those laws'.[6] According to Andrew

Dowling, too, manliness was not only a personal code, a public school cult, or even a way of claiming authority: it constituted a world-view, and entailed the application in the moral sphere of ideas of universal order, conveyed through a powerful metaphoric language: 'Ideals of Victorian manhood exerted power, not necessarily by repressing individuals but by constructing a "knowledge" and "truth" of what it meant to be a man. The hegemonic truth about manliness in the nineteenth century was established through metaphors of control, reserve, and discipline [...].'[7] Its influence was not confined to the middle classes: increasingly, in the latter half of the century, the philanthropic movement to combat the squalor of the cities and improve the living conditions of the urban poor adopted the language and behavioural codes of manliness as a patriotic, quasi-religious, but non-sectarian, form of culture that the middle class could promote among the working class. The adherents of 'muscular Christianity' and other, more secular variants had, indeed, a sense of mission as they ventured into the inner cities to show the poor how to improve their lives. Manliness, as J. A. Mangan and James Walvin have argued, was perceived as 'an antidote to a variety of human and social problems'.[8]

While such ideals and values were circulated in print media and popularized from the pulpit and lecture desk, there was a demand for thoughtful explanation of the religious and philosophical basis for such ideals. From the 1820s until well into the second half of the century, Coleridge's published prose writings lent themselves to the development of this influential Victorian ideal of manliness, even while what was known or believed about his private life (including his consumption of opium) detracted from his credibility as a teacher.

The Coleridge that appeared most necessary for British and American readers in the decades following Waterloo, and until the 1860s, was the philosopher and religious thinker, the author of *The Friend*, *Aids to Reflection*, *Lay Sermons*, and *Church and State*. These works, though criticized upon publication for their obscurity and digressive form, lent their authority to the disciplined, Protestant, socially and politically active model of manliness developed by Anglican churchmen and educators such as J. C. Hare, Frederick Denison Maurice, Thomas Arnold, Charles Kingsley, Thomas Hughes, and Coleridge's own son Derwent, as well as to a model of intellectual life associated with the 'Cambridge Apostles', privileging liberal enquiry and male friendship. Across the Atlantic, too, Coleridge was seen as an influential teacher of the rising generation of intellectuals: Ralph Waldo Emerson, writing to J. H. Stirling in 1868, remarked that Coleridge 'was so efficient a benefactor to that generation of which he had the teaching, that I think his merits under-stated'.[9] In the last 15 years of his life, Coleridge certainly aspired to the role of educator of younger men, gathering around him a circle of gifted and serious-minded students whom he would prepare for their careers in the professions. In February 1822, he placed an advertisement in the *Courier* offering to meet regularly with 'a small and select number of gentlemen, not younger than 19 or 20, for the purposes of assisting them in the formation of their minds, and the regulation of their studies'.[10] At this time, indeed, he was already working with two such young men, drafting the work we know as the *Logic*. Coleridge clearly gave much time and thought to developing a theory of the intellectual and moral discipline necessary for the formation of the 'gentleman' or *homo liberalis*, the man whose conduct is regulated by consciously adopted principles, not driven by appetites, and who has an informed, histori-cally deepened understanding of his place in society and his duties towards it. As Coleridge wrote in 1826, in a letter to James Gillman Jr: 'He alone is *free* & entitled to the name of a Gentleman, who knows himself and walks in the light of his own consciousness'.[11] These ideas perme-ate not only the *Logic* (which did not appear in print during Coleridge's lifetime), but also the *Lay Sermons*, *Aids to Reflection*, and *Church and State*, and thus exercised some influence on many clergy and teachers who were not among the select group that had been tutored in Coleridge's notions of the principles necessary to build 'manly character'. For Anglican educators such as Thomas Arnold, it was perhaps Coleridge's definition of the role of the 'National Church' that was most significant. It places Coleridge in a tradition of political thought that emphasized the complementary functions of the clerisy (comprising both religious and educational institutions) and the state, a tradition leading from Edmund Burke to Christian socialism and ultimately, in a secularized version, to Matthew Arnold. Alderson usefully summarizes the centrality of Coleridge's work to this tradition:

> The national clerisy's role, according to Coleridge, should be a broadly educational one, and the means of achieving national unity would be specifically through the 'cultivation' of the population, a term which, as in Burke, refers to the inculcation of those standards of civility which were the prerequisite of citizenship. The role of the clerisy should be to ensure 'the harmonious development of those qualities and faculties that characterise our humanity. We must be men in order to be citizens.'
>
> (Alderson, 30–1)[12]

However, doubts and hesitations about whether Coleridge was reliable as advocate of a renewed Anglicanism and defender of the clerisy run through nearly all the nineteenth-century comments on his work. The anonymous reviewer of *Aids to Reflection* for the evangelical magazine *The British Critic* welcomed Coleridge's endorsement of the idea 'that the *Christian faith is the perfection of human intelligence*', but condemned his 'minute researches through the subtleties of metaphysics and the refinements of philosophy' as tending to overcomplicate what should be straightforward and accessible to the general reader. 'We want', the reviewer concludes, 'men of other qualities, and of another stamp; men of sound judgment and sober views, as well as of extensive learning; with less of the pretensions, and more of the power of *human reason*, modest, cautious, and circumspect [...]'.[13] *Aids to Reflection* had too many florid, excursive displays of the author's reading – too much German philosophy – to be considered modest or circumspect. Such severe judgements became rarer in the first years after Coleridge's death, partly because of the growing prominence of such 'Coleridgean' thinkers as J. C. Hare and F. D. Maurice, as well as the efforts of Coleridge's daughter Sara, and his nephew H. N. Coleridge, to demonstrate that he had left an impressive body of serious prose work. Yet still the approach many commentators took was to praise Coleridge's goal of inculcating a deeper, more intellectually vigorous religious life, but to express deep regret (genuine or feigned) over either his metaphysical researches, or his opium habit. The publication of Joseph Cottle's *Early Recollections*, for instance, prompted the *Eclectic Review* to remark on the 'humiliating and melancholy spectacle' of 'a mind at once of vast comprehension and minute and exquisite perception [...] ardent in admiration of the great, the noble, the sublime; but subjected, enslaved, degraded, and tormented by one tyrant habit [...]'.[14]

The willingness of Broad Churchmen to admit to Coleridge's influence on them, and to proclaim his significance, went some way towards creating a climate in which Coleridge's personal weaknesses, and even his taste for German metaphysics, could be forgiven. Maurice, who never met Coleridge in person (though he was a close friend of both J. C. Hare and Coleridge's disciple John Sterling), addressing Derwent Coleridge in the dedication to one of his books, almost makes Coleridge a hero of a reinvigorated and more virile Anglicanism when he praises him for his 'manly denunciation of the sentimental school'. Maurice points out that Coleridge's misfortune was to have been rejected by those well-meaning but unreflective, sentimentally pious people who, if they only understood him better, should have welcomed him as an ally against the trivialization of religion. His opposition to the 'sentimental' in religion must be 'painful', Maurice adds, to 'many in our day who have practically adopted the Rousseau cant [...]. The whole object of his book is to draw us from the study of mere worldly and external moral- ity, to that which concerns the heart and the inner man. But here, again, he is so unfortunate, that those who have turned "heart religion" into a phrase – who substitute the feelings and experiences of their minds for the laws to which those feelings and experiences may, if rightly used, conduct us – will be sure to regard him as peculiarly their enemy'.[15] In this way, Maurice casts the Coleridge of *Aids to Reflection* in the role of the stalwart defender of a grown-up, English Christianity in opposition to the immature religiosity he associates with the Rousseauan culture of feelings.

The most telling of early nineteenth-century claims for Coleridge's significance as a thinker, however, was arguably not Maurice's, but J. S. Mill's. This essay – nominally a review of several of Coleridge's prose works – begins by predicting that Coleridge's name would 'be oftener pronounced [...] in proportion as the inward workings of the age manifest themselves more and more in outward facts'.[16] It then goes on to develop the now-classic contrast between Coleridge and the one thinker to have left an even deeper impression on the serious minds of the age, Jeremy Bentham. Bentham, Mill suggests, evaluated every received opin- ion from the 'outside', and 'judged a proposition true or false as it accorded or not with the result of his own inquiries', while Coleridge would characteristically approach 'from within' any doctrine that 'had been believed by thoughtful men', asking 'What is the meaning of it?'[17] Despite the objections to Coleridge's philosophical ideas that Mill raises later in the essay, and his reduction of not only Coleridge himself, but the entire Kantian school, to the role of devil's advocates who actually assisted the eventual triumph of the Locke–Hartley tradition by cri- tiquing its more superficial manifestations, Mill clearly did Coleridge's reputation some service. For our purposes here, the point to seize on is that Mill says nothing about Coleridge's personal weaknesses, nor does he hint that Coleridge's earlier wanderings in the realm of fancy, or his unmanly conduct, might have been a dubious preparation for the role of one of the two leading philosophical minds of the age. Mill represents Coleridge as a worthy English representative of post-Kantian idealism, who had a formative influence on intellectual life in Britain. He and Bentham were 'the men who, in their age and country, did most to enforce, by precept and example, the necessity of a philosophy', and to teach their readers that 'sound theory is the only foundation for sound practice'.[18] The most negative reflection on Coleridge's character is the suggestion in Mill's essay that Coleridge drank too deeply from his German sources: that he 'was anticipated in all the essentials of his doctrine by the great Germans of the latter half of the last century, and was accompanied in it by the remarkable series of their French expositors and followers'.[19] But this is in the context of praise for Coleridge's ability to probe the deficiencies of the Lockean system as it had been formulated by the thinkers of his own time.

Later in the century there were fewer accolades for Coleridge as defender of a philosophical and religious tradition. John Tulloch's essay in the *Fortnightly Review* (1885), which uses Carlyle rather than Bentham as the point of contrast to Coleridge, finds some virtue – even virtue of a manly kind – in Coleridge's 'delicacy', by which Tulloch means his freedom from the fierceness and irascibility that mars many of Carlyle's writings:

> To speak of Coleridge [...] as a great spiritual power, an eminently healthy writer in the higher regions of thought, may seem absurd to some who think mainly of his life, and the fatal failure which characterised it. It is the shadow of this failure of manliness in his conduct, as in that of his life-long friend Charles Lamb, which no doubt prompted the great genius who carried manliness, if little sweetness, from his Annandale home, to paint both the one and the other in such darkened colours. We have not a word to say on behalf of the failings of either. They were deplorable and unworthy; but it is the fact, notwithstanding, that the mind of both retained a serenity and a certain touch of respectfulness which are lacking in their great Scottish contemporary. They were both finer-edged than Carlyle. They inherited a more delicate and polite personal culture; and delicacy can never be far distant from true manliness.[20]

Tulloch's essay made what could evidently be seen, in the 1880s, as a necessary concession concerning the 'failure of manliness' in Coleridge. The attempts of his editors, disciples, and admirers to configure Coleridge as an eminent (proto-) Victorian had achieved some success, but could not wholly suppress the awkward fact of his 'deplorable' conduct in private life. Tulloch tries to limit the damage by suggesting that at least Coleridge, like Lamb, avoided the *excessive* masculinism of Carlyle and was free from the rugged contempt that Carlyle often showed towards old ideas.

In many Victorian accounts, however, there is a half-acknowledged fascination with Coleridge's Dark Side, as if the writer sensed the restrictiveness of conventional masculinity, and unconsciously resented the expectation that men should be always strong and clean-living. Such fascination might also lend support to the argument put forward by Andrew Dowling: that the rage for discipline depends on the very present possibility of deviance, the threat of chaos within the male psyche which makes the *appearance* of stern control necessary (22). One account that can be viewed in this way is John Campbell Colquhoun's biographical sketch of Coleridge in his 1864 collection, *Scattered Leaves of Biography*. Colquhoun's verdict on Coleridge the Christian philosopher is that, in the final analysis, he is trustworthy. He cites Coleridge's admiration for Luther, Bunyan, Hooker, Donne, and Andrewes to prove his basic soundness in doctrinal matters. This is a Coleridge who came perilously close to collapse but was saved by taking to heart Luther's 'clear, firm view' of faith, as 'handed down by the worthies of the English Reformation'.[21] But Colquhoun's sketch also contains an entire chapter headed 'The Weakness of the Man', in which Wordsworth sets the virtuous standard, and Coleridge is cast in the role of the dissolute Romantic artist. Colquhoun claims that whereas the older poet's 'visionary fancies yielded to more sober views', Coleridge 'began in a trance, and the trance of the dreamer passed into the life of the man'.[22] Such a life has its inevitable consequences. Drawing, probably, on De Quincey's account of the 1808 lectures, Colquhoun uses the vocabulary of gothic horror to conjure Coleridge's ghastly appearance as he struggled to address a roomful of London literati at the Royal Institution, Albemarle Street: 'Even when he appeared, his looks betrayed his condition. The lips were parched and black, the tongue cleaved to his mouth, the voice was scarcely audible. [...] [T]hese symptoms, not to be mistaken, clouded the brilliant intellect, and depressed the encumbered powers'.[23] Coleridge's practice while staying at Allan Bank of studying metaphysics throughout the night, and keeping to his bed until well into the afternoon, is described as a 'peculiar' habit, as if it were part of some sinister Faustian aspect of his character: 'He sat up great part of the night devouring German books, and seldom came down stairs till four in the afternoon'.[24] This is Coleridge as haunted Mariner, wrestling with unknown demons and dreaming impossible metaphysical dreams, though it is opium rather than an albatross that has all but destroyed his humanity.

Yet Colquhoun's sketch also testifies to the entrancing power Coleridge could exercise when in full conversational flow. Evidently paraphrasing an account by an unnamed witness of his conversations with the preacher Edward Irving, Colquhoun offers this description of the impassioned, enthusiastic Coleridge: 'a low, sweet, musical voice, which rolled forth a continuous stream of eloquent discourse, rising at times to high elevation, and seeming to soar into the clouds, like distant music fading into the air with a faint dreamy sound,—then dropping down, and coming to objects nearer his audience, to books, and records, and the characters of men,—at times lost in labyrinths of reasoning, yet always at last, as by some sure clue, extricating itself [...]'.[25] Colquhoun's portrait, in sum, is that of a man who never completely escaped the lotus-land of his visionary youth, and never quite measured up to the mysterious criteria by which manliness would be assessed, but nevertheless managed to lay hold of the saving doctrines of English Protestantism just in time to avoid complete collapse. But there is a counter-narrative, too, which seems to hint that Coleridge's irregular habits and unstable nature actually made him a more attractive and effective teacher, and certainly a better conversationalist, than Wordsworth with his 'sober views' and more upright character.

Interestingly, Matthew Arnold, in an essay published the same year as Colquhoun's sketch (1864), also seems to suggest that it was Coleridge's *lack* of Wordsworthian sobriety and Carlylean ruggedness that made him such an entrancing and influential teacher. Arnold first characterizes Coleridge's overall literary achievement as unsatisfactory – 'How little either of his poetry, or of his criticism, or of his philosophy, can we expect permanently to stand!' – and makes the further, astonishing judgement that Coleridge 'had no morals'.[26] After this condemnation, one wonders what Arnold could possibly find to praise. It turns out to be what Arnold considers his 'continual instinctive effort [...] to get at and to lay bare the real truth of his matter in hand, whether that matter were literary, or philosophical, or political, or religious; and this in a country where at that moment such an effort was almost unknown [...]'.[27] Arnold seems strangely reluctant to allow Coleridge the credit of possessing any degree of personal resolve or willpower, explaining his influence over such men as Hare, Maurice, and Mill – themselves men of no mean intelligence and determination – as the result of a blind instinctual struggle towards the light of the more advanced views emanating from the Continent. Coleridge's vast, if rather inchoate, productivity must be put down to 'instinctive effort' – though this seems, perversely, to render his achievement more, not less, impressive than a carefully planned, logically cohesive series of writings would have been. The resulting portrait is that of a rather indeterminate figure who escapes all the recognized categories for influential thinkers, a strangely ungendered intellect never quite embodied in human form.

That the issue of Coleridge's gender identity was still present to Victorian readers is very evident, however, in Swinburne's essay on Coleridge as poet, published in 1875 as the preface to an edition of

'Christabel' and other 'lyrical and imaginative' poems of Coleridge. Like
Arnold, Swinburne considers Coleridge's work uneven in quality; but,
unlike Arnold, he is effusive with praise when he considers a poem successful; and his praise is nearly always couched in gender-coded language. Like many of his predecessors in the field of Coleridge criticism,
Swinburne represents Coleridge as ill-fitted to handle the things of this
earth, an exotic creature, whose natural realm was that of the dream:
'There is a graceful Asiatic legend cited by his friend Southey of "the
footless birds of Paradise" who have only wings to sustain them, and
live their lives out in a perpetual flight through the clearest air of
heaven. [...] Such a footless bird of Paradise was Coleridge; and had his
wings always held out it had been well for him and us. Unhappily this
winged and footless creature would perforce too often furl his wings in
mid air and try his footing on earth, where his gait was like a swan's on
shore.'[28] Adopting an image reminiscent of Baudelaire's 1859 poem
'L'Albatros', Swinburne virtually removes Coleridge from the sphere of
politics and ideas, those weighty matters reserved for the attention of
serious men, and assigns him to the ungendered and attractively weight-
less realm of poetry. Casually dismissing Coleridge's own political and
ideological engagements ('for Coleridge no warning word was needed
against the shriek of the press-gang from this side or that'[29]), and ignoring the efforts of his editors to present him as an intelligible, authoritative philosopher-critic, Swinburne constructs Coleridge as a pure poetic
voice that lives in a paradisal realm beyond gender, not so much sexless
as uniting both sexes in a joyous state of prelapsarian harmony.

Of 'The Ancient Mariner', Swinburne writes: 'the tenderness of sentiment which touches with significant colour the pure white imagination
is here no longer morbid or languid, as in the earlier poems of feeling
and emotion. It is soft and piteous enough, but womanly rather than
effeminate; and thus serves indeed to set off the strange splendours and
boundless beauties of the story'.[30] Even 'The Rime' has a little too much
materiality for Swinburne's taste, however – that is to say, more materiality than is appropriate for the ungendered or bi-gendered poet he is
imagining. It is 'Kubla Khan' and 'Christabel' that receive his highest
praise. These surpass even the 'Rime' in their sheer uniqueness. Only
Shelley could approach the 'absolute melody' of 'Kubla Khan', perhaps
'the most wonderful of all poems': 'An exquisite instinct married to a
subtle science of verse has made it the supreme model of music in our
language, a model unapproachable except by Shelley. All the elements
that compose the perfect form of English metre, as limbs and veins and
features a beautiful body of man, were more familiar, more subject as it

were, to this great poet than to any other'.[31] The association of Coleridge
with Shelley helps Swinburne to reanimate Coleridge's famous description of the poet as one who 'brings the whole soul of man into activity'
in the more carnal but still idealized 'beautiful body of man', though
Swinburne transfers the image from the poet to the poetry.[32] This is
Coleridge recontextualized for readers of Pater, Rossetti, and the early
Wilde. Even more significantly, when Swinburne turns to 'Christabel'
he appears to see in it nothing repellent or disturbing. As Swinburne
reads it, the poem is entirely purged of the sinister sexual innuendo that
had led Coleridge's contemporaries to censure it, and his later admirers
to make excuses for it:

> The very terror and mystery of magical evil is imbued with this
> sweetness; the witch has no less of it than the maiden; their contact
> has in it nothing dissonant or disfiguring, nothing to jar or to deface
> the beauty and harmony of the whole imagination. As for the
> melody, here again it is incomparable with any other poet's. Shelley
> indeed comes nearest; but for purity and volume of music Shelley is
> to Coleridge as a lark to a nightingale; his song heaven-high and
> clear as heaven, but the other's more rich and weighty, more pas-
> sionately various, and warmer in effusion of sound. On the other
> hand, the nobler nature, the clearer spirit of Shelley, fills his verse
> with a divine force of meaning, which Coleridge, who had it not in
> him, could not affect to give.[33]

Clearly, for Swinburne to place Coleridge alongside Shelley is to accord
him high praise, but Coleridge has to pay a high price for this distinction.
Coleridge's poetry wins the palm for passion and warmth, but it is
Shelley's that is credited with more 'force of meaning'. The lark and
nightingale analogies make both poets curiously bodiless and (therefore)
sexless, but while Coleridge, as the nightingale, has a voice rich with
passion and warmth, it is Shelley who sings the purer song and delivers
more insight and spiritual uplift.

   Swinburne's androgynous portrait of Coleridge is achieved, however,
by a process of rigorous exclusion. The blank verse poems are largely
dismissed as inappropriately emotional, while a lyric such as 'Lewti',
though anticipating the finer melody of later work, is condemned as
'effeminate in build, loose hung, weak of eye and foot'.[34] The blank
verse meditation, 'Fears in Solitude', is characterized as 'nerveless and
hysterical', and contrasted with Wordsworth's 'majestic and masculine'
sonnet on the threat of invasion. Coleridge's prose Swinburne considers

as at best a matter of 'splendid fragments', concluding 'I doubt his being remembered, except by a small body of his elect, as other than a poet'.[35] The 'supernatural' poems receive the highest praise, for their 'womanly' sentiment and 'sensuous fluctuation of soul'.[36]

Swinburne's Coleridge is a remarkable portrait, then: hardly recognizable to us, but not very far removed from the figure emerging in other late nineteenth-century accounts. Hall Caine's biography (1887) is one of the few that tries to combat the prevailing picture of Coleridge as having been from the first hopelessly unpractical and weak-willed. His attractive description of Coleridge at the age of 31 strikes a balance between 'masculine' and 'feminine' traits. Alluding to his habit of climbing the fells in all weathers, Caine portrays him as 'a man of great animal spirits and (strange as it may sound) of extraordinary physical energy', with a 'sweet and affectionate' character: 'a man made to love, and to be beloved'. From the summer of 1803, Caine suggests, opium dependency sapped his willpower and periodically threw him into deep depression. Up to that point, however, 'he was a strong man, strongly equipped, working well against great odds'.[37] Leslie Stephen is much less forgiving. Severe on Coleridge's moral failings, and unsympathetic to his philosophy, he excuses Coleridge's philosophical incompleteness on the grounds that he was born to be a poet, not a systematic thinker. 'Dreamland was his reality', Stephen remarks: 'Coleridge was, above all, essentially and intrinsically a poet.'[38]

These *fin-de-siècle* characterizations show that the process by which Coleridge's poetry was first carefully sifted (the poems of the supernatural being given pride of place), and then praised for its detachment from both mundane particularities and serious argument, also succeeded in delivering a curiously ethereal and sometimes oddly sexless author. Gender, it seems, had first of all polarized evaluations of Coleridge, some critics forthrightly condemning him for lacking the 'manly' virtues while others approved his rehabilitation as Sage of Highgate, a reassuringly male figure, though perhaps avuncular rather than patriarchal. Later in the century, the most valued poems – 'The Rime of the Ancient Mariner', 'Kubla Khan', and 'Christabel' – were praised as evidence of a unique poetic gift, and the poet correspondingly elevated to a special realm, where gender boundaries were miraculously dissolved, and the poet was credited with the qualities of 'womanly' sentiment and 'sensuous fluctuation of soul'.[39] If there is more than a little projection happening here – nineteenth-century aestheticism seeing in a safely distant, romantic-era figure the androgynous ideal it was beginning to find attractive in its own art and literature – it is also significant that it was Coleridge, even more than the similarly ambivalent Shelley, who was depicted in this way. Coleridge's character as man and as writer could not easily be defined by conventional markers of masculinity or femininity. In other words, his life and writing themselves tended to destabilize received notions of gender identity; and that in itself is a question worth examining.

At the beginning of this essay, I referred to the recent debate around whether Coleridge was sympathetic to and insightful about women, or almost the opposite, a man who not only shared the conventional misogyny of his time but was even unusually hostile towards the intel-lectual aspirations of women, and whose poetry betrays an almost pathological distrust of the female. It seems that what is recorded of Coleridge's life, psychology and opinions continues to challenge the arbitrariness of our expectations about how men and women should behave towards each other, just as it did in the nineteenth century. The Coleridge presented or deduced from his writing by modern critics cov-ers a range of identities, from the generous though indisputably mascu-line moralist who has the gift of understanding women exceptionally well and sympathizing with their struggles to the insecure, troubled, pathetically dependent grown boy, who shamelessly exploited the women of his circle. For critics who focus on his poetry, the most provocative poems for this debate have usually been the same ones that were found troubling by the early nineteenth-century critics such as Hazlitt and Thomas Moore, and – later in the century – singled out for their unique qualities: 'The Ancient Mariner', 'Kubla Khan', and 'Christabel'. Recently, feminist critics have pointed out that the female figures in these poems perpetuate the insidious mythological, literary, and religious tradition of portraying women as either pious virgins or dangerous vampires and whores. Feminists draw attention to the fact that these females are either inarticulate or, if capable of speech, use it to seduce and entrap (Geraldine, the Nightmare Life-in-Death). Critics who see such nightmarish female figures as having their origin in Coleridge's own psychological and emotional landscape argue that they expose to our view a more than ordinary degree of male distrust, fear, and hatred of women. This is the argument made by Diane Long Hoeveler, who concludes from her analysis of 'Christabel' that Coleridge harboured a 'conscious and unconscious opinion of [women] as perverse, sexually voracious, predatory, and duplicitous.'[40] A different approach, emphasizing Coleridge's relationship to the literary culture of his time rather than his emotional disposition and relationships with actual women, is taken by Karen Swann, for whom Geraldine is more a plot-function than an archetype. Geraldine enters the poem, at a point of 'interpretive crisis', as a recognizable literary artefact. Consequently, the poem exposes the 'cultural fantasy' that is '"feminine" genre and gender alike'.[41]

If 'Christabel' reveals Coleridge's investment in a contemporary masculinist culture that associated the growth of literacy, and the popular market for romances and fantasy literature, with a threatening and uncontrollable female readership, his recorded statements about actual contemporaries such as Mary Wollstonecraft and Matilda Betham can be cited as evidence on the other side suggesting that he took a positive view of women's intellectual capacities and advocated their fuller participation in public and political life. Jeanie Watson finds evidence of Coleridge's support for women's rights in his assertion of their full humanity (their 'Identity' with men 'in the Substance'), and of his acceptance and endorsement of androgyny as an intellectual ideal.[42] Watson's argument is elaborated by Anya Taylor, who argues that 'Coleridge was remarkably sympathetic in his prose writings to certain aspects of the feminist agenda of his day', 'a friend and supporter of many women and one of the earliest proponents of women's suffrage, if there was to be suffrage at all'.[43] Demonstrating the extent to which Coleridge shared Wollstonecraft's critical view of the demeaning and infantilizing education, then considered appropriate for girls and young women, Taylor finds that Wollstonecraft remained a powerful 'voice' in 'the dialogic interplay of Coleridge's chosen voices'.[44] In another contribution to the debate, Taylor offers a reading of 'Christabel' that answers the strictures of Hoeveler and others by suggesting that the poem explores 'fluctuations of power and weakness' and is an exceptionally insightful analysis of experiences common to many young women: 'The poem and the principles that it embodies are rooted in Coleridge's affinity with women'.[45]

The case made by these defenders of Coleridge, that he was relatively free from the anti-woman prejudices of his time, nevertheless has to confront some troubling evidence on the opposite side. As Taylor admits, during the debate about the 1832 Reform Bill, Coleridge was very far from supporting universal suffrage, or any significant extension of the franchise on the basis of a citizen's alleged 'right' to representation. Rather than making a genuine case for extending the franchise to women of the 'higher and middle classes' (to borrow from the title of *A Lay Sermon*) while excluding labouring-class men – though this is a possible reading of his view – he could have been using the argument about some well-educated women's 'moral right' to the vote as a way of exposing logical shortcomings in the position of the reformers. In other words, since he would have assumed that extending the franchise to women was unthinkable anyway in nineteenth-century Britain, he would have felt safe in arguing, against the reformers' proposal to give the vote to poorer men, that middle- and upper-class women, having achieved a certain level of education, should surely be entrusted with the vote before labouring-class men. Moreover, Coleridge's support and admiration for certain *individual* women – Wollstonecraft's imaginative gifts (he did not admire her writings), Dorothy Wordsworth's sensibility, his daughter Sara's knowledge of languages – must be placed in the context of his over-all view that it was not in the nature of womankind to enter the highest intellectual realm – namely, philosophy – and that women should find their fulfilment in being supportive companions of men, not in developing their own independent critical, moral, or social perspectives.

A remark from *Table Talk* (24 June 1827) encapsulates this view: 'The qualities correspond. The courage of the man is loved by the woman, whose fortitude is coveted as it were by the man – his vigorous intellect is answered by her infallible tact'.[46] As Heather Jackson points out, despite his agreement with Wollstonecraft on the need for young women to receive a better quality of education than was then custom-ary, Coleridge 'believed firmly that boys and girls were spiritually and psychologically, as well as physically, different from the start, created for different purposes', and that 'women could not be expected ever to contribute significantly to the realm of intellect [...]'.[47]

More recently, Anne Mellor and Julie Carlson have weighed the con-siderable evidence presented by Jackson, as well as additional evidence not explicitly discussed by her, and have reached similar conclusions. Mellor notes that Coleridge's poetry never portrays a woman as 'a "free and equal companion"', and that his 1819 'Letter on Marriage' enshrines sexual difference as the basis of marriage 'in a way that finally necessitated the absorption of the female into the higher unity of the male'.[48] Mellor's persuasive conclusion is that Coleridge was troubled and even threatened by talented women.[49] Julie Carlson concurs, adding the provocative observation that 'living women were intertextual, sub-stitutable, at times even expendable, and fictional women were often substitutes for beloved men'.[50] Carlson here alludes to the possibility – an hypothesis favoured by some twentieth-century biographers – that not only fictional women such as Christabel, but also actual women such as Sara Hutchinson, played the role of surrogates or tokens in the series of homosocial relationships Coleridge formed with more dominant, outwardly more virile men.[51] Such an interpretation would fit the pattern described in Eve Kosofsky Sedgwick's *Between Men*, in which Sedgwick focuses on the effects upon women of the (mostly unacknowledged) homosocial desires of men, and in particular examines 'the routing through women of male homosocial desire'.[52]

Even if we are not convinced by the suggestion that Coleridge's feelings towards Wordsworth and other admired men were an expression of unacknowledged homosocial desires, the undeniable pattern of dependency that Stephen Weissman and others have pointed to in Coleridge's life, and his conflicted, predominantly negative attitude towards women who refused the subservient domestic role, illustrates what I have called the chameleon quality of Coleridge so far as gender identity is concerned. Impelled by the fear that he lacked 'manliness', Coleridge tried to make 'manly character' one of the goals of his writing and teaching during the Highgate years, only to be viewed with suspicion by most Victorian commentators, and later to have some of his poetry praised for transcending gender in a way that he would hardly have approved. These Coleridgean contradictions now appear especially valuable as an example of the shifting boundaries of gender identity. The varying portraits of Coleridge left us by the Victorian critics, which are themselves a product of changing expectations about the ideas, personality, and private conduct appropriate to an influential poet-philosopher, anticipate the multitude of not-always-harmonious expectations we ourselves bring to the life and works of a writer who was himself at odds with most of the trends of his era. For one aspect of the Romantic period we may now understand a little better is that it was a time when modern masculinity itself was in a formative stage; and few, if any, prominent men can be said to have measured up to the more militant, more overtly politicized Victorian and twentieth-century ideals of masculinity.

Notes

1. Joseph Devey, 'Coleridge', *A Comparative Estimate of Modern Poets* (1873), rpt in Carmen Joseph Dello Buono, ed., *Rare Early Essays on Samuel Taylor Coleridge* (Darby, PA: Norwood Editions, 1981), p. 103. Hereafter cited as Dello Buono.
2. Julie Carlson, 'Gender', *The Cambridge Companion to Coleridge*, ed. Lucy Newlyn (Cambridge: Cambridge University Press, 2002), p. 203. Hereafter cited as Carlson.
3. Jane Rendall, 'Bluestockings and Reviewers: Gender, Power, and Culture in Britain, c. 1800–1830', *Nineteenth-Century Contexts* 26:4 (December 2004): 357. On the way the periodical press accelerated the exclusion of women from the public sphere, see also Clifford Siskin, *The Work of Writing: Literature and Social Change in Britain, 1700–1830* (Baltimore: John Hopkins University Press, 1999), p. 224.

4. Tim Fulford, *Romanticism and Masculinity: Gender, Politics and Poetics in the Writings of Burke, Coleridge, Cobbett, Wordsworth, De Quincey, and Hazlitt* (Basingstoke: Macmillan, 1999), p. 23. The concept of the 'performance' of gender derives from the work of Judith Butler, especially *Gender Trouble: Feminism and the Subversion of Identity* (New York: Routledge, 1990).
5. John Campbell Colquhoun, 'Life of Samuel Taylor Coleridge', *Scattered Leaves of Biography* (London: William Macintosh, 1864), 223–70, rpt. in Carmen Joseph Dello Buono, ed., *Rare Early Essays on Samuel Taylor Coleridge* (Darby, PA: Norwood editions, 1981), 59; 'D.', 'The Poets of Our Age, Considered as to Their Philosophic Tendencies', *London and Westminster Review* 25 (April 1836): 67–8; rpt. in J. R. de J. Jackson, ed., *Coleridge: The Critical Heritage Volume 2: 1834–1900* (London: Routledge, 1991), 64. Hereafter cited as Jackson.
6. David Alderson, *Mansex fine: Religion, manliness and imperialism in nineteenth-century British culture* (Manchester: Manchester University Press, 1998), p. 13.
7. Andrew Dowling, *Manliness and the Male Novelist in Victorian Literature* (Aldershot: Ashgate, 2001), p. 13.
8. 'Introduction', *Manliness and Morality: Middle-Class Masculinity in Britain and America 1800–1940*, ed. J. A. Mangan, and James Walvin (Manchester: Manchester University Press, 1987), p. 4. For fuller discussion of the effort by churchmen and teachers to promote 'Christian manliness' among the working class, and its derivation from the 'moral earnestness' of the Rugby ethos, see John Springhall, 'Building character in the British boy: the attempt to extend Christian manliness to working-class adolescents, 1880–1914', *Manliness and Morality*, 52–74. On the spread of Arnoldian 'manliness' beyond the public school itself see John Tosh, 'Domesticity and Manliness in the Victorian Middle Class: the family of Edward White Benson', *Manful Assertions: Masculinities in Britain since 1800*, ed. Michael Roper, and John Tosh (London: Routledge, 1991), pp. 44–73; and, on the adoption of the public school ethos as the 'language of a national culture', see Jonathan Rutherford, *Forever England: Reflections on Race, Masculinity and Empire* (London: Lawrence and Wishart, 1997), p. 15.
9. *Letters of Ralph Waldo Emerson*, ed. Ralph L. Rusk, 6 vols (New York: Columbia University Press, 1939), 6:19. Note also George Ripley's remark to Emerson, in a letter of 5 October 1835: 'It will be a curious fact, if Carlyle, as well as Coleridge & Wordsworth should find his warmest admirers in old Massachusetts […]' (*Letters of Ralph Waldo Emerson* 1:433).
10. Quoted in J. R. de J. Jackson, 'Introduction', *Logic*, xliv. On this topic see also Anthony John Harding, 'Coleridge as Mentor and the Origins of Masculinist Modernity', *European Romantic Review* 14 (2003): 453–66.
11. *The Collected Letters of Samuel Taylor Coleridge*, 6 vols, ed. Earl Leslie Griggs (Oxford: Clarendon Press, 1956–71), VI, 629. Hereafter cited as *CL*.
12. Alderson is quoting *On the Constitution of the Church and State*, ed. John Colmer (Princeton, NJ: Princeton University Press, 1976), pp. 42–3.
13. Unsigned review from the *British Critic* 3 (October, 1826), rpt in J. R. de J. Jackson, ed., *Coleridge: The Critical Heritage* (London: Routledge and Kegan Paul, 1970), pp. 486, 504.
14. Unsigned review of Cottle's *Early Recollections*, *Eclectic Review* 2 (August 1837), rpt in J. R. de J. Jackson, ed., *Coleridge: The Critical Heritage Volume 2: 1834–1900* (London: Routledge, 1991), p. 65. On the emergence of Hare and

Maurice as Coleridgeans when it was not quite respectable to be so, see Stephen Prickett, *Romanticism and Religion: The Tradition of Coleridge and Wordsworth in the Victorian Church* (Cambridge: Cambridge University Press, 1976), pp. 123–4.

15. F. D. Maurice, Dedication to *The Kingdom of Christ* (1842), rpt in Jackson, ed. (1991), p. 126.
16. J. S. Mill, review of *Table Talk* and other works, *London and Westminster Review*, 1840, rpt in Jackson, ed. (1991), p. 67.
17. Ibid.
18. Ibid., pp. 68–9.
19. Ibid., pp. 69–70.
20. John Tulloch, 'Coleridge as a Spiritual Thinker', *Fortnightly Review* 37 (January, 1885), rpt in Jackson, ed. (1991), p. 158.
21. John Campbell Colquhoun, 'Life of Samuel Taylor Coleridge', *Scattered Leaves of Biography* (1864), rpt in Dello Buono, ed., p. 88.
22. Ibid., p. 59.
23. Ibid., p. 68.
24. Ibid., p. 67.
25. Ibid., p. 52.
26. Matthew Arnold, 'Joubert, or a French Coleridge', *National Review* 18 (January, 1864), rpt in Jackson, ed. (1991), p. 142.
27. Ibid.
28. Algernon Charles Swinburne, preface to his edition of *Christabel* (1875), rpt in Jackson, ed. (1991), pp. 147–8.
29. Ibid., p.149.
30. Ibid.
31. Ibid., pp. 149–50.
32. *Biographia Literaria*, 2 vols, ed. James Engell and W. Jackson Bate (Princeton, NJ: Princeton University Press, 1983), II, 15–16.
33. Swinburne, preface to *Christabel*, in Jackson, ed. (1991), p. 150.
34. Ibid., p. 147.
35. Ibid., pp. 152, 155.
36. Ibid., pp. 149–50.
37. Hall Caine, *Life of Samuel Taylor Coleridge* (London: Walter Scott, 1887), pp. 86, 90–1.
38. Leslie Stephen, *Hours in a Library*, revised edition, 3 vols (London: Smith, Elder, & Co., 1892), 3:345, 358.
39. Swinburne, preface to *Christabel*, in Jackson, ed. (1991), pp. 149–50.
40. Diane Long Hoeveler, *Romantic Androgyny: The Women Within* (University Park, PA: Pennsylvania State University Press, 1990), p. 176.
41. Karen Swann, '"Christabel": The Wandering Mother and the Enigma of Form', *Studies in Romanticism* 23 (1984): 540–1.
42. Jeanie Watson, 'Coleridge's Androgynous Ideal', *Prose Studies* 6:1 (1983): 41. The passage affirming that men and women shared an 'Identity in the Substance' is quoted from *CL* III: 305. The statement that 'a great mind must be androgynous' is reported in *Table Talk* for 1 September 1832 (*TT* II: 190–1).
43. Anya Taylor, 'Coleridge, Wollstonecraft, and the Rights of Woman', *Coleridge's Visionary Languages*, ed. Tim Fulford, and Morton D. Paley (Cambridge: D. S. Brewer, 1993), pp. 84, 86.

44. Ibid., p. 92.
45. Anya Taylor, 'Coleridge's *Christabel* and the Phantom Soul', *Studies in English Literature 1500–1900* 42.4 (2002): 711.
46. *Table Talk*, 2 vols, ed. Carl Woodring (Princeton, NJ: Princeton University Press, 1990), II, 74–5.
47. Heather Jackson, 'Coleridge's Women, or Girls, Girls, Girls Are Made to Love', *Studies in Romanticism* 32.4 (Winter 1993): 582, 585.
48. Anne K. Mellor, 'Coleridge and the Question of Female Talents', *Romanticism* 8.2 (2002): 121, 123.
49. Ibid., see p. 127.
50. Carlson, p. 206.
51. For example: citing a notebook entry in which Coleridge describes Wordsworth as 'more *manly*, and altogether more attractive to any the purest woman': *The Notebooks of Samuel Taylor Coleridge*, 5 vols, ed. Kathleen Coburn, Merton Christenson, and Anthony John Harding (Princeton, NJ: Princeton University Press, 1957–2002), II, 3148. Stephen Weissman discerns a recurring pattern in Coleridge's life: his attempts to form 'a harmonious brotherly quartet' by attaching himself emotionally to the sister or sister-in-law of a stronger man. Weissman suggests of course that the beloved woman's function is to act as 'go-between' or 'fantasy-vehicle' for Coleridge's 'unconsciously homosexual attachment' to the brother-figure. See *His Brother's Keeper: A Psychobiography of Samuel Taylor Coleridge*, Applied Psychoanalysis Monograph Series of the Chicago Institute for Psychoanalysis: I (Madison, CT: International Universities Press, 1989), pp. xiv, 266. For a more positive description of Coleridge's relationship to the Wordsworths, see John Worthen, *The Gang: Coleridge, the Hutchinsons and the Wordsworths in 1802* (New Haven: Yale University Press, 2001), pp. 15, 29–30. Richard Holmes also gives a more positive account of Coleridge's relationships, though observing that 'He would not – could not – break out of his cage; but he would make it a place to sing, his "whole Note". From his wife, from Asra, from the Wordsworths, from Lamb, from all his friends – he simply asked for love and understanding in return'. *Coleridge: Early Visions* (London: Hodder and Stoughton, 1989), p. 315.
52. Eve Kosofsky Sedgwick, *Between Men: English Literature and Male Homosocial Desire* (New York: Columbia University Press, 1985), p. 118.

6
'The Luther of Brahminism': Coleridge and the Reformation of Hinduism

Daniel Sanjiv Roberts

The name of Coleridge is one of the few English names of our time which are likely to be oftener pronounced, and to become symbolical of more important things, in proportion as the inward workings of the age manifest themselves more and more in outward facts.

(J. S. Mill, 'Coleridge,' *Mill on Bentham and Coleridge*)

Oh name of Coleridge, that hast mixed so much with the trepidations of our own agitated life, mixed with the beatings of our love, our gratitude, our trembling hope; name destined to move so much of reverential sympathy and so much of ennobling strife in the generations yet to come, of our England at home, of our other Englands on the St Lawrence, on the Mississippi, on the Indus and Ganges, and on the pastoral solitudes of Austral climes!

(De Quincey, 'Conversation and S. T. Coleridge,'
Works)

Echoing J. S. Mill's prognosis of 1840, De Quincey's fervid hopes for Coleridge's reputation not only in England, but also abroad, in the context of nineteenth-century colonial expansion, deserves surely to be quoted in a collection of essays dedicated to *Coleridge's Afterlives*.[1] Coleridge's famous comment in his *Table Talk* about colonization as an 'imperative duty' on Britain, 'God seems to hold out his finger to us over the sea,' encapsulates well the growing consciousness of Romantic writers that Britain's destiny – and with it their own posterity – was bound in with imperialism. In so envisaging Coleridge's 'afterlife,'

85

De Quincey's anticipation of 'reverential sympathy' and 'ennobling strife' attending on Coleridge's name points suggestively to the sagacious and controversial aspects of Coleridge's religious thought in his later prose works, which, during the colonialist Victorian period, took precedence over the poetry and earlier radical writing privileged by the twentieth century. My purpose in this essay is to explore an aspect of Coleridge's afterlife in the colonies; specifically, the relation of his religious, aesthetic and cultural criticisms to the reformulations of Hinduism (within the wider framework of Indian nation formation) attempted by two key figures of the Bengali intelligentsia during the nineteenth century: Raja Rammohun Roy (1772?–1833) and Bankim Chandra Chattopadhyay (1838–94).[2] Both Indian writers were among the leaders of the Bengal Renaissance, the intellectual and reformist movement of nineteenth-century India which questioned the orthodoxies and traditions of Hindu society, seeking to establish Hinduism on a new foundation of scriptural and cultural authority and to purge it of the supposed accretions and corruptions of later times. Such arguments as I wish to indicate were embedded in colonialist discourses regarding the constitutive culture of Hinduism, the modes and manners of Hindu practices apart from its doctrines. 'Hinduism,' it should be noted, is a comparatively new term in this period, denoting a synthetic impulse to categorize and unify the various traditions, practices and beliefs of India, in contradistinction to the more recognizable forms of codified religion, i.e., Islam, Christianity and Judaism, also prevalent in the region.[3] It is worth noting that Coleridge's understanding of Hinduism is largely based on the Brahminical model, and he distinguishes it sharply from Buddhism[4] (which other accounts often treat as complementary to or a branch of Hinduism).

Coleridge's explicit interest in just such a project as that of the Bengal Renaissance with regard to Hinduism may be gauged by his excited remarks on Rammohun Roy in a letter to Southey of 31 January 1819: 'A Brahmin has, I hear, arisen to attempt what we have both so often wished – viz, to be the Luther of Brahminism – and with all the effect, that could be wished – considering the times'.[5] Coleridge's notice to Southey that Rammohun Roy's work was an attempt to accomplish what he and Southey had 'both so often wished' clearly reveals a long-standing and shared concern regarding Hinduism on the part of both poets, a concern that Southey had effectively translated into poetry in his epic, *The Curse of Kehama* (1810), a work he appended with extensive notes reflecting his immersion in Indological researches of the period.[6] Like Southey, Coleridge remained deeply interested in Hinduism throughout his life, first learning of its classical traditions and history through the pioneering work of the British Orientalist, Sir William Jones and his colleagues and heirs of the Asiatic Society which he founded, Charles Wilkins and Thomas Maurice among others. In this early phase, Hinduism clearly melded well with Coleridge's own tendencies to Unitarianism and natural religion, and was consistent with his radical criticisms of institutionalized Christianity. The impact of Coleridge's c.1796 reading of the first volume of Thomas Maurice's *The History of Hindostan* (1795) which included a description of the birth of Brahma out of a lotus and a plate of the Indian god Vishnu 'reposing during [...] a thousand Ages' is reflected in a letter of 14 October 1797 to Thelwall in which his yearnings for a simpler, monotheistic and natural form of religion, tending towards though distinguished from pantheism, yield to a death-wish of sorts. This desire is expressed in a vision of dreamy and eternal bliss such as he identifies with the consciousness of the Hindu god Vishnu:

> My mind feels as if it ached to behold & know something *great* – something *one* & *indivisible* – and it is only in the faith of this that rocks or waterfalls, mountains or caverns give me the sense of sublimity or majesty! – But in this faith *all things* counterfeit infinity! [...] It is but seldom that I raise & spiritualize my intellect to this height – & at other times I adopt the Brahman Creed, & say – It is better to sit than to stand, it is better to lie than to sit, it is better to sleep than to wake – but Death is the best of all! – I should much wish, like the Indian Vishna, [Vishnu] to float about along an infinite ocean cradled in the flower of the Lotos, & wake once in a million years for a few minutes – just to know that I was going to sleep for a million years more.[7]

Coleridge's identification here of Hindu thought as a philosophy of indolence and detachment is clearly attractive to him at a personal level, suggestive of his shared sense with Thelwall of a beleaguered radical politics in the late 1790s. Yet the comment is not without its satirical edge, introducing an element of self-deprecation on Coleridge's part, as Hinduism, now classified as the original or native religion of India, came under increasing criticism in the early nineteenth century, for its supposed political and social weaknesses. As the argument went, the alleged despotism and priestcraft of the religion had inculcated in India a weak and corrupted political order conducive to social stagnation and to imperial domination. Quoting, in fact, the very same passage from the 'Brahman creed' cited by Coleridge, James Mill, in the chapter on Hindu 'Manners'[8] in his influential *History of British India*

(1817), identified the trait of indolence as the national characteristic of the Hindus:

> The love of repose reigns in India with more powerful sway, than in any other region probably of the globe. 'It is more happy to be seated than to walk; it is more happy to sleep than to be awake; but the happiest of all is death.'[9] Such is one of the favourite sayings, most frequently in the mouths of this listless tribe, and most descriptive of their habitual propensities. Phlegmatic indolence pervades the nation.

In Mill's analysis, however, this trait was attributable most directly to the political order of India, and not to other commonly ascribed reasons which he dismisses – such as the tropical climate or the alleged barbarity of the people:

> there is but one cause, to which, among the Hindus, the absence of the motives for labour can be ascribed; their subjection to a wretched government, under which the fruits of labour were never secure.
>
> (I: 333)

Such criticisms of the Hindus, and the Indian nation identified with them, would become increasingly strident through the nineteenth century, legitimizing the growth of imperialism through the period.

In his illuminating study of the development of British Orientalism through the late eighteenth and nineteenth centuries, *Aryans and British India*, Thomas Trautmann has shown how early enthusiasm for Indian antiquity by the Orientalists of the William Jones school (which Trautmann terms 'Indomania') yielded early in the nineteenth century to a far more negative and critical attitude to India ('Indophobia') due to the interventions of the utilitarians and the missionaries, each with their different agendas for the development of India.[10] While the *classical* Hinduism of the Vedic tradition continued to attract respectful notices from the favourably inclined Orientalist scholars, it was felt that the *modern* practice of the religion was severely debased. Polytheism, idolatry and customs such as *sati* (widow immolation) and the *devadasi* tradition (named 'temple prostitution' by colonialists) were viewed as evils, to be rooted out variously through legislation and religious conversion. Linked to these concerns was the whole issue of education in India: whether it was to be conducted in the traditional way through the classical languages of India (as the Orientalists argued), or to be placed on a western scientific footing and taught through English (as the Anglicists wished).

Following the success of the Anglicists, the latter model prevailed, and English achieved a disciplinary status, helping to resolve the conflicting strains of missionary and utilitarian goals in colonial education.[11] Such a model of education, it was hoped, would drive out the allegedly superstitious and outmoded beliefs and practices of Hindus in India. Educated Bengali elites of the nineteenth century often echoed such sentiments. Yet the resultant form of national modernity spawned by English education in India although often satirized as a form of western imitation may be seen in retrospect to have provided for the new cultural development that was to emerge later in the century as Indian nationalism.

Coleridge's attitude to India and to Hinduism has been characterized rightly as one of disenchantment and growing disillusionment in his later years,[12] though his scattered remarks have not been placed in the wider context of the hardening of colonial attitudes and the development of English education described above. Yet Coleridge's importance to these arguments and the new overseas reading audiences in English should not be underestimated. His significance here, as I'd like to suggest, is that of a cultural critic, one of the first of the Victorian sages, who sought to reconcile English civil society with theological orthodoxy through the promotion of a national culture. Such a programme, though addressed to English Christian audiences, was not without its consequences in a wider colonial arena, as De Quincey had anticipated, of his growing overseas readership. Despite his growing discontent with Hinduism, Coleridge continued to recognize a certain degree of doctrinal truth in the Brahminical tradition, though sadly overcome in his view by mythological and doctrinal contradictions. The persistence of his optimism that Hinduism *could* be reformed is suggestive of a residue of revolutionary optimism in his outlook, despite the growing conservatism of his later years. In his *Aids to Reflection* (1825), he argued that the Christian doctrine of original sin – for him a self-evident 'Fact' – was embedded in the Hindu scriptures, though also obscured through the contradictions of their mythology:

> in the most ancient Books of the Brahmins, the deep sense of this Fact, and the doctrines grounded on obscure traditions of the promised remedy, are seen struggling, and now gleaming, now flashing, through the Mists of Pantheism, and producing the incongruities and gross contradictions of the Brahmin Mythology.
>
> (283)

Such a recognition is consistent, of course, with his remarks quoted earlier on the need for reform of the religion, and bespeaks the transition from radicalism to reform which Coleridge's political trajectory displays.[13] His qualified respect for the 'ancient Books of the Brahmins' is tempered by 'the incongruities and gross contradictions' that have overcome its mythology.

Coleridge was probably influenced at this point by his earlier reading of the Abbé J. A. Dubois's *Description of the Character, Manners, and Customs of the People of India* (1817), a work which he annotated with close engagement.[14] While disagreeing with Dubois on the several details of his doctrinal interpretation of Brahminism, his recognition of the 'gleams' and 'flashes' of true doctrine hidden within their ancient books seems indebted to Dubois's theory that Brahminical teaching had gone astray from the wisdom of original sources, mistaking allegory or symbol for literal truths and hence materializing the religion's spiritual content. In Dubois's account:

> Their mythology originally consisted of allegories made intelligible by means of visible and material objects, so that religious knowledge may not die out of the minds of men who appeared to be little influenced by anything that failed to make a direct impression on their senses. But a coarse, ignorant, indolent, and superstitious race soon forgot the spirit of its creed, and ended by believing solely in the forms and emblems which had been employed; so that, before long, they quite lost sight of the spiritual beings of which these emblems were only symbolical.[15]

Dubois's hypothesis of an original symbolic truth lost to the Hindus on account of a gross material construction of it clearly accords well with Coleridge's simultaneously expressed theology and poetics of the symbol in the *The Statesman's Manual*, which read the Biblical histories in symbolic terms as 'the living *educts* of the Imagination'.[16] Indeed, Dubois's suggestion that symbolic truth was somehow overwhelmed by allegories based on 'visible and material objects' seems to reflect interestingly Coleridge's famous distinction in *The Statesman's Manual* between symbol and allegory, the former being sensationalist and the latter idealist. For Coleridge, this distinction between symbol and allegory was made in the context of his criticisms of English culture which he felt had been contaminated by sensationalist and mechanical philosophies:

> The histories and political economies of the present and preceding century partake in the general contagion of its mechanic philosophy, and are the product of an unenlivened generalizing understanding.
>
> (*Lay Sermons*, 29)

As I will indicate, Rammohun Roy and Bankim may be seen as heirs of a Coleridgean legacy in this regard, seeking to reform Hinduism theologically as well as culturally by turning Coleridge's conception of a clerisy or 'national church' to the Hindu/Indian national context, and thus fulfilling De Quincey's colonialist and expansionist expectations for his mentor in unexpected ways. The inheritance I am suggesting, however, should not be conceived of along the lines of a strict identity of thought, or of explicit literary allegiances – indeed both Rammohun Roy and Bankim come to different conclusions from each other, let alone from Coleridge – but rather in terms of their cohabitation within a broader discursive sphere in which their writings may be seen to interact and develop in analogous and comparable ways.

* * *

It was in the context of the Christian apologetics of his later years that Coleridge emerged as a cultural critic for the Victorian period. These apologetics were, as Coleridge emphasized, not merely speculative and doctrinal matters, but were bound up with historical and social change, and the praxes of new branches of learning. Recognizing these factors, Coleridge addressed himself specifically to an English Christian audience. *Aids to Reflection* commences with an exhortation to the manly Christian reader to engage in spiritual reflection, a necessity which, as Coleridge sees it, is under threat from the ever-greater specialisms of knowledge:

> READER! – You have been bred in a land abounding with men, able in arts, learning, and knowledges manifold, this man in one, this in another, few in many, none in all. But there is one art of which every man should be master, the art of REFLECTION. If you are not a *thinking* man, to what purpose are you a *man* at all?
>
> (9)

Coleridge's fears in this respect are an exact opposite of those of T. B. Macaulay, ten years later, addressing the issue of education in India. The opposition lies evidently in the differing social bodies, the kinds of men, envisaged by these very different thinkers. For the utilitarian Macaulay, the education of Indians in their own languages was prone to dissolve the native subject into abstruse metaphysical and theological speculations, 'all the mysteries of absorption into the Deity' that 'the Sacred Books of the Hindoos' could offer.[17] The problem besetting Indians was not a failure to reflect, but the opposite of it, the failure to acquire 'knowledges manifold.' Macaulay's solution, famously, was to recommend the study of English as the only robust and practical way forward for India, English as he saw it being the language in which 'full and correct information respecting every experimental science which tends to preserve the health, to increase the comfort, or to expand the intellect of man' was available (182–3).

Coleridge's opposition to the utilitarian zeitgeist, however, was evident to his contemporaries and was enshrined for the latter part of the nineteenth century in the classically polarized essays of J. S. Mill on Bentham and Coleridge in 1838. These writers – Bentham and Coleridge, J. S. Mill and his father James Mill, along with the canonical Romantics, Wordsworth, Byron and Shelley – became part of the staple reading for the newly instituted discipline of English studies in India. In his essays on Bentham and Coleridge, Mill identified them as 'the two great seminal minds of England in their age' and went on to characterize their thinking as 'Progressive' and 'Conservative,' respectively:

> The writings of both contain severe lessons to their own side, on many of the errors and faults they are addicted to: but to Bentham it was given to discern more particularly those truths with which existing doctrines and institutions were at variance; to Coleridge, the neglected truths which lay *in* them.[18]

While utilitarian thinking has been well studied in relation to colonial India[19] and the rise of what Macaulay presciently labelled 'a class [...] of interpreters between us and the millions whom we govern' (190), a corresponding use of Coleridge, as a crucial oppositional figure to Benthamite philosophy, is worth developing in relation to his colonial readership and influence.[20] Reading the later Coleridge of the post-Napoleonic era as a religious and cultural critic in this way, we may recognize in Mill's insightful comments Coleridge's tendency to advocate a conservative position in religion as in politics – recovering 'neglected truths' – even while criticizing English intellectual culture for its negligence in overlooking these. Such a recognition can be viewed not only in relation to English literary culture, but also as a viable model for cultural criticism in a colonial context. The following remarks, focussing selectively on two writers of the Bengal Renaissance, are offered as a step in this direction. Rammohun Roy and Bankim Chandra Chattopadhyay both wrote widely in English and in Bengali – the latter gravitating towards Bengali in his later years in reaction against the deracination as he perceived it of English-educated ('Baboo') Indians. This article will focus on a few of their significant Hindu reformatory texts, Rammohun Roy's Vedantic translations and commentaries mostly published piece-meal in Bengali, Hindi and English versions by the author in Kolkata between 1816 and 1817, and republished in London in 1817 under the title of *Translation of an Abridgement of the Vedant*, as well as Bankim's *Dharmatattva* published in Bengali 1888 (and translated into English by Apratim Ray in 2003). These texts are significant in challenging and engaging with the powerful imperialist constructions of Hinduism in the colonial period, mediating between European and native perspectives, and seeking to reinterpret and reform the religion for the purposes of a conservative recovery of tradition. In this respect they may be seen to take their bearings from Coleridge's critical example against the secular and utilitarian model which was its polar opposite.

The writings of Rammohun and Bankim reveal the development of an elite educated cultural formation in India along the lines of Coleridge's ideal in *On the Constitution of the Church and State* (1830) of a national church or 'clerisy' who would harmonize and ground the development of civilization in a wider humanistic concern which could be called cul-ture. Carrying echoes of his earlier revolutionary critique of a corrupt and over-refined aristocracy, Coleridge's 'desynonymizing' analysis sep-arates carefully between civilization and culture:

> civilization is itself but a mixed good, if not far more a corrupting influence, the hectic of disease, not the bloom of health, and a nation so distinguished more fitly to be called a varnished than a polished people; where this civilization is not grounded in *cultivation*, in the harmonious development of those qualities and faculties that charac-terize our *humanity*.[21]

This analysis leads to his conclusion, exemplifying the 'most valuable of the lessons taught by history [...] – that a nation can never be a too culti-vated, but may easily become an over-civilized race' (43). This distinction, in Coleridge's thinking, was particularly relevant to classical Hinduism in that it reflected what he had described in the *Aids to Reflection* as the 'highly *civilized*, though fearfully *uncultivated*, inhabitants of ancient India' (22).[22] Responding to the influential criticisms of Mill, Coleridge's distinction was a crucial one for both Rammohun Roy and Bankim. For both writers, Hindu passiveness to the unfair criticisms and taunts of Christian missionaries was a fault of the Hindus' own making, deriving from their gentle and ultimately over-civilized nature. Here Hindu civilization is represented in the colonialist mould of being effeminately constituted, and hence open to imperial/cultural conquest. In Rammohun Roy's analysis in the *Brahmunical Magazine* (1821) which he edited:

> We have been subjected to such insults for about nine centuries, and the cause of such degradation has been our excess in civilization and abstinence from the slaughter even of animals; as well as our division into castes, which has been the source of want of unity among us.[23]

In his *Dharmatattva*, Bankim, as we will see, goes even further with this critique of the excessive development of Indian civilization, identifying the Hindu concept of *dharma* (piety/duty/religion) with culture in order to issue a corrective, and rejecting the suggestion that culture is a western notion: 'There is nothing Western about culture. Culture is the very substance of Hindu dharma'.[24] As we will see, however, both writers, Rammohun Roy and Bankim, launch their reform(ul)atory projects for Hinduism on their ability to mediate a new conception of Hindu tradition and culture to the emerging reading audiences of modern India.

* * *

Coleridge's comment on Rammohun Roy quoted at the start of this essay, recognizing Rammohun Roy as a 'Luther' of the Brahmins, was made in 1819, after the latter had published a series of articles in the Unitarian *Monthly Magazine* between 1817 and 1818. These articles were extracts from his earlier work, *Translation of an Abridgement of the Vedant*, first published in Calcutta in 1816 and republished in London the next year. While Rammohun Roy's work was, in fact, contemporaneous with Coleridge's, it is quite likely that he would have encountered Coleridge's reputation as a radical preacher – such as Hazlitt testifies to his in his 1823 essay 'On My First Acquaintance with Poets' – in the context of the Unitarian movement with which he was associated in India and which provided a context too for some of his public appearances in Britain in the 1830s. Rammohun Roy's ability to reconcile his Hinduism with his Unitarianism suggests how closely his outlook may be aligned with Coleridge's earlier attitude to Hinduism during his radical phase. Though there is no record of Rammohun Roy's formal study of English literature, it is clear that by 1815 at least he was well read in English, probably through his own intellectual drive and his work for the East India Company between 1803 and 1815. In the debate regarding education in India, he supported English rather than Sanskrit in an address to Lord

Amherst, Governor-General of India in 1823, arguing the case in strikingly similar (utilitarian) terms to those put forward by Macaulay twelve years later. Some of these aspects of his work, including his well-known campaign against *sati*, may have prompted Bentham's admiring response when he wrote to Rammohun Roy in 1828: 'I read a style which but for the name of a Hindoo I should certainly have ascribed to the pen of a superiorly educated and instructed Englishman'.[25] Yet Rammohun Roy's development of the Vedantic tradition in Hinduism through his translations and commentaries, and his foundation of the Bramho Samaj, the institutionalized embodiment of his reformatory principles, all denote far more than a Benthamite utilitarian perspective would allow. Coleridge's recognition of Rammohun Roy needs to be placed, as I've suggested earlier, in the context of the growing evangelical criticisms of Hinduism, and of his own attempts to argue for a national church or clerisy in opposition to the mechanical nature of the utilitarian philosophy. Rammohun Roy's construction of Hinduism can be seen likewise to address several of the common criticisms of missionaries and utilitarians, predicating a textual authority for the religion and recovering as it were an idealist tradition for Hindu philosophy within this framework.

A fundamental difficulty with Hinduism in the eyes of its early missionary critics was the absence of any textual basis on which to secure its religious doctrine. As Geoffrey Oddie has argued in his book, *Imagined Hinduism: British Protestant Missionary Constructions of Hinduism, 1793–1800*, it is important to recognize in any comparative study of Hindu and Christian thinking, that the concept of religion in this context is largely a post-enlightenment western one, emphasizing belief and doctrine over performative religion, the ceremonies, customs and traditions that characterized native religious practices in all their diversity across the Indian subcontinent.[26] The construction of Hinduism as a religious creed was stymied, therefore, by the difficulty of establishing any sort of textual authority for the religion. Not only was there a lack of central authority to determine doctrinal orthodoxy, but the various texts of Hindu scriptures were not codified or collected in any single canonical or authorized version. In this respect, Rammohun Roy's programme of privileging the text of the Vedanta may be seen to fulfil a Christian scripturalist imperative:

> The whole body of the Hindoo Theology, Law, and Literature, is contained in the Veds, which are affirmed to be coeval with the creation! These works are extremely voluminous, and being written in the most elevated and metaphorical style are, as may be well supposed,

in many passages seemingly confused and contradictory. Upwards of two thousand years ago, the great Byas, reflecting on the perpetual difficulty arising from these sources, composed with great discrimination a complete and compendious abstract of the whole, and also reconciled those texts which appeared to stand at variance. This work he termed *The Vedant*, which, compounded of two Sungscrit words, signifies *The Resolution of all the Veds*.

(Rammohun Roy, 3)

The Vedas are here presented as a compendium of Hindu doctrine, pre-dating Christianity certainly in historical terms, and viewed by its adherents as a revealed work, its origins 'coeval with the creation.' However, their voluminousness and the metaphorical style in which they were written conspire to render their meaning opaque to a modern age.

Whereas, however the Christian scriptures had been canonized by the Church fathers through an institutional process, Rammohun Roy bases his privileging of the Vedant on popular acceptance by the Hindus themselves: 'It has continued to be most highly revered by all Hindoos, and in place of the more diffuse arguments of the Veds, is always referred to as of equal authority' (3). Yet, Rammohun Roy's appeal here to popular acceptance of the authority of the text is carefully discriminated from popular practice of the religion: 'the Vedant, although perpetually quoted, is little known to the public: and the practice of few Hindoos indeed bears the least accordance with its precepts!' (4). By thus discriminating popular acceptance of the authority of the text from popular practice, Rammohun Roy prepares the ground for his cultural critique of Hinduism.[27] The problem, however, besetting a return to the true Vedantic philosophy of Hinduism was that the text of the Vedant, like that of the Latin Bible, had been obscured from public knowledge, 'being concealed within the dark curtain of the Sungscrit language' which was known to the Brahmins alone, and not to the common people (4). The translation and interpretations of the Vedant he offers, based on the philosophy of the ninth-century Hindu theologian Śankarā, thus not only attempts to locate a doctrinal centrality within Hinduism, but also to develop a mode of cultural criticism, directing his versions of the Vedantic text against the various corruptions of modern Hindu practice as also the criticisms of European detractors.

Despite its basis in a textual tradition it is important to stress that Rammohun Roy's turn to Vedantic Hinduism as an antidote to the largely dismissive criticisms of the colonial establishment was, in the context of the plurality of Hindu philosophical traditions, a judiciously selective and carefully calculated attempt to mediate between Hindu tradition and the new emerging colonial culture in Bengal. Among the traditions of Hindu philosophy which the Orientalists first made known to European audiences, the Advaitic philosophy of Śankarā was initially received in very positive terms. Coleridge's passing comment that in the context of his marginalia on Dubois that 'Spinosa was no Materialist, but the sternest & most consistent of *Adwitamists'* (*Collected Marginalia*, II: 340) indicates the high intellectual regard in which he held the Advaitic philosophy, Spinosa being the philosopher of his 'head' though not his 'heart' as described in the *Biographia Literaria*.[28] Rammohun Roy's singling out of the Advaitic tradition as in many ways the most appealing and compatible of Hindu traditions to the new rationalist and westernizing impulse in India was anticipated to an extent by the praise bestowed on this tradition by Sir William Jones, the founder of the Asiatic Society of Bengal and the most eminent of the early British Orientalists. In his eleventh-anniversary discourse of 1794, 'On the Philosophy of the Asiaticks,' Sir William Jones had signalled the piety and purity of the Vedantic school in terms that link this philosophy with Western idealist traditions:

The fundamental tent of the *Védántí* school, to which in a more modern age the incomparable SANCARA was a firm and illustrious adherent, consisted, not in denying the existence of matter, [...] but, in correcting the popular notion of it, and in contending, that it has no essence independent of mental perception, that existence and perceptibility are convertible terms, that external appearances and sensations are illusory, and would vanish into nothing, if the divine energy, which along sustains them, were suspended but for a moment; an opinion, which EPICHARMUS and PLATO seem to have adopted, and which has been maintained in the present century with great elegance, but with little public applause; partly because it has been misunderstood, and partly because it has been misapplied by the false reasoning of some unpopular writers [...]: nothing can be further removed from impiety than a system wholly built on the purest devotion [...]; though we cannot but admit, that, if the common opinions of mankind be the criterion of philosophical truth, we must adhere to the system of GO'TAMA, which the *Bráhmens* of this province almost certainly follow.[29]

While Jones's admiration of Śankarā and his idealistic philosophy no doubt anticipates Rammohun Roy significantly, it is instructive to compare their very different attitudes with regard to the contemporary value of this philosophy. While both Jones and Rammohun Roy agree that Vedantism had fallen into disregard in the modern period, only the latter sees this as an opportunity to revive its popularity and assert its utility in modern times. Jones, in contrast, is more objective in attitude, placing the Vedantic school among other traditions of Hindu philosophy, and indeed seeing few prospects for its revival given the popularity of the Nyaya philosophy represented by Gotama. His attitude to Vedantism measures its significance in relation to Greek classical writers such as Epicharmus and Plato, rather than to its contemporary significance for modern India which he regards as marginal.

In contrast to Jones, it is evident that the targets of Rammohun Roy's translations, in spite of their basis in medieval textual sources, were extremely contemporaneous. Most striking of these in doctrinal terms was the prevalence of idolatry and polytheism evident in the multitudinous images worshipped in Hindu temples throughout India. Criticizing wrongly liberal-minded Europeans for romanticizing popular Hinduism by regarding the objects of its worship as 'emblematical representations of the Supreme Divinity,' Rammohun Roy is in fact quite uncompromising in his view of the obtaining practice, 'the truth is, the Hindoos of the present day have no such views of the subject, but firmly believe in the real existence of innumerable gods and goddesses' (4). While agreeing with the missionaries that popular Hinduism was ridden by a false idolatry, Rammohun Roy argued, however, that the Vedanta was in fact free from polytheism and image worship. The disjunction between scriptural and contemporary Hinduism thus presented a radical problem, that its present-day ritualized forms bore little relation to the sublime monotheism of the Vedic scriptures, a form of religion he aligned with Unitarian Christianity. The credulity and superstitiousness of prevailing Hinduism seemed to undermine the essential doctrines of the faith. The admission of this hiatus, however, could be seen by other critics of Hinduism, such as the hostile evangelical faction, not as a prelude to reform, but rather as an admission of defeat and a recognition of the need for conversion. Rammohun Roy's solution, however, was a careful mediation between cultural and theological perspectives. He steers a careful path between current practice and doctrinal belief in his criticisms of modern Hindu ritualism, turning to allegorical or symbolic meaning in order to argue his case:

> There can be no doubt, however, [...] that every rite has its derivation from the allegorical adoration of the true Deity; but at the present day all this is forgotten, and among many it is even heresy to mention it.
>
> (4)

Hence, Rammohun Roy's translations would have the effect not of destroying popular Hinduism, but rather of reminding Hindus of their neglected or 'forgotten' heritage and theology, reading the traces of true religious doctrine in the debased practices of popular Hinduism.

The linguistic obscuration of the Vedas in their Sanskrit form was, of course, in Rammohun Roy's view, no coincidence. As he makes clear from the start, his translations and activities had exposed him to the criticisms of the members of his own caste and even of his relations:

> By taking the path which conscience and sincerity direct, I, born a Brahmun, have exposed myself to the complainings and reproaches, even of some of my relations, whose prejudices are strong, and whose temporal advantage depends upon the present system.
>
> (5)

The preservation of esoteric knowledge in order to maintain power was a feature he identified in the priestly Brahmin caste of India who had by virtue of the caste system maintained a monopoly of the scriptural truths of the Vedas. This criticism emerges openly in his translation of the Ishopanishad from the *Yajurveda*:

> Many learned Brahmins are perfectly aware of the absurdity of idolatry, and are well informed of the nature of the purer mode of divine worship. But as in the rites, ceremonies, and festivals of idolatry, they find the source of their comforts and fortune, they not only never fail to protect idol worship from all attacks, but even advance and encourage it to the utmost of their power, by keeping the knowledge of their scriptures concealed from the rest of the people.
>
> (77)

By addressing his English version of the text to a Western audience, Rammohun Roy hoped for a sympathetic response from his Christian readers, not necessarily to convert them to Hinduism – as Hinduism being nondogmatic had never sought converts – but rather to obtain a sympathetic regard among them for the religion founded on universalist principles. As his commentary on the *Céna Upanishad* suggests:

> Such benevolent people will, perhaps, rise from a perusal of them with the conviction that in the most ancient of times the inhabitants of this part of the globe (at least the more intelligent class) were not unacquainted with metaphysical subjects; that allegorical language or

description was very frequently employed to represent the attributes of the Creator, which were sometimes designated as independent existences; and that, however suitable this method might be to the refined understandings of men of learning, it had the most mischievous effect when literature and philosophy decayed, producing all those absurdities and idolatrous notions which have checked, or rather destroyed every mark of reason, and darkened every beam of understanding.

(40)

By returning his appeal to the 'benevolent' members of the colonial establishment, Rammohun Roy may be seen to negotiate a subtle path between the reformation of a native tradition and the conscription of the political elite in India at the time. His theology may be seen therefore as genuinely of a hybrid nature, mediating between imperialist criticisms of Hinduism, and the recovery of a tradition based on a discrete cultural identity.

* * *

The careers of Rammohun Roy and Bankim Chandra Chattopadhyay follow similar paths in many ways. Both were Brahmins who worked for the colonial establishment, and made their mark as writers in apparent opposition both to traditional and colonialist points of view, conducting running arguments with both sides in their publications. However, while Rammohun Roy was fond of employing a serious form of irony in his arguments – for instance, reversing missionary arguments against superstition to attack Christian Trinitarianism effectively on the same grounds – Bankim on the other hand was far more prone to use humour and subtle invective as his rhetorical mode,[30] poking fun at his adversaries – such as his arch-opponent the Rev. William Hastie – while professing to be not a whit bothered by their supposedly feeble arguments. This attitude perhaps emanates from his irreverent 'Young Bengal' influence in youth, an attitude associated with the Hindu College admirers of Henry Derozio who drew on the radical traditions of Enlightenment thought as well as on missionary arguments to attack traditionalist Hindu thinking in Bengal.[31] Both Rammohun Roy and Bankim are often classed as reformers of Hinduism, but though the latter was influenced by Rammohun Roy's Bramho doctrines with regard to his reformatory ideals, he disagreed profoundly with him on the nature of popular religion, accepting the polytheism and idol worship of popular Hinduism as crucial aspects of devotionality. Their theologies are thus fundamentally different.

While Rammohun Roy was educated in the classical traditions of India, learning Persian and Arabic in Patna between the ages of nine and twelve, and thereafter Sanskrit in Benares until the age of 16, before he acquired English (apparently without a formal training and through his service for the East India Company), Bankim on the other hand was more formally educated in English, reading the prescribed literary canon in English at school and developing a classical taste in literature.[32] Yet Bankim too was deeply educated in his early years in the Sanskrit tradition, which he was born into, and he returned to the *Mahabharata* as the basis for his excavation of a historical Hinduism through the figure of Krishna in his later work entitled *Krishnacharitra* (1886). His wittiest and most destabilizing work, however, is the satirical *Kamalakanta Duptar* (1875), in which he introduced the eccentric distinctive voice of the opium-eating Bengali narrator, Kamalakanta, modelled on the romantic figures of Coleridge and De Quincey, dispensing wisdom and sometimes bathos in a disturbing mix of narrative traditions and styles. The latter work, however, is almost untranslatable from the Bengali original (which puns interestingly between Bengali and English) and it is his later work, *Dharmatattva* (1885), more seminal to our discussion, that I turn to for an illumination of Coleridgean discursive inheritance. The following analysis, it should be emphasized, does not constitute a comprehensive commentary on the text, but focuses on those aspects of Bankim's work – his definitions of culture and aesthetics – that appear analogous to Coleridgean thinking.

In his introduction to the *Dharmatattva* for the recent Oxford edition, Amiya Sen distinguishes between the critical methods of Rammohun Roy and Bankim:

> If the charges of 'innovation' levelled against Raja Rammohun Roy by his orthodox contemporaries are true, they would be more so in the case of Bankimchandra for, in many ways, the latter's reformulation of certain key elements in Hindu religion differed more sharply from the way these were understood in tradition. Both Rammohun Roy and Bankimchandra were to deny the charges of innovation, arguing that they were only bringing back to life what in their opinion was 'authentic' Hinduism. Even, so, we cannot help observing that, while the two remain united in their defence, their hermeneutics are far from identical. While the Raja stuck, more or less, to the time-tested methods of textual exegesis, Bankimchandra never considered himself to be bound by these.
>
> (25)

The *Dharmatattva* launches itself in the form of a dialogue between an apparently traditional guru figure (the 'Master') and his Disciple. While there is no doubt that this is a philosophical conversation in the Indian guru–sishya tradition wherein the Master's words are revealed as wisdom and the Disciple is engaged in a learning process, the Disciple's evident scepticism and even cheekiness at times reveals the work as being located in a more contested space, akin to the Bakhtinian notion of dialogism. In the context of a Coleridgean afterlife, Bankim's sceptical voice in the Disciple, a trace emergence of his Young Bengal attitude, corresponds interestingly to Coleridge's youthful radicalism, suppressed though never fully overcome in his later critical thinking.

In a chapter surveying Bankim's thought in relation to the emergence of Indian nationalism, Tapan Raychaudhuri, in his book, *Europe Reconsidered: Perceptions of the West in Nineteenth-Century Bengal*, has lucidly discriminated Bankim's view on culture in the *Dharmatattva* from Benthamite utilitarianism by which he was influenced but which he never found sufficient:

> He sees Utilitarianism as a worship of the good and hence attributes to it the characteristics of religion. But it is an incomplete religion, because it does not include the worship of the Beautiful and the True as well. [...] The lengthy discussion on the subject in Dharmatattva accepts the Utilitarian ideal almost in its entirety, but argues that it is not enough and must be subsumed by the doctrine of culture.
>
> (200)

In the following analysis I shall concentrate on a Coleridgean dimension to this corrective aspect of Bankim's critique, arguing that it is in Coleridge that Bankim's religious thinking finds the most significant parallel among his western influences, though clearly he himself arrives at this understanding without a direct application of Coleridge's work. The later Coleridge, certainly, would have been less than pleased to be associated with the more martial and explicitly Hindu aspects of Bankim's writings (especially in novels such as *Anandamath* [1882] and *Sitaram* [1886] which seem to delight in military victories over Muslim forces), though the two writers can be seen to work out a parallel development of religious culture in their own spheres. Bankim himself tends to credit Auguste Comte's Positivism and Robert Seeley's humanistic view of Christianity as his major influences, and mentions Matthew Arnold's views of culture in passing, though none of these writers is fully adequate by his admission. Instead he develops the traditional

Hindu notion of 'dharma' which he insists anticipates, contains and even surpasses the notion expressed by the English word 'culture.'

Throughout his writings, a troubling aspect of Bengali culture for Bankim is undoubtedly that of the physical weakness of the Hindus.[33] This attitude to Indian physicality, deriving from colonialist criticisms (such as James Mill's quoted earlier) of alleged indolence and lack of physical vigour, explains the unedifying, though unavoidable, fact of colonial rule in India, not only of the British, but also of the earlier Muslim rulers whom Bankim resents quite as much as their British usurpers. His notion of culture therefore includes a strong emphasis on physical development along with mental discipline, while all along asserting the superiority of Hinduism's spirituality. The text which elaborates this doctrine unfolds its message gradually, but this is clearly the first understanding of it that the Disciple achieves:

> DISCIPLE: I take it therefore that, in your opinion, it is only the training and management of our bodily and mental faculties that constitute piety, and the lack of this training and management is impiety.
> MASTER: The doctrines of piety are the most profound of all and cannot be dealt with in a few words. But suppose it is so!
> DISCIPLE: But this is the Western doctrine of Culture!
> MASTER: There is nothing Western about culture. Culture is the very substance of Hindu dharma.
> DISCIPLE: How can it be? There is not a single equivalent of the word "Culture" in any of our native languages.
> MASTER: It is because we grope around for words and do not look for the real meaning that we are reduced to this miserable state. What do you think the four stages in the life of the twice-born signify?
> DISCIPLE: A system of Culture?
> MASTER: Indeed, and so profound is this system that it is doubtful if Western exponents of Culture, like Matthew Arnold, have the capacity to comprehend it.
>
> (*Dharmatattva*, 36)

The English word 'culture' is first introduced to the text by the Disciple. Despite the Master's careful avoidance of the term so far, this is the most readily apprehensible way of approaching the concept for the Disciple. The Master, however, corrects him by establishing that though the word is English/Western, the practice can easily be recognized in the theory of Brahminical spiritual development, and the concept is anticipated and in fact more deeply comprehended in the Sanskrit word 'dharma,' which in turn is then introduced for the first time in the text. The Master, however, is not a novice with regard to Western thinking and immediately shows knowledge of the major exponents of culture, including Arnold.

Yet, the first difficulty with the Western notion of culture for the Master is precisely its secularized even 'atheistic' nature. The Disciple judiciously provides the example of Auguste Comte, whose 'rejection of the personal god' implies that his notion of culture is 'little more than a set of procedures.' The Master endorses this analysis resoundingly:

> You are absolutely right. I cannot say whether this absence of a god is the reason for the Western doctrine remaining undeveloped, or the result of it. Hindus are, by nature, great devotees, and their system is dedicated to the lotus-feet of the Supreme Being.
>
> (37)

Hindu devotionalism – which had been rejected by the utilitarians as empty of content, and by the more strident missionaries as idolatrous and degraded – is here restored to a normative role in Indian culture. The imputed Western scepticism regarding religious belief in God is ambiguously positioned in relation to culture: it is either the reason for it, or the result of it. The ambiguity is revealing because it does not pre-judge the issue of God's prior and independent existence: God is a notion coextensive with human culture, and requires to be developed within this framework. Much of the detail of Bankim's text concerns itself with the details of various devotional traditions and practices, from which he extracts, perhaps disappointingly to minoritarian national sensibilities, a fairly Hindu-bourgeois cultural package: of love for the family, devotion to God, respect for social authority and government, the privileges of the cow, etc. His recuperation of these traditional virtues can be better understood as a reaction against the limitations of English education, too focussed on mere knowledge for utilitarian ends, which as the Master agrees with his disciple is at the root of the problem.

In comparison with Rammohun Roy, Bankim's procedures are eclectic, deriving from a wide variety of textual sources and social practices a theory of culture that reconciles a modern rationalistic outlook with a respect for various Hindu religious practices that had come under attack from some of the colonial establishment in India. Against the Advaitic tradition favoured by Rammohun Roy, he asserts a personal rather than an impersonal God, and insists that religious devotion can only be achieved within a humanistic perspective. Perhaps the most interesting aspect of his work, however, and one relevant to the present discussion is his treatment of aesthetic theory, with which he concludes the argument of *Dharmatattva*. At an earlier point in the text, in the context of a discussion of bhakti (or devotion), the Master seems to denigrate popular religious practices, apparently in tacit agreement with Rammohun Roy's disregard for such practices:

> The singing of God's praises, the paying of homage by offering flowers, the singing of hymns, the worship of idols – all these are manifestations of an inferior form of worship.
>
> (178)

However in the context of his aesthetic theory he seeks to demonstrate the artistic nature of Hindu worship and to reconcile this with devotion, restoring the intimate connection between religion and art, which he considered western civilization to have lost.

> The purpose of flowers, sandalpaste, garlands, incense, lamps, music, song and dance, and all other paraphernalia of Hindu worship is to synchronize the cultivation of the aesthetic faculties with that of bhakti or, at least, to awaken and excite feelings of devotion. Even in the religious practices of ancient Greece and in the Roman Catholicism of medieval Europe, there was a considerable endeavour to inspire and satisfy man's aesthetic urge. [...] All the skills and talents of painters, sculptors, architects and musicians were given over to the serving of spiritual ends.
>
> (224)

Bankim's formulation clearly operates to reconcile the material realm of sensuous perception with that of religious belief and devotion. The ritualism of Hindu culture, which was so appealing and emotionally attractive to the Hindus, was self-justified insofar as it expressed an artistic endeavour by the participants. The implicit separation between modern Evangelical Christians, and the medieval Catholics and ancient Greeks is instructive in that Bankim's argument is more concerned with the immediate representatives of western culture, than a full-scale attack on it. His understanding here of the aesthetics of Hindu worship answers the uncomprehending vision of colonial commentators who criticized these activities as degrading or at best meaningless. The lacunae, however, in the religion were the lack of formal codification of these practices and their integration with religious doctrine: 'what has existed so long as mere folk culture must now be formally codified as gospels and integrated into the main body of the faith' (225). The *Dharmatattva* thus constitutes Bankim's attempted reconciliation of Hindu doctrine with culture, a notion that is evidently English and modern, but which he paradoxically reclaims for Hindu tradition.

* * *

In seeking to relate Rammohun Roy and Bankim with Coleridge's critical influence, it is important to stress that we do not thereby imply a negation of the traditional (classical and popular) Indian texts and sources that both Rammohun Roy and Bankim emphasized with good reason as primary to their thinking. Bankim's aesthetic theory in the *Dharmatattva* returns in the end to the ineffable doctine of satchitānanda (that blissful state of consciousness which evidently Coleridge had desired in his identification with the God Vishnu in the letter to Thelwall):

> MASTER: The aesthetic faculties constitute those means [the means to acquire ānanda or bliss]. Their complete and comprehensive cultivation can reveal to us the satchitānanda that pervades the entire universe and an universe that overflows with satchitānanda. Without this cultivation dharma remains half-accomplished.
>
> (227)

However, it is Bankim's *recovery* of these ideas that are interesting, played out in a context of colonial politics and culture to which Coleridge too responded deeply. This reading of Coleridge's afterlife in nineteenth-century critical thinking of India, should demonstrate, therefore, the subtle mediation of tradition that Coleridge's critical thinking enables in such a context. In their own ways, each of the three writers we have considered addressed their criticisms to a changing and profoundly challenging new order of culture which they diagnosed as being in danger of the loss of religious sensibility. Confronting the stout stick of utilitarianism, which threatened to beat the religious sensibilities of their age into submission, each of them affirmed the importance of a religious tradition and culture for their societies. In doing so, each of these writers sought to recover a selective notion of religious culture for their age and in relation to their different audiences.

The development of Hindu spiritualism from the nineteenth century – labelled 'guru English' by Srinivas Aravamudan – has been described by him as a vigorous but derivative afterlife of Romanticism in which 'what seems most natural, organic, and authentic about Indian culture – whether in its national or cosmopolitan version – is shown to be invented, prosthetic, and supplementary'.[34] Paradoxically however, as Partha Chatterjee has argued, the derivativeness of this spiritualized language from western Orientalist and utilitarian critiques was to result in the formation of national identity in the spiritual realm long before it was formulated in terms of an independence movement. Viewed from an Indian point of view, Rammohun Roy and Bankim fulfil in the Hindu context what Coleridge envisaged for his national Church or clerisy in England, albeit, ironically, that Coleridge's attitude to Hinduism had turned antagonistic on account of his later subscription to the very criticisms that his critical heirs in India sought to challenge. Despite Bankim's mystical tendencies, neither of the Indian writers appears pantheistic in the way that Coleridge identified essentially with Hinduism. Neither of the Indian writers too could be described as 'nationalist' in an explicit sense in that neither of them challenged British rule directly; but their writings may be seen to map the areas of what Partha Chatterjee (in a critique of Benedict Anderson's theory of nationalism) insightfully describes as the 'inner space' of nationalism:

> This account of nationalism flies in the face of a whole mass of evidence on the continued legitimacy of nationalist claims to cultural autonomy and self-determination. More importantly, by directing its inquiry towards the domain of the institutional forms of the modern nation-state, it misses entirely the site where the nationalist imagination is most creative. The very separation of culture into the material and the spiritual domains affords nationalism an inner space over which it declares its sovereignty long before the political battle with colonial rule is fought out.[35]

Our examination of Rammohun Roy and Bankim in relation to Coleridgean thinking affirms Chatterjee's counter-argument regarding Indian nationalism, and shows too that the traditions of Indian cultural autonomy were forged in the crucible of colonial encounter, and were never available in any pristine form. In retrospect, this can be recognized as inevitable given the course of Indian history in the wake of the English education bill of 1835. By focussing on the Hindu religion and a discovery of its culture, both Indian writers confronted the colonial elites of their day in terms that oddly enough would have been welcomed by Coleridge who wished for a reformation of Hinduism, and himself hypothesized a reformation of Protestant Christian culture in post-revolutionary England through his notion of a clerisy. All three writers under consideration may be considered as late Enlightenment thinkers for whom religious belief required to be squared with rationality; each of them sought to cast tradition in a way that would allow for rational belief based on it; and all of them responded in various ways to cultural changes in society, recognizing variously the challenges of modernity and seeking to adapt religious culture to regenerate the nation. Transplanted to India, however, the seeds of Coleridge's thought seem to be productive of new and exotic blooms of spiritualized nationalism, more a hybrid growth perhaps than an 'afterlife' in the canonical sense – though who is to say less significant for that?

Notes

1. 'Conversation and S.T. Coleridge' is a posthumously published essay of De Quincey's which can be dated to the late 1840s or the 1850s. The article includes an internal dating of 1849, though possibly it was reworked in the 1850s. See Grevel Lindop's headnote in *The Works of Thomas De Quincey*, 21 vols. (London: Pickering & Chatto, 2000–2003), XXI: 42–43.
2. Both names are commonly spelt in a whole variety of different ways and have not yet been standardized. This makes their works particularly difficult to access in English catalogues. It may be worth noting that Chattopadhyay is now the favoured form of the common Bengali surname 'Chatterjee' which was corrupted to the latter form by colonial administrators who found it difficult to pronounce. However, the convention of surnames was not in practice among Bengalis through much of the nineteenth century, and hence both writers are referred to by their first names, Ram Mohun or Rammohun, and Bankim or Bankimchandra, respectively. The 'Raja' which commonly prefixes Rammohun Roy's name is a title bestowed by Akbar II. For consistency's sake I shall use the forms which are prevalent in current scholarly use, referring to them as Rammohun Roy and Bankim, respectively.
3. The earliest use of 'Hindooism' I am aware of is in Michael Symes, *An Account of an Embassy to the Kingdom of Ava*, 1800, 'the Shaster proscribes the whole world, and denies the cord of Hindooism to all mankind.' (99n.). Rammohun Roy is credited as the first Indian to use the term. The *OED* (second edition) cites the use of 'Hinduism' from 1829 onwards.
4. See his comment in *Aids to Reflection* on the 'rival Sect' of Buddhism which he sees evidently as based on materialist thinking and which he describes as 'religious Atheism': 'God is only universal Matter considered abstractedly from all particular forms'. See *Aids to Reflection*, ed. J.B. Beer (Princeton, NJ: Princeton University Press, 1993), p. 283.
5. *The Collected Letters of Samuel Taylor Coleridge*, ed. Earl Leslie Griggs, 6 vols. (Oxford: Oxford University Press, 1956–71), IV: 917. Hereafter cited as *CL*. Nigel Leask has quoted Coleridge's letter and treated Rammohun Roy's influence on the Romantics, particularly Shelley, in his *British Romantic*

Writers and the East (135–54), but aside from his pioneering work, there has been little exploration of Rammohun Roy's writings in the scholarship of Romanticism. See Nigel Leask, *British Romantic Writers and the East: Anxieties of Empire* (Cambridge: Cambridge University Press, 1992).

6. The extent of Southey's Indological scholarship has been traced in detail in my edition of *The Curse of Kehama*, Vol. 4 of *Robert Southey: Poetical Works, 1793–1810*, 5 vols., gen. ed., Lynda Pratt (London: Pickering and Chatto, 2004). Southey's wide reading in Orientalist and indological literature, and his increasingly hardline attitude favouring forced conversions to Christianity are explored in the introduction and editorial notes to this edition.

7. *CL* I: 350.

8. 'Manners' here anticipates the critical term 'culture' as used by Coleridge and Arnold. In Mill's words: 'By the manners of a nation are understood the peculiar modes in which the ordinary business of human life is carried on. The business itself is everywhere essentially the same. In all nations men eat and drink; they meet, converse, transact, and sport together. But the manner in which these and other things are performed is as different as the nations are numerous into which the race is divided' (Mill, I: 303). 'Manners' are here equated with what we might call a national culture. See James Mill, *The History of British India*, ed. H.H. Wilson, 9 vols. (London: J. Madden, 1840–46).

9. In his edition of Mill's *History of British India*, the eminent Orientalist Horace Hayman Wilson added the following footnote to Mill's unsubstantiated quotation: 'It is not true that this is a favourite saying. I never heard it uttered during a long residence in Bengal, and doubt its genuineness' (Mill, I: 333n.). Coleridge and Mill may have encountered this attribution to Brahmin philosophy in Henry Home Kames's *Sketches of the History of Man* (1796 edition). Kames writes: 'One great maxim of the Bramins contained in their ancient books is, that it is better to sit than to walk, better to lie than to sit, better to sleep than to wake, better to die than to live.' Kames, the philosopher of civility, adds severely: 'This is directly subversive of industry, and consequently of morality'. See Henry Home Kames, *Sketches of the History of Man*, 4 vols. (Basil: J.J. Tourneiser, 1796), IV: 265–6.

10. Thomas Trautmann, *Aryans and British India* (Berkeley: University of California Press, 1997), pp. 62–130.

11. A full-length study of this development is to be found in Gauri Viswanathan's book *Masks of Conquest: Literary Study and British Rule in India* (London: Faber and Faber, 1989).

12. John Drew, *India and the Romantic Imagination* (New Delhi: Oxford University Press, 1987), pp. 185–227.

13. Coleridge's later Victorian writings perhaps suffer neglect from the strain of this periodization now enshrined in literary curricula, as he himself is largely pigeonholed in literary syllabi as a Romantic.

14. *Marginalia*, ed. George Whalley and H.J. Jackson, 6 vols. (Princeton, NJ: Princeton University Press, 1980–2001) II: 339–49.

15. J.A. Dubois, *Hindu Manners, Customs and Ceremonies* (3rd edn., Oxford: Clarendon Press, 1906), p. 105.

16. *Lay Sermons*, ed. R.J. White (Princeton, NJ: Princeton University Press, 1972), p. 29.

17. It is worth noting that Macaulay does include 'works of imagination' and 'speculations on metaphysics' as among the resources available in English: but it is evident that for him these are precisely *resources* that are valued insofar as they are *useful*. He dismisses 'the whole native literature of India and Arabia' as not worth 'a single shelf of a good European library'. See his 'On Education for India' in *Imperialism*, ed. Philip D. Curtin (London: Macmillan, 1971), p. 182.
18. John Stuart Mill, *On Bentham and Coleridge*, ed. F.R. Leavis (London: Chatto & Windus, 1950), p. 40.
19. The classic study of nineteenth-century Utilitarianism in India is Eric Stokes's *The English Utilitarians and India* (Oxford: Oxford University Press, 1959), while a more focussed study of James Mill's *History* in relation to Orientalism is Javed Majeed's book, *Ungoverned Imaginings: James Mill's 'The History of British India' and Orientalism* (Oxford: Oxford University Press, 1992). Yet another relevant study in relation to this topic is David Kopf's book focussing on the early period of the Bengal Renaissance, *British Orientalism and the Bengal Renaissance* (Berkeley: University of California Press, 1969), which represents Macaulay's intervention as a 'defeat' of the Orientalists. My essay seeks to augment and continue the arguments of these works through a consideration of Coleridge's potential as an over-looked oppositional figure in the English critical tradition to the dominant discourse of Victorian ulititarianism.
20. Exhibiting the obviousness of such a mode of critical discrimination to the Indian critic even in the twentieth century, the historian S.N. Mukherjee delineates Bankim's Victorian intellectual heritage thus: 'Mill shared with Bentham the eighteenth-century enthusiasm for individualism and reason, but excessive individualism and the neglect of feelings worried Mill. He turned to Coleridge and regarded the conservatism of the Romantic a powerful, critical weapon in favour of reform. [...] Bankim Chandra was no more conservative than Mill had been and like Coleridge he wrote some of the severest satires "upon existing evils"'. See S.N. Mukherjee, *Sir William Jones: A Study of Eighteenth-Century British Attitudes to India* (London: Cambridge University Press, 1968), p. 17.
21. *On the Constitution of the Church and State*, ed. John Colmer (Princeton, NJ: Princeton University Press, 1976), p. 43.
22. This is a distinction that his predecessor James Mill overlooked in *The History of British India*. Criticizing Hindu culture for its attitude to women, and quoting the harsh dictates of Manu with regard to the treatment of women, Mill concluded that Hinduism was uncivilized as a consequence. The terms are congruent when Mill generalizes as follows:

> The history of uncultivated nations uniformly represents the women as in a state of abject slavery, from which they slowly emerge, as civilization advances.
>
> (I: 309)

23. *The English Works of Raja Ram Mohun Roy*, ed. Jogendra Chandra Ghose (Calcutta: Bhowanipore Oriental Press, 1885), p. 170.

24. *Dharmatattva*, trans. Apratim Ray. (New Delhi: Oxford University Press, 2003), p. 36.
25. *The Works of Jeremy Bentham*, 11 vols. (Edinburgh: W. Tait, 1843), X: 589.
26. Geoffrey Oddie, *Imagined Hinduism: British Protestant Missionary Constructions of Hinduism, 1793–1800* (New Delhi: Sage, 2006), p. 13.
27. It should be noted that Rammohun Roy unlike Bankim does not explicitly refer to his criticism in terms of culture; hence we may speak of his critique more strictly as being proto-cultural. My point is that he anticipates Bankim even if he does not use quite the same terminology.
28. Coleridge's comments on Spinoza indicate that he was intellectually enamoured of his philosophy, though it was Christianity that he found emotionally satisfying: 'For a very long time indeed I could not reconcile personality with infinity; and my head was with Spinoza, though my whole heart remained with Paul and John'. Here, Coleridge may be seen to be casting his philosophical growth in a revisionary light, or at least interpreting it in a tendentious way. *Biographia Literaria*, ed. James Engell and W. Jackson Bate, 2 vols. (Princeton, NJ: Princeton University Press, 1983), I: 259.
29. *The Works of Sir William Jones*, ed. Anna Maria Jones, 6 vols. (London: G.G. Robinson, 1799) I: 165–6.
30. This is an important aspect of his work if his often conflicted texts are to be appreciated; a full-length treatment of Bankim's rhetorically transgressive nature as a writer caught between traditionality and modernity may be found in Sudipta Kaviraj's book, *The Unhappy Consciousness: Bankimchandra Chattopadhyay and the Formation of Nationalist Discourse in India* (New Delhi: Oxford University Press, 1995).
31. Tapan Raychaudhuri, *Europe Reconsidered: Perceptions of the West in Nineteenth-Century Bengal* (2nd edn., New Delhi: Oxford University Press, 2002), p. 201.
32. Raychaudhuri details Bankim's English reading at school and the formidable syllabus of the newly established Calcutta University from which he graduated as an autodidact in 1858 (125). He continued to read widely in English throughout his life, showing acquaintance with a wide range of European literature.
33. In an rewarding chapter on Bankim's significance for Indian nationalism Partha Chatterjee identifies culture as the crucial aspect of Bankim's critique: 'Bankim's explanation of the subjection of India is not in terms of material or physical strength. It is an explanation in terms of *culture*' ('The Moment of Departure,' 55). While agreeing with Chatterjee's broader analysis of Bankim's career, my essay seeks to focus on the Coleridgean aspects of Bankim's cultural critique, in counter-distinction to the more obvious Benthamite influence which Chatterjee highlights (showing its corresponding limitations). See Partha Chatterjee, 'The Moment of Departure: Culture and Power in the Thought of Bankimchandra' in *Nationalist Thought and the Colonial World: A Derivative Discourse* (London: Zed Books, 1986).
34. Srinivasa Aravamudan, 'The Colonial Logic of Late Romanticism', *South Atlantic Quarterly* 102:1 (2003), p. 209.
35. Partha Chatterjee, 'In their Own Words: An Essay for Edward Said' in *Edward Said: A Critical Reader* (Oxford: Blackwell, 1992), p. 195.

7

Ralph Waldo Emerson and Coleridge's American Legacy

Laura Dassow Walls

Emerson without Coleridge can scarcely be imagined, so central is the Englishman to the American's development as a writer, philosopher, and public intellectual. Yet this very fact raises a question: how is it that a British author gave voice to an American, and hence to a new, national American literature? The short answer is that Coleridge gave Emerson a decentralized center, a 'focal' instead of a 'central' body. In *On the Constitution of the Church and State*, Coleridge insisted that in the heavens and the intellect the center is everywhere, the circumference nowhere. Every system is unified by the power of its own 'sun or focal orb' which like gravity connects all with all.[1] There could be no single center of unity or power, mind or culture, but rather a constellation of focal points – Coleridge one, Emerson another. In effect, Coleridge showed Emerson how to focus his own thoughts in his own way. Thus, although no writer was more important to Emerson than Coleridge, he refocused Coleridge's ideas into a distinctively Emersonian vision and a distinctively American Romanticism: away from British centralized hierarchy toward a sprawling democratic American national literature, away from religious orthodoxy toward a new church of science and the intellect. Democracy and atheism! Coleridge would have been horrified.[2]

At the crisis point of his life, in 1833 in his 30th year, Emerson broke away from America and traveled to Europe, where he made a point of visiting those British luminaries, Coleridge, Wordsworth, and Carlyle, who were crucial to the development of American Transcendentalism. Of the three visits, that with Coleridge was by far the least satisfactory. The elderly Wordsworth treated the young American kindly, reciting poetry like a schoolboy as they strolled the garden-walk together; in Carlyle Emerson discovered one of his lifelong friends. With Coleridge, Emerson felt rebuffed. On 5 August, he made his way to Highgate and after some difficulty in locating Coleridge received word that the great man was in bed but would see Emerson at one o'clock. Upon Emerson's return, Coleridge appeared, 'a short thick old man with bright blue eyes' and 'a fine complexion' who presently soiled his cravat and 'neat black suit' with snuff while he harangued Emerson on 'the folly & ignorance of Unitarianism.' When he finally paused to draw breath, Emerson admitted that he himself was a Unitarian. 'Yes, he said, I supposed so, & continued as before,' noted Emerson in his journal.[3] Afterward, Emerson observed that 'much of the discourse was like so many printed paragraphs in his book, perhaps the same; not to be easily followed' (*JMN* IV, 411). Not that Emerson was a follower: having sought out the greatest minds of his day, the very fact that he was not intimidated by them was liberating. Three weeks later, waiting at Liverpool for the ship home, Emerson reviewed his encounters with greatness and vowed, 'I shall judge more justly, less timidly, of wise men forevermore' (*JMN* IV, 78). None overawed him; he knew he was at least their equal. By the time Emerson had returned to Boston he had laid his own plans for greatness.

What had drawn Emerson to Highgate, and what effect did this one-sided interview have on the American pilgrim? Emerson had known Coleridge's name for many years and had gleaned passages from *Biographia Literaria* for his notebooks, but it was not until late in 1829, shortly after his marriage to Ellen Tucker, that his interest was ignited. The preceding March he had been ordained as pastor at Boston's Second Church, founded in 1650 and home to the great Puritan ministers Increase and Cotton Mather. This was a time of tremendous intellectual growth for Emerson. He was now writing weekly sermons, and he was reading widely, in Plato, Bacon, Montaigne, Rousseau and Carlyle, Lucretius and Herder. He had taken his place as a rising young minister in the most liberal wing of New England's most liberal church, the Unitarians led by their famous preacher, William Ellery Channing. Well before reading Coleridge, Emerson had already absorbed from Channing the conviction that we know the spirit of God through the unfolding of his principle in our own mind and heart. As Channing preached in 1828, 'God is another name for human intelligence, raised above all error and imperfection, and extended to all possible truth. [...] It is the lawgiver in our own breasts, which gives us the idea of divine authority and binds us to obey it.'[4] Encountering Coleridge afresh, Emerson's wide-ranging reading began to fuse into a dynamic intellectual program which he soon was advancing to his Second Church congregation.

The first record appears in December 1829 in a letter to his aunt Mary Moody Emerson. That October, Mary had written him that Coleridge was a 'blockhead' for placing his intellect on a par with Plato and Milton. Her nephew responded with a spirited defense of Coleridge, whose *Friend* he is reading 'with great interest.' Yes, Waldo agrees, he 'has a tone a little lower than greatness – but what a living Soul what a universal knowledge [...] there are few or no books of pure literature so self impr[inti]ng, that is, so often remembered, as Coleridge's.' To those who 'wag their heads & say I cant understand Coleridge,' Emerson answers, 'I say a man so learned & a man so bold has a right to be heard [...]. At least I become acquainted with one new mind I never saw before.'[5] Early in January he alerted his brothers William and Edward to his new passion: he is reading 'Coleridge's Friend – with great interest; Coleridge's *Aids to reflection* with yet deeper' (*L* I, 191). Throughout the winter and spring of 1830 he and Mary read Coleridge simultaneously, forging a significant step in the development of Transcendentalism. As her biographer Phyllis Cole observes, 'Through Coleridge, Mary felt an influx of self-confidence that counterbalanced' her fear of German higher criticism, for Coleridge allowed her to affirm 'my reason my nature – this divine identity' no matter what the 'barbarian innovators' say about the divine authority of the Bible. Waldo would in time make Coleridgean reason a fundamental term of Transcendentalism, but it was Mary Moody Emerson who first employed it as a solution to her own sense of religious crisis.[6]

One reason American readers were so quick to grasp the implications of Coleridgean Reason was the extraordinary introduction provided by James Marsh to his American edition of *Aids to Reflection*, published in November 1829. In 1826, Marsh had become president of the University of Vermont with the intention of building 'a curriculum along Coleridgean transcendental lines,' going 'beyond the limitations of the Understanding' to allow the students 'to develop their higher power of Reason.' Marsh deeply influenced a generation of students, who carried his Coleridgean philosophy across the country as far as Oregon and Hawaii.[7] Down in Boston, Marsh's edition of *Aids* was read avidly by Emerson as well as other young ministers and intellectuals who in a ferment of growing excitement came together in 1836 to discuss the 'new philosophy' of Coleridge, Carlyle, and the German metaphysicians. Their meeting led to the foundation of the Transcendentalist movement, which used the new philosophy as a basis for reform in religion, philosophy, science, poetics, education, and politics. Octavius Brooks Frothingham, a second-generation Transcendentalist, recalled that 'the name of Coleridge was spoken with profound reverence, his books were studied industriously, and the terminology of transcendentalism was as familiar as commonplace in the circles of divines and men of letters.' Marsh himself was unimpressed with the Boston crowd, noting in a letter of 1841 that he takes 'the whole of Boston Transcendentalism [...] to be a rather superficial affair.' Lacking the 'manly logic and strong systematizing tendency' of the German writers, they 'pretend to no system of unity, but each utters, it seems, the inspiration of the moment, assuming that it all comes from the universal heart, while ten to one it comes from the stomach.'[8]

In his 'Preliminary Essay,' Marsh outlined the grounds for discontent with the old and progress toward the new. The philosophy of Locke gives us a false metaphysics that makes us doubt God, reducing us to the level of beasts completely subject to natural law and 'bound by that law, as by an adamantine chain.' But we are more than merely 'a better sort of animal,' for we feel the moral obligation to fulfill a higher law. If our philosophy is 'unsafe,' by limiting us to what Coleridge calls the 'understanding,' reflection shows that we have peculiar powers of our own, Coleridge's 'reason.' As for the difficulty of reading Coleridge, Marsh in defense rises to eloquence: Coleridge's language becomes 'a living power, "consubstantial" with the power of thought, that gave birth to it, and awakening and calling into action a corresponding energy in our own minds.'[9]

Mary Moody Emerson was right: Coleridge's concept of Reason answered the urgent need to combat skepticism. As Lawrence Buell states, 'the concept of a higher Reason is the heart of what came to be called Transcendentalism.'[10] Coleridge gave these breakaway radicals, born of old-style Harvard rationalism, the means to claim 'reason' of a higher order, trumping their soulless forefathers on their own ground. In his lecture 'The Transcendentalist' (1841), Emerson pointed to Kant as the originator of the term 'transcendental,' as a reply to the skepticism of Locke who claimed that all thought originated in the senses; as Emerson wrote, Kant showed by contrast the existence of Transcendental ideas that 'did not come by experience, but through which experience was acquired; that these were intuitions of the mind itself.'[11] This was, of course, a creative reading of Kant, who would never have condoned the notion that intuition could reveal the absolute; Emerson's more immediate sources were in fact Channing and Coleridge. But few Transcendentalists read Kant, while all read Coleridge; over and over they celebrated the release from Locke's materialism. Kant's new Copernican revolution had put the mind of man at the center of the universe, and now Coleridge's Reason became the sun or 'focal orb' that illumined the universe into meaning, the lens that brought it into focus.

While reading *Aids* in 1829, Emerson began a new notebook, inscribing on the cover a motto derived from Coleridge: 'Quantum scimus sumus,' 'We are what we know.' As his editors note, what followed was of special importance to Emerson: 'That which we find within ourselves, which is more than ourselves, and yet the ground of whatever is good and permanent therein, is the substance and life of all other knowledge' (*JMN* III, 164). Coleridge confirmed for Emerson what he had already suspected, and he began to use Coleridgean themes in his sermons: the divinity within each human being, the necessity of self-knowledge and self-reflection, reason as the true basis for self-reliance. After Ellen's tragic death in February 1831, he turned twice to Coleridge's translation of Schiller's *Wallenstein* for comfort; in later years he would allude to the opening in responding to the deaths of his brothers Edward and Charles.[12] Perhaps most important, as Emerson began to question orthodox Christianity, he found in Coleridge the foundation for his restorative turn to a new faith grounded not in the Bible but in Nature, as interpreted not by Lockean empiricists but by Coleridgean scientific Method. By the time of his interview with Coleridge, Emerson had resigned from his post as pastor and determined to pursue instead what he called, in his farewell letter to his congregation, 'the ministry of truth.'[13]

His quest led him not only to the great minds of Europe, but to the Paris Muséum d'Histoire Naturelle, where he experienced an intense, Coleridgean vision of the fundamental principle uniting all living forms: 'The Universe is a more amazing puzzle than ever as you glance along this bewildering series of animated forms, – the hazy butterflies, the carved shells, the birds, beasts, fishes, insects, snakes, – & the upheaving principle of life everywhere incipient in the very rock aping organized forms. [...] I am moved by strange sympathies, I say continually "I will be a naturalist"' (*JMN* IV, 199–200). Barely three weeks later he would be sitting in Coleridge's Highgate rooms, in no mood to defend the Unitarianism he had already left behind, and frustrated in his attempt to connect with the man, himself a lapsed Unitarian who had also once been a rising star in the ministry, whose writings had so profoundly changed his life. However, unlike James Marsh, Emerson had no intention of becoming a disciple, and he returned to America intent on becoming not a planet in Coleridge's orbit but the sun of his own system.

Emerson's disappointment at Highgate did not diminish but invigorated his interest in Coleridge's ideas. Upon his return he re-engaged Coleridge's concept of Method in lectures on natural science and on British literature. He first explored just what his vow to 'be a naturalist' might mean. It clearly was not the collection and identification of spec- imens. Emerson would be Coleridge's 'enlightened naturalist,' who sees that all such specimens derive their existence as parts of nature from 'the antecedent method, or self-organizing PURPOSE' (*Friend* I, 498). The Coleridgean direction of Emerson's thinking on science became most clear in his May 1834 lecture 'The Naturalist.' Two days before, he ruminated in his journal on the problem of 'classification,' concluding that Coleridge writes 'well on this matter of Theory in his Friend.' Do not enumerate facts without a method, but let the method 'make its own fact, create its own form,' presenting not a catalogue but 'an idea of which the flying wasp & the grazing ox are developments' (*JMN* IV, 290). Two days later he presented Coleridge's ideas on method to his audience at the Boston Society of Natural History, capping his develop- ing critique of empiricism and his recommendations for the renovation of science.

In *The Friend*, Coleridge had stated that the true method of science was the enlightenment of Understanding by Reason, 'the scientific fac- ulty,' which identified the 'essential properties of things by means of the Laws that constitute them'.[14] Not all sciences had reached this state of maturity – botany, for example, remained 'little more than an enor- mous nomenclature; a huge catalogue' still awaiting its philosopher. In his turn, facing an audience composed largely of botanists, Emerson agrees that 'Natural History is now little but a nomenclature.'[15] While we need nomenclature, it, together with retort, scalpel, and scales, must be subordinated as '*Means*' which flow from the 'passion, the enthusi- asm for nature, the love of the Whole.' Science must ascend from nomenclature through classification to laws and finally to 'the elemental law, the *causa causans*, the supernatural force' (*EL* I, 80). The naturalist who will do this, who will see 'the Idea in the particulars, the Type in the manifold forms,' will be more than merely a naturalist – he will be 'a poet in his severest analysis' (*EL* I, 82). Thus, Emerson announces, 'I fully believe in both, in the poetry and in the dissection,' for the studies of naturalists 'point more and more steadily at Method, at a Theory.' Moreover, 'no truth can be more self-evident than that the highest state of man, physical, intellectual, and moral, can only coexist with a perfect Theory of Animated Nature' (*EL* I, 79, 82–3).

In this peroration – which points directly to the opening of *Nature* two years later, with its call for 'a theory of nature' (*CW* I, 8) – Emerson echoes Coleridge's statement that only the idea of a universal law man- ifested in opposite and interdependent forces would enable man to comprehend 'the relation of each to the other, of each to all, and of all to each' (*Friend* I, 511). This idea led Emerson, in his lectures on British literature, to articulate Coleridge's concept of Imagination. His poem 'Each and All' recalls his boyish joy in collecting shells at the beach and disappointment when once home 'the poor, unsightly, noisome things / Had left their beauty on the shore, / With the sun, and the sand, and the wild uproar.'[16] In Shakespeare Emerson saw again his boyhood lesson: 'The most elegant shell in a cabinet does not please the eye like the contrast and combination of a group of the most ordinary sea shells lying together wet upon the beach.' Even so with our thoughts: gathered one at a time, a week past or ten years past, they lie dry and isolated until fused into life by 'Composition or methodical union,' 'the most powerful secret of Nature's workmanship.' This was Shakespeare's gift, to fuse the catalogue of his library, his thought, his experiences, into 'a quite new collective power' (*EL* I, 318).

Just so, Emerson attempted to fuse his own library, thought, and experiences into a greater composition, a new collective power. Thus he sought not to chronicle the British poets but to see literature as 'holden and determined by firm laws,' laws that will lead us to 'the Theory of Literature' (*EL* I, 218, 225). The first law is that we are 'the prisoner of thoughts,' the ideas that 'tyrannize' over us, dictate our every word and action: 'There are no walls like the invisible ones of an idea. [...] Rebellion against the thought which rules me is absurdity' (*EL* I, 218). Such ideas – 'God, order, freedom, justice, love, time, space, self, matter' – are the true realities of our experience, as they clothe themselves 'with societies, houses, cities, language, ceremonies, newspapers.' Around each abstraction 'timber, brick, lime, and iron have flown into convenient shape, obedient to the master idea reigning in the minds of many persons' (*EL* I, 219). Objects in turn are themselves ideas, as they become 'vehicles and symbols of thought' (*EL* I, 221). In short, to free himself from that prison of ideas Emerson has moved from Reason to Imagination, the faculty that 'dissolves, diffuses, dissipates, in order to re-create,' the idealizing and unifying faculty that is 'essentially *vital*, even as all objects (*as* objects) are essentially fixed and dead'.[17]

Emerson used Shakespeare to exemplify the Imagination. As he said in *Nature*, the poet 'unfixes the land and the sea, makes them revolve around the axis of his primary thought, and disposes them anew' (*CW* I, 31).[18] But the power of Imagination by itself is not enough to produce a Shakespeare. Alone and untempered, Imagination 'would be a disease,' 'morbid from its own excess.' The antidote to such partiality lies in a 'vision of all being we call Reason,' the 'mind's Eye' (*EL* I, 296–7).

In adding to his 'towering Imagination' this 'self-recovering, self-collecting force' of Reason, as well as the powers of reflection, Shakespeare turns into poet, philosopher, and practical man, with all the greatness of universality (*EL* I, 297, 305). By contrast, Francis Bacon, exemplar of 'the dissection,' falls short precisely through the absence of Reason, pointing to the troubling inadequacy of empirical, inductive science. Bacon, too, was a 'universal mind' with 'an imagination as despotic as Shakespear's [sic],' but he employed his imagination merely 'to illustrate and adorn the objects presented under the agency of the Understanding' (*EL* I, 321). In the balance of Each and All, Bacon's virtue was in knowing the value of Each – he was wise enough to know that each single object had value (*EL* I, 327) – but his weakness lay in his lack of 'an intrinsic Unity, a method derived from the Mind,' so his unceasing collection of facts lay scattered along the ground, 'a vast unfinished city' (*EL* I, 334–5), the raw materials out of which later generations might build empires.

In *Nature* (1836), his first major publication, Emerson used Coleridge to correct Bacon and show 'the *metaphysics* of conchology, of botany, of the arts,' to 'build science upon ideas' (*CW* I, 40). Coleridge's influence on *Nature* is widely recognized, although interestingly, Emerson repressed his source, acknowledging Coleridge only once – and that in a parenthetical misquotation.[19] Yet his groundbreaking essay is saturated with Coleridgean concepts, centered on the concept of 'Reason.' Emerson first took up this term in a letter to his brother Edward of 31 May 1834, where he gave an excellent working definition:[20]

> Reason is the highest faculty of the soul – what we mean often by the soul itself; it never *reasons*, never proves, it simply perceives; it is vision. The Understanding toils all the time, compares, contrives, adds, argues, near sighted but strong-sighted, dwelling in the present the expedient the customary. Beasts have some understanding but no Reason. Reason is potentially perfect in every man – Understanding in very different degrees of strength.
>
> (*L* I, 412–13)

Here, he concludes, is a key 'to Literature to the Church to Life [...]. So hallelujah to the Reason forevermore' (*L* I, 413). In democratic America, the Understanding can be cultivated, and Reason opened to all men. Soon the paired terms pepper the pages of his journal. A year later, in June 1835, Emerson began a new journal volume by declaring his intent 'to announce some of the laws of the First Philosophy,' the 'original laws of the mind' that are 'Ideas of the Reason' and that astonish the Understanding. *Nature*, which so astonished the Understanding that it catalyzed the Transcendentalist movement, was completed and published the following year.

The opening image of *Nature* literalizes the metaphor of reason as 'the mind's Eye-ball' in a passage that earned Emerson undying notoriety. Crossing a bare common at twilight, dodging snow puddles, Emerson experiences a moment's pure revelation: 'I became a transparent eye-ball. I am nothing. I see all. The currents of the Universal Being circulate through me; I am part or particle of God' (*CW* I, 10). Soon after, in a paraphrase of Coleridge, he identifies this Universal Being or Soul as 'Reason: it is not mine or thine or his, but we are its [...]. That which, intellectually considered, we call Reason, considered in relation to nature, we call Spirit. Spirit is the Creator. Spirit hath life in itself. And man in all ages and countries, embodies it in his language, as the FATHER' (*CW* I, 19; *Aids* 217–18). While the senses see man and nature as 'indissolubly joined' in a lower sense, the 'eye of Reason' will 'relax this despotism of the senses.' To its 'more earnest vision, outlines and surfaces become transparent, and are no longer seen; causes and spirits are seen through them' (*CW* I, 30). Once Reason dissolves the world to reveal its underlying laws, imagination steps in to recreate that world, 'to unfix land and sea' and conform them to his thoughts; 'The imagination may be defined to be, the use which Reason makes of the material world' (*CW* I, 31). Understanding buys back our kingdom inch by inch; Reason vaults us at once back into the throne, and, as the essay concludes, 'The kingdom of man over nature, which cometh not with observation, – a dominion such as now is beyond his dream of God, – he shall enter without more wonder than the blind man feels who is gradually restored to perfect sight' (*CW* I, 45). Thanks to Coleridge's philosophy, Bacon's empire will be realized after all.

In essence, Emerson has already achieved his 'theory of nature.' *Nature* opens with the philosophical definition of Nature as the 'NOT ME,' the opposite of the Soul, which would seem to alienate the mind from nature. Yet, near the conclusion, the essay arrives at an image of organic union: 'spirit, that is, the Supreme Being, does not build up nature around us, but puts it forth through us, as the life of the tree puts forth new branches and leaves through the pores of the old. As a plant upon the earth, so a man rests upon the bosom of God; he is nourished by unfailing fountains, and draws, at his need, inexhaustible power' (*CW* I, 38). This vision of a concentered mind does not displace the earlier vision of alienation; rather, the two coexist as a function of Coleridge's 'universal Law of Polarity or essential Dualism' whereby 'every power in Nature and in Spirit must evolve an opposite, as the sole means and condition of its manifestation' (*Friend* I, 94–5).[21] Alienation from nature gives us the necessary power of the understanding to abstract and generalize, to use nature for our own ends. But this static, materialistic stance deploys nature as product only. To truly gain access to the 'inexhaustible power' of natural processes, the mind must assimilate nature to itself by identifying with the 'antecedent method, or self-organizing PURPOSE' from which all products of nature derive their existence (*Friend* I, 499).[22] Or as Emerson put it, paraphrasing Coleridge, the philosopher not less than the poet 'postpones the apparent order and relations of things to the empire of thought.' Philosophy's need for an 'unconditioned and absolute' ground for all that is conditional leads it to the 'faith that a law determines all phenomena, which being known, the phenomena can be predicted. That law, when in the mind, is an idea.'[23] Philosopher and poet are one, each seeking a truth which is beauty, and a beauty which is truth (*CW* I, 33, 34).

In short, the eye of Reason overcomes our experience of alienation by dissolving the phenomenal world to reveal the laws, principles, or ideas which are its origin; the hands of Imagination then remake that world to our own design. 'Build, therefore, your own world,' Emerson exhorts his readers in his conclusion; 'As fast as you conform your life to the pure idea in your mind, that will unfold its great proportions' (*CW* I, 45). As he had said in 'The Naturalist,' ideas do build the world, assimilating to themselves timber, brick, lime, and iron. Emerson's idealism was his Archimedes lever, giving him the power to move the world, to remake Nature into America, forests and rivers into fields and cities, canals, railroads, machines, factories, and universities. Far from a meditation on the dappled woods, *Nature* is a blueprint for modernity.

Ideas which in human hands become machines and cathedrals become through divine agency rocks, trees, flowers and leaves – and flesh and blood. Emerson was an early convert to evolution, starting in the 1820s with his reading in geology, which convinced him of the earth's gradual development over untold millennia. From *The Friend* he took Coleridge's idea of method as 'progressive arrangement' (*JMN* VI, 222), and from *Aids* the expression that 'All things strive to ascend, and ascend in their striving.' As he off-rhymed in the epigraph for his 1849 reissue of *Nature*, 'And, striving to be man, the worm / Mounts through all the spires of form' (*CW* I, 7). Starting in 1844, his understanding of evolution came together when, following his reading of *Vestiges of the Natural History of Creation*,[24] he coined the phrase 'arrested and progressive development' to encapsulate his understanding of life's upward striving against the resistance offered by a hostile environment. It is unclear whether Emerson read Coleridge's *Theory of Life* (although this work was important to Thoreau),[25] but Coleridge's vision of upward ascent culminating in maximum individuality combined with maximum interdependence accorded well with Emerson's thinking. Charles Darwin failed to impress Emerson, who saw the great theorist of evolution as a latecomer adding little to an already established truth.

One feature of evolution did trouble Emerson. As he remarked in his journal, 'The whole circle of animal life, internecine war, a yelp of pain & a grunt of triumph, until, at last, the whole mass is mellowed & refined for higher use, – pleases at a sufficient perspective' (*JMN* XIII, 87). Evolution might work from a cosmic perspective, but what of the individual ground underfoot by the long march of progress? – or burned away with the rest of the phenomenal world by the fire of Reason? In later years, Emerson turned with increasing interest to the problem of the individual in society. His essay 'Self-Reliance' (1840) advanced the Coleridgean view that our Reason simultaneously creates us each as distinctive, self-reliant individuals and relates us to all humanity, for it is Reason only insofar as it is universal: as Coleridge said of the Body Politic, 'There is one heart for the whole mighty mass of Humanity, and every pulse in each particular vessel strives to beat in concert with it' (*Friend* I, 97). Similarly in *Nature*, what might seem to be alienating distance resolved itself, in the light of Reason, as a common bond: the prophet, espying the future from the alpine heights of 'Prospects,' returns to the valley to minister to the commoners.[26] The Poet, too, must go it alone, severing himself from his companions in order to rejoin them on the higher plane of the Imagination. Emerson's model continued to be Coleridgean polarity, in which opposite powers produce each other and are drawn together toward union or synthesis.

Coleridge had turned to the physical sciences to find an analogue in the poles of a magnet or of electricity, and Emerson romanced the magnetic analogy throughout his life as a figure for the alignment of individuals with each other and the whole. In *On the Constitution of the Church and State*, which Emerson read in 1834, Coleridge used magnetism as an image of the law of balance by which the constitution of the State was established and preserved: the two 'antagonist powers' of the State, Permanence and Progression, 'like the magnetic forces, suppose and require each other' (*CS* 24). In his 1841 lecture 'The Conservative,' Emerson expounded a parallel idea, the 'irreconcilable antagonism' of 'Conservatism' and 'Innovation': 'It is the opposition of Past and Future, of Memory and Hope, of the Understanding and the Reason.

It is the primal antagonism, the appearance in trifles of the two poles of nature,' the 'counteraction of the centripetal and centrifugal forces' (*CW* I, 184–5). Although grounded by his family heritage in Conservatism, Emerson cast himself on the side of Innovation, the Future, and Hope. Throughout his life he would attempt to moderate and control the explosive energies unleashed by America's founding radicals, Tom Paine and Thomas Jefferson, by bringing to America the principled vision of Reason.

Coleridge had insisted that no man can be treated as a thing: all citizens must participate, through the act of self-making, in the making of the State (*CS* 14–15). Similarly, Emerson's foundational idea was 'the infinitude of the private man.' Since every person carries the divine within, every person must have the freedom to realize the divine idea which made them. In the antebellum United States, such notions flatly contradicted the law of the land, which mandated and supported slavery. For years, Emerson worried over the problem in private without committing himself to a public statement. Slavery and other government injustices, such as the forced removal of the Cherokee from their ancestral homelands and the armed invasion of Mexico, seemed like excrescences on the body politic that would divert him from his true, philosophical calling. Over the time and the pressure of events, his view changed, as he realized, first, how the 'each' of particular injustices was intrinsically related to the 'all' of the State; and second, that, as Coleridge warned, the idea of the State can fail. The former insight prompted Emerson to plunge into the antislavery movement of his day with his 1844 'Address on the Emancipation of the Negroes in the British West Indies,' which showed slavery to be a violation of the constitution of the universe. But his faith in progress allowed him to mute his message: in time, the universe would correct itself, the body politic would heal, in America just as it had in England. *Vox populi vox Dei*: the voice of the people would articulate the will of God and shake off the moral atrocity of slavery. But passage in 1850 of the Fugitive Slave Act shocked Emerson into realizing that progress was not inevitable, that Imagination was failing, the Idea of the American state crumbling away. The voice of the people needed guidance, a vision. Thereafter, Emerson argued in passionate antislavery addresses that the failed, 'quadruped' constitution of 1787 must give way before the true and higher Constitution of the universe itself, founded as it was on the Idea of self-organization that necessitated freedom for all beings capable of self-realization.[27]

Starting in the 1840s, Emerson's growing prominence as a public intellectual positioned him at the center of what Coleridge called the 'third Estate,' those clergy and educators engaged in cultivating the knowledge that makes us human in order 'to secure and improve that civilization, without which the nation could be neither permanent nor progressive' (*CS* 43–4). As a member of America's emergent Clerisy, Emerson through his popular lectures, essays, and poems labored to educate and inspire the greater democratic public to take up their responsibilities as free citizens of America. Emerson was also instrumental in organizing other members of America's Clerisy into activist societies of educated gentlemen, most remarkably the original Transcendentalist movement, and two decades later the Saturday Club, an association of New England's leading intellectuals – writers, poets, scientists, lawyers, doctors, musicians, historians, a Senator – that self-consciously sought to offer guidance to America's political leadership and to its general reading population.[28] Coleridge's social philosophy was for Emerson not theoretical but deeply practical, and through Emerson and his colleagues, Coleridge's theories had a profound impact on the political and social organization of the United States.

In one significant respect, however, Emerson departed widely from his model, who had offered his philosophy as a means to bolster Christian orthodoxy. By the time of his visit to Highgate, Emerson had already resigned his ministerial position rather than practice an orthodoxy in which he had ceased to believe, and as the years passed he departed ever farther from conventional Christianity – most publicly in his 1838 address to the Harvard Divinity School, in which he declared that the church was dying and Jesus was not the son of God. Emerson's own 'national church' would be based not on Christianity but on science. On his lecture tour of Great Britain in 1847–8, he openly proposed to a London audience a new religion of science; 12 years later he developed these radical ideas in his essay 'Worship,' in which he proposed that 'the scientific mind must have a faith which is science' (*CW* VI, 128). His lectures and essays made him the darling of British Dissenters – from Alexander Ireland (who organized Emerson's tour) to the radical publisher John Chapman, free-thinker Harriet Martineau, notorious atheist George Jacob Holyoake, and the agnostic physicist John Tyndall – who entertained Emerson during his tour of Britain and followed his career in their journals.[29] Had Coleridge known what a viper he was entertaining that afternoon, he might have accused Emerson and his Unitarian friends of far worse than 'quackery' (*JMN* IV, 410).

Early in the 1840s, Emerson's active engagement with Coleridge dropped off, as he moved from his early idealism to a performative pragmatism that built on his insight that ideas create their reality in a flux of change: 'We are golden averages, volitant stabilities [...] houses founded on the sea' (*CW* 4, 91). The energizing polarity of the later Emerson was not reason and understanding but the interchanging dance of matter and mind, reality and illusion.[30] Emerson always used his reading as a catalyst for his own thought, a process of 'creative reading' that he recommended to all American intellectuals as a shield against America's courtly European past (*CW* I, 58). His 1836 lecture on Coleridge emphasized the English writer's unpopularity and played up his role as a literary critic, the one role Emerson himself did not take on. Thus even in publicly acknowledging his intellectual mentor, Emerson stressed not consanguinity but distance, a theme finalized in *English Traits* (1856) where his visit with Coleridge two decades earlier became an anecdote illustrating England's decline in the face of America's rise. Now England was the past, and America the divinely ordained future – a dynamic contest that Emerson was certain he would win. He did, at least in the United States, but he did so by assimilating Coleridge's ideas so thoroughly they became part of his own nature and thence, part of American literary and cultural history. By the time of his death, Emerson had succeeded in transmuting the dangerous, atomistic, and revolutionary ideals of his American rationalist forefathers into a moderate and principled ideology that used Coleridge's ideas to inspire, and to contain, the masses of an emergent, modern and democratic America.

Notes

1. *On the Constitution of the Church and State*, ed. John Colmer (Princeton, NJ: Princeton University Press, 1976), pp. 118–9. Hereafter cited as *CS*.
2. As Alexander Kern asserts, the Transcendentalists 'became Romantics with a difference': see 'Coleridge and American Romanticism' in Donald Sultana, ed. *New Approaches to Coleridge* (London; Totowa, NJ: Vision; Barnes and Noble, 1981): 113–36. Other recent studies include Kenneth Walter Cameron, *Emerson the Essayist*, Vol. 1 (Hartford: Transcendental Books, 1972); Gregory Miller Haynes, *Coleridge, Emerson, and the Prophet's Vocation* (Ph.D. dissertation, University of Virginia, 1984); Kenneth Marc Harris, 'Reason and Understanding Reconsidered: Coleridge, Carlyle and Emerson,' *Studies in Literature* 13.2 (Fall 1986): 263–82, and see also Patrick J. Keane's fine study, *Emerson, Romanticism, and Intuitive Reason: The Transatlantic 'Light of All Our Day'* (Columbia: University of Missouri Press, 2005), which came out after this essay was written. Many of the arguments in this essay are further developed in my book *Emerson's Life in Science: The Culture of Truth* (Ithaca: Cornell University Press, 2003).
3. *The Journals and Miscellaneous Notebooks of Ralph Waldo Emerson*, ed. William H. Gilman, Alfred R. Ferguson, George P. Clark, Merrell R. Davis, Merton M. Sealts, Jr., Ralph H. Orth, A.W. Plumstead, Harrison Hayford, J.E. Parsons,

Linda Allardt, Susan Sutton Smith, Ronald A. Bosco, and Glen M. Johnson, 16 vols (Cambridge: Harvard University Press, 1960–82), IV, 409. Hereafter referred to in parenthetical citations as *JMN*.

4. William Ellery Channing, 'Likeness to God,' in Joel Myerson, ed. *Transcendentalism: A Reader* (Oxford: Oxford University Press, 2000), 7.

5. *The Letters of Ralph Waldo Emerson*, vols I–VI ed. Ralph L. Rusk (New York: Columbia University Press, 1939); vols VII–X, ed. Eleanor M. Tilton (New York: Columbia University Press, 1990–5), VII, 188–9. Hereafter referred to as *L*.

6. Phyllis Cole, *Mary Moody Emerson and the Origins of Transcendentalism* (Oxford: Oxford University Press, 1998), 209, 212.

7. John J. Duffy, ed., *Coleridge's American Disciples: The Selected Correspondence of James Marsh* (Amherst: University of Massachusetts Press, 1973), 2, 7.

8. Octavius Brooks Frothingham, *Transcendentalism in New England* (Philadelphia: University of Pennsylvania Press, 1959), 89; Duffy 3.

9. James Marsh, 'Preliminary Essay,' in Coleridge, *Aids to Reflection*, 1840 (Port Washington, NY: Kennikat, 1971), 36, 52.

10. Lawrence Buell, *Literary Transcendentalism* (Ithaca: Cornell University Press, 1973), 5. Crucial to Emerson was his reading of Frederick Henry Hedge's article 'Coleridge's Literary Character–German Metaphysics,' *Christian Examiner* 14 (March 1833): 108–29.

11. *The Collected Works of Ralph Waldo Emerson*, ed. Alfred R. Ferguson, Robert E. Spiller, Joseph Slater, Jean Ferguson Carr, Wallace E. Williams, Douglas Emory Wilson, Philip Nicoloff, Robert E. Burkholder, Barbara Packer, and Ronald A. Bosco, 7 vols to date (Cambridge, Mass.: Harvard University Press, 1971–), I, 206–7. Hereafter referred to as *CW*.

12. Cameron 165–70, 173.

13. *The Complete Sermons of Ralph Waldo Emerson*, ed. Albert J. von Frank, Teresa Toulouse, Andrew Delbanco, Ronald A. Bosco, and Wesley T. Mott, 4 vols (Columbia: Univerisity of Missouri Press, 1989–92), IV, 305.

14. *The Friend*, 2 vols, ed. Barbara E. Rooke (Princeton, NJ: Princeton University Press, 1969), I, 158.

15. *The Early Lectures of Ralph Waldo Emerson, 1833–1842*, ed. Stephen E. Whicher, Robert E. Spiller, and Wallace E. Williams, 3 vols (Cambridge, Mass.: Harvard University Press, 1959–72), I, 79. Hereafter referred to as *EL*.

16. *Collected Poems and Translations* (New York: Library of America, 1994), 9. See also *JMN* IV, 291.

17. *Biographia Literaria*, 2 vols, ed. James Engell, and W. Jackson Bate (Princeton, NJ: Princeton University Press, 1983), I, 304.

18. As several commentators note, Transcendentalists tended to emphasize the primary imagination and downplay the formal aesthetic demands of the secondary. See Kerns 129; Frank Lentricchia, 'Coleridge and Emerson: Prophets of Silence, Prophets of Language,' *Journal of Aesthetics and Art Criticism*, 32.1 (Autumn 1973): 37–46.

19. '"A Gothic church," said Coleridge, "is a petrified religion"' (*CW* I, 27). As Haynes shows, Emerson borrowed the quotation from *Literary Remains*, in which Coleridge was reported to have said, 'A Gothic cathedral is the petrifaction of our religion.' Haynes details how the misquote 'sepulchres the mentor-father' (203). For documentation of Emerson's borrowings from Coleridge in *Nature*, see Cameron 200–23; Haynes 201–45.

20. As J. Edward Schamberger notes, Emerson was familiar with the concept already through the Scottish Common Sense philosophers Dugald Stewart and Richard Price, although after his study of Coleridge he reversed the terms in accordance with Coleridge's usage. See 'The Influence of Dugald Stewart and Richard Price on Emerson's Concept of the 'Reason,' *ESQ* vol. 18 (3rd quarter 1972): 179–83.

21. For a classic analysis of *Nature* in terms of Coleridge's polar dialectic, see Barry Wood, 'The Growth of the Soul: Coleridge's Dialectical Method and the Strategy of Emerson's *Nature*,' in Merton M. Sealts, Jr., and Alfred R. Ferguson, ed., *Emerson's Nature: Origin, Growth, Meaning*, 2nd edn (Carbondale: Southern Illinois University Press, 1979).

22. For an extension of these ideas in Emerson's later work, see his 1844 essay 'Nature,' which develops at length the paired terms of nature as product, *natura naturata*, versus nature as process, *natura naturans*, a distinction derived from Coleridge. See Owen Barfield, *What Coleridge Thought* (Middletown: Wesleyan University Press, 1971): 22–5.

23. Joseph Warren Beach points out that it was Kant, not Plato, who called for an unconditioned and absolute ground for knowledge; see *The Concept of Nature in Nineteenth-Century English Poetry* (New York: Russell and Russell, 1966), 220–1. Coleridge, however, credits this to Plato (*Friend* I, 461), one further reminder of Emerson's actual source.

24. *Vestiges*, by the Scottish journalist Robert Chambers, was published anonymously in 1844. Chambers never admitted authorship, although many, including Emerson, guessed it; Emerson met Chambers during his second tour of England, in 1848.

25. See Robert Sattelmeyer and Richard A. Hocks, 'Thoreau and Coleridge's *Theory of Life*,' *Studies in the American Renaissance*, ed. Joel Myerson (Charlottesville: University of Virginia Press, 1985): 269–84.

26. See Haynes, 165; Haynes argues throughout that among all the authors he read, Emerson chose Coleridge as a personal model for his role as the 'perturbed prophet,' who compensates for alienation from society by turning prophet to humanity.

27. For a longer discussion of this, see Walls, '"As Planets Faithful Be": The Higher Law in Emerson's Anti-Slavery Lectures,' *Nineteenth-Century Prose* 30.1–2 (Spring–Fall 2003): 171–94. Republished in *Ralph Waldo Emerson: Bicentenary Appraisals*, ed. Barry Tharaud (Trier: WVT Wissenschaftlicher Verlag Trier, 2006): 235–53.

28. Members of the Saturday Club helped to found the Republican Party and in 1860 succeeded in electing, and in 1864 reelecting, Abraham Lincoln to the presidency; they also founded *The Atlantic*, a general-interest intellectual magazine still published today.

29. For a discussion of Emerson's relationship with British Dissenters and the scientific naturalism of Tyndall and T. H. Huxley, see Walls, '"If Body Can Sing": Emerson and Victorian Science,' *Emerson Bicentennial Essays*, ed. Ronald A. Bosco, and Joel Myerson (Massachusetts Historical Society/ University of Virginia Press, 2006), 334–66.

30. The shift is most notable starting with Emerson's 1844 essay 'Experience.' See Harris, 277–9; Eric Wilson, 'Coleridge, Emerson, and Electromagnetic Hermeticism,' *Wordsworth Circle* 32.3 (Summer 2001): 134–8.

8
'I Have Strange Power of Speech': Narrative Compulsion after Coleridge

Daniel Karlin

> *The yarns of seamen have a direct simplicity, the whole meaning of which lies within the shell of a cracked nut. But Marlow was not typical ...*[1]

In the Thames below Gravesend, towards sunset, a small yacht lies at anchor, waiting for the ebb-tide which will take her out to sea. On board are five men, one of whom, without being prompted, begins to tell a story. The story concerns a journey up a river in Africa, to find a man called Kurtz. As the story progresses, an earlier tale takes shape behind it, shadowy, impalpable, not directly invoked, yet a sensible presence. This earlier tale contains, in a different configuration to be sure, many of the elements of the later: a nightmarish journey by water, spectral and skeletal figures, guilt and remorse, terrifying retribution; yet this is not what makes the connection between them potent. Where *Heart of Darkness* most takes after *The Rime of the Ancient Mariner* is in its evocation, and framing, of a compulsive and compelling voice.

The 'afterlife' of *The Rime of the Ancient Mariner* is rich in terms of character and theme and can be summed up in a series of images and phrases whose enduring power is barely diminished by their having become such clichés: the Mariner's glittering eye; the shooting of the albatross; water, water everywhere; all things both great and small; a sadder and a wiser man. Yet the narrative design of the poem – the relation between its authorial frame and narrative 'action', and what that says about narrative power – has arguably had as great an influence, though one which is harder to trace because of its curious obliquity. It is a paradox, or mystery, worthy of Coleridge that while the poem's influence on storytelling can be traced in the evolution of an entire genre, that of dramatic monologue, specific imitations of its *mise-en-scène* are vanishingly few in number. (The paradox begins with Coleridge himself, for *The Rime of the Ancient Mariner* is one of those singular masterpieces which are unrepeatable by their own authors.) I shall attempt, in this essay, to suggest something of what happens to the poem's narrative design in subsequent writing; but I shall return at the end to *Heart of Darkness* because it is that surprisingly rare thing, a literary work in which Coleridge's meditation on telling and listening is drawn out to its fullest extent and touches the circumference of its meaning.

The Rime of the Ancient Mariner begins with a scene which has become so famous, and therefore so familiar, that we may need reminding of its double peculiarity:

> It is an ancient Mariner,
> And he stoppeth one of three.
> 'By thy long grey beard and glittering eye,
> Now wherefore stopp'st thou me?
>
> 'The Bridegroom's doors are opened wide,
> And I am next of kin;
> The guests are met, the feast is set:
> May'st hear the merry din.'
>
> He holds him with his skinny hand,
> 'There was a ship,' quoth he.
> 'Hold off! unhand me, grey-beard loon!'
> Eftsoons his hand dropt he.
>
> He holds him with his glittering eye—
> The Wedding-Guest stood still,
> And listens like a three years' child:
> The Mariner hath his will.[2]

The 'Advertisement' to the 1798 *Lyrical Ballads* states that the poem was 'professedly written in imitation of the *style* as well as of the spirit of the elder poets'. It is generally agreed that these 'elder poets' are those of the so-called 'ballad tradition' (extending roughly from the 12th to the 15th centuries), whose renewed popularity dated from Thomas Percy's *Reliques of Ancient English Poetry* (1765); but what, precisely, does 'style' comprise? The 'imitation' of archaic metre and diction (especially in the 1798 text) is obvious enough, but if we extend the term to cover narrative method the picture is less clear. To begin with there is no parallel in the traditional ballad for the element of compulsion in Coleridge's poem – compulsion to listen, that is. Spells are cast (by witches, fairies, gipsies) and characters are struck motionless or dumb, but never with the intention of forcing them to listen to a story.[3] Ballads often begin by soliciting an audience ('Hearken to me gentlemen, / Come and you shall heare'; 'Lythe and listen, gentilmen, / That be of frebore bloode', etc.);[4] it is, after all, of the essence of the relation between ballad-singer and audience that he cannot compel them to 'gather round'. In any case, the Mariner's capture of the wedding-guest as his spellbound listener is not the opening of the poem, which is started (as it will be finished) by an unnamed and impersonal narrator. Coleridge's 'Rime', as opposed to the Mariner's tale, begins not by addressing an audience, but by narrating how a particular person compels another to listen to his story. (This helps to account for its subtitle in the three editions of *Lyrical Ballads* after 1798, 'A Poet's Reverie'.)[5] This, too, is unprecedented: no traditional ballad has the telling of a story *as its subject*. A character in a ballad (as opposed to an impersonal narrator) may tell the story in question-and-answer format:

> O where ha' you been, Lord Randal my son?
> And where ha' you been, my handsome young man?
> I ha' been at the greenwood; mother, mak my bed soon,
> For I'm wearied wi' hunting and fain wad lie down.

> ('Lord Randal')[6]

But in such cases the action is separate from the circumstances of its relation. In Coleridge's poem, on the other hand, the telling of the story is the primary action of the poem, governing the Mariner's relation of his experiences. The Mariner's selection of the wedding-guest is not arbitrary, but purposive, and springs from a compulsion which grips not the listener of the tale, but its teller. At the end of the poem, we learn the reason for the action of the opening lines: they spring from the original telling of the story, the Mariner's response to the Hermit:

> 'O shrieve me, shrieve me, holy man!'
> The Hermit crossed his brow.
> 'Say quick,' quoth he, 'I bid thee say—
> What manner of man art thou?'

> Forthwith this frame of mine was wrenched
> With a woful agony,
> Which forced me to begin my tale;
> And then it left me free.

Since then, at an uncertain hour,
That agony returns:
And till my ghastly tale is told,
This heart within me burns.

I pass, like night, from land to land;
I have strange power of speech;
That moment that his face I see,
I know the man that must hear me:
To him my tale I teach.

(ll. 574–90)[7]

The Mariner had looked forward to being absolved by the Hermit ('He'll shrieve my soul, he'll wash away / The Albatross's blood', ll. 512–13), but when it comes to the point the tale is 'wrenched' from him 'With a woful agony', and it is this painful, physical catharsis which '[leaves him] free'. The Mariner does not make a voluntary confession, and the Hermit noticeably does *not* 'shrieve' him, or impose the telling of the story on him as a penance. That happens of itself, in fulfilment of the prophecy made by the second spirit at ll. 408–9: 'The man hath penance done, / And penance more will do'.[8] Confession, leading to absolution and penance, may be a recurring sacrament, but the substance of what is confessed is not the same. The Mariner, by contrast, tells the same story, again and again, and is purged each time – until the next time. He travels the world but makes no progress; in today's jargon he cannot 'move on'. Only his death could bring this series to an end, but the poem makes no mention of such a horizon and if anything suggests the opposite – that the Mariner, like the Wandering Jew, is doomed to travel the earth and tell his tale until the Day of Judgment.

It turns out, therefore, that the scene at the beginning of the poem has a hidden cause, the Mariner's seizure by a recurring 'agony', and his 'stopping one of three' was not random but determined by definite, if occult signs, those by which the Mariner recognizes his destined listener. His listeners are not priests, and cannot give him permanent absolution; but he can, and does, have a permanent impact on them. For after the first telling a second purpose is added, which relates not to the teller but the listener.[9] Each is the recipient of a (presumably invariable) moral lesson:

He prayeth best, who loveth best
All things both great and small;

> For the dear God who loveth us,
> He made and loveth all.
>
> (ll. 614–17)

Perhaps all these listeners are, actually or metaphorically, 'wedding-guests', people whose unthinking hedonism needs to be corrected; each is selected as one who will rise 'A sadder and a wiser man' on 'the morrow morn' (ll. 624–5).[10] But whether this is the case or not, the fact remains that the telling of the story acquires a second purpose after its original outburst. And this purpose is communicated to the listener: the wedding-guest is told both about the Mariner's experiences, and about his own function as compelled listener to a compulsive narrative.

I note in passing that the Mariner's compulsion is not intended to be contagious. The wedding-guest (and in this respect, too, we may think of him as typical) is not expected to become a carrier of the story. Each listener is affected, perhaps in the same way, but in any case as an individual; the Mariner is distributing his tale but not seeding it. As far as the listeners are concerned, to borrow Toni Morrison's phrase at the end of *Beloved*, 'this is not a story to pass on'.[11]

The Rime of the Ancient Mariner thus presents us with a narrative design unprecedented in the genre to which it ostensibly belongs, that of the ballad; but it may be asked whether Coleridge drew on other sources, either for the figure of the compulsive storyteller, or for that of the compelled listener. Such sources are surprisingly hard to find. The bard Demodocus in book 8 of the *Odyssey* tells Odysseus's own story to him, so powerfully that Odysseus weeps; but though the hero pays him fulsome tribute, Demodocus is still no more than a glorified ballad-singer, who performs at request and whose authority is a kind of courtesy-title. In the *Arabian Nights* Scheherazade resumes, each night, the thread of a story on whose success in holding the King's attention her life depends; but her 'power of speech' is an innate gift and not an infliction. Nor is she compelled to narrate, except insofar as storytelling constitutes her stratagem; and she cannot, of course, repeat herself. As for the King, he too is not compelled to listen; his being continuously captivated by Scheherazade's art is a testimony to her skill but is not, in any meaningful sense of the term, involuntary.[12] The closest parallels, as you might expect with Coleridge, are Shakespearean. Othello (a middle-aged if not an ancient mariner) is accused by Brabantio of seducing Desdemona (not just a wedding-guest, but the bride herself) by occult means; he admits to using 'conjuration, and ... mighty magic' (I. iii. 92), but it turns out that this refers to storytelling: after hearing him relate his 'travel's history', Othello claims, Desdemona 'bade me, if I had a friend that lov'd her, / I should but teach him how to tell my story, / And that would woo her ... This only is the witchcraft I have us'd' (I. iii. 164–6, 169). Shakespeare intends us, I think, to take Othello's denial of having used magic as both true and disingenuous – true in that he did not do so in the vulgar literal way that Brabantio suspects, 'By spells and medicines bought of mountebanks' (I. iii. 61); disingenuous in that storytelling is indeed a form of magic, capable of casting a spell on its listener. We might say, then, that Coleridge has made explicit and (within a fiction) 'literalized' this suggestion that the storyteller can indeed bewitch his audience; he may also have taken a hint from *The Tempest* (III. iii. 53–82), in which Ariel casts a spell on the 'three men of sin', Alonso, Antonio, and Sebastian, who must listen to his denunciation of them.

In Act I, scene 5 of *Hamlet* the Ghost is certainly an imperative story-teller and Hamlet a compelled listener: 'Mark me', the Ghost adjures Hamlet, who replies 'I will'; and again, 'lend me thy serious hearing', to which Hamlet replies 'Speak; I am bound to hear'. The verbal parallels are much stronger in the 1798 text, which clearly remembers the Ghost's 'List, list, O list!' in lines which were cut from 1800 onwards:

> Listen, O listen, thou wedding-guest!
>   "Marinere! thou hast thy will:
>   "For that, which comes out of thine eye, doth make
>   "My body and soul to be still."[13]

Yet the differences are as striking as the resemblances. The Mariner and the wedding-guest are not related; Hamlet is 'bound to hear' because of the fil-ial bond, not because the Ghost has any occult power over him. Nor is the Mariner a spirit; he explicitly reassures the wedding-guest on this point (ll. 230–1). The Ghost himself is under a compulsion not to talk but to walk: 'Doom'd for a certain term to walk the night ... Till the foul crimes done in my days of nature / Are burnt and purg'd away' (I. v. 10–13). Far from being compelled to tell tales, he is 'forbid / To tell the secrets of my prison-house' (ll. 13–14). It is not his own 'foul crimes' that he wants Hamlet to know about, but the foul crime done to *him*. His motive in telling his story is not to purge himself, but to provoke Hamlet to act.

If we move away from the specific act of storytelling, we can find plenty of instances of spellbinding song – Orpheus, Amphion, David, among others – but these figures, are, precisely, *singers* not narrators. Their power is lyric, embodied in music, and is exercised over natural or supernatural phenomena. They tame wild beasts, or raise the walls of a city, or charm the gods of the underworld, or drive out an evil spirit. The Ancient Mariner is not like these singers (except, possibly, in playing David to his own Saul) in that the aesthetic qualities of his performance, however much those qualities matter to us, have no bearing on its purpose and (as far as we can judge) make no impact on the wedding-guest. The Mariner's story may be one of the most 'compelling' ever told, but it is not that which compels the wedding-guest to sit through it.

I can best illustrate the peculiarity of Coleridge's invention by presenting two examples of the poem's direct influence on a subsequent work, but in which this very peculiarity is either absent or turned in on itself. The first example comes from chapter 14 of Elizabeth Gaskell's *Mary Barton* (1848). Esther, Mary's aunt, has become a prostitute after an affair with an army officer, who abandons her and her illegitimate child. She fears that her niece, who is being courted by the mill-owner's son Henry Carson, will '[follow] in the same downward path to vice'. She tries to warn John Barton, Mary's father, but he rebuffs her. 'She must speak; to that she was soul-compelled; but to whom?' She decides to approach Mary's other (and respectable) suitor, Jem Wilson, and accosts him in the street.

> She laid her hand on his arm. As she expected, after a momentary glance at the person who thus endeavoured to detain him, he made an effort to shake it off and pass on. But trembling as she was, she had provided against this by a firm and unusual grasp.
>
> "You must listen to me, Jem Wilson," she said, with almost an accent of command.
>
> "Go away, missis; I've nought to do with you, either in hearkening or talking."
>
> He made another struggle.
>
> "You must listen," she said again, authoritatively, "for Mary Barton's sake."
>
> The spell of her name was as potent as that of the mariner's glittering eye. "He listened like a three-year child."
>
> "I know you care enough for her to wish to save her from harm."
>
> He interrupted his earnest gaze into her face, with the exclamation—
>
> "And who can yo be to know Mary Barton, or to know that she's ought to me?"
>
> There was a strife in Esther's mind for an instant, between the shame of acknowledging herself, and the additional weight to her revelation which such acknowledgment would give. Then she spoke.

"Do you remember Esther, the sister of John Barton's wife? the aunt to Mary? And the Valentine I sent you last February ten years?"

"Yes, I mind her well! But yo are not Esther, are you?" He looked again into her face, and seeing that indeed it was his boyhood's friend, he took her hand, and shook it with a cordiality that forgot the present in the past.

"Why, Esther! Where han ye been this many a year? Where han ye been wandering that we none of us could find you out?"

The question was asked thoughtlessly, but answered with fierce earnestness.

"Where have I been? What have I been doing? Why do you torment me with questions like these? Can you not guess? But the story of my life is wanted to give force to my speech, afterwards I will tell it you. Nay! don't change your fickle mind now, and say you don't want to hear it. You must hear it, and I must tell it; and then see after Mary, and take care she does not become like me. As she is loving now, so did I love once; one above me far." She remarked not, in her own absorption, the change in Jem's breathing, the sudden clutch at the wall which told the fearfully vivid interest he took in what she said. "He was so handsome, so kind! Well, the regiment was ordered to Chester (did I tell you he was an officer?), and he could not bear to part from me, nor I from him, so he took me with him. I never thought poor Mary would have taken it so to heart! I always meant to send for her to pay me a visit when I was married; for, mark you! he promised me marriage. They all do. Then came three years of happiness. I suppose I ought not to have been happy, but I was. I had a little girl, too. Oh! the sweetest darling that ever was seen! But I must not think of her," putting her hand wildly up to her forehead, "or I shall go mad; I shall."

"Don't tell me any more about yoursel," said Jem, soothingly.

"What! you're tired already, are you? but I will tell you; as you've asked for it, you shall hear it. I won't recall the agony of the past for nothing. I will have the relief of telling it. Oh, how happy I was!"[14]

Gaskell's reworking of the opening scene of Coleridge's poem (she assumes the reader will instantly recognize it, an impressive testimony to its popularity) introduces a significant, and from our viewpoint disabling, variation. Like the Mariner, Esther is 'soul-compelled' to speak, but unlike him her motive for 'stopping' Jem *in particular* is personal, and she in turn cannot compel his attention without appealing to his own interest. Her strong grasp of him is physically 'unusual' but not uncanny; she has no 'glittering eye' and is indeed rebuffed by his 'momentary glance'; her first imperative, 'You must listen to me', is uttered 'with *almost* an accent of command'. In order to overcome Jem's resistance she has to appeal to him, even though this appeal is disguised as a command: '"You must listen," she said again, authoritatively, "for Mary Barton's sake."' Esther's *authority* here is not, so to speak, authorial; it is borrowed from her knowledge of Jem's situation. In turn, he responds only to this secondary imperative: 'The spell of her name was *as* potent as the mariner's glittering eye' tells you that Esther does not, herself, possess this 'eye'. It is true that Gaskell was too good an artist to leave matters there. Esther's unselfish motive, to warn Jem that what happened to her might happen to Mary (even though that involves the revelation of her own shameful history) gets mixed up with the impulse to tell her story for her own sake. She ends the passage more truly like the Ancient Mariner than she was at the beginning, gripped by 'the agony of the past' and impelled to seek 'the relief of telling it'. The trigger for this is Jem's 'thoughtless' question, which acts on Esther with the same abrupt violence as the Hermit's question to the Mariner, 'What manner of man art thou?' Gaskell clearly apprehends the dual compulsion of the poem, for whose 'plot' she incidentally provides an admirably succinct formula: 'You must hear it, and I must tell it.' Yet her own plot cannot fully implement this formula. Jem remains under Esther's spell because of her relation to Mary; the 'fearfully vivid inter- est' he shows is not in what has happened to Esther – even though, as we shall see, he is moved by her plight – but in what might happen to the woman he loves, and who is in danger of being seduced by 'one above [her] far'. In this light Esther's repeated imperatives ('You must hear it ... you shall hear it') have a merely token force. Jem will listen not because he must but because he wants to. His interest chimes with that of his author, who at this point in her novel is concerned not with narrative but with plot; the use she makes of *The Rime of the Ancient Mariner* is in the end rhetorical and circumstantial, and Esther's fiery response to Jem is left as an undeveloped motif.

My second example comes from Samuel Beckett's *Not I* (1972).[15] The imprint of the Ancient Mariner (on reflection it is there from the start) comes into clear focus towards the end of the play, when Mouth speaks the history of her speech:

> speechless all her days ... practically speechless ... even to herself ... never out loud ... but not completely ... sometimes sudden urge ... once or twice a year ... always winter some strange reason ... the long

evenings ... hours of darkness ... sudden urge to ... tell ... then rush out stop the first she saw ... nearest lavatory ... start pouring it out ... steady stream ... mad stuff ... half the vowels wrong ... no one could follow ... till she saw the stare she was getting ... then die of shame ... crawl back in ... once or twice a year ... always winter some strange reason ... long hours of darkness ...[16]

Mouth experiences her compulsion a little more predictably than the Mariner ('always winter some strange reason') but in other respects the parallel is much closer than in the case of *Mary Barton*. The 'sudden urge to [...] tell' (the word is tellingly isolated) is followed by the arbitrary seizure of a listener ('rush out stop the first she saw', the word *stop* making the connection with the poem evident). The apparent coarseness of Beckett's image of this unwilling listener as the 'nearest lavatory' is mitigated by the older meaning of that term as a laver, or vessel for washing, one of whose figurative meanings is that of spiritual cleansing, so that Mouth, in a characteristically Beckettian compacting of opposites, is both excreting and purifying herself. (The exact content of what is told is not specified, and doesn't really matter; it is in any case not a question of a single guilty action but an entire life of wracked lovelessness, not a deed but a predicament.) The action of narrating leads to no good result, either for Mouth or for the recipient of her tale. Beckett makes the point by inversion: the 'glittering eye' of the Mariner becomes 'the stare she was getting' – getting, not giving. It is the speaker, not the listener, who experiences the eye's power, not to cast a spell but to penetrate with shame.

Beckett's imagining of the dynamic of compulsive speech and compelled listening is, in one way, closer to Coleridge than Gaskell's, because Beckett sees the significance of there being no prior relation between speaker and listener ('He stoppeth one of three' – 'rush out stop the first she saw'); but it turns away from Coleridge just where Gaskell draws nearer, at the point where speaker and listener actually make contact. The second purpose of the Mariner's tale, to inculcate the lesson of God's universal love, is beautifully transmuted by Gaskell into the creation, in Jem Wilson, of human sympathy for Esther. In this sense the behaviour of the Mariner himself in his own tale, first cursing and rejecting the 'slimy things' in the sea, then blessing them, is divided between John Barton, Esther's brother-in-law, who curses and rejects her, and Jem Wilson, whose initial revulsion turns to compassion; Jem is also the wedding-guest (he is 'on his way' in the novel to his marriage with Mary) whose 'heart's sympathy' for Esther is the product of her terrible history.[17] In *Not I*, however, Beckett is remorseless towards the 'wedding-guest' figures, each of whom responds to Mouth with a 'stare' which makes her 'crawl back in' (painfully reversing the initial *rush out*). But Beckett has not left matters there. There is another listener in *Not I*, whose responses displace those of the 'wedding-guests'. I am not referring to the officially designated 'Auditor', the silent figure who stands stage left and raises its arms at intervals in a decreasingly perceptible gesture of 'helpless compassion', but to the internal listener, the one within the consciousness of Mouth herself.[18] This listener is identified with one desperate aim, to make the voice pouring out of Mouth, the voice which we hear unintelligibly before the curtain rises and which sinks back into unintelligibility as it falls, to make this voice *stop*.[19] Yet we know of this aim only because the words which express it are spoken by the same voice:

> stream of words ... in her ear ... practically in her ear ... not catching the half ... not the quarter ... no idea what she's saying ... imagine! ... no idea what she's saying! ... and can't stop ... no stopping it ... she who but a moment before ... but a moment! ... could not make a sound ... no sound of any kind ... now can't stop ... imagine! ... can't stop the stream ... and the whole brain begging ... something begging in the brain ... begging the mouth to stop ... pause a moment ... if only for a moment ... and no response ... as if it hadn't heard ... or couldn't ... couldn't pause a second ... like maddened ... all that together ... straining to hear ... piece it together ... and the brain ... raving away on its own ... trying to make sense of it ... or make it stop ... or in the past ... dragging up the past ...

By rhetorical involution the voice which speaks, and the voice of the wish that it should stop speaking, intolerable bore and intolerably bored, are fused in a single impossible Mariner-guest, 'dragging up the past' in order to convey a message from and to herself. It is the same message as in *The Rime of the Ancient Mariner*, Beckett's lyric distillation of Romantic 'natural supernaturalism': 'God is love ... she'll be purged ... back in the field ... morning sun ... April ... sink face down in the grass ... nothing but the larks ...'; it is perpetually arriving, and never getting through.[20]

If the poem's partial precursors and successors do no more than return us to the originality of Coleridge's invention, at least they give us a clue as to what that originality consists of. No one, after all, really believes in the power of storytellers to compel their audience to listen, or their readers to read. Poets, novelists, dramatists may like to imagine that they have power over their audience, and a loose critical vocabulary colludes in their fantasy, but no one is really fooled. When Coleridge coined the phrase 'that willing suspension of disbelief for the moment, which constitutes poetic faith',[21] he was articulating a truth about the relation between teller and listener which is the very opposite of that which he describes *within* 'The Rime of the Ancient Mariner', though it corresponds exactly to the way in which he expected readers *of* the poem to respond. No reader of *The Rime of the Ancient Mariner*, in other words, duplicates the involuntary fascination of the wedding-guest, for the very good reason that the poet is not, himself, an Ancient Mariner, and cannot hold us with his glittering eye; the phrase used of the wedding-guest, 'He cannot chuse but hear', does not and cannot apply to us *in our capacity as readers*.

I make this qualification because there are, of course, circumstances in life in which we are compelled to listen to other people telling stories. Many of these situations are socially determined – sitting next to someone at a dinner, or in a railway carriage, or on board an aeroplane. We may feel coerced by family obligation, or conventions of politeness, or subservience within a hierarchy, and though strictly speaking even these do not constitute compulsion the distinction is often hard to make in practice. If your boss enjoys telling interminable anecdotes, or you are stuck with a garrulous fellow-passenger on a transatlantic flight, you may well feel that you 'cannot chuse but hear'. Writers have been drawn to such socially-determined compulsions: in chapter 22 of Jane Austen's *Sense and Sensibility*, for example, Elinor Dashwood is trapped into becoming the confidante of Lucy Steele, who maliciously torments her by forcing her to listen to the history of Lucy's secret engagement to Edward Ferrars, the man Elinor loves (and whom Lucy knows she loves); in *Emma*, by contrast, Miss Bates has a 'power of speech' which Emma must learn to suffer gladly (the most stinging rebuke she elicits from Mr Knightley, during the excursion to Box Hill in chapter 43, springs precisely from her attempt to shut the well-meaning old lady up). *Mrs Caudle's Curtain-Lectures*, by Douglas Jerrold, brilliantly exploits the hapless nightly constraint of the hen-pecked husband going to roost. Crushed beneath the condescending weight of his grand host's interminable after-dinner *apologia*, the young journalist Gigadibs, in Robert Browning's poem 'Bishop Blougram's Apology', 'played with spoons, explored his plate's design, / And ranged the olive-stones about its edge' – behaviour which can no doubt be seen every night at one High Table or another. Other social situations are more painfully constraining.

Robert Lowell, in 'Under the Dentist', realizes the exquisite irony of a poet famous for his manic (real-life) harangues subjected to the dentist's patter, as unstoppable as a drill. In *The Hitch-Hiker's Guide to the Galaxy*, Ford Prefect tells Arthur Dent that if they are very unlucky their expulsion from the Vogon spaceship into outer space will be preceded by being made to listen to the Vogon captain recite his poetry. Pedro Almodóvar's film *Talk to Her* portrays a special modern form of narrative compulsion, that of the coma patient hooked up to the drip of her carer's assiduous, interminable gossip. And how many spouses chat by their partners' gravesides, relaying news of their own and their children's doings? This, too, is a scene which has found its way into literature and film. The most extreme example, and the most formally inventive, comes in the bleakly 'comic' denouement of Evelyn Waugh's *A Handful of Dust*: trapped in the Amazon jungle, Tony Last is forced to read Dickens aloud, forever, to his mad 'rescuer', Mr Todd: the wedding-guest is tormented by being made to tell, not even his own but another's stories, to act the part of the Mariner but without forgiveness or remission.[22]

The number of real-life situations in which we may compel others to listen to us may be great or small, but in literature, I repeat, it is simply nil. A literary work which, like *The Rime of the Ancient Mariner*, represents such a situation is subject to an implacable irony, that its own audience is not compelled to pay attention. The opening of the poem is, in this light, knowingly impersonal, making no claims on its reader but staging a kind of universal fantasy of authorial power. What the Mariner does to the wedding-guest will remain forever out of reach for the poet himself; art is a transaction in which literal power dematerialises, to be replaced by the gift, priceless because uncompelled and gratuitous, of attention.

It seems therefore that the true afterlife of *The Rime of the Ancient Mariner* lies in the storyteller's return to a problem which cannot be resolved – a transposition of the Mariner's own recurring 'agony' from the psychological to the aesthetic domain. The dramatic monologue has been the most fertile ground for this transposition, but within this genre we need to distinguish 'strong' works, in which the scenario is actually or at least potentially recurrent, and in which the scenario comprises both a compulsive speaker and a compelled listener, from 'weak' ones, in which these conditions are lacking or defective. Tennyson's Ulysses is under no real compulsion to make a farewell speech before he sets out, though Telemachus and the other Ithacans (where, incidentally, is Penelope?) are admittedly bound to listen to it, since he is still king and they must at least look interested until he is out of the harbour; still, it is a speech he is only going to make once. Tithonus, on the other hand, is trapped in a condition (that of unendingly growing older) where recurrence never amounts to renewal, so that his complaining about it to Aurora, the goddess of dawn who 'renew[s] [her] beauty morn by morn' (l. 74), is fittingly recurrent, and her having to listen to it is a matter of clever timing on his part (she can't leave the house till it's time for her to go to work).[23] Browning's Duke in 'My Last Duchess' is evidently expert at contriving the situation in which he can inflict on selected listeners the story (a matter for him of obsessive self-justification) of how he dealt with his too-agreeable wife; the particular instance in the poem is heightened by the listener's being an envoy sent to negotiate a second marriage, but this is merely an embellishment to a scene which has taken place before and will take place again, requiring only a listener who is a social inferior and unable to protest or depart. Andrea del Sarto will always quarrel and plead with Lucrezia in the same tone, and she will always listen because the outcome is that he gives her money and condones her adultery. The Bishop of Saint Praxed's, on the other hand, surrounded by his 'nephews' on his deathbed, can force them to listen to his tirade of sinful memory and thwarted desire, but like Ulysses his hold on his audience lasts only as long as the poem. If Fra Lippo Lippi is caught out of bounds in Florence again, or if Mr Sludge is caught cheating at another séance (each of these poems begins with someone's hand at the speaker's throat), they may well try to wriggle out of it in the same way (they carry their 'story' within themselves, like a grievance), but there is no necessity for the officer of the watch, or the outraged patron, to react in the same way and settle down to hear their story. A later Browning monologue, 'Martin Relph', has every Coleridgean element on the narrator's side – guilt, remorse, penance, compulsive narration (doubly powerful in that it is associated with a return to the scene of the crime) – but is 'weak' on the other side, that of the audience. The action of the poem takes place during the '45 rebellion. Martin Relph has the chance to save the woman he loves (but who does not love him) from execution as a Jacobite spy, by pointing out to the commanding officer of the firing-party, from his vantage-point on a hill, the imminent arrival of her pardon, borne by her frantically hastening lover, Martin's rival. He makes no sign, the execution takes place, and the rival dies of despair. Each year Martin returns to the hill and makes a public confession, yet what he seeks is ambivalently poised between redemption and evasion of his guilt. He wants his audience, who treat him as a madman and public spectacle, to help him convince himself that his inaction was the result of mere human cowardice, of fear for his own safety if he intervened. The alternative, that he was motivated by diabolical dog-in-the-manger jealousy ('She were better dead than happy and his!'), is likelier to be true, but is too painful to face; yet every year he returns to face it. Subtle, acute, persuasive though the poem's treatment of Martin is, it leaves his audience nothing really to do. Their reactions are necessary to Martin's act, but not necessary in themselves; if they were not there he would make them up. By the same token they have no compelling motive to listen to him, except the crowd's motive of idle and cruel fun; and his speech leaves as it finds them.[24]

Although the dramatic monologue clearly derives some of its energy from the situation imagined in *The Rime of the Ancient Mariner*, its field is more various and its excellence does not depend, or only in rare instances, on fidelity to Coleridge's model ('Ulysses' is a great poem despite Ulysses not being a true Ancient Mariner, and would indeed be less great if he were represented as setting off and returning at intervals). Not that 'fidelity' should be taken too literally here. Stories which carry Coleridge's colours include the 'Scylla and Charybdis' chapter of Joyce's *Ulysses* and William Faulkner's *Absalom, Absalom*. The artistic problem to which Coleridge gave an indelible shape, the fantasy of authorial power which he thematized, recur in these works because their authors, like Coleridge, consciously represent the compelling power of narrative within works which cannot, themselves, exercise that power. Stephen Dedalus, expounding his biographical theory of Shakespeare on the steps of the University Library to a doubting group of doubtful friends, and 'begging with a swift glance their hearing', has a power which gathers strength as the chapter progresses, to the point where the storyteller occupies the position both of the Ghost in *Hamlet* and of Claudius, his murderer: 'They list. And in the porches of their ears I pour.'[25] *Absalom, Absalom* opens with a scene of enforced listening (by Quentin Compson) to a compulsive narrator (Miss Coldfield), and is structured throughout by the compulsive need (shared between Miss Coldfield, Quentin, his father and grandfather, his friend Shreve) to tell, fully, the story of Thomas Sutpen and the lost world he embodied, as well as by the fearful toll which this telling exacts on all of them, on Quentin most of all.[26] The complexity of the book's narrative method culminates in part 8: during the course of a single night in their rooms in Harvard, Quentin and Shreve work through the story to the brink of its terrible denouement, a night in which they not only exchange roles as narrator and listener, but become an impossible conjoined being that tells and

hears, in 'some happy marriage of speaking and hearing wherein each
before the demand, the requirement, forgave condoned and forgot the
faulting of the other' (261) – Faulkner's syntax enacting the melting
together of demand and response. Like many happy marriages this one
does not last. How could it? Quentin and Shreve aim 'to overpass to
love, where there might be paradox and inconsistency but nothing fault
nor false'; a union between teller and hearer based not on compulsion
but on mutual surrender, in which these coupled storytellers might
truly reflect the relation between an author and his readers.

In *Heart of Darkness* the entanglement and exchange of narrative roles
(teller and listener, Mariner and wedding-guest) is 'realized' in its most
complex and powerfully baffled form. The book begins, conventionally
enough, by presenting a situation in which the compulsion to speak is
matched by the necessity to listen. This necessity is not magical –
Marlow casts no spell – or rather we might say that the spell is cast by
circumstance, and is marked by a pun on the word 'bound'. The *Nellie*
is 'bound down the river' (her purpose is seaward) but is 'bound'
(obliged) by that very fact to anchor and 'wait for the turn of the tide'.
The scene is described for us by an anonymous narrator, who, as in *The
Rime of the Ancient Mariner*, opens (and will close) the narrative. He is
one of five men on board the yacht, who are also 'bound' together, by
what the narrator calls 'the bond of the sea'. They sit in silence, and
when Marlow begins to speak he already has a captive audience, con-
strained, as the narrator emphasizes, by circumstance as much as by the
force of his character:

> We looked on, waiting patiently—there was nothing else to do till
> the end of the flood; but it was only after a long silence, when he said
> in a hesitating voice, "I suppose you fellows remember that I did
> once turn fresh-water sailor for a bit," that we knew we were fated,
> before the ebb began to run, to hear about one of Marlow's incon-
> clusive experiences.[27]

Within this frame-narrative, Marlow's four companions play the part of
the 'wedding guest'; yet Marlow, who has them under a kind of spell,
immediately begins casting himself as spell-bound, first by the map of
Africa in a shop-window which 'fascinated me as a snake would a bird –
a silly little bird', then by the old woman in the Company offices in
Brussels ('An eerie feeling came over me. She seemed uncanny and
fateful').[28] The imagery of enchantment proliferates uncontrollably
from this point on: it takes in the 'faithless pilgrims bewitched inside

a rotten fence' in the Station (23), the trees by the river whose stillness 'seemed unnatural, like a state of trance' (39), the approach to Kurtz which seems 'beset by as many dangers as though he had been an enchanted princess sleeping in an enchanted castle' (42).[29] Kurtz's own fascination – 'He had the power to charm or frighten rudimentary souls into an aggravated witch-dance in his honour' (50) – is offset by 'the heavy mute spell of the wilderness' which Marlow tries in vain to break. It is he, instead, who is spell-bound ('transfixed', 69) by Kurtz's condition.[30] But not by his voice, whose power leaves Marlow appalled but not deceived. 'A voice! a voice! It was grave, profound, vibrating, while the man did not seem capable of a whisper' (60).[31] 'Kurtz discoursed. A voice! a voice! It rang deep to the very last. It survived his strength to hide in the magnificent folds of eloquence the barren darkness of his heart' (68).[32] As listener Marlow can be 'held' but not subjugated; and this applies both to Kurtz's voice, and to that of his Intended, for Marlow has to endure both the 'spell' of darkness and corruption, and that of innocence and purity, the second as fearful as the first. More fearful perhaps, for the Intended's delusion about Kurtz is specifically linked to her having fallen under the spell of his voice, which has infected her own with its sick enchantment:

> And the girl talked, easing her pain in the certitude of my sympathy she talked, as thirsty men drank. ...
>
> '"... Who was not his friend who had heard him speak once?' she was saying. 'He drew men towards him by what was best in them.' She looked at me with intensity. 'It is the gift of the great,' she went on and the sound of her low voice seemed to have the accompaniment of all the other sounds full of mystery, desolation, and sorrow I had ever heard—the ripple of the river, the soughing of the trees swayed by the wind, the murmurs of the crowds, the faint ring of incomprehensible words cried from afar, the whisper of a voice speaking from beyond the threshold of an eternal darkness. 'But you have heard him. You know!' she cried.[33]

The look which the Intended gives Marlow has, in its 'intensity', an affinity with the Mariner's eye, as though at this late stage she were making an effort to compel him to believe in her vision of Kurtz's life; yet the real ground of her conviction (that Marlow *must* share this vision) is the effect on him, as she imagines it from her own experience, of Kurtz's voice. And her delusion, it is made clear, springs from a trustfulness as hollow as Kurtz's eloquence: when Marlow looks at her photograph, before going to see her, she seems to him 'ready to listen, without mental reservation, without suspicion, without a thought for herself' (72).[34] You might say she listened to Kurtz 'like a three-year child'; but Marlow will not surrender himself in this way, either to Kurtz or to her.

Marlow's refusal leaves him in a complex position as storyteller and listener. He is like the 'wedding-guest' in that he emerges 'a sadder and a wiser man' from the spell both of Kurtz's voice, and that of the Intended; he is like the Mariner in that he takes on the burden of these voices, the obligation (or curse) to reproduce them. Yet the culmination of his story is a *refusal*: 'I could not tell her. It would have been too dark—too dark altogether' (77). As for his own listeners, their response is just as blocked and deflected:

> Nobody moved for a time. "We have lost the first of the ebb," said the Director suddenly. I raised my head. The offing was barred by a black bank of clouds, and the tranquil waterway leading to the uttermost ends of the earth flowed sombre under an overcast sky— seemed to lead into the heart of an immense darkness.[35]

These images return us to the enforced stillness of the opening; even though the tide has turned, the way out to sea is 'barred', and the flow of the tide itself has become sinister, fateful. Might the 'immense darkness' be an image of that final act of 'telling' from which Marlow recoiled? 'It would have been too dark—too dark altogether.' Yet we must remember that what Marlow spares the Intended he does not spare his listeners. They are compelled to sit through his story to the end – even if it is the end of an 'inconclusive experience'.

Notes

All quotations from the poem, unless otherwise indicated, are from the *Poetical Works* of 1834, the last edition published in Coleridge's lifetime. There is clearly a case for using the poem's original version, 'The Rime of the Ancyent Marinere', published anonymously in *Lyrical Ballads* (1798), or even the revised text from the subsequent editions of that work (1800, 1802, 1805). Coleridge first printed the poem under his own name in *Sibylline Leaves* (1817), though his authorship of it was known from the beginning. In truth the question of which text to use is (fittingly perhaps, for anything involving Coleridge, but exasperatingly) unresolvable. The deliberately archaic spellings and idioms of 1798 are neither here nor there as far as my purpose in this essay goes; what matters more is that the narrative framework is slightly but still significantly different, both more elaborate at the start and with more interjections by the Mariner and the wedding-guest in the course of the narrative. However, to speak of the poem's 'afterlife' or influence, even in the qualified sense in which I take these terms, requires reference to a text more widely disseminated than the 1798 version. Needless to say one of the few direct mentions of the poem in Victorian fiction immediately contradicts this notion, and incidentally confirms George Eliot's acute historical sense. In chapter 5 of *Adam Bede* (1859), which is set at the end of the eighteenth century, Arthur Donnithorne, knowing his godmother, Mrs Irwine, is fond of 'queer, wizard-like stories', offers her a book which 'came down in a par-cel from London the other day': 'It's a volume of poems, "Lyrical Ballads": most of them seem to be twaddling stuff; but the first is in a different style—"The Ancient Mariner" is the title. I can hardly make head or tail of it as a story, but it's a strange, striking thing.' This must be the 1798 edition, since that was the only one in which *The Rime of the Ancient Mariner* was the lead item. In general, though, I think the later text is likely to have been more widely known. I note the 1798 readings where they affect the narrative aspect of the poem.

1. Joseph Conrad, *Heart of Darkness*, ed. P. B. Armstrong (New York and London: W. W. Norton, 2006), p. 5. Hereafter Conrad.
2. The 1798 opening makes more of the wedding-guest's resistance: 'But still he holds the wedding-guest— / There was a Ship, quoth he— / "Nay, if thou'st got a laughsome tale, / Marinere! come with me." // He holds him with his skinny hand, / Quoth he, there was a Ship— / "Now get thee hence, thou grey-beard Loon! / Or my Staff shall make thee skip." // He holds him with his glittering eye— / The wedding guest stood still / And listens like a three year's child; / The Marinere hath his will' (ll. 9–20).
3. For possible Shakespearean sources, see below, pp. 132–3. Along with tradi-tional forms of spellbinding Coleridge may have had in mind the more recent, and fashionable, practice of mesmerism, though the mesmeric trance was usually induced not by gaze but by 'passes' of the mesmerist's hands. Nor was mesmerism used as a means of getting someone to listen to a story; indeed, the development of hypnosis as a technique in psychotherapy had the opposite aim – to get the subject to speak.
4. The openings of 'King Estmere' and 'A Gest of Robyn Hode', in James Kinsley (ed.), *The Oxford Book of Ballads* (Oxford: Oxford University Press, 1969), pp. 127, 420.
5. Michael Mason (*Lyrical Ballads*, London: Longman 1992), 177, argues that 'the implication of this subtitle is [...] in some measure maintained by the [Latin] epigraph in later editions'.
6. *Oxford Book of Ballads*, 243; other mother–son dialogues include 'Edward, Edward' (p. 239) and 'Son David' (p. 241).
7. In 1798 ll. 582–5 read: 'Since then at an uncertain hour, / Now oftimes and now fewer, / That anguish comes and makes me tell / My ghastly aventure.' The revision dates from the *Lyrical Ballads* text of 1800, where however 'That agony' was felicitously misprinted as 'That agency'.
8. The 1817 text was printed with marginal glosses; opposite ll. 574–81 the gloss reads: 'The ancient Mariner earnestly entreateth the Hermit to shrieve him; and the penance of life falls on him', a form of words which avoids stating that the Hermit imposes the penance.
9. We are not given the Hermit's reaction, but in any case we know that the Mariner cannot intend to 'teach' him a moral lesson.

10. These closing lines of the poem are anticipated in the 1798 text by the Mariner himself, in lines which were cut from 1800 onwards: 'Never sadder tale was told / To a man of woman born: / Sadder and wiser thou wedding-guest! / Thou'lt rise to morrow morn' (ll. 366–9 in 1798, in a passage following l. 372 in the final version; see also 133 and n. 13). Michael Mason points out that though the primary meaning of 'sadder' is 'more serious', 'the dismaying nature of the Mariner's experiences ... must be relevant too' (204). Mason goes on to suggest that 'The Mariner does seem to wish to inculcate a less hedonistic attitude in the wedding-guest', a point reinforced by the biblical resonance, in the 1798 lines, of the phrase 'man of woman born': 'Man that is born of woman is of few days, and full of trouble' (Job 14: 1).
11. Toni Morrison, *Beloved* (London: Chatto and Windus, 1987), p. 274.
12. Coleridge does mention the *Arabian Nights* in connection with the poem, but not in the context of its narrative frame; he is responding to Mrs Barbauld's complaint that the poem 'had no moral' (*Table Talk*, 31 May 1830, cited in Mason, p. 367).
13. Lines 362–5 in 1798, in a passage following l. 372 in the final version (see above, n. 10). The quotations from *Hamlet* are from Act I, scene 5. In the 1798 text, the phrase 'Listen, Stranger!' also occurs at ll. 45 and 49 (after l. 40 in the final version), and the parenthesis '(Listen, O Stranger! to me)' at l. 205 (after l. 198); the first two were retained in the 1800 edition of *Lyrical Ballads*, but disappeared from 1802; the third survived in all editions of *Lyrical Ballads* but was cut when Coleridge reprinted the poem in *Sibylline Leaves* in 1817. The wedding-guest's tribute to the Mariner's power echoes another Shakespearean storytelling scene, in Act I scene 2 of *The Tempest*, where Prospero, in the course of telling Miranda how they came to the island, suspects that she is not paying attention: 'Dost thou attend me? ... Thou attend'st not ... Dost thou hear?' (ll. 78, 87, 106). To the last question Miranda replies 'Your tale, sir, would cure deafness'.
14. Elizabeth Gaskell, *Mary Barton*, ed. M. Lane (London: J. M. Dent, 1977 [Everyman's Library]), pp. 149–51.
15. I am grateful to Christopher Ricks for drawing my attention to this work.
16. Samuel Beckett, *The Complete Dramatic Works* (London: Faber and Faber, 1986), p. 382. Hereafter Beckett.
17. The encounter between John Barton and Esther, stormy with Coleridgean intimations of guilt and unforgiveness, is in chapter 10 (116–17). He holds her morally responsible for the death of his wife, her sister: 'Dost thou know it was thee who killed her, as sure as ever Cain killed Abel [...] at the judgment day she'll rise, and point to thee as her murderer'. Jem's 'heart's sympathy' is on p. 152, one of a cluster of such terms: 'the sympathy of Jem's countenance ... He deeply pitied her ... deep sympathy'. It is part of Gaskell's own moral rigour that she represents Jem as willing, but not quite willing enough, to turn his 'heart's sympathy' into practical help for Esther.
18. Beckett's 'Note' on the Auditor's movement is on p. 375.
19. It is possible that Beckett had in mind Keats's famous description of Coleridge's unstoppable 'conversation' as he experienced it on Hampstead Heath: 'I heard his voice as he came towards me—I heard it as he moved away—I had heard it all the interval—if it may be called so' (to George

and Georgiana Keats, 14 February–3 May 1819, *Letters of John Keats*, ed. Robert Gittings (Oxford: Oxford University Press, 1975), p. 237.

20. Beckett, pp. 380–1.

21. *Biographia Literaria* (1817), chapter 14; Coleridge is speaking generally about the poems he was to contribute to *Lyrical Ballads*, not specifically about the Ancient Mariner.

22. *Mrs Caudle's Curtain Lectures* began life as contributions to *Punch*, and appeared in volume form in 1846. 'Bishop Blougram's Apology' was published in *Men and Women* (1855). 'Under the Dentist' was published in *History* (1973). *Talk to Her* (*Hable con ella*) was released in 2002. The first volume of *The Hitchhiker's Guide to the Galaxy* was published in 1979, having begun as a BBC Radio 4 serial the previous year; the Vogon poetry episode comes at the end of chapter 6 and beginning of chapter 7. *A Handful of Dust* was published in 1934; Tony Last's fate is described in chapter 6. In the film *Shenandoah* (1965), the widowed Charlie Anderson (James Stewart) talks to his wife at her graveside.

23. 'Ulysses' was published in *Poems* (1842), 'Tithonus' in *Enoch Arden and Other Poems* (1864); both had been drafted in 1833.

24. 'My Last Duchess' was published in *Dramatic Lyrics* (1842); 'The Bishop Orders His Tomb at Saint Praxed's Church' in *Dramatic Romances and Lyrics* (1845); 'Andrea del Sarto' and 'Fra Lippo Lippi' in *Men and Women* (1855); 'Mr Sludge, "the Medium"' in *Dramatis Personae* (1864); 'Martin Relph' in *Dramatic Idyls* (1873).

25. James Joyce, *Ulysses* (Harmondsworth: Penguin, 1984 [reprint of 1971 edition]), p. 197.

26. The effect on Quentin is double: despair (the action ends shortly before his suicide, described in the second section of *The Sound and the Fury*, published seven years earlier in 1929), and a precarious, negatively phrased affirmation of love, in the book's closing words, replying to Shreve's accusing question, 'Why do you hate the South?': '"I dont hate it," Quentin said, quickly, at once, immediately; "I dont hate it," he said. *I dont hate it* he thought, panting in the cold air, the iron New England dark; *I dont. I dont! I dont hate it! I dont hate it!*'

27. Conrad, p. 7.

28. Ibid., pp. 8, 11.

29. Ibid., pp. 23, 39, 42.

30. Ibid., pp. 50, 69.

31. Ibid., p. 60.

32. Ibid., p. 68.

33. Ibid., p. 75.

34. Ibid., p. 72.

35. Ibid., p. 77.

9
The Sin in Sincerity: Ethics, Aesthetics, and a Critical Tradition from Coleridge to Wilde

Jane Wright

On 6 April 1897, a little over a month before his release from Reading jail, Oscar Wilde wrote to Robert Ross asking him to gather together some books in time for Wilde's release:

> You know the sort of books I want: Flaubert, Stevenson, Baudelaire, Maeterlinck, Dumas *père*, Keats, Marlowe, Chatterton, Coleridge, Anatole France, Gautier, Dante and all Dante literature; Goethe and ditto; and so on.[1]

Although direct evidence of Wilde's reading of Coleridge is slight, the Highgate Sage was clearly one of only a handful of English authors uppermost in Wilde's mind when thinking of life after prison. Literary critics have rarely, and usually only in passing, drawn links between the work of Samuel Taylor Coleridge and the work of Oscar Wilde.[2] At first this seems unsurprising. No one, after all, would claim that the two men shared religious beliefs in any organised or obvious sense. Nor, at first sight, do they seem to share much stylistically or in terms of literary critical perspectives: Coleridge often championed the careful application of 'general' principles, while Wilde sought to encourage the 'particular' response of the individual critic. Nor would one wish to compare Wilde's comparatively slight literary production with the abundance of Coleridge's, even if the extent of the latter's output took some time to come fully to light.[3] Yet the more one reads both authors' work, the more evident become the similarities in their patterns of self-borrowing and apparent self-contradiction, and further connections present themselves. Both men have been considered infamous literary plagiarists. Each was accused of writing immoral works. And in both cases these were works representing exotic and ambiguous subjects – which were, furthermore, often specifically linked by critics with the imputed immorality of the author's own personal life. Vincent O'Sullivan, in 1918, went so far as to assert that, as a writer, 'Wilde's sexual aberration [...] did to him what opium did to Coleridge'.[4] He seems to intend to level charges of addiction against the two men; addiction which he considers the cause of 'indolence'. Yet despite the absurdity of the charge in some senses, if one considers that an acute awareness of the moral complexity of their needs and desires was, for varying reasons, characteristic of Coleridge and Wilde, O'Sullivan's statement becomes more apt than he knew.[5] Overtly valuing the significance of individuals' pleasures and desires shapes the critical perspectives of both men.

As literary figures, Coleridge and Wilde are chief among those who draw our attention to a tendency of nineteenth-century criticism to collapse the life and literature even of writers who try explicitly to assert marked distinctions between the two. In their different ways, both are men with a sometime Dandy-esque image. Both are renowned talkers whose actual literary output is considered to be only part of the story, and each was well-known for a capacity for long, continuous and (sometimes) mesmerising speech. In this respect both (to twist Wilde's own description of himself) are men whose lives have seemed to demonstrate their genius as much as their works do.[6] Peter Ackroyd, for instance, comments that 'It is plausible to suggest that only half of Oscar Wilde's genius resides in his published works. He belongs in the company of other conversationalists, such as Johnson and Coleridge, whose wit and inventiveness were too exuberant to be confined to their written words.'[7] In different ways (though both invoking Plato) each is, moreover, a writer for whom dialogue, or at least a dialogic procedure, plays a fundamental role in his writing – whether in the interplay of 'Aphorism' and 'Comment' in Coleridge's *Aids to Reflection* (1825) or in the critical dialogues (sometimes called 'duologues' as expressions of the author's divided thinking) of Wilde.

The present chapter aims to contribute to a long-held critical debate about Wilde's views on art and morality, aesthetics and ethics. What I want to suggest is that some of Wilde's most awkward but central critical views find an important antecedent in Coleridge. By reflecting later upon links between 'sin' and 'sincerity', the chapter proposes that Wilde is indebted to Coleridge for the bold critical associations he makes between the two.

Art and morality

One of the reasons that *Biographia Literaria* (1817) places Coleridge as forefather of the literary critical development of the New Criticism is that there he focuses on the significance of form, and on assessment of the successful realisation of form as the most important task of the critic. It is a critical focus that has the potential to prompt a thorough-going separation of aesthetic from moral concerns, dividing attention to form from attention to content.[8] Writing about the division between art and morality in Coleridge's criticism, Michael Kooy finds that 'The assertions about aesthetic autonomy that appear throughout *Biographia* make it plain that in Coleridge's view art can have no direct influence on morals'.[9] As Wilde would argue in defence of *The Picture of Dorian Gray* (1891), 'The sphere of art and the sphere of ethics are absolutely distinct and separate'.[10] But distinctness and separateness will not, of course, preclude relation.

In *Biographia*, Coleridge criticises Wordsworth for not really describing characters 'of some low profession' (as he professes to do) so much as using such characters as so many mouthpieces for his own moral ideas. Wordsworth, Coleridge suggests, has turned the aim of his poetry into 'truth' rather than 'pleasure', and this is an error. As Coleridge famously explains, 'A poem is that species of composition, which is opposed to the works of science, by proposing for its *immediate* object pleasure, not truth'. This was a critical pronouncement that had a far-reaching impact on subsequent writing on art.[11] Wilde also complains of Wordsworth 'moralizing about the district'; but that this did not leave him wholly unsympathetic to Wordsworth's poems also suggests a tempering of response that is in sympathy with Coleridge.[12] The faults that Coleridge finds with Wordsworth's contributions to *Lyrical Ballads* and describes in volume two of *Biographia* are comparable to those faults that Wilde finds with 'realism' as he feels it has been degraded by the surge in production of cumbrous and pettily moralistic three-decker novels in the second half of the nineteenth century. Vivian, in 'The Decay of Lying' (1891), disapproves of Wordsworth's finding 'in stones the sermons he had already hidden there'.[13] The artistic method such 'finding' implies is a problem. The resulting art work is unlikely to prompt an aesthetic experience in which the mind is freed of didactic limitations; it therefore cannot offer a sense of freedom from within which the reader may realise him or herself as an independent moral agent. An aesthetic experience distinct from an ethical message may contain or invoke contradictions.

But it will be an experience that accords with Coleridge's description of Plato, because it will offer a 'higher' sense of knowledge by leading the reader or viewer 'to see that contradictory propositions are each true— [and] therefore *must* belong to a higher Logic—that of Ideas'.[14] Coleridge's 'higher Logic', I shall explain later, provides the cultural model for Wilde's 'higher ethics', and each of these 'higher' realms may be accessed by an art object or piece of criticism that works in a seemingly paradoxical or self-contradictory way.[15]

One of the reasons that aesthetic and moral concerns are separate, Coleridge explains, is not the result of any ultimate division between them; the separation is merely necessary given the social circumstances of life as we experience it. 'Blest indeed is that state of society, in which the immediate purpose [of art – i.e. to produce pleasure] would be baffled by the perversion of the proper ultimate end; in which no charm of diction or imagery could exempt the Bathyllus even of an Anacreon, or the Alexis of Virgil, from disgust and aversion!' (*BL* II, 12). That 'proper ultimate end' of art may be moral, and, in a different state of society – one 'Blest indeed' – aesthetic value might be marred or destroyed in the process of representing evil or vicious characters or acts. But this is not the case in society as it exists – in our own fragile, fragmentary universe. In works of high aesthetic value, there remains something to admire that may be separated from the work's possible moral implications. 'Is this dangerous?' Wilde's Gilbert asks rhetorically having explained his own separation of aesthetics and ethics, 'Yes; it is dangerous – all ideas, as I told you, are so [...] It is Criticism that leads us. The Critical Spirit and the World-Spirit are one'.[16] Criticism has a vital role to play in recognising and negotiating the diverse claims of art upon us, discerning which aesthetic productions work in a way that places them beyond moral censure.

Frank Kermode finds *The Critic as Artist* instrumental as he thinks about the language of organicism and the reconciliation of opposites in Romanticism, and he links Wilde and Coleridge when he writes that 'irritating as most people now find [*The Critic as Artist*], [...] by ruthlessly abstracting some of its arguments we may be able to indicate some of the disguised similarities between poetic periods [Romantic and nineteenth-century *fin de siècle*] usually considered antithetical'.[17] In the duologue, Gilbert states that 'All the arts are immoral except those baser forms of sensual or didactic art that seek to excite to action of evil or of good', and Kermode explains that 'The word "immoral" here represents a coarsening of the aesthetic in the interests of paradox; but the descent of the idea is obvious enough, and Wilde is concerned, in modern terms, to distinguish art from both propaganda and entertainment'.

There is a troubled connection between Wilde's word 'immoral' and the aesthetic debates of Romanticism. The 'descent of the idea' Gilbert expresses, Kermode suggests, is Coleridgean. In response to Wilde's assertion that 'all artistic creation is absolutely subjective', Kermode remarks that this 'might, with certain metaphysical qualifications, be Coleridge [speaking]'[18] and a little later, he comments: 'Form is organic (Coleridge distinguishes it from what he calls "shape", or mechanical design) and nature is only the symbolical potential, meaningful only in perception informed by the moral act of imagination. (The meaning of "moral" here, by the way, is not very remote from what Wilde meant by "immoral". If the act of imagination is incorrupt, the product cannot possibly meddle in ethics or have a design upon the reader.)'.[19] In Kermode's discussion, the indirect relationship between ethics and aesthetics is identified by the near-synonymy of 'moral' and 'immoral' that reaches between these authors' works. Gilbert calls all art 'immoral' because he believes that real art reaches to a higher ethical plane than that of common social morality. Coleridge considers acts of imagination 'moral' because they too will offer access to this realm. As Michael Kooy remarks on Coleridge: 'The aesthetic does no more than not offend against the moral law; in other respects it remains neutral towards it and only in so far as it is neutral, offers the greatest aesthetic pleasure and the greatest possibility of effecting action'.[20]

Coleridge is an important figure for De Quincey, in illustrating another instance of the necessary division between aesthetic and moral realms that Wilde will later seize upon, in 'On Murder Considered as One of the Fine Arts' (1827). In this satirical work, De Quincey explains that 'Everything in this world' has two handles. Murder, for instance, may be laid hold of by its moral handle [...] or it may also be treated *aesthetically* [...], that is, in relation to good taste'.[21] Taking Coleridge for an authority on this point, De Quincey cites an evening during which he and Coleridge witnessed a fire at a piano-forte maker's near Berners' Street in London. Being called away, De Quincey recounts that he never saw 'how that very promising exhibition [the fire] had terminated', and that on enquiring of Coleridge about the outcome, the latter had replied: 'Oh sir, it turned out so ill, that we damned it unanimously'. De Quincey concludes: 'Now does any man suppose that Mr Coleridge, – who, for all he is too fat to be a person of active virtue, is undoubtedly a worthy Christian, – that this good S.T.C., I say, was an incendiary, or capable of wishing any ill to the poor man and his piano-fortes [...]?'[22] Poking fun at Coleridge, De Quincey played upon a separation of moral and aesthetic concerns popularly deducible not only from Coleridge's actions in life but from the principles of literary criticism he had published in *Biographia*.

Continuing with some remarks upon thieves and ulcers, De Quincey states that 'They are both imperfections, it is true; but to be imperfect being their essence, the very greatness of their imperfection becomes their perfection'.[23] Coleridge would have had a problem with the lack of attention to the contrast between addressing differences in *degree* and differences in *kind*, but his name and something of his aesthetic principles gave force to De Quincey's wit. 'Virtue has had her day; and henceforward, *Vertu* and Connoisseurship have leave to provide for themselves'.[24] I will return to the Wildean twists that might occur to Coleridgean 'virtue' and the question of taste ('*Vertu*') in my discussion of Wilde's reliance upon Coleridge's definition of 'beauty' later.

Wilde drew on De Quincey's 'On Murder' as the forerunner of his own 'Pen, Pencil and Poison' (1891), and, in so doing, also called on Coleridge. What began as a joke at Coleridge's expense became part of a serious aesthetic perspective of Wilde's, but in the process a serious feature of Coleridge's critical thinking reemerges, and that is a link between sin and personality. Wilde repeatedly implies both a human and aesthetic relationship between 'sin' and 'sincerity' in his writing, and the division between aesthetic and moral worth is marked and cross-cut by this linking; he deliberately embroiders on his ability to apply each term in both moral and aesthetic statements. Writing of Thomas Griffiths Wainewright (1794–1852), painter, forger, and murderer, Wilde considers that Wainewright's writing on art possesses 'ardent sincerity and strange fervour' and he notes approvingly De Quincey's description of Wainewright on the Italian Masters: 'There seemed a tone of sincerity and of native sensibility as in one who spoke for himself'.[25] But here was part of the conundrum; Wainewright's ability to speak for himself (which is part of his sincerity) is related by Wilde to his crimes, and Wilde repeatedly refers to these crimes as Wainwright's 'sins', noting humorously that sins may also be either moral or aesthetic. 'Sin' for Wilde is an expansive concept, in more ways than one. He explains of Wainewright that 'His crimes seem to have had an important effect upon his art. They gave a strong personality to his style, a quality that his early work certainly lacked'.[26] 'One can fancy', he continues, 'an intense personality being created out of sin', but: 'That [Wainewright] had a sincere love of art and nature seems to me quite certain. There is no essential incongruity between crime and culture [...]'.[27] Having looked further at this connection in the following section, I shall return to consider, in the last part, the implications of linking sin and personality in *The Critic as Artist*.

Like *Biographia, The Critic as Artist* is divided into two: the first part focusing upon biography and the role of a critic's own subjectivity in his work, the second upon principles of criticism (and this is where the questions of sin, beauty, and sincerity are explored most explicitly). Throughout book two of *Biographia*, Coleridge is careful to explain that the pleasure afforded by art has at least an indirect moral power: that 'the communication of pleasure is the introductory means by which alone the poet must expect to moralize his readers' (*BL* II, 131).[28] This indirectly moralizing role for pleasure would, for Wilde, demand a revision of popular morality and bring ideas about sin, sincerity, and the self-realizing process of the critical endeavour inextricably together.

Thinking, paradox, and higher things

In *The Critic as Artist*, Gilbert tells Ernest that 'some one should teach [the honest beaming folk who frequent art galleries and similar public places] that while, in the opinion of society, Contemplation is the gravest sin of which any citizen can be guilty, in the opinion of the highest culture it is the proper occupation of man. [...] [T]o do nothing at all is the most difficult thing in the world, the most difficult and the most intellectual. To Plato, with his passion for wisdom, it was the noblest form of energy'.[29] Although he does not say so directly, it soon becomes apparent that one of the reasons that contemplation seems to be a 'sin' in Gilbert's 'society' is that contemplation is 'Unlimited'. Unlike action, which, he explains, is both 'limited and relative', the intellectual experiences of someone who truly thinks open endless potential for further new ways of thinking, new ways of becoming, a boundless supply of sources of the self. (As Coleridge had remarked in Notebook entries of 1801, there can seem to be 'Something inherently mean in action', whereas '*Thinking* as distinguished from *Thoughts*' may take place as an 'Abstract [...] as a pure act & energy'.[30]) Thinking offers Wilde's speakers the opportunity for the creation of multiple selves (a purely imaginative version of what Hopkins had also been formulating as his more physically active and therefore explicitly moral 'selving').[31] Gilbert implies that true contemplation would lead the way to 'the *fruitio Dei*' (enjoyment of God). But, all too aware that in the present age 'Metaphysics' have been rejected and 'religious ecstasy is out of date'; that scepticism rules; and that for the present age the 'world through which the Academic philosopher becomes "the spectator of all time and of all existence" is not really an ideal world, but simply a world of abstract ideas', Gilbert offers two (combined) solutions for attempting to reclaim the abstract and reconnect it with the ideal. The foremost is aesthetic experience. But subsidiary to this, and combining with it, is his notion of sin. Having identified the current rejection of the metaphysical and spiritual among his contemporaries, Gilbert concludes: 'No, Ernest, no. We cannot go back to the saint. There is far more to be learned from the sinner'.[32] Here Gilbert opts for just the kind of separation of the aesthetic from the ethical that Coleridge had described at the start of the century. There is more to learn from the sinner because the sinner (for the purposes of *The Critic as Artist*) is a figure who embodies the rejection of moral law and to that extent may also be made to embody, or represent, freedom from that moral law. If the appellation 'sinner' seems incongruous from this perspective (given that it implies its own limiting frame) it is because Wilde retains the moral term as a means of highlighting the disparity between art and morality, even though what he will go on to describe is a reintegration of aesthetic and moral concerns along Coleridgean lines. Wilde's 'sinner' – who is also, as we shall see, the sincere critic – represents the necessary indirection of the link between aesthetics and morality which is played out in Coleridge's aesthetic criticism (in, for example, the 'Lectures on Shakespeare', *Biographia Literaria*, and the marginalia). The critic announces, and even stands for, the interplay of ethics and aesthetics, of sincerity and sin.

Art, says Gilbert, presents us with 'those who have stained the world with the beauty of their sin'.[33] 'The ancient flame wakes within us. Our blood quickens through terrible pulses. [...] Wild tears of anguish break from us, and we bow our heads to the ground, for we know we have sinned'.[34] In this way 'the sorrow with which Art fills us both purifies and initiates'.[35] Coleridge had written: 'An hour of solitude passed in sincere and earnest prayer, or the conflict with, and conquest over, a single passion or "subtle bosom sin," will teach us more of thought, will more effectually awaken the faculty, and form the habit, of reflection, than a year's study in the Schools without them'.[36] Through the contemplation of (imaginative) sin, Gilbert argues, one becomes a more sincere critic, more aware of the world's variety.

In a world of moral limitation, both aesthetic experience and sin offer 'modes' (a favourite word of Wilde's) of breaking down or challenging limitation. Each might offer the individual a pleasurable sense of freedom from limitation; freedom, at least, from imposed codes of conduct, if not from pangs of conscience. Kooy offers the following description of aesthetic experience in his discussion of Coleridge and Schiller; he writes that during an aesthetic experience 'We are momentarily released from the prejudices, the tendency to disbelieve, the awareness of self and we are cast instead into a "temporary oblivion". And in that "oblivion", free from moral and physical determination, that state of aesthetic indeterminacy, we are brought to an awareness of our moral freedom.'[37]

A number of the central terms and ideas that are explored by the speakers of Wilde's dialogues might be subtly linked with those which Coleridge presents early in *Aids to Reflection* as foundational to the process of self-critical enquiry which that book is intended to support. Already within the first dozen aphorisms of *Aids*, are remarks upon the importance of 'novelty'; 'reflection' (which provides, via Matthew Arnold, one cultural model for the significance of 'thinking' and 'contemplation' in Wilde's work); the sometime necessity of 'paradox' or the meeting of extremes; and the process of 'becoming' oneself, developing one's 'personality', which will all strike chords that resonate through Wilde's essays. In sentiment, if not in style, the following passage from *Aids* could be Gilbert explaining his own notions to Ernest: 'In a world, the opinions of which are drawn from outside shows, many things may be *paradoxical*, (that is, contrary to the common notion) and nevertheless true: nay, paradoxical, *because* they are true' (*Aids*, 17). When Gilbert says of sin that 'it is one with the higher ethics', this is because he uses 'sin' to denote both the contemplation that his contemporaries condemn and, therefore, the self-realisation that it enables. It is one with the higher ethics because, in making 'sin' mean something beneficial, Gilbert brings seeming opposites together and lifts his notion of sin above the domain of conventional social mores. Like Coleridge's 'higher logic', the 'higher ethics' result from the clash of simultaneously true but opposed conditions (imaginative and material). For Wilde, opposition came from the truth of social convention.[38] The apparent contradictions inherent in expressing something 'higher', therefore, offer him a perfect combination of audacity and indirection – a method for truth-telling that does not require telling the truth straight out.

Personality and the critic's sincere sins

I now want to bring the indirect relationship between ethics and aesthetics to bear upon the personal elements of the critic's work, via a consideration of taste. The category that falls between aesthetic and moral considerations, and that highlights the potential disjunction between them, is beauty. Coleridge was careful to relate the problem of beauty to taste in the arts, and, with a nod to Plato, he defined beauty as 'a pleasurable sense of the Many [...] reduced into unity'.[39] (This became 'the many seen as one' in 'Lectures on European Literature'

(1818) and, most famously, 'Multëity in Unity' in 'On the Principle of Genial Criticism' (1814).[40]) Here Coleridge noted a difficulty with language that relates to the question of taste and virtue that I mentioned above; and here again a subtle aspect of Wilde's pressing commitment to beauty, taste, individuality, and the necessity of flexibility in language (all preoccupations in *The Critic as Artist*) can be seen to find a cultural authority in Coleridge. Developing Wilde's link between sin and culture, Gilbert imagines sin as a version of cultural heredity and tells Ernest of Heredity:

> It is sick with many maladies, and has memories of curious sins. It is wiser than we are, and its wisdom is bitter. It fills us with impossible desires, and makes us follow what we know we cannot gain. One thing, however, Ernest, it can do for us. It can lead us away from surroundings whose beauty is dimmed to us by the mist of familiarity, or whose ignoble ugliness and sordid claims are marring the perfection of our development. [...] Do you think that it is the imagination that enables us to live these countless lives? Yes: it is the imagination [...] [W]ho is the true critic but he who bears within himself the dreams, the ideas, and feelings of myriad generations, and to whom no form of thought is alien, no emotional impulse obscure?[41]

In his desire to assert the liberating and productive possibilities of multiplicity, Wilde applies a term to the critic which Coleridge had applied to 'our *myriad-minded* Shakespear [sic]' (*BL* II, 19). Wilde earlier states that it is

> the beholder who lends to the beautiful thing its myriad meanings, and makes it marvellous for us, and sets it in some new relation to the age, so that it becomes a vital portion of our lives, and a symbol of what we pray for, or perhaps of what, having prayed for, we fear that we may receive. [...] Tonight [the work of art (he refers to *Tannhäuser*)] may fill one with that ΕΡΩΣ ΤΩΝ ΑΔΥΝΑΤΩΝ, that *Amour de l'Impossible*, which falls like a madness on many who think they live securely out of reach of harm, so that they sicken suddenly with the poison of unlimited desire [...]. Beauty is the symbol of symbols. Beauty reveals everything, because it expresses nothing. When it shows us itself, its shows us the whole fiery-coloured world.[42]

Once the dangerous multëities of contemplating beauty are accepted, taste comes most fully into play.

Taste, in Coleridge's definition, is a comment upon, or articulation of, the concept of multëity. It is an expression of the individuality and diversity of human preferences without being a rejection of shared experience. In the first of his 'Lectures on Principle in Poetry' (1808), which became the later 'Essay on Taste' (1810), Coleridge writes that 'Taste [...] as opposed to Vision and Sound will teach us to expect in its metaphorical use a certain reference of any given Object to our own Being, and not merely a distinct notion of the Object as in itself or [in] its independent properties' (*LL* I, 36–7). Matthew Arnold, of course, would apply Vision metaphorically and make 'see[ing] the object as in itself it really is' central to his own view of the function of criticism. When Wilde's Gilbert famously inverts this Arnoldian principle, he draws, I suggest, Coleridge's definition of taste into his own definition of Criticism. Gilbert dismisses Arnold's view as 'a very serious error, [which] takes no cognizance of Criticism's most perfect form, which is in its essence purely subjective, and seeks to reveal its own secret and not the secret of another'.[43] This temporarily becomes, in Ernest's mouth, the starker statement that 'the primary aim of the critic is to see the object as in itself it really is not',[44] but this extremity is re-poised at the close of Part I of *The Critic as Artist* when Gilbert – surely making a joke about 'taste' – states that '[after supper] we will pass on to the question of the critic considered in the light of interpreter'. 'Ah!', Ernest responds, 'you admit, then, that the critic may occasionally be allowed to see the object as in itself it really is. GILBERT: I am not quite sure. Perhaps I may admit it after supper. There is a subtle influence in supper'.[45] Gilbert explains what Coleridge had described as the 'reference of any given Object to our own Being', playing on the idea of taste as he does so. The question Wilde raises here of 'Criticism's most perfect form' is suggestive, finally, of the extent to which the critic really is an artist committed to a Coleridgean view of imagination and form, and seeking (as Wilde would put it to Lord Alfred Douglas in *De Profundis*) a 'mode of existence [...] in which the outward is expressive of the inward'.[46]

Following the second of the Prudential Aphorisms in *Aids*, in which Leighton writes that 'It is one of Epicurus's fixed maxims, "That life can never be pleasant without virtue"', Coleridge adds the qualifying comment that 'the dictates of virtue are the very same with those of self-interest, tending *to*, though they do not proceed *from*, the same point. For the outward object of virtue being the greatest producible sum of happiness of all men, it must needs include the object of an intelligent self-love, which is the greatest possible happiness of one individual; [...]' (*Aids*, 48–9). Wilde, one could say, both adopts and inverts this view in his definition of the true critic, nevertheless remaining true to the spirit of it. Coleridge continues:

> If then the time has not yet come for any thing higher, act on the maxim of seeking the most pleasure with the least pain: and, if only you do not seek where you yourself *know* it will not be found, this very pleasure and this freedom from the disquietude of pain may produce in you a state of being directly and indirectly favourable to the germination and up-spring of a nobler seed. If it be true, that men are miserable because they are wicked, it is likewise true, that many are wicked because they are miserable. [...] —Pleasure, I say, consists in the harmony between the specific excitability of a living creature, and the exciting causes correspondent thereto. Considered therefore exclusively in and for itself, the only question is, quantum, not quale? How much on the whole? the contrary, *i.e.* the painful and disagree-able, having been subtracted. The quality is a matter of *taste:* et de *gustibus* non est disputandum. No man can judge for another.
>
> This, I repeat, appears to me a safer language than the sentence quoted above, (that virtue alone is happiness; that happiness consists in virtue, and the like)'.
>
> (*Aids*, 49–51)

'Pleasure [...] consists in the harmony between the specific excitability of a living creature, and the exciting causes correspondent thereto': truly discovering the nature of that harmony might involve commit-ment to unending and self-conscious self-interrogation – the life of a Romantic artist isolated by the unity (or perhaps one ought to say of Coleridge and Wilde, the unities) of his vision and necessarily suffering because of it. If 'virtue', in Coleridge's formulation in *Aids*, is 'manly', the opposed quality, 'vice', is perhaps a necessary counter for Wilde, but Coleridge nevertheless becomes a supportive forebear in Wilde's ability to develop aesthetic ideas and critical principles that indirectly offer a greater scope of possibility to homosexual expression. Appearing as it does in a work subtitled '*in the Formation of a Manly Character*', Coleridge's justification of 'the specific excitability of a living creature'; the need for that specific excitability to find its correspondent causes in order to achieve pleasure; and the role of pleasure as a basis for virtuous (which is also to say 'manly') advancement, all combines to qualify Leighton's assertion that 'virtue alone is happiness' and to endorse a license not to the degree but certainly to the kind of an individual's choices. For Wilde, such a qualification might offer a perfect aid in the formation of his own manly character, and articulate links between pleasure, taste, and virtue that corroborate the sinful sincerity of the critic who sees the Object with reference to his own Being.

Linda Dowling has examined the profound effect of philological studies (and Coleridge's central role in them) upon the later sense of linguistic decay rife at the *fin de siècle*; and she gives a suggestive account of Coleridge's afterlife during this period in her study of his transmission of the German Romantic tradition of the new philology. Discussing debates about the difference between spoken and written language, Dowling emphasises what she sees as Coleridge's preference for the written word, and in this way she places him foremost in establishing conditions from which ideas about literary decay and decadence proliferate. Dowling writes that 'In the new linguistic order ushered in by the new comparative philology, the only instance of decay in language was writing, and the only monuments of dead language were works of literature embalmed as books on the shelves of libraries. The threat to Victorian values was manifest and convulsive, and out of that convulsion would emerge the movement known as literary Decadence'.[47] As an alternative to this view, I suggest that among Coleridge's multiple afterlives there is one which, rather than fixing the written word, accentuates the flexibility of written language as well as the critical creativity of 'talk', and which lives on in the voices of Oscar Wilde's essay duologues.[48] Dowling argues that Wilde made conversation as polished as the written word; that he thereby made speech less mutable, more fixed; and that, in turn, he sped the decline of art that sought to mimic speech by exposing the frangibility of precise language through the paradoxes and apparent superficialities of his characters. But Wilde's interest in the spoken word is an important element of his commitment to a suppleness of thinking and to an ideal immediacy and intimacy of communication also inspired by the ghost of Coleridge.[49] That Coleridge's work is central to the establishment of the *Oxford English Dictionary* and a sense of increased precision in words does not mean that he offers a rigid view of language.[50] Precision, after all, will enable greater subtlety and nuance and ambiguity: flexibilities that will guard against decay, if not against decadence.

Wilde is famous for his apparent promotion of 'insincerity' in art. But his work also repeatedly highlights the importance of allowing flexibility to words and how they are used, and in his own supple and varied applications of 'insincerity', 'sincerity', and 'sin', he ensures that the terms become delicately but ineluctably entangled. In *The Critic as Artist*, Gilbert grumbles that 'men are the slaves of words' and goes on to describe a notion of 'sin' that might (presumably were men not the slaves of words) be considered a strain of (not just on) sincerity. Gilbert explains:

> Each little thing that we do passes into the great machine of life which may grind our virtues to powder and make them worthless, or transform our sins into elements of a new civilization, more marvellous and more splendid than any that has gone before. But men are the slaves of words. They rage against Materialism, as they call it, forgetting that there have been few, if any spiritual awakenings that have not wasted the world's faculties in barren hopes, and fruitless aspirations, and empty or trammelling creeds. What is termed Sin is an essential element of progress. Without it the world would stagnate, or grow old and colourless. By its curiosity Sin increases the experience of the race. Through its intensified assertion of individualism, it saves us from monotony of type. In its rejection of the current notions about morality, it is one with the higher ethics.[51]

Wilde differs markedly from Coleridge in denying, or at least seeking to negate, the difficulties engendered by use of words. As Coleridge noted in *Aids*: 'I can see no advantage in the improper use of words, [...] but, on the contrary, much mischief. [...] We should accustom ourselves to *think*, and *reason*, in precise and stedfast terms; even when custom, or deficiency, or the corruption of the language will not permit the same strictness in speaking' (*Aids*, 46). However, that the same strictness might not be permitted in speaking is another good reason for Wilde's choice of the dialogue, in which speakers directly challenge matters of word-use, even while they speak and potentially introduce further confusion. In the second part of *The Critic as Artist*, Gilbert complains again about the supposed limitedness of words, but this time it is 'sincerity' that saves 'from monotony of type', because although 'A little sincerity is a dangerous thing, and a great deal of it is absolutely fatal[,] The true critic will, indeed, always be sincere in his devotion to the principle of beauty'. This latter sincerity will drive the critic to 'seek for beauty in every age and in each school, and [he] will never suffer himself to be limited to any settled custom of thought, or stereotyped mode of looking at things.' In his emphasis on the critic's commitment to beauty and on finding beauty in what amounts to multëity in unity, Gilbert asserts a strongly Coleridgean principle. He continues (with an additional echo of Pater):

> You must not be frightened by words, Ernest. What people call insincerity is simply a method by which we can multiply our personalities.[52]

The word 'we' is nicely caught between denoting self and community. Here, once more, is the invocation of finding a 'method' for change around which 'sincerity' is fraught and wrought anew. If 'sincerity', Gilbert suggests, can be unpicked from the pettiness of popular morality and applied to the flexible, critical aim of widening experience, it might start to look remarkably similar to sin and it will entail a person's being better able to recognise and respond to beauty. Though Wilde often invokes Matthew Arnold's words only to refute or heavily qualify them, this last quotation remains an echo of Arnold's famous assertion that 'criticism must be sincere, simple, flexible, ardent, ever widening its knowledge.'[53] For Wilde, this meant subverting what he framed as social conventions. His revision of Pope's 'A little learning is a dangerous thing' ('Essay on Criticism'), also ensures that Gilbert's earlier reference to sincerity is poised associatively between knowledge and ignorance.[54] When Gilbert later remarks that 'There is no sin except stupidity', therefore, he both demonstrates the flexibility of words that he is trying to promote (using 'sin' now to describe the negation of his progressive ideal) and hints a further potential for the collapse between sincerity (as self-developing self-expression) and sin (which has become a version of the same process).[55]

Critical sincerity may seem insincere by popular standards, because the sincere critical endeavour demands the capacity to see from many perspectives at once. Wilde finds the word 'sincerity' so freighted with critical import that it may suggest both an absolutely singular and defined perspective and yet also the indefinable integrity of holding together multiple or divergent views. And so he simply lifts the word 'sincerity' and (in an apparently anti-Coleridgean way) exploits the multiplicity of its implications. He thereby demonstrates, however, a rather Coleridgean capacity for holding all this potential contradictoriness in suspension and then picking his own path through it. His apparently anti-Coleridgean rejection of fixing words' meanings nevertheless marks a debt to Coleridge in the subtlety of the arguments it enables him maintain. The 'critical spirit', as Gilbert calls it, is not only significant for its exercise in the interpretation of aesthetic experience; it also plays a primary role in the development of self.[56] Summarising his own view of Coleridge's treatment of morality, Laurence Lockridge writes that 'the most encompassing moral endeavour is not so much the performance of right acts as it is the greatest development of the self'.[57] In *The Friend*, Coleridge explains that 'The nurture and evolution of humanity is the final aim [of developing personality]'. Stated perhaps most explicitly in the *Opus Maximum*, which Wilde could not have read, 'personality', as *The Friend* and *Aids* also make clear, cannot (as Lockridge remarks) be 'predicated on limitation'.[58] Personality becomes associable with sin when, about to establish the pleonasmic character of the phrase 'Original Sin', Coleridge writes that 'A Sin is an Evil which has its ground and origin in the Agent, and not in the compulsion of circumstance' (*Aids*, 266). (Life, of course, is 'a thing narrowed by circumstance', as Gilbert reminds us; but sin and aesthetic experience need not be.[59]) In the *Opus*, Coleridge would elaborate the association by explaining that persons have 'personality' where God has 'personeity' and that original sin is not to be linked to the fall of Adam and Eve, but is the act of willing independence which defines the human spirit as other-than-God and, for that reason, other than Good.[60]

When Gilbert explains, then, that 'It seems to me that with the development of the critical spirit we shall be able to realize, not merely our own lives, but the collective life of the race', Wilde is working in distinctly Coleridgean terms, seeking to reconcile awareness of the division between art and morality specifically with awareness of the larger and (though he would not have said so in these words) still-ethical process that reintegrates the two beyond that necessary division. Sin becomes 'one with the higher ethics', because it advances individual development. In relation to art, the figure embodying the necessary indirection of this process of reconciliation is, no less than the artists, the figure of the critic, who works through a series of seemingly indirect processes to ensure that there is 'no mood with which one cannot sympathize, no dead mode of life that one cannot make alive'.[61] The critic's sin – which is to say his or her personality – will continue to express itself by lending itself out to the work of art in the act of sympathy, 'reveal[ing] its own secret and not the secret of another'. It will be there in the specific tastes that draw him or her back to certain subjects or procedures, like an artist with an addiction.

Conclusion

When the celebrated poet Anna Laetitia Barbauld complained that the *Ancient Mariner* 'had no moral', Coleridge responded by remarking that, on the contrary,

> the chief fault of the poem was that it had too much moral, and that too openly obtruded on the reader. It ought to have had no more moral than the story of the merchant sitting down to eat dates by the side of a well and throwing the shells aside, and the Genii starting up and saying he must kill the merchant, because a date shell had put out the eye of the Genii's son.

In other versions of this anecdote, Coleridge emphasises in particular the problem of having a moral in 'a work of such pure imagination' – a view with which Wilde would have agreed.[62] At least into the first half of the twentieth century, critics can too often be found confusing the moral tenor of Coleridge's works with the author's biography. D. W. Harding writes that, 'Creeping back defeated into the social convoy, the mariner is obviously not represented as having advanced through his sufferings to a fuller life; and he no more achieves a full rebirth than Coleridge ever could'.[63] Reviewers also tangled Wilde's life (his views and actions) with the lives of characters in his works; and in defending *Dorian Gray* he was careful to point out that 'Each man sees his own sin in Dorian Gray. What Dorian Gray's sins are no one knows'.[64]

Responding to the attacks of immorality laid against *Dorian Gray*, Wilde found himself engaged in correspondence with the Editors of the *St James's Gazette*, the *Daily Chronicle*, and the *Scots Observer*. In one of his typically witty responses to the *Chronicle*, he explains that the paper's critic has accused him of trying to '"vamp up" a moral in my story', but Wilde notes politely, 'I must candidly confess that I do not know what "vamping" is. I see, from time to time, mysterious advertisements in the newspapers about "How to Vamp", but what vamping really means remains a mystery to me – a mystery that, like all other mysteries, I hope some day to explore.'[65] If Wilde had explored that mystery he would have known that in denying that he vamped his story he was, in one sense, also denying that the story was insincere, since the old etymology of sincere, which Coleridge acknowledges and remarks upon on a number of occasions, was *sine cera*, 'without wax', and in art and craft terms it was often held to mean that an object had not had its flaws hidden by filling them with wax.[66] If Wilde had not vamped up a moral in his story and yet had felt that there was a moral present, that moral itself must have been a sincere one, pure and unvamped. Like Coleridge, although Wilde repeatedly champions the separation of art (or the aesthetic) and morals (or ethics), he could not and did not assert that distinction as fully effective in the case of his own work. As he wrote in the 'Preface' to *Dorian Gray*, 'The moral life of a man forms part of the subject-matter of the artist, but *the morality of art* consists in the perfect use of an imperfect medium' (emphasis added).[67]

Wilde's letters to the papers are comical, but each has its own moral insinuations to make. Just as Barbauld found no moral in *The Ancient Mariner*, a significant number of Wilde's critics could not find a strong or worthy enough moral in *Dorian Gray*. But Wilde offered the critics an explanation very similar to that which Coleridge offered to Barbauld, averring that

> so far from wishing to emphasize any moral in my story, the real trou-ble I experienced in writing the story was that of keeping the extremely obvious moral subordinate to the artistic and dramatic effect. [...] I felt that, from an aesthetic point of view, it would be difficult to keep the moral in its proper secondary place; and even now I do not feel quite sure that I have been able to do so. I think the moral too apparent.[68]

Wilde's 'real trouble' was rather like Coleridge's 'chief fault'. And the phrase 'secondary place' is obviously significant. By defending himself in such terms, each writer also defended the view that aesthetic experience ought finally to be experience free from the constraints of morality. But neither denied that there was nevertheless significant moral import in their works. On the contrary, they foregrounded the fact. 'As for what the moral is,' Wilde continued to the *Chronicle*, 'your critic states that it is this – that when a man feels himself becoming "too angelic" he should rush out and "make a beast of himself!" I cannot say that I consider this a moral'. Wilde explained that the 'real moral' was that 'all excess, as well as all renunciation, brings its punishment'. The 'only question', we might remember, 'is *quantum*, not *quale*? [...] No man can judge for another'. Wilde's parenthetical commas here cradle a point that was dear to him. This syntax manages at once to introduce the significance of the pain of renunciation but to place its mention at a protective, apparently second-ary distance. With this parenthesis, and the affirmative words 'as well as', Wilde makes his assertion that excess brings punishment seem like a new or more pressing point that he is making alongside the more obvious or widely-held view that renunciation brings punishment too. This was a quiet statement about the nature of pleasure; about an identity defined by its division from the centre – human, sinful; about an unending process of self-realisation enabled only by sincere dedication to a critical endeav-our that demanded the exploration (not the renunciation) of pleasure.

Writing of Coleridge in 1887 and of 'the magic of his wonderful personality' (which Wilde felt that Hall Caine had missed in his biog-raphy of the Highgate Sage), he noted in closing that 'It is said that every man's life is a Soul's Tragedy. Coleridge's certainly was so, and though we may not be able to pluck out the heart of his mystery, still let us recognize that mystery is there'.[69] Coleridge is a powerful initiator of a fragmentation of the concept of sincerity that occurred during the course of the nineteenth century.[70] And sin might be one way of thinking about some writers' explorations of fragmentation. But it is from the fragmentation that a new multëity – and so a different unity and newly articulate sincerity – emerges. This sincerity allows for, indeed necessitates, a multiplicity of perspectives that may look at first like inconsistency or sincerity's own opposites (insincerity, hypocrisy, even sin). The critic will possess this quality, as Gilbert remarks, in his or her dedication to beauty. The critic, that is, is sincere insofar as he or she accepts and explores those 'sins of the imagination' to which Gilbert refers. For all his work to desynonymise terms, Coleridge becomes a vital authority for something like a new synonymy that seems to lurk between the terms 'sin' and 'sincerity' for Wilde.[71] Coleridge emerges, as he does repeatedly in this volume of essays, as a cultural authority on walking fine lines. One facet of his afterlife in this regard might be thought of as the method that his example offers to later writers of progression by opposition – the paradoxical, the dialogical, even the sinful becoming more explicit means and modes of self-realisation. Wilde may have found in such methods a perfect balance of audacity and hiddenness, an ambiguity appealing for its potential to aid his own self-expression.[72] He certainly found in them the means of at once reflecting upon and deflecting criticism by hinting the autobiographical impulses of the critic's work.

Notes

1. *Selected Letters of Oscar Wilde* ed. Rupert Hart-Davis (Oxford: Oxford University Press, 1979), p. 248.
2. See, for example, good but brief discussions of such connections by Burton R. Pollin, 'The Influence of "The Ancient Mariner" upon "The Ballad of Reading Gaol"', *Revue Des Langues Vivantes. Tijdschrift Voor Levende Talen*, 40:3 (1974), pp. 228–34; and Richard Ellmann, *Oscar Wilde* (London: Hamish Hamilton, 1987), p. 224n and pp. 500–1.
3. In his chapter (pp. 1–19) James Vigus remarks upon the accusations of poor productivity laid against Coleridge by Victorians who could not have known better (p. 1).
4. See Karl Beckson (ed.), *Oscar Wilde: The Critical Heritage* (New York: Barnes & Noble, 1970), p. 387.
5. Arthur Symons, *The Romantic Movement in English Poetry* (London: Archibald Constable & Co., 1909), writes: 'If Coleridge had been more callous towards what he felt to be his duties [...] he would have been more complete, more effectual, as a man' (p. 127). Coleridge begins to emerge from Symons' discussion as a proto-aesthete figure. Hereafter Symons.
6. Wilde is reported to have said: 'I have put all my genius into my life; I have put only my talent into my works'. See André Gide, *Oscar Wilde: A Study*, intro. Stuart Mason (Oxford: The Holywell Press, 1905), p. 17.
7. Peter Ackroyd, Foreword to *Table Talk of Oscar Wilde*, ed. Thomas Wright (London: Cassell and Co., 2000), p. 8.
8. For an excellent recent discussion of the vital concept of *'forma efformans'* (forming form) in Coleridge's writing, see Angela Leighton, *On Form: Poetry,*

Aestheticism, and the Legacy of a Word (Oxford: Oxford University Press, 2007), pp. 7–9 and p. 19.

9. Michael Kooy, *Coleridge, Schiller and Aesthetic Education* (Basingstoke: Palgrave, 2002), p. 115. Hereafter cited as Kooy.

10. Letter to the Editor of the *St James's Gazette*, 25 June [1890], in Linda Dowling (ed), *The Soul of Man Under Socialism & Selected Critical Prose* (London: Penguin, 2001), p. 105. Hereafter cited as *Selected*.

11. *Biographia Literaria*, 2 vols, ed. James Engell and W. Jackson Bate (Princeton, NJ: Princeton University Press, 1983), II, 13. Hereafter cited as *BL*. Writing in 1866, E. S. Dallas stated confidently that 'We in England [...] are most familiar with the doctrine that art is for pleasure, as it has been put by Coleridge; and it is not unlikely that some of the repugnance which the doctrine meets in minds of a certain order may be due to his ragged analysis and awkward statement'; *The Gay Science*, 2 vols (London: Chapman and Hall, 1866), I, 109.

12. 'The Decay of Lying', *Selected*, p. 173. Hereafter cited as 'Decay'. George Stavros, in 'Oscar Wilde on the Romantics', *English Literature in Transition, 1880–1920*, 20:1 (1977), pp. 35–45, remarks upon Wilde's responses to Wordsworth without noting any Coleridgean sympathy.

13. 'Decay', p. 173.

14. *Table Talk*, 2 vols, ed. Carl Woodring (Princeton, NJ: Princeton University Press, 1990), I, 98. For similar remarks on the 'higher logic', see: *Logic*, ed. J. R. de J. Jackson (Princeton, NJ: Princeton University Press, 1981), pp. 130–40 and *The Notebooks of Samuel Taylor Coleridge*, 5 vols, ed. Kathleen Coburn, Merton Christenson, and Anthony John Harding (Princeton, NJ: Princeton University Press, 1957–2002), V, 5495.

15. Accusations of elitism levelled against Wilde are in this respect comparable to those which critics have also directed at Matthew Arnold; and both can be related to the privileged role of esoteric knowledge in Coleridge's work.

16. *CA* II, p. 278.

17. Frank Kermode, *Romantic Image* (London: Routledge and Kegan Paul, 1957), p. 44.

18. Ibid., pp. 44–5. The quotation of Wilde is from *The Critic as Artist* – Part II, in *Selected*, p. 260. Hereafter cited as *CA* I or *CA* II.

19. Ibid., p. 47.

20. Kooy, p. 117.

21. *The Works of Thomas De Quincey*, 21 vols (London: Pickering & Chatto, 2000), vol. 6, p. 114 (emphasis original).

22. Ibid.

23. Ibid., p. 115.

24. Ibid., p. 116.

25. 'Pen, Pencil, and Poison', *Selected*, pp. 194, 199. Hereafter cited as 'PPP'.

26. 'PPP', p. 210.

27. 'PPP', p. 211.

28. For a full discussion of the indirect relation between aesthetics and morality, via Schiller, in *Biographia* and the marginalia, see Kooy, pp. 115–23.

29. *CA* II, pp. 252–3.

30. *CN* I, entries 1072 and 923.

31. For Hopkins's most explicit description of 'selving' in his poems, see the sonnet 'As kingfishers catch fire', in *Gerard Manley Hopkins: The Major Works*, ed. Catherine Phillips (Oxford: Oxford University Press, 1986, rpt 2002), p. 129.

32. *CA* II, p. 253.
33. *CA* II, p. 248.
34. *CA* II, p. 249.
35. *CA* II, p. 251.
36. *Aids to Reflection*, ed. John Beer (Princeton, NJ: Princeton University Press, 1993), p. 16. Hereafter cited as *Aids*.
37. Kooy, p. 122.
38. For discussion of Coleridge's perception of himself as the recipient of critical attack, and of others as 'out of all sympathy with him', see Michael Macovski, 'Coleridge, the "Rime", and the Instantiation of Outness', in *Dialogue and Literature: Apostrophe, Auditors, and the Collapse of Romantic Discourse* (Oxford: Oxford University Press, 1994), pp. 67–101 (p. 77).
39. *Lectures 1808–1819 On Literature*, 2 vols, ed. R. A. Foakes (Princeton, NJ: Princeton University Press, 1987), I, 35. Hereafter cited as *LL*.
40. See *LL* II, p. 220 and n. 'Multëity', of course, is Coleridge's coinage, first used in *Principles of Genial Criticism*.
41. *CA* II, p. 255. For related discussion, see David Alderman, *Mansex fine: Religion, manliness and imperialism in Nineteenth-Century British Culture* (Manchester: Manchester University Press, 1998), especially pp. 154–9 (hereafter cited as Alderman). Where Alderman describes Wilde's 'rejection of sincerity' by '[t]he critical spirit' (p. 155), I suggest that Wilde instead attempted to recreate sincerity through its importance to the critical endeavour – an endeavour that demands the multiplication of personality.
42. *CA* I, pp. 239–40. The Greek means 'love of the impossible'.
43. *CA* I, p. 238.
44. *CA* I, p. 240.
45. *CA* I, p. 243.
46. *De Profundis*, in *De Profundis and Other Writings*, intro. by Hesketh Pearson (London: Penguin, 1954, rpt 1986), pp. 160–1.
47. Linda Dowling, *Language and Decadence in the Victorian Fin de Siècle* (Princeton, NJ: Princeton University Press, 1986), p. 84.
48. Symons pertinently considers Coleridge's prose criticism 'a kind of thinking aloud' (p. 136).
49. Paul K. Saint-Amour, 'Oscar Wilde: Orality, Literary Property, and Crimes of Writing', *Nineteenth-Century Literature*, 55:1 (June 2000), pp. 59–91, makes passing reference to Coleridge in relation to Wilde's commitment to spoken language in his Chatterton lecture of 1886. Coleridge's idea of a 'clerisy' of educated men (which left traces in Thomas Carlyle's 'hero' and Matthew Arnold's 'critic') also endorses Wilde's definitions of the 'thinker' and 'critic'.
50. For further discussion, see James C. McKusick, '"Living Words": Samuel Taylor Coleridge and the genesis of the "OED"', *Modern Philology*, 90:1 (August 1992), pp. 1–45.
51. *CA* I, p. 232. The passage identifies the post-Darwinian perspective available to Wilde. For discussion of Wilde's 'evolutionism', see Jonathan Dollimore, *Sexual Dissidence: Augustus to Wilde, Freud to Foucault* (Oxford: Clarendon, 1991), pp. 3–18; Lawrence Danson, *Wilde's Intentions: The Artist in his Criticism* (Oxford: Clarendon, 1997), pp. 18–19; and Alderman (op. cit.), pp. 154–9.
52. *CA* II, p. 264.

53. 'The Function of Criticism', in *The Complete Prose Works of Matthew Arnold*, ed. R. H. Super, 11 vols (Ann Arbor: University of Michigan Press, 1960–1977), vol. III, p. 285.
54. 'Essay on Criticism', l. 215, in *Alexander Pope. Collected Poems*, ed. Bonamy Dobrée (London: Everyman, 1983), pp. 58–76.
55. *CA* II, p. 277.
56. *CA* II, p. 254.
57. Laurence S. Lockridge, *Coleridge the Moralist* (London and Ithaca: Cornell University Press, 1977), p. 194.
58. Ibid., p. 193. See *The Friend*, 2 vols, ed. Barbara E. Rooke (Princeton, NJ: Princeton University Press, 1969), I, 508.
59. *CA* II, p. 251.
60. See *Opus*, pp. 164–5 and pp. 237–8; and *Aids*, p. 257.
61. *CA* II, p. 254.
62. *TT* I, pp. 272–3. See, also, 31 May 1830, *Table Talk*, ed. H. N. Coleridge (London: Murray, 1852), p. 86.
63. 'The Theme of the *Ancient Mariner*', *Scrutiny*, IX (1941), p. 341.
64. Letter to the Editor of the Scots Observer, 9 July 1890, *Selected*, p. 116.
65. Letter to the Editor of the *Daily Chronicle*, 30 June [1890], *Selected*, p. 113.
66. J. C. Hare, for example, in his 'Introduction' to John Sterling, *Essays and Tales* (London, 1848), p. v, writes: 'Among the anecdotes which I have heard of his boyhood, the following seems characteristic enough to be worth recording. He used to relate that, when he was about nine years old, he was much struck by his master's telling him that the word *sincere* was derived from the practice of filling up flaws in furniture with wax, whence *sine cera* came to mean *pure, not vampt up*. This explanation, he said, gave him great pleasure, and abode in his memory, as having first shown him that there is a reason in words as well as in other things [...]'. For one of Coleridge's references to the supposed etymology *sine cera*, see his letter to Joseph Cottle of 7 March 1815, in *The Selected Letters*, ed. H. J. Jackson (Oxford: Oxford University Press, 1988), p. 183.
67. *The Picture of Dorian Gray*, ed. Peter Ackroyd (London: Penguin, 1985), 'Preface', p. 3. Anthony Savile, 'Kant and the Ideal of Beauty', in *Art and Morality*, ed. Jose Luis Bermudez and Sebastian Gardner (London: Routledge, 2003), pp. 185–203, discusses the 'Heternomists, who hold [ethics and aesthetics] to be intimately and inextricably intertwined' (p. 185) and he inappropriately sets Wilde in critical and philosophical opposition to such a view.
68. To the Editor of the *Daily Chronicle*, 30 June [1890], *Selected*, p. 113.
69. 'Great Writers by Little Men', *Pall Mall Gazette*, March 28, 1887, p. 5.
70. I have been unable to discuss here the implications of *The Friend* in this regard. But, in its first hundred or so pages, Coleridge suggests associations between sincerity and wholeness, and sincerity and long chains of reasoning, as opposed to aphorisms. He then pursues his own course aphoristically.
71. For a direct discussion of the importance of desynonymizing words, and the historical progression of this process, see *BL* I, pp. 82–3.
72. Cp. Gilbert's remark on 'dialogue': 'By its means [the thinker] can both reveal and conceal himself' (*CA* II, p. 262).

10
Coleridge's German 'Absolutism'

Ross Wilson

This essay attempts to chart an aspect of the afterlife of an afterlife. Explorations of Coleridge's reception of German thinking, and especially of his role in the transmission of that thinking to a wider British audience, are doomed to formulate their procedure in such a seemingly over-complex way. The complexity of the undertaking does not arise only from the difficulty of the attempt exactly to describe the lineaments of Coleridge's own reception of German thought. It arises neither, more generally, from the difficulties involved in describing the influence of Coleridge's reception of German culture on later receptions of German philosophy. Perhaps the chief cause of the complexity of this undertaking arises from the fact that the earliest responses to this reception took the form of charges that Coleridge had copied from German philosophical sources – chiefly Schelling, but also the little-known Maas, the better-known Tennemann, and the well-known Kant. These responses were followed then by defences against those charges. In turn, these defences were then followed by a scepticism, less dependent on the charge of plagiarism than previously, as to the motivation and the value of Coleridge's interpretation of German culture at all. Finally, while increasingly positive accounts of Coleridge's relationship with German philosophy began to emerge, the mid- to late-nineteenth-century saw a growth in British interest in German culture the impetus for which it would be difficult to explain by reference chiefly, or at least exclusively and directly, to Coleridge.

Nevertheless, the relationship between Coleridge and Germany, as well as the numerous responses to that relationship both throughout the nineteenth century and today remain significant features of his authorship and legacy. In examining this relationship and its aftermath this essay attempts to perform three tasks. First, it offers a sketch of the history of responses to Coleridge's German-reception. Unsurprisingly, these responses cannot be reduced to consensus, not least, of course, because initial responses to Coleridge's German criticism were involved in a conflict regarding his alleged plagiarism from German sources. However, the second task of this essay is to attempt a more general characterisation of the way in which Coleridge's relationship with German philosophy was viewed in the nineteenth century. This task is performed by way of an examination of Walter Pater's important evaluation of Coleridge's achievement and legacy, in particular his assessment of why Coleridge turned to German thought and of how he, according to Pater, put to use what he found there in the development of his aesthetics and philosophy of art. Pater views Coleridge's recourse to German philosophy as an attempt to satisfy a need for metaphysical, absolutist dogma. Pater's critique is characteristic of much of the response to Coleridge's German-reception in its view, first, of German Idealist philosophy stemming from or reacting to Kant as always and straightforwardly dogmatic, and, second, in its ascription of the motivation of Coleridge's use of German philosophy to the pathology of his idiosyncratic intellectual constitution. Most significantly, Coleridge's absolutism is especially registered for Pater in his philosophy of art which, according to Pater, is the aspect of his thought most derived from German philosophy. The final section of this essay will argue instead that one important aspect of Coleridge's philosophy of art derived from German sources – that is, his assimilation of Kant's aesthetics, with their basis in an account of reflective judgement – is meant precisely to refuse such absolutism.

The sketch of responses to Coleridge's German-reception and the examination of Pater's view of Coleridge fulfil the essay's promise to examine the afterlife of an afterlife. The final section of the essay re-examines Coleridge's reception of Kant's aesthetics and argues that, contrary to a very strong trend in the nineteenth-century reading of Coleridge's use of German philosophy, Coleridge found in Kant a specifically anti-dogmatic account of aesthetic judgement that was, crucially, anti-relativistic at the same time. All of this, of course, has significant consequences for Coleridge's Kant today. Rather than being easily reducible to the apparently absolutist consensus of German philosophy, Kant, as important recent work has re-emphasised, emerges as negotiating a path between relativism and absolutism. This essay explains that, contrary to Pater's characterisation, Coleridge recognised this feature of

Kant's aesthetics and his response to it is central to his development of a view of criticism.

*

Coleridge's role in the transmission of German thinking to British audiences has usually been described as being of great significance. Ever since I. A. Richards's attempt to overturn T. S. Eliot's doubt regarding the virtues of what in Coleridge was not traceable to 'his own delicacy and subtlety', there has been a renewal of interest in the twentieth century both in Coleridge's turn to German philosophy, and in the estimation and influence of this among his contemporaries.[1] By some, Coleridge's communication of German thinking to English readers has been seen as his only real merit. René Wellek's generally low estimation of Coleridge as a philosophical innovator, and his lukewarm view of him as a critic, is directly connected to his estimation of Coleridge's 'very great' importance in the transmission of German thinking to the Anglophone world.[2] 'But if we look at Coleridge from an international perspective [...] we must, I think, come to a considerably lower estimate of his significance, however great and useful his role was in mediating between Germany and England.'[3] A more enthusiastic exponent of Coleridge's merits, Rosemary Ashton, claims in her frequently cited historico-biographical account of the reception of the 'German idea' in Coleridge, Carlyle, Lewes, and Eliot, that, of all these writers, 'Coleridge was undoubtedly the most important interpreter of Kant.'[4] Indeed, in a comparison that has recently been renewed and developed by Michael John Kooy, Ashton evaluates Schiller and Coleridge as interpreters of Kant of equal and independent significance.[5] Thus both detractors from and defenders of Coleridge's legacy take it rather as a given that he played a major role in the development of interest in German thought witnessed in the early to mid nineteenth century. However, this assumption may not necessarily be a safe one, at least in the rather bold form in which it is to be found in Wellek and Ashton. Indeed, Coleridge himself notes in the *Biographia Literaria* that a 'notion' of Kant was already extant at the time of writing, albeit a false one, propagated by 'Reviewers and Frenchmen'.[6] The view of Coleridge as the main English propagator of German culture has also been questioned in later scholarship; for example, in a detailed study of the transmission of German thinking to British audiences through the periodical press between around 1760 and 1830, John Boening mentions Coleridge only once, describing his role in the growth of the British interest in German thinking as, in fact, 'minimal'.[7] (Boening's candidate for the leading role

in communicating German culture to Britain is William Taylor of
Norwich, with a supporting part played by Carlyle.) When Matthew
Arnold stated his own claim that Heine was the most important modern German author, Carlyle, and not Coleridge, was described as having
been the most active mediator of German culture to British readers.[8]
And by the time that John Watson wrote his overview of the reception
of Kant's philosophy in England during the nineteenth century, Spencer
and Sidgwick are seen to be the chief exponents of German thinking in
Britain, having superseded Coleridge's role as mediator to such an
extent that he does not even warrant a mention.[9]

Such a straightforward overturning of such a straightforward assumption does not, of course, tell the whole story. Carlyle is for Arnold, writing
thirty-one years after Coleridge's death, '[t]he *living* writer who has done
most to make England acquainted with German authors'.[10] In 'The
Function of Criticism at the Present Time', Coleridge stands out (along
with Shelley) from the other romantics for his 'immense reading'.[11] For
Arnold, such immense reading would, of course, imply an international
context, which would in turn have to include the 'unfettered thinking
of a large body of Germans', whose 'force of learning and criticism'
could not be matched by anything English during the time of Coleridge
and Shelley.[12] While Watson has no room for Coleridge in his examination of the role of Kant's philosophy in Spencer and Sidgwick, that
book appears as a very truncated account of Kant and his English critics,
as truncated as, at least, Spencer's engagement with German philosophy appears when compared with Coleridge's.

*

The influence of Coleridge's reception of German philosophy is hardly,
then, uniform. Along with the rival claims to the role of chief mediator
of German thinking to English readers, one of the main obstacles to
establishing a coherent view of Coleridge's reception of German philosophy, and of the subsequent reception of that reception, is, of course,
the well-documented controversy surrounding his alleged plagiarism,
chiefly in the *Biographia Literaria*, of German sources. While the so-called
'plagiarism controversy' quickly made Coleridge's relationship to German
philosophy an important topic in the debate regarding his legacy,
substantive interpretation of his understanding and deployment of
German thinking was somewhat stifled. This might be seen as an
inevitable implication of the charge of plagiarism because what is then
at issue is not so much the interpretation of those passages under
scrutiny but rather the identification of the sources from which they

were taken, and hence the legitimacy or illegitimacy of their borrowing and deployment. The explicit curtailment of interpretation of Coleridge's German-reception, and the limitation of engagement with it to the citation of evidence in the case against him, is perhaps most clearly exemplified in one of the most pungent and systematic charges of plagiarism against him, that made by J. F. Ferrier. Ferrier is dismissive of what he takes to be De Quincey's woolly case for the prosecution of the charge of plagiarism against Coleridge, and he thus seeks to quantify the details of the charge more boldly and thoroughly. Ferrier's essay is full of metaphors of dubious financial gain and of outright fraud, and with Coleridge's unacknowledged borrowings irresponsibly disturbing the balance of trade between Britain and her competitors, Ferrier refuses to 'have foreign productions palmed off upon [a literature] as the indigenous growth of its own soil'.[13] Ferrier's article is an over-fastidious attempt – he is ostentatiously honest about his debts to others as well as the limitations to his own competence – merely to catalogue Coleridge's thefts and thence to condemn. Even evaluative interpretation of Coleridge's German-reception is explicitly disavowed: '[our limits] will permit us to offer little or no criticism on the merits either of the borrowed or the original passage; and still less will they allow us to enter into any explanation touching the transcendental philosophy in general; but we can at least state the exact pages of Coleridge in which the plagiarisms occur, and the corresponding pages of Schelling from which they are taken' (293). Ferrier allows himself just enough room here to denounce Coleridge's use of Schelling. It is already 'little', not 'no', criticism to note that Coleridge 'adds nothing to the original remarks from which his observation is borrowed' (294). And it is more criticism still to state that, when he does change the original, Coleridge's 'interpolations [...] rather detract from than add to' Schelling's original. Coleridge's additions are, according to Ferrier's paradoxical quip, 'improvements for the worse' (295).[14]

So, while such explicit refusal of interpretative interference is qualified by Ferrier's note, for good measure, that, needless to say, where Coleridge does add anything to Schelling it is to the latter's detriment, all that can really be offered by way of a gloss on any aspect of Coleridge's relationship with German thinking is a cursory attempt at an explanation as to why he should have felt the need to copy. Opium, a poor memory, and peculiar habits might account for Coleridge's plagiarisms. The significance of the 'transcendental philosophy', let alone anything like Coleridge's thoughts, if there can even be said to be such, regarding it, cannot be discussed. What emerges from Ferrier's attempted demolition of Coleridge's *Biographia* is the insistence that his adoption of German philosophy shall not be interpreted because plagiarised sections of text do not require interpretation over and above that which they would demand in their original, legitimate source. Coleridge's use of his German sources is, rather, to be explained. This kind of psychologism might seem only to have currency so long as the question of Coleridge's German-reception was identified with the legitimacy or illegitimacy of his use of sources. However, in the following section, it will be seen that Pater does not really attempt to develop an interpretation of Coleridge's German-reception any further than merely explaining the turn to German philosophy by Coleridge's addiction to the absolute.

*

While the ferocity of the plagiarism controversy abated fairly early on, the charge of plagiarism, as well as the need to defend Coleridge against it, has not exactly gone away. A recent account of Coleridge's use of Kant in the *Aids to Reflection* by Elinor Shaffer, one of the main twentieth-century interpreters of Coleridge's use of German philosophy, hopes that at last Coleridge's German-reception can be explored in terms other than the legitimacy or illegitimacy of his use of sources.[15] This is a wish already implicit in, for example, Thomas McFarland's extensive study of Coleridge and the largely German 'pantheist tradition', which begins with an attempt to demonstrate Coleridge's intellectual independence from those sources upon which he was thought to be entirely dependent.[16] The expression of such a wish for freedom from the plagiarism controversy is meant to serve as a propaedeutic to the sustained attempt to interpret and evaluate Coleridge's inheritance of German philosophy. However, the focus, characteristic of the plagiarism controversy, on the explanation rather than the interpretation of Coleridge's deployment of German philosophy was shared by a great deal of nineteenth-century discussion of Coleridge's German-reception not necessarily, or not explicitly, concerned with plagiarism. Wariness, weariness, blank incomprehension, and mockery, were common responses to Coleridge's adoption of German thinking from the contemporary reviews onward. Thomas Barnes thought it extremely regrettable that Coleridge had become enchanted with Kant's philosophy to the detriment of his poetical output, the 'British Critic' found Kant inscrutable, the 'Monthly Reviewer' thought that Coleridge's tremendously horrible Kantianism would be too much even for the current taste for 'wonders and horrors', while Hazlitt was perhaps most excoriating of all, finding in Kant nothing short of intellectual dishonesty and in Coleridge's devotion to him a lonely idolatry.[17] As well as such summary rejections of Coleridge because of his alleged infatuation with Kantian obfuscation, James Hutchison Stirling expressed dissatisfaction with Coleridge's interpretation of Kant on what Stirling took to be the key topics of the difference between reason and understanding, the difference between the terms 'subjective' and 'objective', and the source of Kant's obscurity, acknowledged by Coleridge and, following Hegel, by Stirling.[18] F. J. A. Hort, however, subtly addresses precisely these central topics in an important and thorough consideration of more or less the entirety of Coleridge's œuvre.[19] In particular, Hort carefully discriminates between Kant's and Coleridge's versions of, for example, reason and understanding, noting, importantly, that Coleridge neither attempted to advance ideas derived without considerable alteration from Kant nor scrupulously to represent Kant's position. Moreover, Kant's role for Coleridge, according to Hort, was as much to clarify his attitude to Plato and Platonism as to furnish him with Kantian doctrine. The great strength of Hort's essay is that it, unlike much of the earlier, vitriolic criticism, neither conflates Kant and Coleridge, thus condemning merely by association, nor, therefore, does it take Coleridge's comments on Kant to be attempts merely somehow to re-package German philosophy for British consumption.

In what follows, I want to leave the largely epistemological and metaphysical focus of the early responses to Coleridge's German-reception. Instead, I will examine an important, and critical, view of his aesthetics that emphasises the effect of supposed German absolutism on it. In turning to the view of Coleridge's reception of German thought set out in Walter Pater's 'Coleridge', the rest of this essay examines the charge of German absolutism, made by Pater, against Coleridge's aesthetics in particular.[20] In many ways, Pater's appreciation of Coleridge, though sympathetic and attentive, inherits much of the suspicion of Coleridge's turn to and use of German philosophy. Whereas, for only the most pugnacious example, Ferrier's article exemplifies the concern with the legitimacy of Coleridge's borrowings, Pater's evaluation of Coleridge's significance typifies the later attempt to account psychologically and, as it were, biographically, for the character of Coleridge's thought, and to explain the use he makes of German thinking from the resulting perspective. In particular, I want here to examine – and to respond to – Pater's claim that Coleridge sees art as subject to absolute, dogmatic, and metaphysical rules. It will, rather, be shown that Coleridge's affinity to Kant involves his adoption of the German philosopher's refusal of absolute rules for aesthetic judgement. Instead, it will be suggested that

Coleridge takes over from Kant the insight that aesthetic judgements are *subjectively universal*: that no-one can make such a judgement on the behalf of anyone else and that agreement in aesthetic judgements cannot be compelled, but that a claim for universal assent is combined with every such judgement nevertheless.

Pater's 'Coleridge' falls roughly into two parts, the first dealing with Coleridge's prose and his attempt in it to assimilate the lessons of German philosophy, and the second dealing with the consequences of this engagement with the absolute spirit of German thinking for Coleridge's poetry, especially as it contrasts with Wordsworth's. Pater's comments are structured throughout by an opposition between the ancient, absolutist, philosophy, including its only apparently modern German variant, and the modern, relativist philosophy, attentive to 'what is here and now' (104), without the need always to refer every part to an all-encompassing whole. The content of the essay is evident from its closing comments that 'Coleridge, with his passion for the absolute, for something fixed where all is moving, his faintness, his broken memory, his intellectual disquiet, may still be ranked among the interpreters of one of the constituent elements of our life.' (ibid.)

As was suggested above, by the time that Pater came to make his assessment of Coleridge, the furore of the plagiarism controversy had largely died down. Of course, Pater still felt the need to offer some sort of account of the charges made against Coleridge, quoting Heine's defence of Schelling that 'There can be no plagiarism in philosophy' (75), although he attempts neither a thoroughly documentary account of Coleridge's borrowings and differences from German philosophers, nor a speculative psychological explanation as to what made him do it. Despite the apparently marginal status of the plagiarism controversy by this time, Pater still seeks rather to explain Coleridge's relationship to German philosophy from an account of his philosophical tendencies and their source in the pathology of his own mind, rather than explicitly to engage with the content of his German-reception.

Coleridge, Pater argues, is an intellectual absolutist. 'Now the literary life of Coleridge was a disinterested struggle against the relative spirit.' For Pater, Coleridge's battle against the relative spirit 'was an effort, surely, an effort of sickly thought, that saddened his mind, and limited the operation of his unique poetic gift' (68–9). While this struggle, and his attempt to establish first principles in all things, is given a patho- logical explanation, it can still be mapped onto an opposition between ancient, absolutist, philosophy, and modern, relativist, philosophy (66). Coleridge's natural philosophical home was Germany, with its apparently aprioristic rationalism. 'In 1798', Pater writes, 'he visited Germany, then, the only half-known, "promised land," of the metaphysical, the "absolute," philosophy' (71). Not now stealing from but applying Schelling 'with an eager, unwearied subtlety' Coleridge attempted 'to reclaim the world of art as a world of fixed laws' (74). All of this was, as has often been stated, part of an attempt 'to present the then recent metaphysics of Germany to English readers, as a legitimate expansion of the older, classical and native masters of what has been variously called the a priori, or absolute, or spiritual, or Platonic, view of things' (81).

Of course, Pater is not altogether unjustified in this view. After all, Coleridge's programme for *The Friend* was aimed at 'not instruction merely, but fundamental instruction':

> To refer men's opinions to their absolute principles, and thence their feelings to the appropriate objects, and in their due degrees; and finally, to apply the principles thus ascertained, to the formation of stedfast convictions concerning the most important questions of Politics, Morality, and Religion—these are to be the objects and the contents of this his work.[21]
>
> (ibid.)

And yet, even such pronouncements might be qualified by the continued insistence not on obedience to absolute rules external to the individual, but faithfulness to a kind of disciplined autonomous judging. Coleridge sought in *The Friend* 'to kindle his own torch for him, and leave it to himself to chuse the particular objects, which he might wish to examine by its light' (ibid.). For Pater, however, Coleridge's intellectual, or, indeed, intellectualist, character, and hence the almost inevitable deployment of German absolutist metaphysics, led not to the kindling of spiritual awareness but to a kind of all-encompassing spiritual ossification. 'In Coleridge's sadder, more purely intellectual, cast of genius, what with Wordsworth was sentiment or instinct became a philosophical idea, or philosophical formula, developed, as much as possible, after the abstract and metaphysical fashion of the transcendental schools of Germany' (87). Such straightforward and regrettable apriorism can only be alleviated, according to Pater, by a relativistic joie de vivre, energetically 'breaking through a thousand rough and brutal classifications' (103) although never, of course, breaking sweat.

*

The view that the Coleridgean adoption of German philosophical concerns was a dangerous detour into the realms of the absolute was common enough for it to be presented by John H. Muirhead as the standard – and false – view of the fate of characteristically British philosophy:

> It is a common view of the course of British philosophy that, starting from the empirical basis laid down by Bacon, Hobbes, and Locke, its chief and characteristic contribution to Western thought has been the development this received from their time to that of Mill, Spencer, and Sidgwick; that in the 'sixties of last century this tradition was broken into by an influx of foreign ideas which diverted it for a generation from its own natural bed into that of Kantian and post-Kantian idealism; finally, that the paradoxes of absolutism to which it had thus been led have created a strong counter-current under the influence of which it is returning repentantly to the older, safer, more national lines.[22]

Muirhead's characterisation of a 'common view' of the admixture of British philosophy with 'foreign ideas' is apt. There is a suggestion that the common viewer would not want British philosophy to have to do with anything as ungraspable as *ideas*, which even in their everyday sense here slide ineluctably towards idealism. It is not just that desertion of the native philosophical soil leads to paradox but that it leads to the 'paradoxes of absolutism'. Foreign, that is, German, philosophy is not empirical but absolutist and hence unavoidably paradoxical. The joke is, for Muirhead, that it was, of course, Kant's *Critique of Pure Reason* that most trenchantly defined the 'paradoxes of absolutism'; paradoxes that result, according to Kant, precisely when attempts are made in theoretical philosophy to step beyond the bounds of experience.[23] This is not to say, though, that post-Kantian idealism was not, indeed, paradoxical and absolutist. But is Coleridge's adoption and adaptation of German philosophy always aimed at the establishment of absolute, fixed metaphysical principles in the battle against the relative spirit, particularly with regard to aesthetics? This final section suggests that at least one aspect of Coleridge's German-reception – his understanding of Kant's account of reflective judgement in general and aesthetic judgement in particular – refuses the bad choice between old metaphysical absolutism on the one hand and new empirical relativism on the other. At first sight, Coleridge's endeavour, throughout his critical authorship, to furnish art and its criticism with fixed rules seems irrevocably to be at odds with a view of aesthetic judgement which asserts that 'There is neither a science of the beautiful, only a critique, nor a beautiful science, only beautiful art.'[24] There is also the case, influentially advanced by G. N. G. Orsini, that the more significant German source for Coleridge's aesthetics is Schelling's theory of art as the finite appearance of the infinite.[25] Coleridge's programme for literary criticism seems most often to demand more the control of aesthetic judgement ordered according to rules, than the emancipation of aesthetic judgement from externally imposed restrictions. The problem with literature, for example, is that access to it is not policed by door-men, as, at least, is the case at the theatre. There is no 'royal mintage for arguments' by which to measure the value of any particular literary judgement and thus no-one can be turned away from the door of literary criticism for presenting false coin (*Friend* I, 277–8). And Mr Boyer, Coleridge's headmaster, who drew up 'a list of interdiction' on which certain poetic devices were placed, had taught Coleridge of the logical rigours of poetry: 'I learnt from him, that Poetry, even that of the loftiest, and, seemingly, that of the wildest odes, had a logic of its own, as severe as that of science; and more difficult, because more subtle, more complex, and dependent on more, and more fugitive causes' (*BL* I, 9).

Despite appearances, Coleridge's attempt to establish principles for criticism is not unambiguously absolutist in opposition to the kind of refusal of absolutism in aesthetics offered by Kant. While Coleridge's anxiety about the use of the word 'taste' is evident in the course of his attempt explicitly to provide a terminology that would distinguish between taste 'as it exists both in the palate and the soul', in that there is a 'Taste *for* Shakespear' but a 'Taste *of* venison' (*Friend* I, 11–12), the definition at which he arrives at the conclusion of a similar discussion in his 1808 'Lectures on the Principles of Poetry' is clearly indebted to Kant's insistence on the autonomy of aesthetic judgement. 'Taste may then be defined—a distinct Perception of any arrangement conceived as external to us co-existi̶n̶g̶ent with some degree of Dislike or Complacency conceived as resulting from that arrangement—and this immediately, without any prospect of consequences—tho' this is indeed implied in the word co-existent'.[26] Moreover, it is not the case, as Coleridge's introduction to the statement of 'the application of the rules, deduced from philosophical principles, to poetry and criticism' at the beginning of the *Biographia* might appear to suggest, that the value of art is to be measured against standards worked out in advance. That the rules of art do not, for Coleridge, come before art itself is most explicitly stated in the *Logic*, a text to which, it should be noted, Pater did not have access:

> [R]ules are in all cases means to some end. A truth the oversight of which is exemplified and may be profitably illustrated by the false conclusions of certain French critics, who, having borrowed the rules of tragedy which Aristotle had abstracted and generalised from the composition[s] of Aeschylus, Sophocles, and other Greek poets, treated them as ends to which all the parts of every tragedy were to be adapted as means. [...] The science of criticism dates its restoration from the time when it was seen that an examination and appreciation of the end was necessarily antecedent to the formation of the rules, supplying at once the principle of the rules themselves and of their application to the given subject.[27]

At first sight, there are a number of features of this passage that seem to put it at some remove from Kant's anti-dogmatic aesthetics. In stating that there is such a thing as a 'science of criticism', this passage seems flatly to contradict Kant. However, this science is taken to be founded upon a view of its principles which, upon closer examination, appear to share much with Kant's view of aesthetic judgement. First, there is a distinct suspicion here of Aristotle's method of abstraction and generalisation, to which 'examination and appreciation' are, in the next sentence, implicitly preferred. For sure, both Aristotle's and Coleridge's methods of arriving at the rules for criticism begin from works of art. However, for the French critics that borrow Aristotle's rules, any given work of art either succeeds or fails insofar – and only insofar – as it fulfils the Aristotelian prescriptions for tragedy. In contrast, 'examination' demands not the application of rules abstracted from supposedly ideal models but rather close attention, foremost, and crucially, first, to the specific features of a particular work of art. Moreover, 'appreciation' echoes the Kantian insistence on the role of individual pleasure in aesthetic judgement, for which neither the application of abstract rules, nor the mere opinions of others, against which Coleridge had been so excoriating in his discussion of critical estimates of Wordsworth (*Friend* I, 40), can be substituted.

Second, in addition to this offer of an alternative to Aristotle's abstractions, Coleridge insists on the primacy of attention to the end – the work – prior to the formation of rules for its judgement. This insistence casts the search for rules by which to judge a work of art according to Kant's account of reflective judgement. Now, the notion of reflective judgement is central to Kant's attempt to articulate an account of aesthetics that would resist the application of abstract rules but would, at the same time, not therefore sacrifice the claim of aesthetic judgement to universality. The role of reflective judgement is assumed in some of Kant's clearest statements of the impossibility that there might be determinate conceptual rules for aesthetic judgement:

> There can be no objective rule of taste that would determine what is beautiful through concepts. For every judgment from this source is aesthetic, i.e., its determining ground is the feeling of the subject and not a concept of an object. To seek a principle of taste that would provide the universal criterion of the beautiful through determinate concepts is a fruitless undertaking, because what is sought is impossible and intrinsically self-contradictory.
>
> (5:231; 116)

The key terms here are 'determining' and its cognates. It is not that Kant thinks that aesthetic judgement has nothing to do with principles, but that those principles must always begin with what they are judging rather than with pre-ordained concepts:

> The power of judgment in general is the faculty for thinking of the particular as contained under the universal. If the universal (the rule, the principle, the law) is given, then the power of judgment, which subsumes the particular under it [...] is determining. If, however, only the particular is given, for which the universal is to be found, then the power of judgment is merely reflecting.
>
> (5:179; 66–7)

Criticism, crucially, starts not with a universal rule by which to judge particular works of art, but rather with particular works of art for which the universal must be sought. Moreover, it is clear from this passage that this process is not undertaken once and for all, but that the judgement of each work of art prompts its own search for its own rule. Coleridge's attempt, therefore, to escape the edicts of pre-ordained aesthetic dogma while maintaining the possibility that universality can be claimed for the judgement of artistic productions is strongly reminiscent of Kant's insistence that judgements of works of art are neither merely relative nor clearly scientific but occupy an easily collapsible space in between. Pater's view that Coleridge turned to German philosophy because of his addiction to the absolute, and that the consequences of this addiction are most clearly registered in his theory of art, is testimony to the way in which a view of aesthetic judgement that refuses both absolutism and relativism can easily be overwhelmed by either of these dogmatic rivals.[28]

The resemblance between Coleridge's mature view of aesthetic judgement and that articulated in the third *Critique* is reinforced by the close verbal resonances between Coleridge's passage and Kant's refusal to be dictated to by supposedly pre-established standards of taste. In the long course of commentary on Coleridge's German-reception, many such verbal resonances between his work and that of his German predecessors have been identified but, in echoing the formulations of Kant's aesthetics, Coleridge does not so much take over a body of doctrine but rather follows Kant's way out of a doctrinal double bind. Kant refuses to allow the circumscription of aesthetic judgement by pre-established rules, whether French, German, or ancient:

> If someone reads me his poem or takes me to a play that in the end fails to please my taste, then he can adduce Batteux or Lessing, or even older and more famous critics of taste, and adduce all the rules they established as proofs that his poem is beautiful; certain passages, which are the very ones that displease me, may even agree with the rules of beauty (as they have been given there and have been universally recognized): I will stop my ears, listen to no reasons and arguments, and would rather believe that those rules of the critics are false or at least that this is not a case for their application than allow that my judgment should be determined by means of a priori grounds of proof [...].
>
> (5:284–5; 165)

The affinity between Coleridge's passage and this account of the singularity of the judgement of taste, despite the commitment of the former to the science of criticism, is clear. Indeed, this is all the more the case because the singularity that is insisted upon here is not reducible to idiosyncrasy or to the merely personal; rather, the singularity of aesthetic judgement is, for Kant, the condition of its universality. While Pater saw Coleridge's philosophy of art as starkly opposed to the spirit of relativism in its attempt conceptually to secure art in the realm of the absolute, Coleridge's affinity with Kant's critique of taste suggests that

that opposition between absolutism and relativism has itself been refused. Coleridge was indeed unusually sensitive to the role that subjective universality, the lynch-pin of Kant's aesthetics, played in Kant's philosophy more generally, especially in his epistemology and its account of the necessary conditions of objective knowledge. Again in the *Logic*, for example, Coleridge comments that the 'universal subjective' is prior to and necessary for the 'properly objective' (*Logic*, 145) and that the sense in which 'objective' might be used to designate that which belongs to the subject universally, that is to all subjects and to all subjects at all times, is again remarked (*Logic*, 203).[29]

In an insightful article on the difficulty Coleridge faced in his attempt to reconcile aspects of German Idealist dialectics, Kantian philosophy of the will, and Christian faith, Tim Milnes has commented on the way in which different strands of Coleridge's thinking have, since the nineteenth-century reception of his work, been disentangled from their original (often confusing) contexts, to be woven into new critical patterns.[30] Something of this operation of Coleridge's critical fate can be seen in that reading of his reception of German thinking of which Pater is a characteristic example. It is not that Coleridge turned – or, at least, always turned – to German philosophy for so much absolutist metaphysics. Rather, at least in Kant's view of aesthetic judgement, he found a model of criticism that required the search for principles but did not lay such principles down prior to any judgement of any work of art. What Coleridge found in German philosophy was not, as so many nineteenth- and twentieth-century attempted demolitions or ambivalent appreciations have thought, merely reducible to absolutism. His turn to Kant's aesthetics at least was precisely in the service of the refusal of arbitrary, absolute rules.

Notes

1. Eliot's *The Use of Poetry*, 80, quoted, and countered, in Richards's *Coleridge on Imagination*, ed. by John Constable, I. A. Richards Selected Works 1919–1938, VI (London: Routledge, 2001; first published, 1934), 11. Richards draws on John H. Muirhead's defence of Coleridge against Wellek's criticisms. See in particular John H. Muirhead, *Coleridge as Philosopher* (London: Allen & Unwin, 1930).
2. 'Coleridge', in *A History of Modern Criticism: 1750–1950*, 8 vols (Cambridge: Cambridge University Press, 1981; first published, 1955), II, 151–87 (187).
3. Ibid., p. 151.
4. Rosemary Ashton, *The German Idea: Four English Writers and the reception of German thought, 1800–1860* (Cambridge: Cambridge University Press, 1980), 72.

5. Ibid., pp. 35–7. Cf. Kooy, *Coleridge, Schiller and Aesthetic Education* (Houndmills: Palgrave, 2002), especially 100–6 on Coleridge's view of Kant's aesthetics.
6. *Biographia Literaria*, 2 vols, ed. James Engell and W. Jackson Bate (Princeton, NJ: Princeton University Press, 1983), I, 153. Hereafter cited as *BL*. For commentary on the political implications of Coleridge's revision of the extant view, see David M. Baulch, 'The "Perpetual Exercise of an Interminable Quest": The *Biographia Literaria* and the Kantian Revolution', *Studies in Romanticism*, 43 (2004), 557–81 (568).
7. 'Pioneers and Precedents: The "Importation of German" and the Emergence of Periodical Criticism in England', *Internationales Archiv für Sozialgeschichte der deutschen Literatur*, 7 (1982), 65–87 (84).
8. 'Heinrich Heine', in *Essays in Criticism, First Series*, ed. by Sister Thomas Marion Hoctor, S. S. J. (Chicago: University of Chicago Press, 1968), 96–117 (97).
9. *Kant and His English Critics: a comparison of critical and empirical philosophy* (Glasgow: MacLehose, 1881).
10. 'Heinrich Heine', 97, emphasis added.
11. In *Culture and Anarchy and other writings*, ed. by Stefan Collini (Cambridge: Cambridge University Press, 1993; repr. 1999), 26–51 (30).
12. Ibid., 31.
13. 'The Plagiarisms of S. T. Coleridge', *Blackwood's Edinburgh Magazine*, 47 (1840), 287–99 (288). Further references are given in the text.
14. Wellek, for one, dissents from this view, arguing that Coleridge did, at least, combine what he took from German philosophy 'in a personal way'. See 'Coleridge', 157–8.
15. 'Coleridge and Kant's "Giant Hand"', in *Anglo-German Affinities and Antipathies*, ed. by Rüdiger Görner, (Munich: Iudicium, 2004), 39–56 (41). See also Shaffer's earlier, 'Illusion and Imagination: Derrida's Parergon and Coleridge's Aid to Reflection. Revisionary readings of Kantian formalist aesthetics', in *Aesthetic Illusion: Theoretical and Historical Approaches*, ed. by Frederick Burwick, and Walter Pape (Berlin: De Gruyter, 1990), 138–57.
16. McFarland, *Coleridge and the Pantheist Tradition* (Oxford: Oxford University Press, 1969), xxiii–xl and 1–52.
17. These reviews can be found most conveniently in *Coleridge: The Critical Heritage*, ed. by J. R. de J. Jackson (London: Routledge and Kegan Paul, 1970). 'Strada' [Thomas Barnes], 'Mr. Coleridge', *Champion*, 26 March 1814, 102–3; repr. *Critical Heritage*, 189–94 (191). Anonymous, review of *Biographia Literaria*, British Critic, November 1817, 8, 460–8; repr. *Critical Heritage*, 355–75 (357). Anonymous, review of *Sibylline Leaves*, Monthly Review, January 1819, 88, 24–38; repr. *Critical Heritage*, 399–412 (400). [William Hazlitt], review of *Biographia Literaria*, Edinburgh Review, August 1817, 28, 488–515; repr. *Critical Heritage*, 295–322 (303–5).
18. James Hutchison Stirling, 'De Quincey and Coleridge Upon Kant', in *Jerrold, Tennyson and Macaulay, with other critical essays* (Edinburgh: Edmonston & Douglas, 1868), 172–224.
19. F. J. A. Hort, 'Coleridge', in *Cambridge Essays, Contributed by Members of the University* (London: Parker and Son, 1856), 292–351.
20. 'Coleridge', in *Appreciations, with an Essay on Style* (London: Macmillan, 1910), 65–104. Further references will be given in the text.

21. *The Friend*, 2 vols, ed. Barbara E. Rooke (Princeton, NJ: Princeton University Press, 1969), I, 16. Hereafter cited as *Friend*.
22. *The Platonic Tradition in Anglo-Saxon Philosophy: Studies in the History of Idealism in England and America* (London: Allen & Unwin, 1931), 13.
23. See the 'Transcendental Dialectic', *Critique of Pure Reason*, trans. by Paul Guyer, and Allen W. Wood (Cambridge: Cambridge University Press, 1997; repr. 1998), 384–623.
24. Kant, *Critique of the Power of Judgment*, ed. by Paul Guyer, trans. by Paul Guyer, and Eric Matthews (Cambridge: Cambridge University Press, 2000; repr. 2001), 184. Further references to this edition, preceded by the volume and page number of the *Akademie-Ausgabe* of Kant's works, will be given in parenthesis in the text.
25. Orsini, *Coleridge and German Idealism: A Study in the History of Philosophy* (Carbondale: Southern Illinois University Press, 1969), especially 167–71 and 236–7. Werner Beierwaltes' introduction to his edition of Schelling's *Texte zur Philosophie der Kunst* (Stuttgart: Reclam, 1982; repr. 2004) includes a good introductory discussion of art as, according to Schelling, the finite appearance of the infinite. See 3–46.
26. *Lectures 1808–1819 On Literature*, 2 vols, ed. R. A. Foakes (Princeton, NJ: Princeton University Press, 1987), I, 30.
27. *Logic*, ed. J. R. de J. Jackson (Princeton, NJ: Princeton University Press, 1981), pp. 66–7. Hereafter cited as *Logic*.
28. For a helpful account of Kant's identification – and rejection – of both relativism and scientism in aesthetics as dogmatic, see Paul Guyer, *Kant and the Claims of Taste*, 2nd edn (Cambridge: Cambridge University Press, 1997), 5–6.
29. This aspect of the relationship between subjective and objective universality, and its importance to Coleridge's reception of Kant, is noted in a sympathetic review of the second edition of *Aids to Reflection* by J. H. Heraud in *Fraser's Magazine*, June 1832, 5, 585–97; repr. in *Critical Heritage*, 585–606 (595–6).
30. 'Through the looking-glass: Coleridge and post-Kantian philosophy', *Comparative Literature*, 51:4 (1999), 309–23.

11
The Consummate Symbol: A Coleridgean Tradition

Paul Hamilton

I once published a book explaining why Coleridge failed to become an English Schelling. The advantages and disadvantages of this falling-short were complicated. I would now put the argument more straightforwardly. Coleridge did not succeed in providing the transcendental deduction, modelled on Schelling's *System*, necessary to the philosophical coherence of two volumes of intellectual self-justification, *Biographia Literaria*. Whatever the expressive compensations and ironic dividends, the gap between the first volume theorising imagination and the second volume of corroborating criticism disabled Coleridge's stated project. Another source for the work's undeniable affective success on its readers had to be found. It appeared that the literary criticism of the second volume might indeed connect with the earlier philosophical effort if the philosophy were viewed as a protracted act of desynonymy. *Biographia Literaria* contains, in embryo, an argument for the homologous development of life and language. Both proliferate through a splitting and regrouping by which what was previously thought to be simple and irreducible actually spawns new individuals. At the levels both of biology and meaning, the philosophical understanding of life and the literary understanding of poetic expression, the same process of individuation is at work. They are different versions, or, in other Schellingian terms, 'potencies' of each other. The first volume's metaphysics and the second volume's critical discriminations belong to an identical activity. An organic view of language can be read reversibly to produce a startlingly modern-sounding grasp of life as the generation of (genetic) information.[1]

Interpreted in this fashion, Coleridge's apparently divergent volumes actually possess a unity of understanding issuing from the common matrix of language. Coleridge shows rather than says this. His demonstration is not the deliberate gesture of Wittgensteinian philosophical effacement at the end of the *Tractatus*. Nor does he offer philosophy as a therapeutic treatment of our need for it, as Wittgenstein does in *Philosophical Investigations*. Nevertheless, the confidence with which Coleridge moves towards the second volume's final assertion of our divine universal spokenness – Logos – evinces a certainty Wittgenstein would have recognised, the certainty of someone caught ineluctably within the linguistic process of immanence of which he is trying to make sense.[2] Many of his remarks elsewhere, published and unpublished, testify to his lasting conception of an 'anti-Babel' made up of diverse 'logoi'. The religious resonance of this overarching Logos, and Coleridge's own tendency to hear himself this way, dulled his followers' sense of his proleptic reliance on the idea of language as the new *prima philosophia*. Subsequently, it became easy to forget the philosophical charge which Coleridge's appropriation of Schelling's 'dynamic' *Naturphilosophie* had dissolved in language. Coleridge's linguistic turn was undervalued. Now it is uncontroversial. Coleridge's formulation of Logos as a collective of 'logoi' can be plausibly juxtaposed with the thought of Heidegger and others instrumental in the 'linguistic turn' which took so many forms in twentieth-century philosophy.[3] Once this topicality was appreciated, however, something historical became obscured as a consequence. For Coleridge had not left Schelling behind when he cast logic in the shape of a philosophy of language.

Another frequently ignored reversible relation in this area is Coleridge's reading of Schelling. For Schelling also read Coleridge. Significantly, his most extended remark on Coleridge concerns language. In a footnote to the historical introduction to his late *Philosophie der Mythologie* (1842), Schelling writes that reading Coleridge is very like reading one of his own earlier works. He doesn't put it quite so simply, and states instead that it is delightful to find one of his own works that had been neglected in Germany so well understood (*Über die Gottheiten von Samothrake*). But the hare of plagiarism is raised. 'One ought not to charge a true fellow-genius (*einem wirklich congenialen Mann*) with that kind of thing', says Schelling handsomely (II / 1, 196n.).[4] Again, the issue of unattributed borrowings, that Schelling is prepared to overlook, has perhaps obscured the more substantial connection between his own understanding of mythology and Coleridge's philosophy of language. To appreciate that link is to agree with Schelling that Coleridge had something to contribute to Schelling's own argument.

For Schelling's discussion annotates *his* borrowing of the word 'tautegorical' from Coleridge's Royal Society of Literature lecture 'On the Prometheus of Aeschylus [...]'. The lecture was published in the Society's

'Transactions' of 1834, nine years after it was delivered. Coleridge's lecture has been ably and convincingly interpreted for the ways in which it might reflect upon his developing notion of a Clerisy or intellectual caste entrusted with the task of educating us in inalienable human qualities that tie us to a particular political and ecclesiastical establishment.[5] The esoteric initiates of Samothrace recall Egyptian precursors and anticipate later formations of an essential theogony, knowledge of which is part of a perennial activity distinguishing intellectuals as the class capable of detecting the constitutional character of the divinely interpreted world. The elite initiates of the Samothracian mysteries arguably figure a pleasingly *recherché* source for intellectual authority. In Coleridge's own day, their sourcing of contemporary mysteries in a still more ancient culture parallels the universality or 'Idea' that Coleridge seeks in his justification of a National Church staffed by his Clerisy. His contemporary *ricorso* of a perennial pattern is divinely potentiated, and this 'potency' makes it impossible to separate out the earlier from the later rationale, however superior to a Christian its current expression might appear to be. This explains Coleridge's use of the words 'tautegory' or 'tautegorical' on which Schelling later seizes.

Schelling's remarks on Coleridge's lecture suddenly crystallise into a pointed analysis that departs from the generalised approval making up the rest of the footnote. It homes in on Coleridge's choice of expression: 'I have called this article wonderful', Schelling writes, 'because of the language; though we want to abandon parts of earlier terminologies (*Kunstausdrucke*), or would like to quit them, if the subject allowed, he – if with some irony – without second thoughts gives his unaccustomed compatriots expressions such as subject – object and the like'. The outmoded subject/object terminology that tautegory's conflation ('subject–object') supersedes does indeed occur in Coleridge's lecture. 'The Prometheus', he claimed, 'is a *philosopheme* and ταυτηγορικον'.[6] This means, as Schelling interprets Coleridge, that myth has to be taken less as figurative than as literal (*eigentlich*). Schelling himself would have preferred to characterise mythology 'not as artistic, but as natural' (II / 1, 195), although this 'natural' turns out to be mythology's own thing, not its explanation in other terms. Coleridge, though, in his *Lay Sermons* and elsewhere, famously bemoaned his age for having no third term, lying between the literal and the figurative, with which to characterise a truth that is *sui generis*. Coleridge christened the missing link a 'symbol'. It takes its shape from outside nature, and so seems figurative, but is partially the same as what it signifies. The symbolic complex thus problematises normal epistemological models based on a subject knowing an object. The difficulties myth creates for both science and rhetoric lead to Coleridge's call for the act of desynonymy that will generate the term 'tautegory'. The myth that does not describe but *is* achieves this knowledge dissolving identity through a performance in which it 'is an object that is its own subject, and *vice versa*, a conception which, if the uncombining and infusile genius of our language allowed it, might be expressed by the term subject – object'.[7] The language does not allow it, inhibited here in finding expression for its mutual implication of knowledge and life, syntax and φυσις (life). Hence Coleridge's difficulty in quitting a terminology Schelling's philosophy has sought to abandon. Tautegory, though, is an up-to-date attempt to find a new term adequate to myth's self-identity.

This problematic self-identity is addressed from the start in Schelling's *Philosophie der Mythologie*. Philosophy and mythology, he concedes to begin with, are two things so 'strange and disparate' (II / 1, 4) that any *rapprochement* seems unlikely. The key to bringing them nearer lies in the recognition that mythology is irreducible. Consequently, it cannot be translated into a set of other natural or historical facts. Mythology is the natural history that its Gods require in order to appear. Not, it is vital to note, that Schelling thinks Gods possess a noumenal reality of which these historical phenomena are partial substitutes. 'The Gods are not something first existing in the abstract outside these historical conditions' (II / 1, 7). They only exist, in an ontological sense, by infusing that same history with a sense of its grounding. We cannot recover some anterior whole (*das Ganze der Mythologie*), out of which *they* might have contracted to their current historical proportions. Their troubling of the historical sense by its *own* power retrospectively to suggest and simultaneously make unattainable such plenitude produces mythology. Or, put most succinctly by Schelling, we can have no theology (*Götterlehre*) without theogony, or the necessarily historical realisation of what makes history (*Göttergeschichte, oder wie die Griechen das natürliche allein hervorhebend sagen, Theogonie* [II / 1, 7]).

Schelling's thought here is enormously suggestive. Despite the professed disappointment of the distinguished audience who attended these Berlin lectures, they seem to have left an inheritance still in need of recognition. We are close here, for example, to Kierkegaard's idea of repetition, or the consciousness of being able to stand beside one's life, seeing it at second-hand, but not as different from its original. Its lack of ontological necessity creates that absurd space in which, for Kierkegaard, God's possibility is infinite. Kierkegaard is pushed to echo the Schellingian language of potencies when he describes this awareness as 'consciousness raised to the second power'.[8] Schelling's refusal to assume an enlightened superiority to the intimations gained through mythology marks him off from the 'higher critics' and young Hegelians of his old age. It also links him to post-modern critics of enlightenment reason. His thought is as different from 'higher criticism' as Foucault's historicism is from Hegelianism. Mythology expresses powers that are replayed in the discourses supposedly demythologising them but actually inaugurating their own terms of mastery and dominance. The history by which we place the past places itself when our reconfiguration of the previous necessarily reveals a history of the present. Precisely this translatability was what infuriated Engels, who attended the lectures, and who saw in their historical fluency, its apparent timeliness for all, a lack of principle.[9]

Insistence on immanence, on the inescapability of overarching determinations, and the implication in their hegemony of the philosophical medium by which we chart them, reaches recent philosophical self-examinations. Scepticism about the foundations of philosophy along with the persistence of a need for philosophy appears in many different shapes and idioms. The temptation to extrapolate from these a universally applicable, authoritative formula immediately rehearses the problem their variety was supposed to displace. We are left with ways of reading our language from the inside. In Wittgensteinian fashion, philosophy can become a form of therapy against its own transcendental aspirations. Once these are abandoned, philosophy becomes the interpreter of discourses to each other, standing in for their ideal communicability without having to postulate some transcendental reality to which they all refer. Foucault was more interested in the historical character and sense of an epoch – the 'spirit', as his opponent Hegel would have put it – thrown up by these philosophical negotiations, Habermas emphasises their counterfactual logic and the extent to which they can model a desirable political generosity. Cavell, summarised by Richard Eldridge, perhaps generalises this situation most acceptably:

> Philosophy should not primarily imitate the sciences in supplying explanations of what has happened and predictions of what will, and it should not primarily draw lines between the scientifically accessible and knowable, on the one hand, and the poetic, superstitious, religious, mythical, and so on, on the other, though it may do these things by the way. Its central business is neither empirical generalization nor legislation, but rather reading, or criticism, or understanding from the inside.[10]

It is this reading from the inside, this understanding and criticising of the network from within which one must work, think and act, that Coleridge so typically practises and encourages, although 'by the way', as if an aside from his ostensible projects. The larger linguistic dimension which interpretative activity throws up by default shadows all his work. For the later Schelling, though, to evoke our production in language is philosophy's whole existence, and that is why he remains helpful and underestimated in estimating Coleridge's legacy, to which we now return.

Coleridge's use of 'tautegory' in *Aids to Reflection* and in the Notebooks primarily opposes the notion of 'allegory'. As its etymology suggests, tautegory is the same as what it figures in a way that allegory is not. In a theological context, Coleridge, like Schelling, wishes to refute any higher criticism that historicises or relativises the truth of Christian doctrine.[11] To the idea that scriptural expression might be allegorical of anything, he opposes the claim that it is consubstantial with its subject. The symmetries here with the real presence at the Eucharist are obvious and pressing, and they tend to commandeer the agenda. Coleridge can sound more like Schelling's friend and opponent, Creuzer, assuming a connection between the symbol's particular intimacy with divine fiat – letting us see the universe as a specific option – and a particular divinity, or monotheism.[12] If, though, the pressure to read Judaeo–Christian conviction back into other religions is resisted, the philosophical issues at stake visibly recompose themselves again. To begin with, though, one must note Coleridge's fundamental premise that tautegory does not, its consubstantiality suggests, change the subject in the interests of interpreting it. No figurative, allegorical or symbolic gloss is provided by tautegory. Tautegory is 'the consummate *Symbol*', according to the explanation given in Notebook 29.[13] It possesses an iconic self-sufficiency. This is what lets it guarantee the unchangeability of God's word. Genuine religious expression obviously changes with different historical circumstances, but its embodiment of truth cannot be superseded: it can only be re-cycled.

The undoubtedly conservative dimension to Coleridge's use of tautegory need not therefore obscure its simultaneous picture of our production by language. Inescapable, immutable Christian truth figures, even if Coleridge does not wish to foreground this homology, our entrapment within a form of words. If, as *Aids to Reflection* has it, we must believe before we can understand, a philosophical dependency becomes as evident as the particular religious dependency Coleridge is usually assumed to be exclusively talking about here. Only by assent to a vocabulary can we activate our essentially linguistic being. This is also the perception of

Schelling's philosophy of mythology, and the reason for his sympathy with Coleridge (and for his interpretation of Coleridge's sympathy for him). Schelling appreciates that Coleridge's use of 'tautegorical' doesn't quite match his own *tautegorisch*. But he does see inscribed in the Royal Society lecture Coleridge's interest in original expression *as* original philosophy. Irrespective of its theistic content, thinks Schelling in the pages surrounding his Coleridge footnote, mythology points up our natural condition. In mythology we cannot distinguish content from form, raw matter from its clothing (II / 1, 195). Let us unpack the logic of this iconicity a bit more.

To say, with Schelling, that myths are tautegorical is to say that they are untranslatable. There is nothing that they stand for, no literal meaning that they allegorise (II / 1, 247). In their identity with their subject, they therefore are instances of the fact that anything anterior to our knowledge can only disclose itself through our knowledge. But knowledge's authority is compromised by possessing this power to be an accessory after the fact. Retrospectively, it apparently legislates against itself. (This retrospective logic of construction is familiar as what makes it possible to think the Freudian Unconscious and Heidegger's 'Being'.) There is no epistemic relation involved here. It is precisely to cater for what happens when epistemology cannot cope with its own ambitions that figures like tautegory are evolved. Less compensatory than the aesthetic, though, tautegory does not so much exonerate epistemological failure as bypass the relation of subject to object necessary for knowing in the first place. For commentators like Douglas Hedley, primarily interested in finding for Coleridge a Trinitarian 'rational theology', it appears that 'the concept tautegoric links insight and the Platonist maxim, homoion hoimoio, "like is known by like"'.[14] But in Schelling's post-transcendentalism and post-*Naturphilosophie* writings, the self-consciousness of spirit, which Hegel so influentially historicised as a progressive search for its own likeness, is displaced by a Being that only has a self or identity through its embodiment. There isn't something that materiality could reflect if that something only *happens* as a consequence of materiality. The logic of reflection is inappropriate here.

Any lack in our understanding, or any remainder left over after our scientific mapping of what is, must still be grasped through Being's choice, as it were, to submit to the kind of form that produces our kind of knowledge of it. That is what makes it an it, capable of being known; and that is also what relativizes our knowledge, making us seek expression for its situatedness, a location we can never get outside. Could we get outside, we could produce that putatively 'higher' criticism to which

Schelling and Coleridge object. Their historicism is of a different kind. Locution for them is always location; but this place is one we can never get a perspective on, and so map in relation to something else. The mythological thus both declares its provisionality and asserts the irreplaceability of its function. It repeats a dilemma we can never get out of. Myth can never be demythologised, in the sense of being rendered obsolete.[15] Subsequent philosophies of mythology can only explain it by historicizing it; not, to repeat, by allegorising it, but by reconceiving its tautegorical structure in a new, contemporary form.

This ontology, isomorphic with tautegory, connects Schelling's middle philosophy (*Freiheitschrift*, *Weltalter*) with his later philosophies of mythology and revelation. The latter, positive philosophy, searches for philosophical expressions of the wonder that there is something rather than nothing. This project links up with the esoteric meaning of freedom used in the earlier works to describe the indeterminate ground (*Ungrund*), learned from Boehme, that fortunately contracts into our knowledge of it rather than producing something else we couldn't know. Clearly this scheme would be attractive to a Christian Trinitarian. The ineffable that freely incarnates itself in a world and allows this predilection to be gratefully intuited can obviously be reworked as the triad of Father, Son, and Holy Ghost. For Thomas McFarland, editor of Coleridge's *Opus Maximum*, Coleridge is to be understood as insisting on the inviolability of this identification of philosophy with theology: 'And if the Trinity was Coleridge's final theological bastion, it was no less important to his ultimate philosophical position. The largest task of the *magnum opus* was to extricate and validate the idea of the Trinity against pantheism and evolutionary materialism'.[16]

The Christian, Trinitarian view, though, looks less like an historicisation of the tautegorical function, more like a revival of allegory. Philosophy, here, actually means theology; despite appearances, its major categories fight a theological crusade, a battle against the very idea of a separate, secular realm in which questions claiming the same scope might be discussed. Tautegory, though, should not mean but be, in different historical ways. This slogan caters for the occasionally existential evocation of Christianity given by Coleridge. It also helps explain his attractiveness to 'new criticism' with its hatred of paraphrase, and the commitment to an immanent criticism of mentors of 'new criticism', such as T. S. Eliot and I. A. Richards. There are important distinctions to be made here though. Eliot and the new critics take their cue primarily from Coleridge's frequent defences of an autonomous aesthetic category opposed to science. They neglect his larger, post-Kantian feeling for an overall articulation whose language we can only repeat as we try to formulate our sense of being dictated by it. Although like Eliot primarily curious about aesthetic definition, Richards, as much as Coleridge and Schelling, strives to formulate the linguistic structure of our lives.

Finally, though, I return to that politicisation of Coleridge's imagination from which this discussion tried to make an original departure. The absolute indifference, which Coleridge and Schelling see as the form of ultimate expression, and which Coleridge figures as our linguistic immanence, looks as if it floats above all political questions. Political issues appear bound to a world divided between the interests of subject and object, conveyed through the relative authority of one or the other within specific epistemologies – empiricist, idealist and so on. Is the object traduced or mastered by the knowing subject? Or is the subject limited in its basic freedoms by being bound to the task of knowing only a specific kind of object? Yet power relations intrinsic to the political require epistemological definition; the refusal or dismantling of them can nevertheless contain their own powerful political charge. It need not be the case, in other words, that ontology consecrates existing establishments or leaves them critically untouched. Its rethinking of our worldly participation can set up a *new* kind of politics. The process begins at home, in disciplinary fashion, with philosophy's necessary distribution of its own mastery among other discourses. Its purpose becomes one of getting us to re-interpret these aesthetic, religious, or affective idioms as telling expressions of the constitutive human situatedness it has discovered through its own limitations. This philosophical hybridity or discursive collaboration is very different from the confrontational disciplinariness that high Romantic theory or Hegelian hierarchies have been thought to encourage. In the new dispensation entrapment becomes proliferation, and immanence a kind of sharing of wisdom. And maybe that too was a Coleridgean destination?

Ruskin's Turner

By its nature this destination would never be fixed but always be an expanding horizon, dilating with the changing knowledge and experience of which it was the boundary. Its consequences would be historical through and through. In keeping with this mutability is Carlyle's early fascination, learned from the Germans, for philosophical cross-dressing of a sort in *Sartor Resartus*, even if conclusively abandoned for the later prejudices of 'Shooting Niagara' and the like. Like Newman's 'idea of a university', Arnold's ostensible side-stepping of politics in favour of a cultural criticism of life can be conceded. But Arnold's work as an inspector of schools which his criticism arguably inspired can also suggest new, more local, practices that in these post-modern days are more readily described as political. One of the most egregious creations of a critical object in the years following Coleridge's era, an object which appears reciprocally to create the discipline adequate to it, was Ruskin's Turner. In Turner, Ruskin found or invented a subject that could expatiate the discourse of art criticism with which he wished to rehabilitate general commentary – commentary on art, clearly, but also on politics, ethics, society, and the host of topics mandatory for a Victorian sage. But Ruskin also intuited collaborative, auxiliary relations between these varieties in a manner deriving from the Coleridgean expansiveness described above. In line with the open-ended drive of Coleridge's thinking, Ruskin's Turner can, without much forcing, be read as fluently applying Coleridge's philosophical idiom and further-ing its project through Ruskin's idiosyncratic socialism.

We start, though, with a contrasting example of censorship.

May 3, 1862. my dear Wornum: As the authorities have not thought it proper to register the reserved parcel of Turner's sketchbooks, and have given no direction about them, and as the grossly obscene drawings contained in them could not be lawfully in anyone's possession, I am satisfied that you had no other course than to burn them, both for the sake of Turner's reputation (they having been assuredly drawn under a certain condition of insanity) and for your own peace. And I am glad to be able to bear witness to their destruction and I hereby declare that a parcel of them was undone by me, and all the obscene drawings it contained burnt in my presence in the month of December 1858.[17]

My argument is that, given Ruskin's full-blown interpretation of Turner, this act of vandalism was a contradictory one. Turner was certainly jealous of his reputation. He rose from humble origins to be a President of the Royal Academy who took his duties very seriously, lecturing students on perspective, helping fellow artists whenever possible, and contributing to annual exhibitions where he appeared to the public as a sort of wonder on 'touching days'. While contemporary accounts generally emphasise the assiduous academician, they also insist that he retained unmistakeable signs of where he came from. It is how his mate-rial origins fit with his later elevation that is in question here. Is the former a riposte to the latter, or the latter a sublimation of the former, or, as the vision Ruskin constructed out of his reading of Turner's paintings startlingly suggests, is there a collaboration of sorts?

Constable recalled first meeting Turner at an Academy dinner of 1813: 'I was a great deal entertained with Turner. I always expected to find him what I did. He is uncouth but has a wonderful range of mind.'[18] Clearly the material integument of Turner's life did not contribute to his admirable understanding. Presumably, on this view, the uncouthness inspired the sketches Ruskin burned. Turner's artistic intimacy with the urges most constructive of his life produced a dissociated rather than an integrated sensibility. Constable's Turner was no better than he should be; his imagination, as Ruskin was to put it, may have inhabited Carthage, but 'practically' he had to live in 'modern Margate'. But Turner's spots of commonness in fact indicated aspects of his sensibility which some of Ruskin's most mesmeric interpretations were to focus. Turner knew the worth of his own labour and was impolite enough to point it out to those who, like Sir Walter Scott, wrote desperately for money but maintained a dignified silence on the subject. According to Scott, 'Turner's palm is as itchy as his fingers are ingenious and he will, take my word for it, do nothing without cash, and any thing for it. He is almost the only man of genius I ever knew who is sordid in these matters'.[19] Early nineteenth-century critics and friends felt that Turner's success was in spite of his social background rather than an expression of it. In his *Recollections*, a fellow artist, George Jones, asks us to remember 'that in early life [Turner's] education had been defective, his associates of a class unlikely to elevate his mind, his reading, nothing. He had no one to impress upon him that disdain of mercenary feeling which ought to accompany genius.'[20]

While Ruskin missed in Turner that disdain of the sordid, he evidently valued the practical contact with the realities of economics and labour demonstrated in his art. The appreciations of Turner in *Modern Painters* are materialist. At first sight, Turner's progress is surely from the material to the immaterial. It is difficult to deny that his art becomes more atmospheric, impressionistic, less monumental, more interested in light. Ruskin builds, perhaps, on insights like those of Hazlitt. Hazlitt allowed Turner to be 'the ablest landscape painter now living'; he also thought his 'representations [to be] not so properly of the objects of nature as the medium through which they are seen'. Such phenomenology can, of course, pose as a form of realism. Hazlitt's frequent citing of Coleridge's opinion that Turner's landscape's 'were *pictures of nothing and very like*' is sympathetically buttressed by explanations of why they *could* be pictures of nothing, 'depicting the first chaos of the world ... [when]

"All is without form and void"'.[21] Coleridge himself elaborated this thought in the conclusion to the fourth of his *Lectures on the History of Philosophy*. There he describes a 'symbol' of death in a trecento painting as adequate to a productive formlessness with reference to the power of music to recall a formative childhood. The enforced synaesthesia, one art helping another, is instructive.[22] Ruskin arguably develops the onto-logical idiom here that links Turner's art to the depiction of the ontol-ogy out of which differentiation is visibly emerging, the differentiation from within which we are obliged retrospectively to construct our ideas of something anterior. Again we need the logic of Coleridge's 'tautegory' to explain why such expression avoids collapsing into the nugatory. Ruskin's interpretations almost always argue for Turner's grasp of the material conditions, ranging from the social to the geological, which produce the scenes he paints. Turner's vision of immanence, in Ruskin's eye, solicits the collaborative activity required to produce the idea of genesis, the idea on which his last paintings close, when he seems able to paint what produces his own art.

Turner's painterly grasp of natural productivity is not, Ruskin insists, disinterested; it significantly places objects in a particular kind of soci-ety, a mutual society, one might say. 'Composition', Ruskin declares, 'may be best defined as the help of everything in the picture by every-thing else'. For Ruskin, this mutual assistance or 'help' lets Turner's rep-resentation of nature describe the kind of society he wants to see established.

> The highest and first law of the universe – and the other name of life is, therefore, 'help'. The other name of death is 'separation'. Government and co-operation are in all things and eternally the laws of life. Anarchy and competition, eternally, and in all things, are the laws of death.[23]

There are undoubtedly limits to Ruskin's socialism, but, as expressed here in *Modern Painters*, these limits are not metaphysical ones. Ruskin's socialism becomes a socialism of nature, a scientific world-view insepa-rable from a politics, a partisan politics directed against the increasingly *laissez-faire* economism of his time. One might expect that paintings inspiring these critical principles would look unusual, or that they might at least transgress aesthetic convention. It is, though, an elaboration of Ruskin's philosophy, to see in Turner's impressionism an immense con-fidence that spectators will feel the pressure of a collaboration of absent powers legitimating the sketch and its sketchiness – making it thinkable as a sketch, an aspect. 'It is as the master of this science of *Aspects*, Ruskin famously concludes in his third volume, 'that [...] Turner must eventually be named always with Bacon, the master of the science of *Essence*'.[24]

If some of Turner's work strains our collaborative sympathy even now, the socialism behind Ruskin's claims for Turner's central representation of 'help' presumably does so as well. 'Help', thus understood, would not just have exonerated Coleridge from plagiarism, but would have made him exemplary: 'The greatest is he who has been oftenest aided.'[25] Sometimes it suggests a liberal idealisation of class difference. Ruskin worked hard to remain an optimist: in *Modern Painters*, he repeatedly makes the move, so enviable for a Victorian, from the idea of a divine principle in the universe to the burgeoning science of geology, so often a main stumbling block at the time to religious belief. The political colouring reflected back to Ruskin by Turner's view of nature's activity must have solved a few other local problems as well. Help came from all quarters, and to Ruskin's ear, 'the "Holy" one' was simply 'softer Saxon' for 'the Helpful One'.[26] Turner, author of the MS poem, 'The Fallacies of Hope', is ostensibly pessimistic, but only, I would venture, to the extent that his cooperative nature is presented as overriding immediate individual interests. Hence the characteristic canvases of disasters he conspicuously informed with the combinatory powers of nature. As negative images of auxiliary possibility, these share their socialising power with the contemporary pessimism of Leopardi. The Marxist critical tradition Leopardi excited was perhaps prefigured by the 'softer Saxon' of Ruskin's response to Turner.

Ruskin typically enhances Turner's wordy titles by telling stories about the paintings or playing games with them. The reader is frequently told to cover up a detail in order to see how the entire composition is affected. Or collaborative plots are uncovered by critical detective work. Here is Ruskin on a scene Turner painted below a waterfall on the Rhine.

> One of the gens-d'armes is flirting with a young lady in a round cap and full sleeves, under pretence of wanting her to show him what she has in her bandbox. The motive of which flirtation is, so far as Turner is concerned in it, primarily the bandbox: this and the millstones below, give him a series of concave lines, which, concentrated by the recumbent soldiers, intensify the hollow sweep of the fall [...].[27]

Victorians are always telling stories in paintings, or indulging in conspicuous literary pictorialism. More grandly, European aesthetic ambition in the nineteenth century arguably develops from Schlegel's *Mischgedicht* towards the Wagnerian *Gesamtkunstwerk* before its original ontological relativity hardens into *fin de siècle* aestheticism. Ruskin's story still retains the ontological resonance, though. The interpretation of aspects brings out the essence of the scene: this is Turner's collaborative design, in which flirting and geometry help each other to depict their natural possibility. The more stories you tell, the further away from the picture you get in your commentary, the more you evoke the mass of pressures helping to make of it the image it is. When Turner paints his homage to Byron, in 'Childe Harold's Pilgrimage – Italy' (1832), the generality of that 'Italy' focuses on the choice of aspect. Other works of the time – Staël's *Corinne, ou l'Italie* or Lady Morgan's (Sydney Owenson) *Italy*, Samuel Rogers' *Italy* (also illustrated by Turner, a copy of which he presented to the boy Ruskin) – are inspired by Italy to a holistic portrait whose implausible range must put into question portraiture itself. In Turner's case, the process of representation is rendered still more self-conscious by its reference to another example. Through his characteristic modifications of Claude's Italianate idiom, the framework within which Hazlitt thought Turner did his best work, he perhaps suggests Byron's own mixture, in Canto 4 of that poem, of regret for an idealised past with the determination of a modern poet to survive with an authority equal to that past, not as a *beau ideal* but as part of our language. But you have to read the whole poem before you can either quarrel with or accept this aspect as representative. Comparably, 'The Field of Waterloo' (1818) had shown the dead, among them the Cameronians (soldiers not covenanters) celebrated in Canto 3 of *Childe Harold*. The painting emphatically marginalised the glory of victory by the light of the burning farm of Hougomont. Byron's stanzas on Waterloo in *Childe Harold* are elevated and moralising, rather like Turner's own poetry. Byron only matches the painting later, in *Don Juan*. Turner's chiaroscuro recalls instead the lurid contrasts of Goya's *Pinturas negras*, the 'black' paintings which horrifically identify with the atrocities of the Peninsular War by lending to human gatherings the aspect of witches' Sabbaths. Turner's morbid aftermath of battle has to be scrutinised before we are sure of the helpfulness of the attitude of the women in the foreground.

In 'Ulysses deriding Polyphemus – Homer's Odyssey' (1829), the whole poem (or Pope's translation of it) is once more evoked, although this time through a recognisable incident. We see the moment when Odysseus mocks the Cyclops, telling him that ουδεις (no one) has blinded him: that is what he should inform his father, Poseidon. The Cyclops reclines in agony, but his blighted strength looks to be of a piece with the brilliant atmospherics and even the monumental geological forms which bring out Turner's painterliness. In the East, the horses of Apollo, another divine enemy against whom Odysseus has blasphemed, are visibly beginning to drag the sun across the sky. The sketch for the painting lacks Apollo and shows how Turner developed the plot. It is curious to try to read the painting in the manner I have attributed to Ruskin so far. For the painting sets story and image in opposition. Odysseus and Polyphemus scarcely *help* each other: the image is of the man's vision pitted against the elemental son of the ocean. The man wins by blinding the primitive, and then triumphing in his difference. But, as a latter-day anti-Hegelian, Adorno, points out, Odysseus's taunt likens him to what he scorns: 'the subject Odysseus denies his own identity, which makes him a subject, and keeps himself alive by imitating the amorphous'.[28] Or, to translate Adorno's perception into a problem for Ruskin, we might ask why we should subscribe to Ruskin's helpful, collaborative socialism of nature if it can be represented by an image of exactly the opposite? The same problem arose with the disaster canvases and Turner's pessimism generally. But Ruskin could argue that what Odysseus sees is not what Turner sees; the magnificence of the painting comes from the victim of the triumph, and the light by which we see it reminds us further of Odysseus's criminality. And this escapes simple moralism when one takes the further implication that the painting represents our own immanence within what produces our supposedly superior viewpoint, whose benevolence in so favouring us should not obscure our dependence upon it.

This returns me to those obscene drawings. In their case, isn't Ruskin a bit like Odysseus, seeing only an unsightly primitivism, uncouthly shrouded in vapour and obfuscation, when he should be seeing something else – the energies that harmonise Turner's paintings? In burning them, as Adorno might point out, Ruskin only imitates the conflagration of powers surrounding Polyphemus. In 1989 the Clore Gallery staged an exhibition called 'Turner and the Human Figure'. Some gestures were made towards including survivals recognisably belonging to Turner's erotica. The catalogue reproduces two nudes in black and white. The kind of thing that distressed Ruskin is described, not exhibited. We are told of the 1834 sketchbook, that 'several pages show two figures entangled. On f. 38, for example, the couple appear embracing as Titianesque lovers.'[29] You can find these two sketches in larger editions of Turner's work. The reason I haven't reproduced them is, I suspect, the reason they did not appear in 'Turner and the Human Figure'. They are steamy in both senses – the more involved the figures, the more atmospheric and indistinct their rendering. Following the painterly logic of 'Ulysses deriding Polyphemus', the logic adduced by Ruskin on other occasions, these sketches reinforce the idea that the most powerful representations of the sources of our individuation are those which impress us with the degree of collaboration they elicit from our reading, the relevant stories they can make us tell, the number of painterly gambits we can see as aspects of an essence. They force on us a kind of grammar of assent, secular assent to the view of nature as a sort of divine cooperative in Ruskin's not Newman's sense. The extant erotic sketches are not graphic, not crudely explicit; but perhaps just because of that, Ruskin destroyed the rest. They were too typical of Turner's art not to do the painter damage, and too much an invitation to Ruskin's storytelling not to compromise the critic. Yet the human figures peopling Turner's later work defer to atmospheric surroundings as the bearer of generative energy; or else they approximate to its entangled, undifferentiated weave. This is true of the vignette, 'The Fall of the Rebel Angels (c. 1834)', and also of that late amalgam of different stories, 'Light and Colour (Goethe's Theory) – the Morning after the Deluge – Moses writing the Book of Genesis' (1843). Moses, unlike Odysseus, is given a viewpoint inside what he is seeing; he helps the composition of what he is writing about; he is a cooperative agent in the history that produces him.

For Turner, colour was a thing, a material to be worked on to a surface with conspicuous labour. From Turner's last work you might surmise that the critical story has taken over from what it glosses, the theory from the representation. Turner's marginalia to Goethe's *Farbenlehre* reveal him thinking of light as an effect of colour, not something in itself. 'The Angel Standing in the Sun' (1846), then, shows the light of spiritual revelation to be a sensuous material thing, a surface scarred and pitted by manual labour. The painting confirms the paganism deduced by many from Turner's deathbed remark that 'the sun is God'; yet his achievement is a kind of *reductio* of the philosophy Ruskin articulated for him. This is because his Romantic explosion of light distils Turner's art down to a painting of how he thinks representation works. Gone is the collaborative invitation, soliciting from the critic the periphrastic indirections whose society implies the impossibility of any single viewpoint on what produces our differentiations of it. Now, paint paints paint. Our situatedness is unforgettably figured in technical self-consciousness, in the impasto that arrests us with its sculpture of its own translucent effect. A painting which signifies its own mode of representation does what all paintings do to some extent, but self-referentiality to the exclusion of everything else produces both a perfect representation and a tautology. Paint paints paint. In this dialectic of representation rather than Enlightenment, we struggle towards perfect representation only to find that, when we achieve it, perfection gets in the way. Perfection turns out not to have been a quality of our representation but what we have represented. Turner's sensuous success makes his lucidity grow opaque; clarity blinds us with the light of revelation. Those of Turner's final works mentioned above can perhaps only be the corollary of Ruskin's reading of Turner from the inside. Their tautology powerfully denies the possibility of an outside. That can be powerful enough, but it is only the premise from which the infinite critical conversation must begin.

Richards's Coleridge

This perception, grasped through the construction of Coleridge not Turner as critical object, is one of the main insights of I. A. Richards's book, *Coleridge on Imagination*, first published in 1934.[30] Coleridge's ambition, for Richards, is to get on terms, philosophically, with our containment within a world-picture of whose painterliness we become aware through the further awareness that we cannot say anything about it directly that isn't tautologous. Like Nietzsche, Richards thinks that all foundational discourses that do claim to describe us from the outside are myths. Science is simply a 'specialized type of myth' (174). Like Schelling and Coleridge, he thinks that we can read into different myths the same relativism, and that some myths are (tautegorically) especially inflected with this consciousness. The 'boundaries of the mythical' are also for Richards 'the bridle of Pegasus'. Myth is the category by which Richards settles the differences between 'projective' and 'realist' views of things, a questionable belief in whose opposition he thinks has been a damaging intellectual inheritance. 'My Coleridge', he tells T. S. Eliot, ' – after having been a goods train heavily if richly laden – has turned into a sort of meteor and gone up into the Heavens. It's now a revelation of the essential mythopoeic faculty [...]'.[31] The external view of the nature to whose reality we contribute is something we can only access in the shape of a further projection that adds to rather than circumscribes that reality.

> We can say nothing of it and think nothing of it without producing a myth. It is the whatever it is in which we live: and there we have to leave it; for to say more of it is not to speak of it, but of the modes of our life in it. For us, it *can* be only – but it also *must* be – such that *all* the modes of our life are supported by it.
>
> (*Coleridge on Imagination*, 181)

Myth, then, signals the abandonment of a monologic science, one that, strictly speaking, ought to be tautologous, to take up a variety of discursive alternatives. It turns the abandonment of a single position of adjudication on the nature of the world into a post-metaphysical one full of collaborative, tautegorical compensations. It is a mistake to think of this immersion in variety as a decline. We should happily court 'every mode of the mythopoeic activity by which we live, shape universes to live in, reshape, inquire, in a thousand varying ways [...]' (212). Richards carries further Coleridge's objection to imposing an 'Act of Uniformity' upon poets and proposes a view of tradition as a confluence rather than a direct, monolithic mode of transmission. He has a lively awareness of the political disasters brewing in Europe at the time, 1934. His interest in Chinese philosophy and culture makes him sense the impending disaster of Japanese imperialism, and he sees no help in the 'Anglo-Catholic tendency' gaining authority in the English letters of his day.[32] His book on Coleridge burst out of a scholarly format to become an essay *in* Coleridge, one in which the ineffability of ultimate truth is a rebuke to 'the exorbitant claims of any one myth' (such as an Anglo-Catholic one) and a spur to diversify intellectually in the awareness that this is sufficient indication of the linguistic scope of our existence.

Richards is an optimist and a modernist. He can sound like an eighteenth-century common sense philosopher searching out a psychology on analogy with Baconian science. He shares the common-sense philosopher's confidence, in his own case inspired by Coleridge, that, powered by a linguistic turn, philosophy can establish a science of mind.

> With Coleridge we step across the threshold of a general theoretical study of language capable of opening to us new powers over our minds comparable to those which systematic physical inquiries are giving us over our environment.
>
> (232)

This optimism must be situated, though, by the anti-foundationalism of the rest of his book. He constantly looks for both/and rather than either/or solutions. He is a partisan modernist to the extent that he can think that the literature of his own time is a progression in some respects over previous literature. But his championing of the enhanced psychological skill he commends in Joyce, Mansfield, Woolf and others never inhibits the philosophical generosity he believes he has learned from Coleridge's demonstration that 'to ask about the meaning of words is to ask about everything' (xi). He privileges poetry over other discourses, and symbolist poetry over other kinds, at the expense of a just consideration of Coleridge's theology. He mistakes Fichte for Schelling in Coleridge's writings (68–9), and doesn't pursue Coleridge's historical understanding of 'philology' to its sources in Schellingian ontology (20–1n.), missing out on crucial historical support for his own argument and so leaving space for mine! But he writes as a 'Benthamite' and a materialist about a thinker he takes to be his opposite, 'an extreme Idealist', and expects his own remarks to be reinterpreted in their turn (18–19). Ruskin, too, had been 'brought continually into collision with the German mind by [his] own steady pursuit of Naturalism as opposed to idealism'. And Richards's biographer, John Paul Russo, claims that 'Richards became a "devotee" of the fourth volume of Ruskin's *Modern Painters* ...'.[33] To champion Coleridge did not mean that Locke and the empiricist tradition were 'false', but, once more, they do show Richards the unfortunate tendency of one of our language-games to arrogate all the others. Like Schlegel, Richards understands the poetic ordering of words in political terms as a broad republic, one ranging from a Lucretian-sounding federation of significant parts to a more centralised model. To call, with Coleridge, the critical preference for one society of words over another an 'act of Uniformity', only resumes his ever-present, sharp sensitivity to the political figurations of linguistic expression.[34] He happily quotes authors as diverse as Lenin and Chuang Tzu in support of his underlying claim that all we can say directly about ontology is that it exists outside our cognition, which non-statement is also the silence of the Tao. The rest is demonstration of the impossibility of cognition thus to get behind itself, and the collaboration of its different discourses in elaborating a consequent sense of situatedness: in bringing, in Coleridge's and Schelling's adaptation of Schiller, 'the whole soul of man into activity' (158–9, 184–6).[35] This 'synaesthesis', as he and his friends called it in the 1920s, propels aesthetics out of isolation and into collaboration.

The example of Richards brings into sharper relief how tautegory can be threatened as much by tautology as it was by allegory and its older Romantic rivals. In Schelling's and Coleridge's day, the reflexivity that could imagine a trans-subjective ontology was newly accredited as a philosophical exercise, whatever existence it already had enjoyed in other expressions. The logic of this achievement, though, was to return the insight to the other discourses, to intersubjectivity generally, since its import was that Being was only to be grasped indirectly through an increased sense of the humanness it had produced. Increasingly, though, the ambition must have arisen to make of that ineluctable mediation a discrete aesthetic object. The truer its representation, though, the more that medium must simply paint itself. Turner's know-ing, final adventures in this field are one thing. Richard's targets are another: the authoritarian presumption either to pronounce, impossi-bly, on one's own production, or to presume over other equally legiti-mate expressions of our mythic condition. Richards's pluralism, learnt from Coleridge's linguistic turn, recovers Schelling's and Coleridge's original resistance to that overweening historicism of the higher critics unproductive of a self-critical history of the present. They also assumed an enlightened power to decode the past that actually restricted their capacity to perceive different ways of being human. They privileged the religious understanding of their own day over those that they believed could be reduced to allegories of it; they thus forgot the mythic status of their own science. Put that way, their sins can be seen clearly to con-verge with those Richards so sharply attributed to his own opponents and his critique to revive the Coleridgean tradition he is describing.

Notes

1. Compare Ross Wilson, 'Coleridge and the Life of Language', *Coleridge Bulletin* n.s. 27 (Summer 2006), 38–44.
2. For speculations on Coleridge's possible etymological grasp of Logos, à la Heidegger, as signifying a 'gathering together', see the editors' 'Prolegomena' to Coleridge's *Opus Maximum*, cix.
3. See Martin Heidegger, *Introduction to Metaphysics*, trans. Ralph Mannheim (New Haven and London: Yale University Press, 1959), p. 128, where the idea of Logos as 'collecting collectedness' is a way of signifying 'neither meaning nor word nor doctrine'. For a convincing comparative reading of Coleridge and Heidegger see A. J. Harding, 'Imagination, Patriarchy and Evil in Coleridge and Heidegger', *Studies in Romanticism*, 35 (1996), 3–26.
4. All references to Schelling are to F. W. J. Schelling, *Sämmtliche Werke*, ed. K. W. F. Schelling, part I, vols 1–10, part II, vols 11–14 (Stuttgart: Cotta, 1856–61).
5. Nigel Leask, *The Politics of Imagination in Coleridge's Political Thought* (Basingstoke: Macmillan, 1988), which set new standards for the political interpretation of Romantic epistemology, is the key text here.
6. 'On the Prometheus of Aeschylus; An Essay, preparatory to a series of Disquisitions respecting the Egyptian in Connection with the Sacerdotal Theology, and in contrast with the Mysteries of Ancient Greece', *SWF* II, 1267–8.
7. *Shorter Works and Fragments*, 2 vols, ed. H. J. Jackson, and J. R de J. Jackson, (1995), II, 1276.
8. Søren Kierkegaard, *Fear and Trembling; Repetition*, ed. and trans. H. V. Hong and E. H. Hong (Princeton, NJ: Princeton University Press, 1983), pp. 229, 304. For Kierkegaard, '*repetition* is a crucial expression for what "recollection" was to the Greeks', pp. 131, 148–9. There are other Schellingian formulations and *reprises* throughout.

9. See Alberto Toscano's lucid discussion of the connections between Schelling's versatility then and his appeal now to many different philosophical approaches in 'Philosophy and the Experience of Construction', in *The New Schelling*, ed. Judith Norman, and Alistair Welchman (London and New York: Continuum Books, 2004), esp. pp. 106–10.

10. Richard Eldridge, *The Persistence of Romanticism; Essays in Philosophy and Literature* (Cambridge: Cambridge University Press, 2001), p. 193.

11. See Edward Allen Beach's knowledgeable and helpful contextualization of Schelling's philosophy of mythology in his 'Introduction' and early chapters of *The Potencies of God(s): Schelling's Philosophy of Mythology* (Albany, NY: SUNY Press, 1994).

12. Ibid., p. 10–11 for a discussion of the controversy raised by Creuzer's work; see Georg Friedrich Creuzer, *Symbolik und Mythologie der alten Völker, besonders der Griechen*, 4 vols (1810–2).

13. *The Notebooks of Samuel Taylor Coleridge*, 5 vols, ed. Kathleen Coburn, Merton Christenson and Anthony John Harding (Princeton, NJ: Princeton University Press, 1957–2002), IV, 4832. Still one of the clearest discussions of the linguistic terminology I am obliged to use here is Umberto Eco, *Semiotics and the Philosophy of Language* (London: Macmillan, 1984).

14. Douglas Hedley, *Coleridge, Philosophy and Religion; 'Aids to Reflection' and the Mirror of the Spirit* (Cambridge: Cambridge University Press, 2000), pp. 144–5, 135.

15. Schelling's main target here is Euhemerism, or 'ungelehrter Euemerismus' (II / 1. 233). He might as well have chosen to attack Vico's socio-economic reductions of myth although he might have felt affinities with his idea of their *ricorsi* or historical recurrence.

16. *Opus Maximum*, ed. Thomas McFarland (Princeton, NJ: Princeton University Press, 2002), xc.

17. Letter discovered by Andrew Wilton, quoted in *J. M. W. Turner*, ed. Guy Weelen (New York and London: Alpine Fine Arts, 1982), 115 n. 2.

18. *John Constable's Correspondence*, II: *Suffolk Records Society*, VI (1964), p. 110. Constable's phrase furnishes the title of John Gage's fine book, *J. M. W. Turner: A Wonderful Range of Mind* (New Haven and London: Yale University Press, 1987).

19. See Jack Lindsay, *Turner: A Critical Biography* (London: Cory, Adams & MacKay, 1960), p. 84. Scott was complimentary enough in his *Journal* an elsewhere about Turner's illustrations to his *Poetical Works*. Scott's publisher at this time, Robert Cadell, found Turner 'very common looking', quoted by Jan Piggott, *Turner's Vignettes* (London: Tate Gallery Publications, 1993), p. 53.

20. *Collected Correspondence of J. M. W. Turner, With an Early Diary and a Memoir by George Jones* (Oxford: Clarendon Press, 1980), p. 2.

21. *The Complete Works of William Hazlitt*, ed. P. P. Howe (London: Dent, 1930–3), 21 vols, IV, 76n.

22. *Lectures 1818–1819: On the History of Philosophy*, 2 vols, ed. J. R. de J. Jackson (Princeton, NJ: Princeton University Press, 2000), I, 195–7.

23. John Ruskin, *Collected Works*, ed. A. Wedderburn and E. T. Cook (London: George Allen, 1903–12), 39 vols, VII, 205, 207.

24. *Works*, VII, 387.

25. 'Finally, touching on plagiarism in general, it is to be remembered that all men who have sense and feeling are being continually helped [...] The greatest is he who has been oftenest aided [...]' *Works*, V, 330.
26. *Works*, VII, 206
27. *Works*, VII, 222.
28. T. Adorno and M. Horkheimer, *The Dialectic of Enlightenment*, trans. John Cumming (London: Verso, 1979), p. 67.
29. *Turner and the Human Figure: Studies of Contemporary Life*, ed. Ann Chumbley, and Ian Worrell (London: Tate Gallery Publications, 1989), p. 30.
30. I. A. Richards, *Coleridge on Imagination* (London: Routledge and Kegan Paul, 1934, 3rd edition with a new Foreword by Kathleen Coburn, 1962). References are made to this edition in the text.
31. *Selected Letters of I. A. Richards*, ed. John Constable (Oxford: Clarendon Press, 1990), p. 77 (to T. S. Eliot, 22 March 1934).
32. Richards's critical biographer, John Paul Russo, is sure that 'the last chapters of *Coleridge on Imagination* should be read with the historical situation of the mid 1930s in mind. Depicting a "wrecked universe" and the competition of warlike myths, Richards never made a more impassioned plea on behalf of the "myth-making" power of imagination as the "necessary channel for reconstitution of order", *I. A. Richards: His Life and Work* (London: Routledge, 1989), p. 384. For his description of how the Japanese invasion of China put paid to Richards's attempts successfully 'to put my recommendations based on Basic English' to the Chinese government, see *Complementarities: Uncollected Essays*, ed. John Paul Russo (Manchester: Carcanet, 1976), pp. 262–3.
33. *Works*, V, 424; Russo, *I. A. Richards: His Life and Work*, p. 593.
34. *Collected Letters*, I. 279 (to John Thelwall).
35. In chapter XV, 'Synaesthesis', of Richards's youthful collaboration with C. K. Ogden and James Wood, this genealogy is noted. 'It is surprising that, whatever its value, Schiller's theory has not attracted more attention. In Germany it seems to have been absorbed into metaphysical speculations such as those of Schelling [...]' *The Foundations of Aesthetics*, reprint of 2nd edition of 1925 (New York: Haskell House Publishers, 1974), p. 86.

12
Imagination Amended: From Coleridge to Collingwood

Douglas Hedley

Mentre ch'alla beltà, ch'i' viddi in prima
Apresso l'alma, che per gli occhi vede,
L'immagin dentro crescie, e quella cede
Quasi vilmente e senza alcuna stima.[1]

One of the most distinguished English philosophers of the twentieth century was R. G. Collingwood (1889–1943). Despite a glitteringly successful career, Collingwood is an oddly isolated figure in twentieth-century philosophy. He had little sympathy for realistic positivism or philosophy as analysis, which he contemptuously rejects as the pedantry and errors of the 'minute philosophers'. His work explores various forms of the spirit in art, science, and religion. Like the Italian philosopher Giambattista Vico (1668–1744), Collingwood places great emphasis upon history and imagination. His work contains quite distinct phases. In *Speculum Mentis* (1924) he takes a conventional Hegelian view of art as superseded; in *The Principles of Art* (1938) art has a more elevated role in the expression of what cannot be otherwise asserted or described. He is often associated with his older contemporary, the Italian idealist aesthetician Benedetto Croce (1866–1952), but Collingwood differs from Croce on salient points; Collingwood's debt to the older 'poetic logic' of Vico may be just as deep.

The enduring legacy of the seminal art critic and social reformer John Ruskin (1819–1900) is, I think, pivotal for the formation of Collingwood's mind. Doubtless it was not merely the melancholy phase of Ruskin's final troubled years in Brantwood in the Lake District that must have left a deep impression upon the young R. G. Collingwood. As the most profound and subtle advocate of the Gothic revival, Ruskin's enthusiasms for Turner and the Pre-Raphaelites, French Gothic and Venetian architecture are all part of a mission to instruct his contemporaries on how to 'see clearly'. As the Slade Professor at Oxford, and through his monthly *Fors Clavigera: Letters to the Workmen and Labourers of Great Britain,* Ruskin exerted a huge influence. William Morris and the Working Men's College Movement are instances of this. Yet I suggest that the trajectory from John Ruskin to R. G. Collingwood in English aesthetics is an instance of the remarkable and enduring legacy of Coleridge.

Born and bred in the lakes, where his father, W. G. Collingwood, was John Ruskin's friend, secretary and biographer, Collingwood was both an historian and a philosopher: at Pembroke College, Oxford, from 1912, and then as Waynflete Professor of Metaphysical Philosophy from 1934–41. Aesthetics was a fundamental concern and he developed the theory that the expression of the creative imagination is the key to genuine art:

> The aesthetic experience, or artistic activity, is the experience of expressing one's emotions; and that which expresses them is the total imaginative activity called indifferently language or art.[2]

This is a paradigmatically Romantic view of the artist as possessor of a unique aesthetic sensibility, reminiscent of Wordsworth's famous definition in the Preface to the *Lyrical Ballads*: 'all good poetry is the spontaneous overflow of powerful feelings'.[3]

Coleridge, Ruskin, and Collingwood share a theory of art that opposes any crudely mimetic, mechanical model of artistic creation, while avoiding the other extreme of aesthetic subjectivism or projectivism. All three share an insistence upon the moral component of true art. All share the Neoplatonic concern for a robustly metaphysical theory of art together with an insistence upon the value of the inner eye of the artist and audience. Coleridge's reflections upon imagination, combined with his theory of the clerisy, provide a good model for appreciating the interests and obsessions of both Ruskin and Collingwood.

Coleridge on imagination

Take Coleridge's much discussed distinction between 'fancy' as 'an aggregative and associative power' and 'imagination' as a 'shaping and modifying power'.[4] The imagination is linked to the unconscious as well as to the will. The imagination is more primordial and inscrutable than fancy. Fancy is a 'mode of Memory emancipated from the order of time and space' (*BL* I, 305). This is the capacity of the mind to represent and combine remembered images. As such the term 'fancy' is not meant pejoratively; fancy is not bad as such, and can have a perfectly respectable and indeed necessary function. It is hard to see how we could negotiate and adapt to the world without the capacity to use memory in this way. Empiricists, from Aristotle to Hobbes, are correct to emphasise the importance of memory employed to such ends, but are wrong to identify this with the imagination in its most important meaning. Imagination is more than the mere reconstitution of items of memory into a new set of relations: it is a fusing power that produces a new unity.

The 'synthetic and magical power' of imagination (*BL* II, 16) is both higher and, as it were, lower than fancy. Imagination, that is, is more closely bound to the primordial unconscious power of the soul and to Divine inspiration than the mundane fancy. The activity of the fancy is more narrowly instrumental: it furnishes the means by which certain images, 'fixities and definites' (*BL* I, 305), are modified though choice for certain ends. The creative imagination is not an agency of expedience or contrivance but the light and energy of soul as it relishes truth: knowledge 'wedded' to feeling. In human beings, pre-eminently the artist of genius, unconscious nature becomes aware of itself as spirit, in articulate self-awareness. In artistic expression, nature is revealed as slumbering spirit: the intelligible fabric of the natural world becomes transparent. This concept of expression is linked to the deeply Romantic-Coleridgean idea of genius. Genius is able to make the external internal and the internal external, 'to make nature thought and thought nature'.[5]

Coleridge's point, however, is that the relatively unproblematic mechanical mental capacity should not be confused with the vastly more mysterious, vital, and creative imagination, which endeavours to see reality as a whole. The artistic imagination experiments with parts in order to create a new and beautiful whole, the attainment of which requires moral effort. The creation of a work of art as world *sui generis* cannot be intelligibly reduced to simple mechanisms of addition and comparison. The poet 'diffuses a tone, and spirit of unity, that blends, and (as it were) *fuses*, each into each, by that synthetic and magical power, to which we have exclusively appropriated the name of imagination' (*BL* II, 16). One might compare Collingwood's emphasis on seeing parts as a whole, a capacity that belongs most distinctively to imagination. As Coleridge declares: 'The poet, described in *ideal* perfection, brings the whole soul of man into activity' (*BL* II, 15–16). Here the artistic imagination is not the unshackled outpouring of emotional forces or the mere receptivity of sensibility; it is a discipline and endeavour to realise one's being. Art for Coleridge is not a skill or craft that effects certain emotions, nor is it the production of certain artefacts, it is rather the imaginative communication with another rational soul, the '*compact* between the poet and his reader', poetry making us poets (*BL* II, 65–6). Collingwood writes in *The Principles of Art*: 'As Coleridge put it, we know a man for a poet by the fact that he makes us poets. We know that he is expressing his emotions by the fact that he is enabling us to express ours' (118).

Collingwood distinguishes crafts like those of the blacksmith or the tailor, whereby the craftsman knows what he is doing with the hammer and the anvil or the needle and the materials – imposing form upon a certain matter in order to achieve a specific end – from arts where the artist characteristically does not know what he is creating until it finds expression. The unconscious is made conscious of itself through the creative imagination. As Coleridge observes:

> [...] the sense of musical delight, with the power of producing it, is a gift of imagination; and this together with the power of reducing multitude into unity of effect, and modifying a series of thoughts by some one predominant thought or feeling, may be cultivated and improved, but can never be learnt. It is in these that "Poeta nascitur non fit."
>
> (*BL* II, 20)

In *The Principles of Art*, first published in 1938, Collingwood argues that art is the manifestation and realization of that which is 'in the head' of the artist. The piece of marble or the paint on the canvas is not strictly the work of art. This view is at odds with the dominant positions of the twentieth century, which tended to define art in external terms: whether functionalist accounts, that define art in terms of particular social ends or purposes; or procedural accounts, which define art in terms of the methods employed in the public domain or institutions to furnish the work with meaning. Even Gadamer's polemic against aesthetics can be seen as a rejection of a romantic tradition of art being inherently 'in the mind'.[6]

Collingwood asserts that the imagination is ubiquitous: 'Regarded as names for a certain kind or level of experience, the words consciousness and imagination are synonymous' (*Principles of Art*, 215). This is an anti-empiricist polemic that he shares with Coleridge and Kant.

Perception of an object always involves more than sense data, it involves the imagining of properties which are not disclosed to the senses, or noticing, i.e. looking at or attending to what is seen. Hence there is a continuity between the imaginative component in habitual perceptual experience and in artistic vision. With a Ruskinian flourish, Collingwood observes: 'Only a person who paints well can see well; and conversely [...] only a person who sees well can paint well' (*Principles of Art*, 304). He suggests that 'one paints a thing in order to see it'. This seeing refers not to sensation but to awareness. Awareness presupposes sensation but involves self-consciousness and the power of the mind itself. Rather than the power of the sensation on the mind (imagine here a raw pain), the mind is asserting itself upon the data of experience, not as a group of unrelated items but as 'a single indivisible unity' (*Principles of Art*, 223).

For both Coleridge and Collingwood there is an analogous relationship between art and religion because of the ineluctable role of imaginative creativity in both domains and the non-mechanical nature of such creativity. There are no rules which can exhaustively define the truly artistic activity. Secondly, true art is imaginative and is thus 'in the head' of both artist and audience because art is a seeing or hearing the invisible or inaudible. Its power lies in that which it evokes through its materials, not in the materials themselves. This is a view of art which is ultimately grounded in Platonic polemics against Stoic materialism, which defined beauty exhaustively in terms of qualities such as proportion and colour.[7] For the Neoplatonists, the inner eye or the imagination can perceive the images of the sensible world as furnishing pointers to the intelligible domain.

Coleridge and Ruskin were both deeply influenced by this lofty strain of Platonic theorising about art as metaphysical. Art mirrors the divine order through the work of imagination. Notwithstanding Ruskin's polemics about the art around Lorenzo de Medici, Ruskin shares the view of art as essentially an index of the spiritual that was immensely influential in the Renaissance. Anthony Blunt writes:

> For Michelangelo it is by means of the imagination that the artist attains to a beauty above that of nature, and in this he appears as a Neoplatonist compared with the rational Alberti. To him beauty is the reflection of the divine in the material world.[8]

Michelangelo (1475–1564) was reared in the intensely Neoplatonic milieu of the Medici circle and came especially under the influence of its *spiritus rector*, Marsilio Ficino (1433–99). Michelangelo was fascinated by the concept of the 'inward image which the beauty of the visible world arouses in his mind'. The creative imagination, rather than formal norms of beauty, determines the work of Michelangelo; interior vision, or the 'concetto', is paramount rather than the formal or material properties of an artistic object. Hence, in carving away at the block of marble, the artist is discovering the idea of the sculpture that existed in his own mind. The sculpture is primarily 'in his head'.

Like Neoplatonists such as Michelangelo or Coleridge, Collingwood is a philosopher who argues for the metaphysical dignity of art. It is on the basis of this high view of art that Collingwood distinguishes art from craft. Collingwood is determined to distinguish between what counts as art *per se*, and then to distinguish between good and bad art. This is very much the Ruskinian legacy in Collingwood: to separate genuine art from that which is bogus, and great art from the rest. The defining characteristic of art is inextricably normative:

> What the artist is trying to do is to express a given emotion. To express it, and to express it well, are the same thing. To express it badly is not one way of expressing it [...], it is failing to express it. A bad work of art is an activity in which the agent tries to express a given emotion, but fails. This is the difference between bad art and art falsely so called [...]. In art falsely so called there is no failure to express, because there is no attempt at expression; there is only an attempt (whether successful or not) to do something else.
>
> (*Principles of Art*, 282)

Bad art is the denial or 'repression' of feelings: the 'corruption of consciousness'. Here Collingwood refers to Freud's language of repression and projection as the disowning of aspects of one's conscious experience and attributing them to other agents. Collingwood links this to Spinoza's ideal of self mastery through transforming passive into active emotions in his *Ethics*. It was Spinoza who best delineated 'the conception of the truthful consciousness and its importance as a foundation for a healthy mental life'.[9]

> Art is not a luxury, and bad art is not a thing we can afford to tolerate. To know ourselves is the foundation of all life that develops beyond the mere psychical level of experience. [...] Every utterance and every gesture that each one of us makes is a work of art. It is important to each one of us that in making them, however much he

deceives others, he should not deceive himself. If he deceives himself in this matter, he has sown in himself a seed which, unless he roots it up again, may grow into any kind of wickedness, any kind of mental disease, any kind of stupidity and folly and insanity. Bad art, the corrupt consciousness, is the true *radix malorum*.

(*Principles of Art*, 284–5)

The theory of art is linked to Collingwood's theory of 'the decay of our civilisation' and his view that most of what passes for art in a decadent civilisation is mere amusement (*Principles of Art*, 332). Both Coleridge and Collingwood present a robustly metaphysical theory of art, linked to both a theory of mind and society.

Art and the clerisy

The artist, on Collingwood's view, fulfils the role of one of Coleridge's clerisy: one who diffuses spiritual cultivation as a counterweight to the dominance of the utilitarian-commercial spirit. Like Coleridge, Collingwood saw philosophy as being tied to the health of the nation, and like Coleridge he claimed that 'the vital warmth at the heart of a civilisation is what we call religion'.[10] Stephan Collini has recently observed: 'Though not normally placed in this company, Collingwood surely belongs in these respects on the conservative wing of the so-called "culture and society tradition", with its deep yearning for the modern world to go away'. This seems a rather harsh judgement upon a man who died in 1943, and who possessed a deep admiration for those parliamentary traditions attacked by both right and left throughout Europe. In the face of communism and fascism as the 'two warring creeds which are dividing the inheritance of nineteenth-century liberalism', Collingwood's cultural pessimism had much empirical justification (*Principles of Art*, 71). But it seems correct to place Collingwood in the company of writers such as Eliot and Dawson, part of an 'anti-Utilitarian, anti-"pagan", consensus'.[11]

As a practising historian, Collingwood's philosophical reflections are often informed by his work on Roman antiquity. But he shares with Vico the anti-Cartesian position that history and art furnish a mode of knowledge which cannot be reduced to experimental methods:

The reason why the civilisation of 1600–1900, based upon natural science, found bankruptcy staring it in the face was because, in its passion for ready-made rules, it had neglected to develop that kind of insight which alone could tell it what rules to apply, not in a situation of a specific type, but in the situation in which it actually found itself. It was precisely because history offered us something altogether different from rules, namely insight, that it could afford us the help we needed in diagnosing our moral and political problems.[12]

One might compare this remark of Collingwood with Coleridge's cognate complaint in the *Lay Sermons* about the 'barren fig tree of the mechanic philosophy' and the 'OVERBALANCE OF THE COMMERCIAL SPIRIT' since 1688.[13] Such 'insight' required in historical judgement, morality or politics is essentially imaginative rather than deductive or inductive, though it must not be confused with make-believe or fantasy. It is fitting that one of the last and greatest of the British Idealists should develop such a Coleridgean theme. He provides a theory of the essence of art and provides a normative theory of what counts as genuine as opposed to bogus art. In conscious opposition to both aesthetical dandyism (e.g. Wilde and the Bloomsbury group) and popular emotive literature and art (like Kipling or left-wing political writers of the day) he upholds a sternly high-minded, even Brahminical, view of the vocation of the artist in society.

From Coleridge to Ruskin

John Ruskin's debt to Coleridge is hard to estimate with any accuracy. *Prima facie* the influence seems deep but unspecific. In Collingwood's *The Art Teaching of John Ruskin* we find a most positive account of Coleridge's influence upon Ruskin:

> The school to which Ruskin belongs in thought is that connected on the one hand with romanticism, and on the other with transcendentalism, originating in Germany, and spreading to England through Coleridge and Carlyle. It is difficult to trace the exact affiliation of the doctrines of *Modern Painters* to any given writings of the school; but in a different way they, and all Mr Ruskin's thought on other matters than Art, run parallel with German thinking, in spite of his disclaimer. In this matter of beauty he seems to have received the first hints from Coleridge, and, finding a justification of his belief in Aristotle, to have worked out his theory independently.[14]

Ruskin was 'really on the side of those who have popularised German philosophy of Kant, Fichte and Hegel in the country. The first of these acclimatisers of Transcendentalism was S. T. Coleridge'.[15] Even though Ruskin was not pursuing Coleridge's specific distinctions or proposals – the particular critical genius of each man lay in very different fields: literature and fine art – Ruskin was following Coleridge in the temper of his thought and some central tenets. Ruskin, like Coleridge, regards beauty as a spiritual phenomenon: quite distinct from the merely agreeable, which is grounded in instinct and desire.[16]

Ruskin is famous for his eloquent defence of the supremely imaginative vision of Turner and a repudiation of sterile models of artistic imitation. 'To see clearly is poetry, prophecy and religion, all in one'.[17] Real art, for Ruskin, cannot be confused with imitation because of the necessarily selective work of imagination and the expressive element involved in depictive representations. The popular contrast between art as mimetic and art as expression is quite erroneous for Ruskin, as it is for Plotinus, Michelangelo or Coleridge, for the Neoplatonic reason that the creative imagination imitates the archetypes not the ectypes of objects. The vision of the true artist is concentrated upon reality not appearances.

Here we have the foundation for an important distinction for Ruskin between real and sham art. Real art is not dependent upon tools or mechanical procedures but is grounded in the exercise of man's spiritual nature; 'the very life of man, considered as a seeing creature'. The 'spiritual seeing' that plays such a central role for Ruskin requires three tenets: Firstly, that earthly beauty bears some analogy to divine glory and that the creative activity of the artist reflects God's creation. Secondly, that the artist cannot be seen in isolation from the values of a particular society, and that art has an inherently moral content. Thirdly, regarding the dynamics of perception, that the 'seeing' is not to be construed in empiricist terms as the recording of verifiable data, but as ineluctably imaginative. Hence Turner's landscapes are discussed in conjunction with the visionary landscapes of poets such as Homer, Dante and Walter Scott. Beauty cannot be constructed out of natural features of the world such as desire, habit or custom, or association of ideas. Beauty is neither arbitrary nor conventional, but an intrinsic quality, an index of the sacramental nature of the created realm. To contemplate nature fully is to see it as the manifestation of divine attributes. Thus Beauty must be understood independently of instrumental considerations, although its habitual force must be appreciated in connection with customs, propensities and practices. The true artist is a seer.

Collingwood's intellectual background

R. G. Collingwood writes of Ruskin:

> It was not till the seventies, when a few enterprising young men in Oxford began to expound Hegel to their pupils, that ideas akin to those which formed Ruskin's philosophy became part of the mainstream of academic thought in this country. Ruskin had been applying in practice since 1840 the philosophical system of which the theory was first published in English by James Hutchison Stirling in that queer, incoherent, isolated book *The Secret of Hegel*, and was taken up in the following decade by Wallace and Bradley and others, and in a modified form by T. H. Green.[18]

John Ruskin was appointed in 1870 to the Slade Professorship of Art. This provided an ideal platform for Ruskin's Platonism, with its intense appeal to art and beauty as providing a basis for fundamental economic and social reforms. The awareness of beauty is linked to a sense of the sacred and Ruskin was the pre-eminent champion of the Gothic revival. But Platonism was also linked to the Oxford interest in Hegel. Benjamin Jowett of Balliol College, Oxford, who translated the dialogues of Plato, was both a Platonist and a Hegelian, an intellectual combination that could claim kinship with Coleridge. Coleridge, for instance, interprets Plato's dialectic in the following manner: 'Plato's works are preparatory exercises of the mind. He leads the mind to see that contradictory propositions are each true—which therefore *must* belong to a higher Logic—that of Ideas. They are contradictory only in the Aristotelean Logic'.[19] Or in another passage 'Plato discovered the insufficiency of the Understanding *indirectly*, by contradictions'.[20] A later translator of Plato, Paul Shorey, diagnosed this version of dialectic as leading to the *coincidentia oppositorum* as contaminating Jowett. 'This Coleridgean poison', thunders Shorey:

> has been widely diffused by Jowett, who attributes to Plato a Hegelian Logic of the future – which is the polar antithesis of the true Platonic dialectic.[...] The higher logic is to philosophy, what the higher law is to a criminal court – an evasion of responsibility.[21]

The leading British Hegelian in Victorian times was T. H. Green, like Jowett a Fellow at Balliol, who argued that the effective force of truth, beauty and goodness cannot be captured by empiricism. Green was appointed to a chair in 1878 and was succeeded by Edward Caird, another Platonic-Hegelian, after Green's untimely death. R. G. Collingwood dedicated *Speculum Mentis* to his father, W. G. Collingwood, as his 'First and Best teacher in Art, Religion Science, History and Philosophy'. Hence the family influence was a clearly deep. William Johnston remarks:

> Collingwood did not achieve a vision of the unity of experience by setting out to resurrect Hegel. Indeed the vision came to him not from books at all. Rather it was transmitted to him by his father, who had received it from John Ruskin. If Collingwood reincarnated many of Hegel's achievements and still more of his goals, the capacity to do so came not from Hegel but from Ruskin.[22]

Johnston notes that 'few of R. G. Collingwood's achievements as a thinker would be conceivable if he had not received from his father a Ruskinian education'.[23]

Imitation and expression

There is a popular story of Western aesthetics which traces a shift from an objectivist mimetic model of art mirroring nature to a more modern, 'Romantic' model of art as expressing the subjectivity of the artist: the paradigm of the 'lamp'.[24] According to this story, Coleridge and Collingwood belong to the latter 'Romantic', i.e. expressivist and subjectivist, paradigm. Aesthetics as a specific philosophical discipline is a very recent development in the history of thought, unknown to ancient and medieval philosophers. The very term 'aesthetics', a coinage of the eighteenth-century German philosopher Alexander Baumgarten, seems to usher an age of subjectivism and expressivism, in contrast with the classical and medieval tradition of art as essentially representative: *mimesis*. However, Stephen Halliwell has eloquently attacked such a schematic view of the history of thinking about art and argues for 'a significant degree of both historical and conceptual continuity'.[25] Halliwell also warns against the misleading assumption that *mimesis* can be straightforwardly translated as 'imitation'; he rightly insists that *mimesis* in some of the key ancient thinkers often includes rather than excludes expression.

Thus the theories of Coleridge and Collingwood may be best seen as 'mimetic' in this wider sense that maintains the centrality of expression. Both writers are adamant that art does far more than merely express subjective emotings. This becomes clear in Coleridge's view of the primary imagination as 'a repetition in the finite mind of the eternal act of creation in the infinite I AM' and hence as imitating the Divine creativity (*BL* II, 304). Collingwood's parallel rejection of subjectivism is most strongly evident in the closing words of *The Principles of Art*, in which he discusses Eliot's *The Waste Land* in a hierophantic tone of Ruskinian solemnity:

> The artist must prophesy not in the sense that he foretells things to come, but in the sense that he tells his audience, at risk of their displeasure, the secrets of their own hearts. His business as an artist is to speak out, to make a clean breast. But what he has to utter is not, as the individualistic theory of art would have us think, his own secrets. As spokesman of his community, the secrets he must utter are theirs. The reason why they need him is that no community altogether knows its own heart; and by failing in this knowledge a community deceives itself on the one subject concerning which ignorance means death. For the evils which come from that ignorance the poet as prophet suggests no remedy, because he has already given one. The remedy is the poem itself. Art is the community's medicine for the worst disease of mind, the corruption of consciousness.
>
> (*Principles of Art*, 336)

It is also clear from this passage that Collingwood's expressivism entails neither non-cognitivism nor individualism in aesthetics. Art provides knowledge of the most vital kind: self-knowledge. The artist tells his audience 'the secrets of their own hearts'. And this knowledge is the self-knowledge of the community. To understand an art work on this model is to share a vision and to be transformed by it. As Coleridge insisted: 'The postulate of philosophy and at the same time the test of philosophic capacity, is no other than the heaven-descended KNOW THYSELF!' (*BL* I, 252). Because art is not just a mirror of the mind, a *speculum mentis*, but of the soul, a *speculum animae*, the imagination can be a vehicle of self-transcendence.

Conclusion

J. S. Mill in his very acute essay 'Coleridge' observed that

> The influence of Coleridge, like that of Bentham, extends far beyond those who share in the peculiarities of his religious or philosophical creed. He has been the great awakener in this country of the spirit of philosophy, within the bounds of traditional opinions.[26]

R. G. Collingwood, one of the most influential and important philosophers of art in the English language, who produced a uniquely elaborate
and sophisticated theory of the imagination for the twentieth century,
was quite literally raised in the milieu of the Lakeland poets, in the
shadow of John Ruskin. In the early life and formative influences of
R. G. Collingwood we can see at work both the tortured genius of
Ruskin and, with it, the tangled legacy of Coleridge; in Collingwood's
metaphysics we find a magnificent development of some of Coleridge's
deepest interests in the relation between art, mind and society.

Notes

1. 'As my soul, looking through the eyes, draws near to beauty as I first saw it,
   the inner image grows, while the other recedes, as though shrinkingly and
   of no account.' Michelangelo, quoted in Anthony Blunt, *Artistic Theory in
   Italy 1450–1600* (Oxford: Oxford University Press, 1962), p. 63.
2. R. G. Collingwood, *The Principles of Art* (Oxford: Clarendon Press, 1945; first
   published 1938) p. 275. Henceforth cited in the text as *Principles of Art*.
3. *Preface* (1800), *The Prose Works of William Wordsworth*, ed. W. J. B. Owen, and
   Jane Worthington Smyser, 3 vols (Oxford: Clarendon, 1974), I, 126.
4. *Biographia Literaria*, 2 vols, ed. James Engell and W. Jackson Bate (Princeton,
   NJ: Princeton University Press, 1983), I, 293, 294. Hereafter cited as *BL*.
5. Coleridge, 'Notes on Poesy or Art', in *Biographia Literaria*, ed. John Shawcross
   (Oxford: Oxford University Press, 1907), II, p. 258.
6. Hans Georg Gadamer, *Wahrheit und Methode* (Tübingen: Mohr Siebeck,
   1990), pp. 48ff.
7. Plotinus, *Ennead* I: 6 (1), 1, in *The Enneads*, tr. Stephen MacKenna, ed. John
   Dillon (London: Penguin, 1991), pp. 45–7.
8. Blunt, *Artistic Theory in Italy 1450–1600* (Oxford: Oxford University Press,
   1962), p. 62.
9. Collingwood, *Principles of Art*, p. 219.
10. R. G. Collingwood, 'Facism and Nazism', *Essays in Political Philosophy*, ed.
    David Boucher (Oxford: Oxford University Press, 1989), p. 187.
11. Collini, *Absent Minds: Intellectuals in Britain* (Oxford: Oxford University Press,
    2006), p. 346.
12. Collingwood, *An Autobiography* (London: Oxford University Press, 1939), p. 101.
13. *Lay Sermons*, ed. R. J. White (Princeton, NJ: Princeton University Press, 1972),
    p. 109, p. 171.
14. W. G. Collingwood, *The Art Teaching of John Ruskin* (London: Percival and
    Co., 1891), p. 117.
15. Ibid., p. 15.
16. Paul L. Sawyer, *Ruskin's Poetic Argument: The Design of the Major Works*
    (Ithaca: Cornell, 1985), esp. pp. 95ff., and Richard Dellamora, 'A Victorian
    Optic: Translucent Landscape in Coleridge, Ruskin and Browning', *Prose
    Studies* 3:3 (1980), 271–86.
17. John Ruskin, *Modern Painters* (London: George Allen, 1898), vol. III, part IV,
    chapter XVI, p. 278.

18. R. G. Collingwood, *Ruskin's Philosophy* (Kendal: Titus Wilson & Son, 1922), p. 28.

19. *Table Talk*, 2 vols, ed. Carl Woodring (Princeton, NJ: Princeton University Press, 1990), I, 98.

20. *The Notebooks of Samuel Taylor Coleridge*, 5 vols, ed. Kathleen Coburn, Merton Christenson, and Anthony John Harding (Princeton, NJ: Princeton University Press, 1957–2002), V, 5495.

21. Shorey, *Platonism Ancient and Modern* (California: California University Press, 1938). pp. 224–5.

22. W. M. Johnston, *The Formative Years of R. G. Collingwood* (The Hague: Martinus Nijhoff, 1967), p. vii.

23. Ibid., p. 145.

24. M. H. Abrams, *The Mirror and the Lamp: Romantic Theory and the Critical Tradition* (London, Oxford and New York: Oxford University Press, 1953).

25. S. Halliwell, *The Aesthetics of Mimesis: Ancient Texts and Modern Problems* (Princeton, NJ: Princeton University Press, 2002), p. 8.

26. J. S. Mill, 'Coleridge', *Utilitarianism and Other Essays,* ed. Alan Ryan (Harmondsworth: Penguin, 1987), p. 177.

13
Eliot and Coleridge

Seamus Perry

T. S. Eliot's anti-romanticism was once famous, and his place within a broader 'classical revival' could seem clear-cut: 'classicist in literature, royalist in politics, and anglo-catholic in religion'. But then none of those terms is exactly self-explanatory, and perhaps especially not 'classicist', as Eliot himself genially conceded as soon as he had declared his position: 'I am quite aware that the first term is completely vague, and easily lends itself to clap-trap.'[1] The 'recurrent theme of Classicism versus Romanticism' that Eliot retrospectively identified in his earlier critical writings was often provoked by disagreement with Middleton Murry, and then the arguments quickly went beyond the merely literary:[2] 'the difference seems to me rather the difference between the complete and the fragmentary, the adult and the immature, the orderly and the chaotic.'[3] The net could spread very comprehensively indeed: '"Romanticism" [...] is a term which is constantly changing in different contexts, and which is now limited to what appear to be purely literary and purely local problems, now expanding to cover almost the whole of the life of a time and of nearly the whole world.'[4] So it might have been with his own expansive habits in mind that he told the audience of his Clark lectures in 1926: 'The words *classic* and *romantic* have been so widely employed that their contrast can easily be reduced to absurdity'; anyway, he swiftly exemplified the point by claiming that Pope, widely known as 'the first "classic" poet (in the Augustan sense)', was 'also one of the first "romantic" poets in my context of the history of emotion or sensibility'.[5] His deploying of the categories often has a scarcely concealed comedy about it like that. Eliot once deprecatingly portrayed his conversational manner as 'so nicely | Restricted to What Precisely | And If and Perhaps and But':[6] it is perhaps not surprising that he should have deployed 'romantic' and 'classic', in particular, with such nice, even fiddly, circumspection ('something which, for want of a better name, we may call classicism').[7] Sometimes he professed the common wish to do without them ('it would perhaps be beneficial if we employed both terms as little as possible, if we even forgot these terms altogether');[8] and sometimes he proposed exchanging the pair for something else, an antithesis more fundamental such as *orthodoxy* and *heterodoxy*.[9] But the words have always proved much too useful for reform, and Eliot utilises them in some of his best *mots* with great polemical verve, inspired by the feline acerbity of Babbitt as well as by T. E. Hulme's rougher stuff – 'Romanticism is a shortcut to the strangeness without the reality [...] there may be a good deal to be said for Romanticism in life, there is no place for it in letters', and so forth.[10]

Murry thought he sniffed out 'an unregenerate and incomplete romantic' beneath Eliot's classicist professions, a smart though obvious countercharge that anticipates a lot of scholarship over the last 50 years or so, not just about Eliot's connections with Romantic literary thinking but about the origins of English modernism more generally.[11] 'It is remarkable how often, in the history of poetry, it is difficult to distinguish *reaction* from *tradition*', Eliot himself observed, offering as an example 'the Romantic poets of the early nineteenth century' who, despite their revolutionary image, seem in retrospect 'merely to prolong with more excitement the language and sentiments of the latter half of the eighteenth' (*Varieties*, 198). In something of the same way, critics have frequently recast the modernists' reaction as prolonging a Romantic tradition. Frank Kermode's *Romantic Image*, for a prominent example, set out to describe a set of assumptions which though '[t]horoughly Romantic [...] are none the less fundamental to much twentieth-century thinking about poetry';[12] and, a few years before that, M. H. Abrams's *The Mirror and the Lamp* had maintained that, in Jonathan Culler's synopsis, 'a whole series of contemporary critical concepts, including those that one had thought of as antiromantic, had in fact been formulated by Coleridge and other Romantic critics.'[13] Actually, Culler makes the discovery sound a bit more of a surprise than it probably was: already by 1953, the year of *The Mirror and the Lamp*, Murray Krieger was complaining that it had become 'almost a commonplace for those who wish to attack modern theories of poetry to claim that the anti-romanticism at their root is itself essentially romantic'.[14] The argument did not need to be a mode of attack, of course. Abrams wasn't trying to undermine the modern theories, merely to trace their genealogy; and Geoffrey Faber meant no animosity when, introducing his collected poems in 1941 with a sketch of recent literary history, he observed that 'the anti-romanticism of the moderns is itself a variety of romanticism':[15] the idea was evidently in the air for a while before the professionals gave it decent footnotes. Faber happened to be one of Eliot's colleagues, and it is difficult to imagine that the poetry editor was entirely absent from his mind while he generalised about 'the moderns'; but either way, several critics and historians have subsequently fitted Eliot into the larger story of a Romantic continuity in one way or another – as they need to, of course, if the story is to hang together at all. 'Eliot found within the Romantic poets themselves, then, most of the ideas which he used in his critique of Romanticism', says Edward Lobb:[16] as a way of putting it that is momentarily puzzling but turns out to be useful, if the implication is that Eliot found something in the 'Romantic poets' (or in *some* of the Romantic poets anyway) besides their 'Romanticism'; and pursuing the point promises to tell us as much about those Romantic poets as it does about Eliot.

It is true, nevertheless, that the noises often sound unambiguously hostile. He memorably told his audience at Harvard that the literary history of the early nineteenth century was full of 'riff-raff' (*Use*, 105). Homage was to be paid to the more salubrious John Dryden, and to the poetry of the seventeenth and eighteenth centuries, which, 'even much of that of inferior inspiration, possesses an elegance and a dignity absent from the popular and pretentious verse of the Romantic Poets and their successors'.[17] It is, as Eliot says or implies in several places, from 'the work of Wordsworth, Shelley, and Keats' that the literary mind of the nineteenth century chiefly descended (*Essays*, 304); and, in the terms of his own historical myth, that lineage served to confirm the 'dissociation of sensibility' which had got into English poetry during the seventeenth century – a dissociation that left in its wake poets who could think, more or less, and poets who could emote, certainly, but left no poets with the absorptive power enjoyed by the metaphysicals, 'a mechanism of sensibility which could devour any kind of experience' (*Essays*, 287).[18] The Romantic period was not the origin of this dissociation but its intensification, leaving a kind of rumbling crisis in nineteenth century letters. Things might have worked out differently, for even within the Romantic age, as Eliot said in an early review, 'four of the greatest minds ... remained apart from the general ideas of the time', meaning Crabbe, Blake, Landor, and Austen. 'But the generation after 1830 preferred to form itself upon a decadence, though a decadence of genius: Wordsworth; and upon an immaturity, though an immaturity of genius: Keats and Shelley; and the development of English literature was retarded.'[19] In fact, Eliot says some warm and generous things about

Keats, particularly in the Norton lectures, where he describes Keats's letters as 'certainly the most notable and the most important ever written
by any English poet' (*Use*, 100); and while he was waspish enough about
Wordsworth – 'the still sad music of infirmity' and so on (*Use*, 69) – there
was manifestly admiration too, something I shall return to presently.
The appearances that Shelley makes in Eliot's prose are much more
consistently disapproving, as though he exemplified Romantic shortcomings embodied less purely or simply in the others (although even
here things are less than single-mindedly hostile once you look).[20] But
a broad picture of rejection and polemical distaste is clear enough, and
hardly to be dismissed as somehow 'merely' rhetorical.

None of this is disinterested literary history, needless to say, but a way
of trying to understand the present and to discriminate between its
various elements: it is the writing of one who is, in Eliot's words,
'absorbed in the present problems of art' (*Sacred Wood*, 37) and using literary history as one way of trying to answer the question (as he put it
later) 'How should poetry be written now?' (*Poetry*, 148). Throughout
Eliot, but especially in and around *The Sacred Wood*, what is wrong
about the Romantic poets (whatever their virtues) matters because it
gathers into the decisive wrongness of the contemporary scene:
'Because we have never learned to criticize Keats, Shelley and
Wordsworth (poets of assured though modest merit), Keats, Shelley and
Wordsworth punish us from their graves with the annual scourge of the
Georgian Anthology.'[21] These are the imperfect critics and the 'incom-
plete artist[s]' whom the young Eliot so deftly anatomises, self-cast in
the role of one who refuses to be taken in: 'What, we ask, is this for?'
(*Sacred Wood*, 7; 4). He was often tough-mindedly unimpressed by
Arnold too, but *The Sacred Wood* begins with an endorsement of
Arnold's view of the 'Romantic Generation' as having 'something pre-
mature' about it (*Sacred Wood*, xi); and for Eliot the immaturity and
incompleteness released into the tradition by the Romantics finally con-
denses into the iconic figure of Swinburne, who crops up again and
again in *The Sacred Wood*, a poet for whom 'the object has ceased to
exist, because the meaning is merely the hallucination of meaning', and
whose words, as Eliot puts it a little later, 'are all suggestions and no
denotation' (*Sacred Wood*, 149; *Homage*, 22). This characterisation of one
lost in a self-invented and self-intoxicating verbal universe of his own
owes a good deal to Arnold's tenacious portrait of Shelley, the 'beautiful
and ineffectual angel';[22] and in the later lectures on metaphysical poetry
Eliot makes an overt connection between the two poets, casting them
as a pair of exemplarily dissociated sensibilities – 'their minds were like

clocks hurriedly put together by the hand of a child [...] there is no real *intimacy* between the thought and the feeling in their verse' (*Varieties*, 175). Everything about Swinburne is dissociated, in an almost comically archetypical way: he 'is one man in his poetry and a different man in his criticism' (*Sacred Wood*, 5); he was, Eliot told his students in 1917, 'The pure romantic'.[23] And his romantic shortcomings are more than just individual flaws; they are the failings of modern literature at large:[24] for someone beginning to write in the first years of the century, as Eliot later remembered, 'The question was still: where do we go from Swinburne? and the answer appeared to be, nowhere' (*Inventions*, 388). It was to the French of Laforgue and Corbiére that Eliot turned: French poetry, anyway, was capable of saving him.

The place of Coleridge within this literary historical myth turns out to be unexpectedly intricate. If romanticism is the stuff of fragmentariness and disorder and chaos, then Coleridge's association with it would look damningly obvious. And indeed Eliot quoted approvingly Pater's 'admirable study' of Coleridge as an exemplarily deracinated modern:[25]

> More than Childe Harold (he says of Coleridge), more than Werther, more than René himself, Coleridge, by what he did, what he was, and what he failed to do, represents that inexhaustible discontent, languor, and homesickness, that endless regret, the chords of which ring through our modern literature.
>
> (*Essays*, 439)

Pater's next sentence, which Eliot does not quote, is: 'It is to the romantic element in literature that those qualities belong.'[26] Nevertheless, despite Coleridge's apparently impeccable credentials as a romantic, Eliot felt a keen and complicating regard too, one that lasted throughout his life. The situation seems to me rather more involved than, say, Eliot coming to realise that he was actually more of a Coleridgean than he had first thought: 'One reason for the gradual progress in Eliot's references to Coleridge from mild vituperation to unqualified praise', says Emerson Marks, 'was surely an awareness of how closely his own evolving conceptions of poetry had come to coinciding with those of his great predecessor'.[27] While there is obviously much that's right about such an overview, it attributes perhaps rather too great a sense of coherence to both writers' 'conceptions of poetry' – as though Coleridge's conception were something settled and singular which Eliot's might more and more nearly resemble as complications and misunderstandings fell away. What might have proven most fertile for Eliot's thinking was an altogether less resolved or consistent sort of inheritance; and the history of his response would then be less one of gradually coming round to Coleridge's view and more a deepening exploration of contradictions and perplexities common to them both.

(i)

Coleridge was the only major nineteenth-century English writer whom he could still read, Eliot said in 1955 – this being Coleridge 'rather as philosopher and theologian and social thinker than as poet'.[28] Eliot's later writings about culture and society are evidently indebted to Coleridge's social criticism:[29] *The Idea of a Christian Society*, especially, advertised its dependence upon *On the Constitution of the Church and State According to the Idea of Each*.[30] But Coleridge was also always, and crucially, a poet for Eliot – and, more crucially still, a poet-critic: indeed, he was the prime instance, along with Johnson and Dryden, of 'the critic whose criticism may be said to be a by-product of his creative activity [...] the critic who is also a poet' – the class in which Eliot 'shyly' placed himself (*Critic*, 13).[31] (And the class from which he excluded Swinburne: 'compared with Swinburne, Coleridge writes much more as a poet might be expected to write about poets' (*Sacred Wood*, 18).) 'To appreciate Johnson', Eliot told an audience in 1956, 'an effort of histor-ical imagination is needed; a modern critic can find much in common with Coleridge. The criticism of to-day, indeed, may be said to be in direct descent from Coleridge', a statement which would seem to include his own criticism among the descendants (*Poetry*, 104). The first critic mentioned in *The Sacred Wood* is Arnold, early in the introduction; but, as though to establish bearings, the first critic to appear in the opening essay is Coleridge, in the first sentence, which asserts an eminence: 'Coleridge was perhaps the greatest of English critics, and in a sense the last' (*Sacred Wood*, 1).[32] A little later in the book, Coleridge is ascribed 'natural abilities [...] more remarkable than those of any other modern critic', even though, as it happens, those abilities turn out to have been hampered by Coleridge's philosophical passions, his readi-ness 'to take leave of the data of criticism' and follow 'a metaphysical hare-and-hounds' (*Sacred Wood*, 12, 13). Eliot made much the same point in a radio talk in the early 1930s, contrasting Coleridge's criticism with Dryden's, and lamenting the way that Coleridge 'disappears in metaphysic clouds'.[33] These have been the formulae of hostile Coleridgean commentary since Hazlitt, of course – which is not to say that they are without their truth; but there is more to Eliot's Coleridge than them. For more even than regard there was evidently a kind of fellow feeling, even if that was not the sort of feeling about which Eliot could always be altogether easy. He told a London Conservative Union luncheon in 1955 that, of the great conservative thinkers, Coleridge was the man 'rather [...] of my own type', adding graciously that his predecessor differed 'chiefly in being immensely more learned, more industrious, and endowed with a more powerful and subtle mind' (*Critic*, 138): 'industrious' there is kindly chosen. Frederick Tomlin's memoir reveals that a picture of STC hung prominently in Eliot's flat;[34] and, according to Lyndall Gordon, Coleridge's *Letters* were one of the things that Eliot read Valerie during his idyllic second marriage, which seems a mark of devotion.[35] The sense of kinship could take droller forms too: in 1940, Virginia Woolf noted in her journal, amused, that Eliot was increasingly given to remarks like, 'Coleridge and I ...'.[36]

In the 'Experiment in Criticism' that he published in 1929, Eliot called *Biographia Literaria* 'one of the wisest and silliest, the most exciting and most exasperating books of criticism ever written':[37] that advertises an ambivalence. Eliot's most extensive account of Coleridge, in the Norton lectures given at Harvard in 1932–3 which were subsequently published as *The Use of Poetry and the Use of Criticism*, catches more subtly the mixed emotions that his fellow feeling could inspire. Eliot's principal concerns in the lecture in question (it is on Wordsworth and Coleridge together) are poetic diction and definitions of fancy and imagination, so the prose work about which most of the discussion centres is naturally *Biographia Literaria*, the title of which throughout the Faber text, oddly, is spelt '*Biographia Litteraria*' (an artful way, one might think, to rubbish your man). But, importantly, a poem informs much of what's going on too, both here and elsewhere in Eliot's long deliberations with Coleridge: 'Dejection: An Ode', which, says Eliot, a little warily, 'in its passionate self-revelation rises almost to the height of great poetry' (*Use*, 67). He quotes from the poem as he begins his lecture on Wordsworth and Coleridge, the longest verse quotation in the book:

> There was a time when, though my path was rough,
> > This joy within me dallied with distress,
> And all misfortunes were but as the stuff
> > Whence Fancy made me dream of happiness: [Coleridge has 'dreams']
> For hope grew round me, like the twining vine,
> And fruits and foliage, not my own, seemed mine.
> But now affliction bows me down to earth: [Coleridge has: 'afflictions bow']

Nor care I that they rob me of my mirth;
    But oh! each visitation
Suspends what nature gave me at my birth,
    My shaping spirit of imagination.
For not to think of what I needs must feel,
    But to be still and patient, all I can;
And haply by abstruse research to steal
      From my own nature all the natural man—
    This was my sole resource, my only plan:
Till that which suits a part infects the whole,
And now is almost grown the habit of my soul.

                            (*Use*, 67–8)

Those lines had long mattered to him: the four beginning 'For not to think' are marked in his copy of the *Poetical Works*;[38] and their terrible pertinence, and indeed that of the whole poem, for a writer preoccupied by the damage of a dissociation between thinking and feeling is very clear ('I see, not feel, how beautiful they are'). 'The lines strike my ear as one of the saddest of confessions that I have ever read', says Eliot, and continues:

Coleridge was one of those unhappy persons – Donne, I suspect, was such another – of whom one might say, that if they had not been poets, they might have made something of their lives, might even have had a career; or conversely, that if they had not been interested in so many things, crossed by such diverse passions, they might have been great poets. It was better for Coleridge, as a poet, to read books of travel and exploration than to read books of metaphysics and political economy. He did genuinely want to read book of metaphysics and political economy, for he had a certain talent for such subjects. But for a few years he had been visited by the Muse (I know of no other poet to whom this hackneyed metaphor is better applicable) and thenceforth was a haunted man; for anyone who has ever been visited by the Muse is thenceforth haunted. He had no vocation for the religious life, for there again somebody like a Muse, or a much higher being, is to be invoked; he was condemned to know that the little poetry he had written was worth more than all he could do with the rest of his life. The author of *Biographia Litteraria* was already a ruined man. Sometimes, however, to be a 'ruined man' is itself a vocation.

                            (*Use*, 68–9)

His audience may have been surprised by the friendly likeness with Donne, who had once been a hero of unified sensibility, one to whom '[a] thought [...] was an experience' (*Essays*, 287) – especially given that elsewhere in the chapter Donne reappears as a test-case of judgment to imply something wanting in Coleridge and Wordsworth.[39] But Eliot's sense of Donne had been quietly shifting since his essay on the metaphysical poets: 'In Donne, there is a manifest fissure between thought and sensibility', he had announced in 1931, as though Donne were now another embodiment of dissociation, rather than an example of consciousness before the fall.[40] The sense you pick up of Coleridge getting entangled with a more private pattern of interest and need increases when you hear the prose whispering one of Eliot's own poems ('Donne, I suppose, was such another / Who found no substitute for sense') and recalling a second ('These fragments I have shored against my ruins');[41] and the possibility of some personal involvement in this portrait deepens further when Eliot, who had 'a certain talent' for metaphysics himself, fleetingly allows an appeal to a more general experience ('for anyone who has ever been visited by the Muse is thenceforth haunted') – an appeal that doesn't rule out, while not exactly confessing, the testimony of his own experience. The flicker of self-portraiture to this version of Coleridge returns in the last lecture of the series, again through Eliot's invoking of a would-be notional case: 'poetry is not a career, but a mug's game [... the poet] may have wasted his time and messed up his life for nothing' (*Use*, 154); and you hardly need to know that he had himself worried, some years before, about seeming to have 'made a mess of my life' (*Letters* I, 266) to detect an oblique piece of self-disclosure going on. Belatedly, the closing words of the lecture series quietly confirm the hovering sense of identification: 'If, as James Thomson observed, "lips only sing when they cannot kiss," it may also be that poets only talk when they cannot sing. I am content to leave my theorising about poetry at this point. The sad ghost of Coleridge beckons to me from the shadows' (*Use*, 156). The graceful joke of the Thomson succeeds to an unannounced, gentler allusion ('What beck'ning ghost, along the moonlight shade | Invites my step, and points to yonder glade?') which unexpectedly invests the figure of Coleridge with something of the elegiac sympathy that Pope felt towards his unfortunate lady.[42]

(ii)

Just as Coleridge's poetry was hampered by his being 'interested in so many things' other than poetry, so what spoilt Coleridge's criticism, according to Eliot in *The Sacred Wood*, was that it was imperfectly literary: 'his centre of interest changes, his feelings are impure', and 'a literary critic should have no emotions except those immediately provoked by a work of art' (*Sacred Wood*, 12). He was, in this sense, an example of the sentimental reader, who allows 'a work of art to arouse all sorts of emotions which have nothing to do with that work of art whatever, but are accidents of association' (*Sacred Wood*, 7); whereas 'the perfect critic', whom Eliot identifies in the essay of that title as Aristotle, possesses a rigorously untainted quality of response and declines on principle to acknowledge within the experience of an art-work the existence of any other variety of possible experience. The standard feels recklessly fierce:[43] it is hard to imagine what criticism that carried the programme off could possibly look like – not much like Aristotle's for a start, or so you would have thought, since no appeal to *mimesis* (such as Aristotle makes) can get very far without the experience of a world without art for that art to represent. Anyway, whatever its imponderables, Eliot's strong attraction to such aesthetic purism makes itself felt in several places in and around *The Sacred Wood*. Poetry, he announced in an essay of 1919, was 'a means of communicating those direct feelings peculiar to art';[44] and writing in the same year, he praised the blank verse of Shakespeare's time for being 'the vehicle of more varied and more intense art-emotions than it has ever conveyed since' (*Sacred Wood*, 87) – such as a favourite passage from Tourneur's *Revenger's Tragedy* in which diverse emotions combine 'to give us a new art emotion' (*Essays*, 20). Eliot was not alone among his generation in his enthusiasm for aesthetic purity – Swinburne's intelligence was 'impure', by contrast, and his poetry exhibited no '*pure* beauty' – nor in entertaining the thought of an ideal aesthetic response of corresponding purity, 'a pure contemplation from which all the accidents of personal emotion are removed' (*Sacred Wood*, 39; 146; 14–15). Louis Menand makes a good connection between this aspect of Eliot and Clive Bell, who wrote about the way works of art evoke 'aesthetic emotions' (as opposed to normal ones), and instructed critics, in consequence, that properly appreciating art required 'nothing from life, no knowledge of its ideas and affairs, no familarity with its emotions'.[45] Eliot was drawn repeatedly by some such notion of a poetry autonomous and separate from the clutter and multitude of ordinary experience and emotion: his literary intelligence was stirred peculiarly by an awareness of what he called 'the limitations of art' (*Essays*, 111) – the categorical line that, by demarcating art from non-art, established 'the integrity of poetry' (*Sacred Wood*, viii). Consequently, his writings, especially but not only the early ones, turn about a refined and complex kind of anti-humanism or anti-naturalism: 'The business of the poet is not to find new emotions, but to use the ordinary ones and, in working them up into poetry, to express feelings which are not in actual emotions at all' (*Essays*, 21). Any criticism which sought to get at the secret of art by invoking the raw materials of the poet's biography was wholly misconceived, for it was precisely in the overcoming of those conditions that the art, as art, consisted. Batting off Herbert Read's and F. W. Bateson's different biographical accounts of Wordsworth, for example, Eliot complains that they are 'not relevant to our understanding of *the poetry as poetry*' – and sometimes offering any kind of explanation at all 'can distract us altogether from *the poem as poetry*' (*Poetry*, 112; 116). Variants of that phrase, and of its sentiment, occur in many Eliotic contexts: one of the problems of Milton, say, was the extreme difficulty of considering 'his poetry simply as poetry' (*Poetry*, 148) – which was the injunction Eliot had offered himself in the preface to the second edition of *The Sacred Wood*: 'when we are considering poetry we must consider it primarily as poetry and not another thing' (*Sacred Wood*, viii). That poetry *might* be taken for another thing – that it might be, for example, taken for religion – was one of the regrettable innovations of Romanticism: 'For Johnson poetry was still poetry, and not another thing' (*Use*, 65).[46]

Now, to find Coleridge wanting in his inability to grasp 'poetry as poetry', is, really, to invoke a Coleridgean criterion (though not the only Coleridgean criterion) against its framer: The phrase 'poetry as poetry' is Coleridge's own: he uses it in *Biographia* ('that poetry as poetry is essentially *ideal*, that it avoids and excludes all *accident*') where it forms a part of his own argument against confusing what's poetic with what's not.[47] The poet at the centre of that argument was Wordsworth, whose poetic experiments with ordinary language at once fascinated and puzzled Coleridge and provoked him over many years to theorise the ways in which poetry was autonomous and distinct from ordinary language. The theme first emerges among the surviving works in a letter about Wordsworth written to Sotheby in 1802:

> [...] *metre itself* implies a *passion*, i.e. a state of excitement, both in the Poet's mind, & is expected in that of the Reader – and tho' I stated this to Wordsworth, & he has in some sort stated it in his preface, yet he has [not] done justice to it, nor has he in my opinion sufficiently answered it. In my opinion, Poetry justifies, as *Poetry* independent of any other Passion, some new combinations of Language, & *commands* the omission of many others allowable in other compositions.[48]

Poetry is properly animated by an organising principle or passion peculiar to itself: as he put it some years later, 'Passion and Imagination are it's [*sic*] *most* appropriate names; but even these say little – for it must be not merely Passion but poetic Passion, poetic Imagination' (*CL* III, 361). In place of the provocatively artless criteria of excellence that Wordsworth adopted in the 'Preface' to *Lyrical Ballads* and elsewhere – 'nature', 'real', 'ordinary', 'common' – Coleridge sets up his own: 'The connexion of the sentences and the position of the words are exquisitely artificial; but the position is rather according to the logic of passion or universal logic, than to the logic of grammar.'[49] In *Biographia* Coleridge attributed the notion to Boyer, his brute of a headmaster: 'Poetry, even that of the loftiest, and, seemingly, that of the wildest odes, had a logic of its own, as severe as that of science; and more difficult, because more subtle, more complex, and dependent on more, and more fugitive causes' (*BL* I, 9). That is not exactly Eliot's sort of language; but the kinship of ideas is nevertheless very remarkable: he writes in the preface to the translation he made of St John Perse's *Anabasis*, 'There is a logic of the imagination as well as a logic of concepts.'[50]

Such a view of poetry and of the poet's mind implies a disparagement of the ordinary world and the usual experiences it might offer.

> O Lady! we receive but what we give,
> And in our life alone does Nature live:
> Ours is her wedding garment, ours her shroud!
>   And would we aught behold, of higher worth,
> Than that inanimate cold world allowed
> To the poor loveless ever-anxious crowd,
>   Ah! from the soul itself must issue forth
> A light, a glory, a fair luminous cloud
>   Enveloping the Earth—

The 'inanimate cold world' is the normal world, the world without imagination where ordinary people live: the doctrine contemns mass experience in favour of imaginative experience, and defines the one against the other. (I suppose the odd saving grace of the thing here is Coleridge's sorry inclusion of himself among the forsaken, which is most characteristic of him, a model of courtesy that his modernist successors did not always follow.) Those lines from 'Dejection' earned their most famous gloss in I. A. Richards's *Coleridge on Imagination*, which appeared the year after Eliot's lectures but drew upon Richards's earlier discussion in *Principles of Literary Criticism*, a work which Eliot quotes in

The Use of Poetry and the Use of Criticism and which, in turn, was full of the influence of the earlier Eliot. This 'inanimate cold world', says Richards in *Coleridge on Imagination*, is 'the usual world of the senses [...] the world of motor-buses, beef-steaks, and acquaintances, the framework of things and events within which we maintain our everyday existence, the world of the routine satisfaction of our minimum exigences':[51] it is this dismal everyday place that imagination transforms – so that, as Eliot once described the effect of the dramatic poetry he wished to write, 'our own sordid, dreary daily world would be suddenly illuminated and transfigured' (*Poetry*, 82).

'[T]he ordinary man [...] goes about in blinkers because what he would otherwise see would upset him', Richards had earlier written in (supposed) explication of Coleridge's theory: 'But the poet through his superior power of ordering experience is freed from this necessity.'[52] His rhetoric of 'ordering' draws on another way of thinking about the poetic mind that elevates it above the merely normal, which is to consider it godlike: the likeness is already implicit in the notion of the imagination as a bringer of light and life, and it is made overtly in many of Coleridge's most resonant utterances, pre-eminently chapter thirteen of *Biographia*, and also many times in the private writings. 'All other men's Worlds', he writes of the '*great* Poet' in the endpapers of Barry Cornwall's works, 'are *his* Chaos';[53] 'Imagination', he writes in the notebooks, is 'the true inward Creatrix';[54] and elsewhere, most strikingly:

> Idly talk they who speak of Poets as mere Indulgers of Fancy, Imagination, Superstition, &c – They are the Bridlers by Delight, the Purifiers, they that combine them with reason & order, the true Protoplasts, Gods of Love who tame the Chaos.
>
> (*CN* II, 2355)[55]

It is scarcely a Romantic brainchild that taming chaos should be a good thing, of course: Swift could hardly have written about orderliness with such testing irony ('Such order from confusion sprung, | Such gaudy *tulips* raised from *dung*'), nor about chaos with such appalled wonder, had the merits of order not felt to most blithely uncontentious.[56] But to allocate the divine task so emphatically to the poet is to place a new sort of grandeur upon verses; and many modernist writers picked up the idea eagerly, not only Eliot. As Kermode argues in *Romantic Image*, many of the central doctrines of the moderns might be tracked back to Coleridge and one or two others: there is no need to assume they all had their heads turned by the French. It is, for instance, in an entirely Coleridgean cast of mind that Eliot welcomes *Ulysses*: while his contemporaries saw a sardonic piece of mock-heroic, Eliot saw an aesthetic achievement. The Homeric parallel is not primarily satirical but a force for order: 'a way of controlling', as Eliot wrote in *The Dial*, 'of ordering, of giving a shape and a significance to the immense panorama of futilty and anarchy which is contemporary history' (*Prose*, 177). '[I]t is ultimately the function of art', he said years later, to 'impos[e] a credible order upon ordinary reality' (*Poetry*, 87). Taking a poor view of ordinary reality in this way is the trademark of a good deal of modernist thinking: that is the subject of Edmund Wilson's *Axël's Castle*. Yeats sounds like no-one but himself when he says that the poet 'is never the bundle of accident and incoherence that sits down to breakfast; he has been reborn as an idea, something intended, complete';[57] but he is nevertheless also very close to Eliot insisting that 'the more perfect the artist, the more completely separate in him will be the man who suffers and the mind which creates' (*Essays*, 18). Coleridge, too, liked sometimes to think of men of genius, 'a Shakespere, a Milton, a Bruno', as '*pure Action*, defecated of all that is material & passive' (*CN* II, 2026): the anti-naturalism of his aesthetic thinking is often very stark – as when he acclaims modern poetry for its 'under consciousness of a sinful nature, a fleeting away of external things, the mind or subject greater than the object'[58] – and its anticipation of the audacities of modernist notions striking.

The list of unconnected things which Richards attributed to the non-poetic mass recalls some celebrated sentences from Eliot's essay on the metaphysical poets, which describe the reformative powers of the poetic mind, and contrast them with the dissociated experiences that occupy the mental space of 'the ordinary man':

> When a poet's mind is perfectly equipped for its work, it is constantly amalgamating disparate experience; the ordinary man's experience is chaotic, irregular, fragmentary. The latter falls in love, or reads Spinoza, and these two experiences have nothing to do with each other, or with the noise of the typewriter or the smell of cooking; in the mind of the poet these experiences are always forming new wholes.
>
> (*Essays*, 287)

'The famous passage is most suggestive', writes John Bayley, 'though one may wonder if it goes much beyond Coleridge's remarks on the imagination as reconciling opposite and discordant qualities'.[59] Saying so is less catching Eliot out than following up his own lead, for in a contemporary essay about the metaphysical wit of Andrew Marvell he quotes the remarks to which Bayley refers:

> [...] the images in the *Coy Mistress* are not only witty, but satisfy the elucidation of Imagination given by Coleridge:
> This power [...] reveals itself in the balance or reconcilement [sic] of opposite or discordant qualities: of sameness, with difference; of the general, with the concrete; the idea, with the image; the individual, with the representative; the sense of novelty and freshness, with old and familiar objects; a more than usual state of emotion with more than usual order; judgment ever awake and steady self-possession with enthusiasm and feeling profound or vehement [...].
>
> (*Essays*, 298)

That is also the passage from *Biographia* (*BL* II, 16–17), in the abbreviated form in which Richards gave it in *Principles*, that Eliot quoted approvingly in *The Use of Poetry and the Use of Criticism* (*Use*, 79): the alliance of interests is clear, and there really isn't much in Eliot's notion of a unified sensibility which isn't already present in Coleridge's idea of the poet, who 'described in *ideal* perfection, brings the whole soul of man into activity, with the subordination of its faculties to each other, according to their relative worth and dignity' (*BL* II, 15–16). (Eliot offers practically a parody of Coleridge's inclusive ideal when he praises poets such as Donne for looking into more than just the 'heart' when they write – 'One must look into the cerebral cortex, the nervous system, and the digestive tracts': *Essays*, 290.) Coleridge often spoke of the poet in terms that combined chemistry and wonder ('He diffuses a tone, and spirit of unity, that blends, and (as it were) *fuses*, each into each, by that synthetic and magical power [...]': *BL* II, 16);[60] and Eliot followed him in that, as in the gas-jar from 'Tradition and the Individual Talent', in which 'numberless feelings, phrases, images [...] unite to form a new compound', and the excellence resides in 'the intensity of the artistic process, the pressure, so to speak, under which the fusion takes place' (*Sacred Wood*, 55). At one point in the Norton lecture, he seems even to credit Wordsworth and Coleridge with such a fusive and unifying sort of sensibility, as though, whatever he might have said elsewhere, they had somehow bucked history and achieved a pre-dissociated distinction after all: 'In Wordsworth and Coleridge we find not merely a variety of interests, even of passionate interests; it is all one passion expressed through them: poetry was for them the expression of a totality of unified interests' (*Use*, 81). Which is to say that they possessed, as Eliot had quoted Coleridge saying two pages before, 'the power of reducing multitude into unity of effect, and modifying a series of thoughts by some one predominant thought or feeling' (*BL* II, 20).

(iii)

Or rather, misquoting Coleridge, Eliot wrote: 'the power of reducing multitude into *variety* of effect' (*Use*, 80; my italics) – which doesn't make a lot of sense, but it is tempting to think it a significant slip since it so nicely implies a complicating preoccupation on Eliot's part: it is as though some aspect of him were unwilling quite to let go of the variety that was otherwise meant to be gathered into the unity of 'new wholes'.[61] That sort of complication, too, seems to me eminently Coleridgean: I have in mind here what Harold Bloom refers to as 'something dear to Coleridge, a principle of difference he knows may be flooded out by his monistic yearnings'.[62] By separating Fancy and Imagination, Coleridge tries to distinguish between legitimate and illegitimate kinds of unity: the first, heedless of any principle of difference, 'brings together images which have no connection natural or moral, but are yoked together by the poet by some accidental coincidence'; but the second somehow achieves unity while permitting the discrete existence of the various parts, a balancing act for which Coleridge habitually resorts to a rhetoric of organicism and 'life'.[63] (Each character in the Bible, for example, 'appears and acts as a self-subsisting individual: each has a life of its own, and yet all are one life'[64]). In his Marvell essay, Eliot is similarly trying to find a way of discriminating between different sorts of amalgamation: there are wholes and wholes, it turns out. Eliot concedes that Marvell is at times guilty of the over-ingenious 'wit' that Johnson had deplored as metaphysical wit in the life of Cowley (and which Coleridge had had in mind in his definition of Fancy): 'a kind of *discordia concors* [...] The most heterogeneous ideas are yoked by violence together';[65] but, at other times, Marvell rises to a richer *discordia concors* with a Coleridgean authority. Marvell exemplifies, in Coleridge's terms, sometimes 'but Fancy, or the aggregating Faculty of the mind', and at other, better, times 'Imagination, or the modifying, and *co-adunating* Faculty' (*CL* II, 866). Eliot worried similarly over distinctions between varieties of wit in his Clark lectures, where the salient contrast was between Dryden and Johnson: Dryden had 'a greater power of cohering a diversity of feeling than Johnson, and a higher conception of Wit', and describing that higher conception brings him very close to a Coleridgean idiom: 'for Johnson there is nothing organic about Wit' (*Varieties*, 192, 191).

The 'mastery at which the poet aims', Eliot wrote in 1931, is 'to mean as many things as possible, to make it both exact and comprehensive, and really to *unite* the disparate and remote, to give them a fusion and a pattern with the word':[66] the wording beautifully sets the numerous and the unified, the disparate and the fused, playing one against the other without settlement. What matters in all of this is less the coherence or otherwise of such nice distinctions, which are in truth curiously unreal; but rather the nature of the poetic scruple that they exist to try and assuage. A part of Eliot, as of Coleridge, evidently wished to hold true to the experience of differentness or opposition or discordance as it made itself felt in the world without art: the full effect of poetry, in that case, should not be the serene evocation of art-emotions left behind once the chaotic raw elements had been transmuted into something rich and strange, but a more hybrid, less pure sort of thing that, mindful of order, nevertheless managed to keep faith with the untamed multitudinousness that preceded it too. 'Dissonance, even cacophony, has its place', said Eliot (*Poetry*, 32): a poetry moved to reconcile opposites may prove as much a thing of opposites as of reconciliations. In the Clark lectures, he praised Donne for managing to represent 'an inward chaos and disjection' and still be 'pleasing': 'In order to get the full flavour out of Donne, you must construe analytically and enjoy synthetically; you must hold the elements in suspension and contiguity in your mind, as he did himself' (*Varieties*, 124). (Hard to believe that the young Empson, an undergraduate at the time, was not in the audience, but he said he wasn't – although he did hear Eliot speak several times during his stay in Cambridge.[67])

Eliot was always alert to the potential that any unity enjoys, or endures, to break down into its constituent parts. The 'substantial unity of the soul', the theory of which he adduced in the course of 'Tradition and the Individual Talent', could soon dissolve into something altogether less substantial or unified: 'a medium [...] in which impressions and experiences combine in peculiar and unexpected ways' (*Essays*, 19). The universe as described in Bradley's philosophy, 'only by an act of faith unified', undergoes something similar: 'Upon inspection, it falls away into the isolated finite experiences out of which it is put together.'[68] (And in a different way, the abiding interest expresses itself in Eliot's recurrent preoccupation with the nature and consequences of civil war.) His verse lives within this same dynamic field, a perpetual interplay between its component parts and its 'unity of effect' – as any poetry does, no doubt, but Eliot's more so, or at least more self-consciously so, as the verse insists vehemently upon the disparateness and multiplicity of its ingredients. So, in as much as such terms can be applied to real works of art at all, John Bayley is entirely right to see in *The Waste Land* a poetry of Fancy, operating through 'a highly deliberate juxtaposition':[69] the violence of the yoking has become a vivid part of the poem's harried emotional world.

> And when we were children, staying at the arch-duke's,
> My cousin's, he took me out on a sled,
> And I was frightened. He said, Marie,
> Marie, hold on tight. And down we went.
> In the mountains, there you feel free.
> I read, much of the night, and go south in the winter.
>
> What are the roots that clutch, what branches grow
> Out of this stony rubbish? Son of man,
> You cannot say, or guess, for you know only
> A heap of broken images, where the sun beats,
> And the dead tree gives no shelter, the cricket no relief,
> And the dry stone no sound of water.

The connection between the poem's starkly various voices is left obscure throughout: it would be off the point, say, to claim one somehow a metaphor or symbol for another, for that would be to invest one with a sort of precedence which the writing won't allow. The preface to *Anabasis* attempts an apology for the 'obscurity' of lines such as those, an obscurity due 'not to incoherence or to the love of the cryptogram' but to 'the suppression of "links in the chain", of explanatory and connecting matter [...]. The reader has to allow the images to fall into his memory successively without questioning the reasonableness of each at the moment, so that, at the end, a total effect is produced' (*Prose*, 77).

Everything depends on the management of the jumps: it is a modernist version of the eighteenth century preoccupation with the correctness of 'transition' in verse.[70] The abrasively heterogeneous Cowley, Johnson thought, followed the irregularity of Pindar altogether slavishly, when he should have been supplying 'smoothness of transition and continuity of thought' (*Lives* I, 47). But if you are after an English precursor for Eliot's obscurely juxtapositional art, a thing of continuity yet discontinuity, then the natural candidate would not be Cowley's odes, but 'Kubla Khan' – in Rosemary Ashton's words, 'perhaps the first great non-discursive poem'[71] – which proceeds, analogously, by the unexplained mosaic of voices and landscapes.[72] Or you might, perhaps, turn to the sort of effect created at the end of the 'Christabel' fragment:

> 'Why, Bracy! dost thou loiter here?
> I bade thee hence!' The bard obeyed;
> And turning from his own sweet maid,
> The agèd knight, Sir Leoline,
> Led forth the lady Geraldine!
>
> *The Conclusion to Part II*
>
> A little child, a limber elf,
> Singing, dancing to itself,
> A fairy thing with red round cheeks,
> That always finds, and never seeks,
> Makes such a vision to the sight
> As fills a father's eyes with light [...]

There is a subterranean connection between these verses which a different sort of poet might have drawn into a formal analogy ('As might a father [...] so did the Baron [...]'); but the poetry does nothing so explicit and quietly plays makes a formal game with its own irresolution ('*The Conclusion to Part II*'), while offering in passing a self-belitting description of its own fanciful procedures: 'Perhaps 'tis pretty to force together / Thoughts so all unlike each other'. You might risk saying that the relationship of one voice to the other is allegorical, but only in the elusive sense of allegory that Coleridge described in one of his lectures: 'difference is every where presented to the eye or imagination while the Likeness is suggested to the mind' (*Lectures* II, 99).

(iv)

A tenacious attachment to varieties of experience beyond the orderly space of art cannot but complicate any dream of aesthetic purism, either of composition or of response. 'I believe that poetry is only poetry so long as it preserves some "impurity" in this sense', said Eliot in 1948, disputing the notion of *la poésie pure*, and implicitly controverting several of his own early utterances (*Critic*, 39). In *The Use of Poetry and the Use of Criticism*, dismissing the idea that one might separate the poetry from the beliefs in Shelley or Wordsworth, he says: 'by using, or abusing, this principle of isolation you are in danger of seeking from poetry some illusory *pure* enjoyment, of separating poetry from every-thing else in the world, and cheating yourself out of a good deal that poetry has to give to your development' (*Use*, 98). Edmund Gosse, for a bad example, 'was interested in literature for literature's sake; and I think that people whose interests are so strictly limited, people who are not gifted with any restless curiosity and not tormented by the demon of thought, somehow miss the keener emotions which literature can give'.[73] The opening of the essay on 'Religion and Literature' embraces as a principle what the younger Eliot might have considered a slipping of categories, that 'Literary criticism should be completed by criticism from a definite ethical and religious standpoint' (*Essays*, 388) – even if, elsewhere, such a lack of purity is regarded as something of a sad neces-sity: '"Pure" artistic appreciation is to my thinking only an ideal, when not merely a figment, and must be, so long as the appreciation of art is an affair of limited and transient human beings existing in space and time' (*Use*, 109). 'A critic who was interested in nothing but "literature" would have very little to say to us, for his literature would be a pure abstraction' (*Poetry*, 116). As though to illustrate the point in his Norton series, Eliot invited his readers to contemplate Wordsworth's poetical career as an expression of his 'public spirit': 'I believe that you will understand a great poem like *Resolution and Independence* better if you understand the purposes and social passions which animated its author; and unless you understand these you will misread Wordsworth's literary criticism entirely' (*Use*, 73). These examples come mostly from Eliot's middle and later prose, when the ethical and social dimensions of the imagination were becoming preoccupying themes; but even in the more purified air of *The Sacred Wood* and its contemporary essays the pressure of a world without art manages to exert itself. In 'The Function of Criticism' (1923) Eliot names the salutary awareness of this pressure 'a very highly developed sense of fact' – Shakespeare's laundry bills are the mildly jokey example he gives there of the sort of possible factual discov-ery which might, in the hands of genius, find its proper critical use (*Essays*, 31, 33); but the teasing shouldn't detract from the importance of the prin-ciple. Incidentally, Eliot attributes his consciousness of its importance to his practical experience as a tutor, speaking to a room of ordinary readers: one good way of interesting the class, he says, is 'to present them with a selection of the simpler kind of facts about a work – its conditions, its set-ting, its genesis' (*Essays*, 32) – which is to say, the raw ingredients, or some of them, before their aesthetic transformation into 'poetry as poetry'.

As it gets itself registered in verse as a matter of style or voice, the 'impurity' that matters is called prose – that large expanse of language which borders upon verse and sometimes gets into it. Here, the most obvious precursor is Wordsworth, 'the poet of unpoetical natures' in Mill's phrase, whose insistence in the 'Preface' to *Lyrical Ballads* that 'a large portion of the language of every good poem can in no respect differ from that of good Prose' roused Coleridge to make his protracted case to the contrary in *Biographia*.[74] The similarity between Wordsworth's wilfully prosey *avant garde* experimentalism and that of the Men of 1914 is not difficult to spot, especially since Eliot drew the comparison himself on a number of occasions: 'a refreshment of poetic diction similar to that brought about by Wordsworth had been called for (whether it has been satisfactorily accomplished or not)' (*Poetry*, 35; and cp. *Varieties*, 388). Like Wordsworth, Eliot tends to conflate the notions of speech and of prose: 'the important changes in the idiom of English verse which are represented by the names of Dryden and Wordsworth, may be characterised as successful attempts to escape from a poetic idiom which had ceased to have a relation to contemporary speech', he says, setting out the reasons for his difficulties with Milton, namely that 'Milton does [...] represent poetry at the extreme limit from prose; and it was one of one of our tenets that verse should have the virtues of prose' – that, as he recalled in his Norton lecture on Wordsworth and Coleridge, 'diction should become assimilated to cultivated contemporary speech, before aspiring to the elevation of poetry' (*Poetry*, 160; *Use*, 71). The axiom that 'poetry must not stray too far from the ordinary everyday language which we use and hear' (*Poetry*, 29) implies a wholly different sort of relationship between the poetic and the ordinary to that implicit in much of his thinking: this aspect of Eliot has something in common with Ford Madox Ford, say, claiming that 'the moment a medium becomes literary it is remote from the life of the people, it is dulled, languishing, moribund and at last dead.'[75]

The assertion that 'verse should have the virtues of prose' (*Poetry*, 160) might seem as far from Coleridge as could be; and it is tempting to rationalise Eliot's romantic inheritance into Wordsworthian and Coleridgean elements, the first seeking to revitalise poetry with the language of men and social engagement, while the second incongruously encourages an emphasis upon the magically autotelic life of the poem. But that would be too simple a dichotomy, for ordinary experience and its language play a role in the rich confusion of Coleridge's literary thinking too. Critics tend to place Eliot within a romantic tradition by including him within 'the line of neo-Coleridgean movements in poetics, all of which in one philosophical context or another had affirmed the autonomous and autotelic nature of the single, lonely poem';[76] but it is the complete

Coleridgean pattern of inclination and counter-inclination that anticipates the great spectacle of the mind of Eliot.[77] Coleridge says in *Biographia* that 'a poem of any length neither can be, or ought to be, all poetry' (*BL* II, 15), a wonderfully ramificatory and in its context slightly surprising remark, but one which picks up on a practitioner's interest long held in the scope of poetry to encompass things other than the poetic: Eliot's interest coincides when he remarks in 'The Music of Poetry' that 'no poet can write a poem of amplitude unless he is a master of the prosaic' (*Poetry*, 32). Coleridge's invented genre, the 'Conversational Poem' (the subtitle to 'The Nightingale'), advertises its proximity to extra-aesthetic speech, and as it does so evinces some formative equivocation or chariness about the poet's readiness to rise to the poetic;[78] as does, in its different way, claiming to reprint 'Kubla Khan' as a 'psychological curiosity' rather than 'on the ground of any supposed *poetic* merits' (*Poetical Works* I, 295). 'The above is perhaps not Poetry', Coleridge wrote of 'Fears in Solitude', 'but rather a sort of middle thing between Poetry and Oratory – sermoni propriora' (*Poetical Works* I, 257): his version of the Horatian tag, properly *sermoni propiora*, also came to serve as the subtitle to 'On Having Left a Place of Retirement', originally called 'Reflections on entering into active life: A Poem which affects not to be Poetry' (*Poetical Works* I, 106).[79] Such self-deprecating gestures pick up on a whole range of intricate Coleridgean feelings of inadequacy, but also, more positively, they draw into the heart of the verse a fruitful hesitation about the absoluteness or exclusivity of a more self-possessed kind of creativity. Perhaps, historically considered, the most important work in this Coleridgean context is 'Dejection: An Ode', among the most audacious and original things he ever wrote. A poem which grows from the impossibility of poetry, it stands at the head of a long tradition of modern verse which discovers imaginative power in the course of lamenting imaginative desolation. Wallace Stevens's 'The Plain Sense of Things' ('the absence of imagination had | Itself to be imagined') would be a highly self-conscious example, but writers as diverse as Auden, Beckett, and Larkin write out of their own versions of such a predicament.[80] And so does Eliot, whose greatest poetry, too, often begins in the collapsed hopes of a grander or more self-assured sort of art ('These fragments I have shored against my ruins'). Eliot was famously a master of the strategically self-deprecating remark (*The Waste Land* was 'just a piece of rhythmical grumbling');[81] but what matters more profoundly than the deadpan humour is the underlying awareness that imperfection is the name of the game, and that consequently, in a sense, 'The poetry does not matter' ('East Coker': *Poems and Plays*, 179). Coleridge's poems repeatedly undermine themselves and throw themselves away ('Well!— | It is a father's tale'[82]), admit imperfection and apologise for their inadequacies: he creates the possibility of poems that are only incompletely poetic, existing somehow to one side of poetry, or at any rate to one side of the full and autonomous idea of poetry that he elsewhere theorised with such assiduity; and Eliot is one of his chief beneficiaries in this paradoxically enabling art – 'That was a way of putting it – not very satisfactory' ('East Coker': *Poems and Plays*, 179).

(v)

'Romanticism stands for *excess* in any direction', Eliot told his French literature class in 1916: 'It splits up into two directions: escape from the world of fact, and devotion to brute fact.'[83] Those extremes were, in various and moderated forms, the alternatives between which his own literary thinking pursued its course, at once wholly convinced of poetry's value as the transmutation of its worldly circumstances, but fully cognisant too of the diverse claims made upon that poetry by the persisting, unaesthetic world without: 'Even the purest literature is alimented from non-literary sources, and has non-literary consequences' ('Idea', 4). 'Romanticism' was often deplored in Eliot's prose for taking those possibilities too far, in one direction or the other; but then Eliot was very good on why going too far was important: 'Of course one can "go too far" and except in directions in which we can go too far there is no interest in going at all; and only those who will risk going too far can possibly find out just how far one can go.'[84]

Notes

1. 'Preface' to *For Lancelot Andrewes* (Faber, 1928, 1970), p. 7. Hereafter *Andrewes*. (Place of publication is always London unless specified.)
2. *To Criticize the Critic and other writings* (Faber, 1965), p. 17. Hereafter *Critic*. The lecture is dated 1961. Elsewhere in it, Eliot says: 'as for Classicism and Romanticism, I find that the terms have no longer the importance to me that they once had' (p. 15).
3. *Selected Essays* (London: Faber, 1932; third edition, 1951; repr., 1980), p. 26. Hereafter *Essays*.
4. Eliot, T. S., *The Use of Poetry and the Use of Criticism. Studies in the Relation of Criticism to Poetry in England* (Faber, 1933), p. 128. Hereafter *Use*.
5. *The Varieties of Metaphysical Poetry. The Clark Lectures at Trinity College, Cambridge, 1926, and The Turnbull Lectures at The Johns Hopkins University, 1933*, ed. Ronald Schuchard (Faber, 1993), p. 203. Hereafter *Varieties*.
6. 'Five-Finger Exercises: V. Lines for Cuscuscaraway and Mirza Murad Ali Beg', ll.5–7: *The Complete Poems and Plays of T. S. Eliot* (Faber, 1969; repr., 1982), p. 137. Hereafter *Poems and Plays*.
7. 'The Idea of a Literary Review'; *New Criterion* 4 (1926), 1–6, p. 5. Hereafter 'Idea'.

8. '"A French Romantic"' (letter), *Times Literary Supplement* 980 (28 October 1920), p. 703.
9. *After Strange Gods. A Primer of Modern Heresy. The Page-Barbour Lectures at the University of Virginia 1933* (Faber, 1934), p. 21.
10. *The Sacred Wood. Essays on Poetry and Criticism* (Methuen, 1920; third edition, 1932), pp. 31–2. Hereafter *Sacred Wood*.
11. Quoted in *Varieties*, p. 75. There is a good account of the long-running dispute with Murry in David Goldie, *A Critical Difference: T. S. Eliot and John Middleton Murry in English Literary Criticism, 1919–1928* (Oxford: Oxford University Press, 1998).
12. *Romantic Image* (Routledge, 1957), p. vii.
13. *High Romantic Argument: Essays for M. H. Abrams*, ed. Lawrence Lipking (Ithaca, NY, Cornell University Press), 149–63, p. 150.
14. Murray Krieger, 'The Ambiguous Anti-Romanticism of T. E. Hulme', *ELH* 20 (1953), 300–14, p. 300. Krieger has Yvor Winters particularly in mind.
15. Geoffrey Faber, *The Buried Stream. Collected Poems 1908 to 1940* (Faber, 1941), 13–22, p. 21.
16. Edward Lobb, *T. S. Eliot and the Romantic Critical Tradition* (Routledge, 1981), p. 74.
17. *Homage to John Dryden: Three Essays on Poetry of the Seventeenth Century* (Hogarth Press, 1924; repr., 1927), p. 9. Hereafter *Homage*.
18. There is a good and sceptical account of the theory in F. W. Bateson, *Essays in Critical Dissent* (Longman, 1972), pp. 143–52.
19 'The Romantic Generation, If It Existed', *The Athenæum* 4655 (18 July, 1919), p. 616; quoted in Louis Menand, *Discovering Modernism: T. S. Eliot and his Context* (New York: Oxford University Press, 1987), p. 126. Blake was not normally gathered among the Romantics until much later in the century.
20. Shelley is credited with 'one or two passages' in 'The Triumph of Life' that show 'traces of a struggle toward unification of sensibility' (*Essays*, 288). Those included, presumably, the section beginning 'Struck to the heart by this sad pageantry' (ll.176–205) that Eliot quoted in his talk 'What Dante Means to Me' (1950) and described as 'some of the greatest and most Dantesque lines in English': after quoting the passage Eliot comments, 'Well, this is better than I could do' (*Critic*, 132–3; 130; 132). Shelley makes one startling appearance in Eliot's verse: Reilly quotes at length from *Prometheus Unbound* ('Ere Babylon was dust, / The Magus Zoroaster, my dead child, | Met his own image walking in the garden ...') in Act III of *The Cocktail Party*: *Poems and Plays*, p. 437.
21. 'Observations'; *The Egoist* V:5 (May 1918), 69–70, p. 69.
22. 'Byron': Matthew Arnold, *Essays on English Literature*, ed. F. W. Bateson (University of London Press, 1965), 165–83, p. 183.
23. 'Syllabus for a Tutorial Class in Modern English Literature, Second Year's Work' (1917); quoted in Ronald Schuchard, *Eliot's Dark Angel: Intersections of Life and Art* (NY, Oxford University Press, 1999), 42. The classes were given under the auspices of the University of London Extension Board.
24. Cp. 'Eliot's countervailing hostility was directed against an etiolated brand of Romanticism that was working its way out in the aestheticism of his time': John Beer, *Romantic Influences: Contemporary, Victorian, Modern* (Basingstoke: Macmillan, 1993), pp. 226–7.

25. Although at the close of the essay Pater himself is said to represent this state of being 'more positively than Coleridge of whom he wrote the words' (*Essays*, 443).
26. Walter Pater, *Appreciations, With an Essay on Style* (1889; Library Edition, Macmillan, 1910; repr., 1920), p. 104.
27. *Taming the Chaos: English Poetic Diction Theory Since the Renaissance* (Detroit, MN: Wayne State University Press, 1998), p. 291.
28. *On Poetry and Poets* (Faber, 1957), p. 209. Hereafter *Poetry*. And his enthusiasm for the prose had its limits. He read Kathleen Coburn's selection of Coleridge's prose, *Inquiring Spirit*, but thought to draw the line at the complete *Notebooks* – 'I am not sure I should ever wake in the middle of the night with an overpowering impulse to consult Coleridge's notes. Speaking just for myself, you know': a letter from the 1950s, quoted in Janet Adam Smith, 'Tom Possum and the Roberts Family'; in *T. S. Eliot: Essays from the Southern Review*, ed. James Olney (Oxford: Clarendon Press, 1988), 213–26, p. 224.
29. They are well set out by Roger Kojecký in *T. S. Eliot's Social Criticism* (Faber, 1971), pp. 19–25. See also Emerson R. Marks, 'T. S. Eliot and the Ghost of S.T.C.', *Sewanee Review* 72 (1964), 262–80, pp. 270–9.
30. Eliot discusses Coleridge's idea of an 'idea' in *The Idea of a Christian Society* (Faber, 1939), 8–9, p. 67. The two works are succinctly compared, not to Eliot's benefit, in the editor's introduction to *On the Constitution of the Church and State*, ed. John Colmer (Princeton, NJ: Princeton University Press, 1976), p. lxvii.
31. Cp.: 'many creative writers have a critical activity which is not all discharged into their work. Some seem to require to keep their critical powers in condition for the real work by exercising them miscellaneously; others, on completing a work, need to continue the critical activity by commenting on it. Coleridge (if you like) had to write about others; Dryden had to write about his own preoccupations': *The Criterion* II (October 1923), p. 39. The sentence that begins with Coleridge was dropped when the essay, 'The Function of Criticism', reappeared in *Selected Essays*: see Christopher Ricks, *Decisions and Revisions in T. S. Eliot. The Panizzi Lectures 2002* (British Library/Faber, 2003), p. 41. In the essay on *Hamlet*, Eliot expands rather upon the dangers of 'the critic with a mind which is naturally of the creative order, but which through some weakness in creative power exercises itself in criticism instead' (*Sacred Wood*, 95). I should report that among Coleridge's excellences, in Eliot's view, was his skill as a '*tale-teller*', at which, more even than Chaucer, he rivalled Byron (*Poetry*, 196) – this making him a pointed contrast to Tennyson, who 'for narrative [...] had no gift at all' (*Essays*, 331).
32. 'The best Shakespeare criticism' was Eliot's succinct advice to his Elizabeth Literature class: *Syllabus for a Tutorial Class in Modern English Literature* (1918); quoted in Schuchard, *Eliot's Dark Angel*, 49.
33. 'John Dryden – III. Dryden the Critic, Defender of Sanity'; *The Listener* V:120 (29 April 1931), 724–5.
34. E. W. F. Tomlin, *T. S. Eliot: A Friendship* (Routledge, 1988), p. 237.
35. Lyndall Gordon, *Eliot's New Life* (Oxford: Oxford University Press, 1988), p. 259.
36. *The Diary of Virginia Woolf*, ed. Anne Olivier Bell, and Andrew McNeillie (Hogarth Press, 1977–84), V, 287 (25 May 1940).

37. 'Experiment in Criticism'; in *Tradition and Experiment in Present-Day Literature: Addresses Delivered at the City Institute* (Oxford University Press, 1929) 198–215, p. 202.
38. As noted by Christopher Ricks: *Inventions of the March Hare: Poems 1909–1917* (Faber, 1996), p. 274.
39. Eliot asks: 'did Wordsworth and Coleridge acclaim Donne? No, when it came to Donne – and Cowley – you will find that Wordsworth and Coleridge were led by the nose by Samuel Johnson' (*Use*, 72). But of course Coleridge *did* acclaim Donne – as Eliot himself later acknowledged, playing down the idea that he was particularly responsible for the Donne revival (*Critic*, 21).
40. 'Donne in our Time'; in *A Garland for John Donne 1631–1931*, ed. Theodore Spencer (1931; repr., Gloucester, MA, Peter Smith, 1958) 1–19, p. 8. Bateson (*Essays in Critical Dissent*, p. 149) remarks that Eliot's apparent repudiation of his earlier position goes unannounced.
41. 'Whispers of Immortality', ll.9–10; *The Waste Land*, l.430: *Poems and Plays*, 52; 75. The second echo is heard by John Beer: *Romantic Influences*, p. 230.
42. 'Elegy to the Memory of an Unfortunate Lady', ll.1–2: *The Poems of Alexander Pope*, ed. John Butt (Twickenham edition; Methuen, 1963; corr. repr., 1968), p. 262. The Thomson line is from his poem 'Art', l.34. Frank Morley, Eliot's friend and colleague, saw in the lectures' final turn to Coleridge a tacit acknowledgment of domestic unhappiness: 'A Few Recollections of Eliot', *Sewanee Review* 74 (1966), 110–33, p. 124. W. W. Robson writes interestingly, if severely, about Eliot's use of Coleridge: 'A Poet's Notebook: *The Use of Poetry and the Use of Criticism*'; in *The Literary Criticism of T. S. Eliot. New Essays*, ed. David Newton-de Molina (Athlone Press, 1977) 139–59, pp. 141–2.
43. Cp.: 'a standard so severe that Eliot sometimes gives the impression that ordinary life has no language to meet it': Menand, p. 130.
44. 'A Brief Treatise on the Criticism of Poetry', *Chapbook* 2/9 (March 1920) 1–10, 3. Quoted in Goldie, 63.
45. Clive Bell, *Art* (1913), pp. 16, 25. See Menand, p. 141.
46. Cp.: 'The most generalised form of my own view is simply this: that nothing in this world or the next is a substitute for anything else; and if you find that you must do without something, such as religious faith or philosophic belief, then you must just do without it' (*Use*, 113).
47. See *Biographia Literaria*, 2 vols, ed. James Engell and W. Jackson Bate (Princeton, NJ: Princeton University Press, 1983), II, 45–6. Hereafter cited as *BL*. See Paul Hamilton, *Coleridge's Poetics* (Oxford, Blackwell, 1983), pp. 135–85.
48. *The Collected Letters of Samuel Taylor Coleridge*, 6 vols, ed. Earl Leslie Griggs (Oxford: Clarendon Press, 1956–71), II, 811. Hereafter cited as *CL*.
49. *Lectures 1808–1819 on Literature*, ed. R. A. Foakes (2 vols; Princeton, NJ, Princeton University Press, 1987) II, 427. Hereafter *Lectures*.
50. *Selected Prose of T. S. Eliot*, ed. Frank Kermode (Faber, 1975), p. 77. Hereafter *Prose*.
51. *Coleridge on Imagination* (Kegan Paul, etc., 1934), p. 58.
52. *Principles of Literary Criticism* (1924; second edition, 1926; repr., 1934), p. 243.
53. *Marginalia*, 6 vols, ed. George Whalley, and H. J. Jackson (Princeton, NJ: Princeton University Press, 1980–2001), IV, 162.

54. *The Notebooks of Samuel Taylor Coleridge*, 5 vols, ed. Kathleen Coburn, Merton Christenson, and Anthony John Harding (Princeton, NJ: Princeton University Press, 1957–2002), III, 4046. Hereafter cited as *CN*.

55. Emerson Marks quotes the passage in his illuminating discussion of Eliot's 'neo-Coleridgean poetics', mentioning that Eliot could not have known the passage because the notebooks were not published until long after: *Taming the Chaos*, p. 300. As it happens, Eliot *could* have known it, since this entry was printed (in a lightly corrected form) in the selection from the notebooks made by H. N. Coleridge: *Anima Poetæ: From the Unpublished Notebooks of Samuel Taylor Coleridge* (Heinemann, 1895), p. 96. However, what matters here is not identifying a particular source so much as establishing a broader pattern of similarity, and many passages in Coleridge attribute to the poet the same sort of divinely ordering agency.

56. 'The Lady's Dressing Room', ll.143–4: Jonathan Swift, *The Complete Poems*, ed. Pat Rogers (Harmondsworth, Penguin, 1983), p. 452.

57. 'A General Introduction for my Own Work'; in *Selected Criticism and Prose*, ed. A. Norman Jeffares (Pan, 1980), p. 255.

58. *Lectures* II, 428.

59. *The Romantic Survival: A Study in Poetic Evolution* (Constable, 1957), p. 56.

60. A. Walton Litz suggests that Eliot's use of 'fused' might be mediated through Arthur Hallam's essay on Tennyson: '"That strange abstraction, 'Nature'": T. S. Eliot's Victorian Inheritance'; in *Nature and the Victorian Imagination*, ed. U. C. Knoepflmacher and G. B. Tennyson (Berkeley, etc., University of California Press, 1977), 470–88, p. 487.

61. The slip is uncorrected in the 1964 reissue of the book (as is the spelling of *Litteraria*).

62. 'Coleridge: The Anxiety of Influence'; in *New Perspectives on Coleridge and Wordsworth. Selected Papers from the English Institute*, ed. Geoffrey H. Hartman (New York: Oxford University Press, 1972), 247–67, p. 253.

63. *Table Talk*, 2 vols, ed. Carl Woodring (Princeton, NJ: Princeton University Press, 1990), I, 489–90.

64. *Lay Sermons*, ed. R. J. White (Princeton, NJ: Princeton University Press, 1990), p. 31.

65. *Lives of the Poets*, ed. George Birkbeck Hill (3 vols; Oxford, Clarendon Press, 1905), I, 20. Hereafter *Lives*.

66. 'Preface' to Harry Crosby, *Transit of Venus: Poems* (Paris, Black Sun Press, 1931), pp. i–ix, viii–ix; viii.

67. See George Watson, 'The Cambridge Lectures of T. S. Eliot', *Sewanee Review* 99 (1991) 566–83, 579.

68. 'Leibniz' Monads and Bradley's Finite Centres'; in *Knowledge and Experience in the Philosophy of F. H. Bradley* (Faber, 1964), pp. 198–207, 202.

69. Bayley, *Romantic Survival*, p. 56. The practical difficulties of trying to use the Fancy-Imagination distinction are nicely on show in Richards's attempt to expound the different uses in Shakespeare (*Coleridge on Imagination*, pp. 76–84), which ultimately relies on numinous criteria such as 'the fulness and self-completing growth of the response' (p. 83) to tell one from the other.

70. See the very useful account by H. J. Jackson, 'Coleridge's Lessons in Transition: The "Logic" of the "Wildest Odes"'; in *Lessons of Romanticism:*

A Critical Companion, ed. Thomas Pfau and Robert F. Gleckner (Durham, NC, Duke University Press, 1998), pp. 213–24; and for a most suggestive account of the matter see Jane Stabler, 'Transition in Byron and Wordsworth', *Essays in Criticism* 50 (2000), 306–29.

71. Rosemary Ashton, *The Life of Samuel Taylor Coleridge* (Oxford, Blackwell, 1996), p. 116.

72. As it happens, Eliot thought 'Kubla Khan' enjoyed an 'exaggerated repute', being somehow incompletely done: 'The imagery of that fragment, certainly, whatever its origins in Coleridge's reading, sank to the depths of Coleridge's feeling, was saturated, transformed there – "those are pearls that were his eyes" – and brought up into daylight again. But it is not *used*: the poem has not been written [...] Organization is necessary as well as inspiration' (*Use*, p. 146). Whatever the gist, let alone the justice, of the accusation, it is a Coleridgean criterion that Coleridge's poem fails; and, once again, allusion hints at private depths of self-entanglement, for the line describing a sea-change is not only quoted from *The Tempest*, but also from *The Waste Land*, quoting it from *The Tempest*.

73. 'A Commentary'; *Criterion* 10 (1930–1), 709–16, p. 716; quoted F. O. Matthiesen, *The Achievement of T. S. Eliot. An Essay on the Nature of Poetry* (1935; second edition, NY, Oxford University Press, 1947), p. 129.

74. *William Wordsworth*, ed. Stephen Gill (*Oxford Authors*; Oxford, Oxford University Press, 1984), p. 602.

75. Quoted in Menand, *Discovering Modernism*, p. 55.

76. Frank Lentricchia's synopsis: *After the New Criticism* (1980; repr., Methuen, 1983), p. 3.

77. Cp. with Eliot's claim, Coleridge's: 'Poetry must be *more* than good sense, or it is not poetry; but it dare not be less, or discrepant' (*CL* III, 470).

78. *The Complete Poetical Works of Samuel Taylor Coleridge*, ed. E. H. Coleridge (2 vols; Oxford, Clarendon Press, 1912), i.264. Hereafter *Poetical Works*.

79. Coleridge's version means 'more suitable for prose'. John Beer notes the variation: S. T. Coleridge, *Poems*, ed. John Beer (revised edition; Everyman, 1999), p. 110, n.

80. *Collected Poems of Wallace Stevens* (Faber, 1953), p. 503.

81. Quoted as the epigraph to *The Waste Land: A Facsimile and Transcript of the Original Drafts including the Annotations of Ezra Pound*, ed. Valerie Eliot (Faber, 1971; repr., 1980), [p. 1].

82. *Poetical Works*, 6 vols, ed. J. C. C. Mays (Princeton, NJ: Princeton University Press, 2001), I, 267.

83. *Syllabus of a Course of Six Lectures on Modern French Literature* (Oxford, 1916); quoted in Schuchard, p. 27.

84. *Transit of Venus*, ix; quoted in Ricks, p. 67.

Afterword

John Beer

As one surveys the rich discussions that have been generated here by the topic of Coleridge's afterlife, the quality of it that must stand out above all is its ambiguity. To adapt the classification offered by Lynda Pratt, those ambiguities were matters not merely of class and intellectual allegiance, but even of gender.

In the decade following the French Revolution, demarcations according to class began to dissolve, though they would continue to exercise an influence for many decades. Lynda Pratt can trace their presence in one of the notable Coleridge accounts of the time – the 'Early Recollections, chiefly relating to the late Samuel Taylor Coleridge', produced by his publisher Joseph Cottle in 1837 – and describe the anger which it produced in some members of the Coleridge family, including Henry Nelson Coleridge, who was married to the poet's daughter and member of a Coleridge dynasty already upwardly mobile, having established themselves among the middle-classes as a legal dynasty that would shortly produce a Chief Justice of England. She is no doubt right to suspect a note of snobbery in their hostile attitudes to Cottle the tradesman; though she also detects a corresponding touch of pride in his own case, directed towards a man who, having been in his youth a notable figure in Bristol society, had yet, like Humphry Davy, deserted his compeers there to seek the more inviting rewards of the metropolis.

It was London, indeed, rather than the Lakes, that provided a natural focus for Coleridge's lasting allegiance. He might align himself briefly with Southey and Wordsworth as they tried to stand aloof from metropolitan civilization, but he was shrewd enough to perceive where the sources of future recognition must lie. Cottle was annoyed that *Biographia Literaria* should contain so few references to the Bristol that could claim importance in having nurtured his career, but Coleridge himself was no doubt still smarting from the hostility that had been shown him there when he returned over a decade later. The part played by Wordsworth himself, meanwhile, was personal rather than geographical.

Personal elements were nevertheless crucial, since the family loyalty that led some such as Henry and Sara to insist that their relative had had an intellectual importance of a kind superior to any that Cottle might appreciate, also created a reluctance to admit some of the failings that writers such as Cottle noticed all too readily – particularly his opium addiction. Here again the contradiction was evident between his status as protagonist of the human will, pontificating from his Highgate dwelling, and as human victim of his own addiction, powerless to resist a craving for the chemical remedy that he was constantly being driven to seek.

Coleridge's reputation in the years following his death was dogged not only by this known addiction but also by his gradually revealed habit of unacknowledged borrowing – or, as it was less kindly branded by some, 'plagiarism'. In the case of both the opium and the borrowings, awareness of his habits was fostered by the journalistic gifts of De Quincey, who discussed them in various memoirs. But as Frederick Burwick has revealed in his painstaking and searching study, the effect of De Quincey's revelations extended well beyond what was warranted by the evidence, and probably well beyond what the author himself had intended. He would spend the latter part of his career trying to modify the effects of their implications in the face of a public only too ready to respond to what was most sensational. But as Burwick also points out, Coleridge's most important gift to De Quincey was to demonstrate the part played by the subconscious in mental activity, so that some of his most triumphant passages, such as his account of the Brocken Spectre, or the climax of his English Mail Coach essay, would display an intermingling of straightforward description and dream-play that owed a great deal of power to his predecessor.

As his defenders saw, posthumous hostility to Coleridge was often due to the fact that his human flaws stood out so much more boldly than his subtler gifts. If there was an ambiguity in his intellectual stance, for example, that was commonly traced to his dealings with the philosophy of Immanuel Kant, where it was all too easy to demonstrate the primacy of the earlier philosopher and the apparently subservient imitations of the later. It was less readily observed, however, that Coleridge's real dilemma had begun earlier, when, fresh from his discussions with Wordsworth concerning their developing philosophy of vitalism, he had found himself closely engaged with German students and their deep interest in pantheism. It was Spinoza who had first engaged his mind, as he tried to reconcile the attractions of his views with the Christian doctrines he had been expounding to Unitarian congregations; and it was from the matrix of that internal discussion that he had later proceeded to follow his German colleagues in looking for solutions by way first of Kant and then of Schlegel.

As Ross Wilson points out, the issues concerning his relationship to German thought were deeply muddied by the controversies over supposed plagiarisms, which led to consequent questionings of his originality. Once it has been accepted that there are within his text unacknowledged borrowings that are hard to explain or justify, however, it becomes possible to move on and examine the degree to which, in spite of that, he also had important things to discuss and question in what he found in the German writing. In this case the ambiguity of his thinking was particularly evident in his dealings with Kant, whom he at one and the same time respected profoundly for his logical mastery yet scorned for what he thought of as the naiveté of his psychological dealings.

Most of the essays in this collection are in some way inturned, devoted to the contradictions and dilemmas of Coleridge's personality and career as an English writer, but Daniel Roberts's piece takes such matters into a different sphere by discussing the degree to which his achievements can be related to world-wide trends of the time. One of the gifts pointed to by some as having constituted Coleridge's most valuable contribution to subsequent Victorian life was his conception of the 'clerisy', by which young men could be encouraged to offer their individual gifts to the service of the Christian community – particularly by way of the established Church. Roberts finds an equivalent pattern in Indian culture, in the persons of men such as Raja Rammohun Roy and Bankim Chandra Chattopadhyay, both of whom, in their varying ways, were endeavouring to restore to the Hindus the spirituality of their traditional religion.

It was not only in India that such a need for recovery of spirituality was felt. In America also, Ralph Waldo Emerson was pursuing the insight offered by John Stuart Mill, who saw in Coleridge's thinking the perfect complement to Bentham's philosophy – and here the matter of chronology becomes important. As one looks at the various influences from Coleridge that became evident in the century after his death, it becomes clear that in any particular instance a certain amount depended on the point in his career that had provided the starting-point. Emerson, for example, picked it up at the point when he had produced *The Friend*, the work that impressed him most and in which the status of Reason became a dominant theme, its superiority over the

Understanding providing the key assertion for what he had to say. When Emerson visited him some years later Coleridge received him coolly, delivering a long diatribe against the Unitarians which largely missed its target as far as his visitor was concerned, since Emerson was already not only disenchanted with his own sect but unhappy with Christian doctrines generally. The position that he was now taking up paid little attention to religious orthodoxy, working instead from a standpoint that embedded the Coleridgean exaltation of Reason's superiority in an enhanced view of Nature. He was thus moving on from Coleridge's delight in animated life to make that central, while ignoring more traditional religious doctrines, whether Unitarian or Anglican.

The need to take account of chronology when evaluating Coleridge's legacy applies equally at the other end of the century. Just as Emerson looked back primarily to the Coleridge of *The Friend,* so Pater, enunciating what he conceived the core of that legacy to have been, looked rather to his aesthetic judgment. Wilson shows, justly, that any attempt to relate that to Kant's *Critique,* if the two men are to be regarded as supporting a need for philosophical absolutism, is unfair to both thinkers. Both, he maintains, were at one and the same time distancing themselves from absolutism and relativism, employing subtle discriminations in order to do so.

By his later years, as Paul Hamilton points out, when he had passed beyond Kant to engage with the more sympathetic Schelling, Coleridge had given his lecture on the *Prometheus*, in which he set forth the concept of the 'tautegorical', which Schelling so much admired. But the focus of his concerns was still in England, where the lasting ambiguity of his legacy can be traced in the aesthetic of Ruskin, the feeling for 'Life' that had dominated his earlier years being enshrined as a central principle, while the materialism that Coleridge combated was given its due in Ruskin's deep respect for Turner's down-to-earth art and a use of paint by him that was winningly 'tautologous'.

With Douglas Hedley's account of R. G. Collingwood, we are closer to the fate of Coleridge's major concepts. As Hedley points out, Collingwood's own philosophy came largely by way of Ruskin, and Ruskin's paralleling of Hegel's work, so that in many ways he was participating in a side path of thought that owed little directly to Coleridge. Yet in one sense, and whether he grasped the fact or not, Ruskin himself, in his attempts to keep alive an emphasis on human spirituality, was plumb in the line of Coleridgean (and Hegelian) insistences. In the same way, Collingwood, sharing Ruskin's hostility to the mechanism of much contemporary thought, can be seen to have been one with Coleridge's honouring of humanity's imagination as its true guiding power.

With this recognition by one of the twentieth century's most interesting philosophers, the wheel was coming full circle, for some of Coleridge's most lasting legacies belong to that world of the imagination. As Daniel Karlin points out, the narrative method at the opening of 'The Rime of the Ancient Mariner' was not only startlingly original but can be shown to have left a clear mark on subsequent fiction. On a broader front, meanwhile, Seamus Perry is able to show that the relationship between Coleridge and T. S. Eliot was so wide-ranging and subtle as easily to transcend the terms of Eliot's supposed hostility to Romanticism. From the first, Coleridge's mind earned his deep respect – but notably as poet and critic, rather than as metaphysician. Here he was evidently influenced by contemporaries, particularly at Harvard, who appreciated most those who could be seen as forerunners of the imagists, with their delight in vivid language, and who were unwilling to look further into philosophical themes that might lie buried in the poetry. Thus Eliot thought 'Kubla Khan' to have acquired an exaggerated reputation, giving as his grounds the view that 'Organization is necessary as well as inspiration' (*Use*, 146); the idea (which I have explored in my own studies of Coleridge) that organization might exist in such a poem, but *below* the level of surface text, was not one that would have appealed to him. Indeed, as Perry acutely observes, the phrase 'poetry as poetry', which he invokes as a concept with which to flagellate many writers – including Coleridge – who, he thought, had mistakenly given weight to personal, biographical or social factors in making their evaluations, is one that can be found in the writings of Coleridge himself.

Eliot met Coleridge's ambiguities with ambiguities of his own, therefore. He was alive to many of the things that made Coleridge a great critic and an acute writer, yet had less sympathy with the searching, inquisitive speculative quality in the man that went along with his status as someone continually questioning the universe, trying to make it yield up the secrets of its meaning.

It has to be acknowledged, meanwhile, that Anthony Harding's piece, on the issues of gender, points the reader to the most complicated ambiguity of all; for it was the case that while his later works were directed towards the cult of 'manliness' his own proclivities were strikingly feminine. At a personal level, and comparing himself to others whom he admired, he might deplore a lack of manliness in himself: when, for example, he considered, rather enviously, Sara Hutchinson's deep respect for Wordsworth, he had to admit that to her he must appear the more manly figure; and when many years later he proceeded to publish one of his major prose works, one detects a touch of self-gratification in his description of it on the title-page as *Aids to Reflection in the Formation of a Manly Character*. Yet his appeal, during his career and long after, was more often to women than to men. His later poetry often appeared in the growingly fashionable annuals and keepsakes, with their predominantly female audience, while his major poems, along with those of Keats, Shelley and Byron, found an increasing audience among female readers of the day. In his Table Talk he pronounced that while strong minds often belonged to males, great minds were always androgynous. His own relations with women were often vexed: he could enjoy the work of a female poet such as Mary Robinson and be happy to accept her compliments, but his own dreams often betrayed his downright fear of aggressive attitudes from members of the female sex. Yet, as Harding has also shown, his own relationships of all kinds could include a concern that was strikingly 'feminine'. In the climate of Victorian England, with its public school training and its fostering of British imperialism, men might find some of Coleridge's sensitive writing sadly out of place; yet there was more of a gender-dialogue involved than is sometimes grasped. When Thomas Arnold, protagonist of 'manliness' in his shaping of Rugby School, was succeeded by his son Matthew as arbiter of British culture, this could seem a very natural progression, just as the stress on muscular achievement would be succeeded by the growth of the Aesthetic Movement with its stress on feminine aspects of the human; indeed, as Jane Wright's contribution argues, in the latter case a fine, and unexpected, line of connection can be traced between the positions of Coleridge and Wilde, since both men, with their androgynous natures, believed themselves to be finding ways of linking the moral and the aesthetic. As she points out, both adopted a similar defence against those who deplored the lack of 'moral' in one of their major works, maintaining that the main fault in their eyes was that each one had *too much*, obtruded too obviously on the reader's attention. The two men would of course characterize the 'moral' rather differently, yet it can be maintained that Coleridge's admiration of Shakespeare's 'myriad-mindedness' was subtly akin to Wilde's psychical adventurousness and willingness to explore new ideas and sensations. The difference was that what in many moods of Coleridge's was matter of hesitation and half-conscious shame would be in Wilde an occasion of bold assertion, with less sense of paradox. Just as Blake believed that Milton was on the devil's side without knowing it, so Coleridge was more attracted by the energy of the diabolic than he would ever have been prepared to acknowledge – and Wilde no doubt appreciated this. It was perhaps a result of this growing sense among contemporary readers of his subterranean adventurousness that led to Coleridge's own writings (as James Vigus's record makes clear) becoming markedly more fashionable at the end of the century, the publication of a selection of his notebooks under the title 'Anima Poetae', along with collections of his letters and new editions of his complete poems, heralding his twentieth-century reputation and finding new audiences even among the late Victorians – the members of which were no doubt distributed equally across the sexes.

Gender, indeed, can be regarded as prompting the most complex of the ambiguities in Coleridge's afterlife. Anthony Harding's detailed and perceptive discussion serves to bring out the variety of attitudes that could be produced in his successors, ranging from Hall Caine's respect for the strong masculinity he evinced in the years of his fell-walking to the suspicions of effeminacy that some of his choices for poetic topics might arouse. He also cites Swinburne's shrewd characterization of his gifts as those of 'womanly sensibility' rather than effeminacy, going on to see it as something of an advantage that 'his life and writings themselves tended to destabilize received notions of gender identity'. This is certainly an issue relevant to his lasting reputation, reminding the reader once again how crucially his legacies bear on issues that have been vividly alive in intelligent debates, both then and now.

Select Bibliography

Chapter 1 provides annotated details of bibliographies of Coleridge (see note 6) and of selected editions of Coleridge's works prior to the modern *Collected Coleridge*. Each individual chapter in this volume contains full publication details of all works referred to. The purpose of this bibliography is to provide a wide but manageable selection of the critical works referred to in this book. The bibliography thus offers suggestions for further reading on the topic of *Coleridge's Afterlives*.

Arnold, Matthew, 'Joubert' (1864) in *The Complete Prose Works of Matthew Arnold*, ed. R. H. Super, 11 vols (Ann Arbor: University of Michigan Press, 1960–77), 3, pp. 183–211.

Armour, Richard W. and Raymond F. Howes, *Coleridge the Talker: A Series of Contemporary Descriptions and Comments* (New York and London: Johnson Reprint Corp., 1969: first published 1940).

Rosemary Ashton, *The Life of Samuel Taylor Coleridge. A Critical Biography* (Oxford: Blackwell, 1996).

Jeffrey W. Barbeau, 'Sara Coleridge the Victorian Theologian: Between Newman's Tractarianism and Wesley's Methodism', *Coleridge Bulletin* n.s. 28 (Winter 2006), 29–36.

Jeffrey W. Barbeau, 'The Quest for System: An Introduction to Coleridge's Lifelong Project', in *Coleridge's Assertion of Religion: Essays on the Opus Maximum*, ed. Jeffrey W. Barbeau (Leuven: Peeters, 2006), pp. 1–32.

Beer, John, *Romantic Influences: Contemporary, Victorian, Modern* (Basingstoke: Palgrave, 1993).

Beer, John, *Romantic Consciousness* and *Post-Romantic Consciousness* (Basingstoke: Palgrave, 2003).

Caine, Hall, *Life of Samuel Taylor Coleridge* (London: Walter Scott, 1887).

Campbell, James Dykes, *Samuel Taylor Coleridge* (London and New York: Macmillan, 1894, 1896).

Coleridge, G. H. B., 'Biographical Notes, Being Chapters of Ernest Hartley Coleridge's Fragmentary and Unpublished Life of Coleridge', in *Coleridge: Studies by Several Hands on the Hundredth Anniversary of His Death*, ed. Edmund Blunden and Earl Leslie Griggs (London: Constable, 1934).

John Payne Collier, *Seven Lectures on Shakespeare and Milton* (London: Chapman and Hall, 1856).

Collingwood, R.G., *The Principles of Art* (Oxford: Clarendon Press, 1945; first published 1938).

Cottle, Joseph, *Early Recollections: Chiefly Relating to the Late Samuel Taylor* Coleridge, 2 vols (London: Longman, Rees and Co., Hamilton, Adams and Co., 1837).

Dello Buono, Joseph, ed., *Rare Early Essays on Samuel Taylor Coleridge* (Darby, PA: Norwood Editions, 1981).

De Quincey, Thomas, 'Coleridge and Opium-Eating', in *The Works of Thomas De Quincey*, 21 vols, ed. Grevel Lindop, Barry Symonds, Thomas McFarland, Robert Woof, Jonathan Wordsworth, Edmund Baxter, Frederick Burwick, Alina Clej,

Robert Morrison, Julian North, Daniel Sanjiv Roberts, Laura Roman, Barry Symonds, and John Whale (London: Pickering & Chatto, 2000–3), vol. 15, 102–25.

De Quincey, Thomas, Conversation and S. T. Coleridge, in *Works* 21: 42–70.

Dowling, Linda, *Language and Decadence in the Victorian Fin de Siècle* (Princeton, NJ: Princeton University Press, 1986).

Duffy, John J., ed., *Coleridge's American Disciples: The Selected Correspondence of James Marsh* (Amherst: University of Massachusetts Press, 1973).

Eliot, T. S., 'Wordsworth and Coleridge', in *The Use of Poetry and the Use of Criticism* (London: Faber, 1933, 1964), 67–85.

Ferrier, James Frederick, 'The Plagiarisms of Coleridge', *Blackwood's Magazine* (March 1840), 287–99.

Gibbs, W. E., 'Unpublished Letters Concerning Cottle's Coleridge', *PMLA*, 49 (1934), 208–28.

Gillman, James, *The Life of Samuel Taylor Coleridge*, vol. I (London: W. Pickering, 1838).

Goodson, A. C., *Verbal Imagination: Coleridge and the Language of Modern Criticism* (New York and Oxford: Oxford University Press, 1988).

Green, J. H., *Spiritual Philosophy: Founded on the Teaching of the Late Samuel Taylor Coleridge*, ed. John Simon, 2 vols (London: Macmillan 1865).

Gregory, Alan, 'Putting Him in His Place: Coleridge in the *Encyclopaedia Britannica*', *Coleridge Bulletin*, n.s. 20 (Winter 2002), 137–40.

Harding, Anthony John, 'Coleridge as Mentor and the Origins of Masculinist Modernity', *European Romantic Review* 14 (2003), 453–66.

Hare, J. C., 'Samuel Taylor Coleridge and the English Opium-Eater', *British Magazine and Monthly Register of Religion and Ecclesiastical Information*, 7:1 (1 January 1835), 15–27.

Harris, Kenneth Marc, 'Reason and Understanding Reconsidered: Coleridge, Carlyle and Emerson,' *Studies in Literature* 13:2 (Fall 1986), 263–82.

Haynes, Gregory Miller, *Coleridge, Emerson, and the Prophet's Vocation* (Ph.D. dissertation, University of Virginia, 1984).

Hedge, Frederick Henry, 'Coleridge's Literary Character – German Metaphysics,' *Christian Examiner* 14 (March 1833).

Hedley, Douglas, *Coleridge, Philosophy and Religion: Aids to Reflection and the Mirror of the Spirit* (Cambridge: Cambridge University Press, 2000).

Holmes, Richard, *Coleridge: Early Visions* (London: Hodder & Stoughton, 1989).

——, *Coleridge: Darker Reflections* (London: HarperCollins, 1998).

Hort, F. J. A., 'Coleridge', in *Cambridge Essays, Contributed by Members of the University* (Cambridge: Cambridge University Press, 1856), pp. 292–351.

Hunt, Leigh, *Imagination and Fancy*, ed. Edmund Gosse (London: Gresham, n.d.; first published 1844).

Jackson, J. R. de J., ed., *Coleridge: The Critical Heritage*, 2 vols (London: Routledge and Kegan Paul, 1970; 1991).

Kern, Alexander, 'Coleridge and American Romanticism', in Donald Sultana, ed. *New Approaches to Coleridge* (London; Totowa, NJ: Vision; Barnes and Noble, 1981), 113–36.

Kooy, Michael, *Coleridge, Schiller and Aesthetic Education* (Basingstoke: Palgrave, 2002).

Marsh, James, 'Preliminary Essay', in Coleridge, *Aids to Reflection*, 1840 (Port Washington, NY: Kennikat, 1971).

McFarland, Thomas, *Coleridge and the Pantheist Tradition* (Oxford: Oxford University Press, 1969).

McKusick, James C., '"Living Words": Samuel Taylor Coleridge and the Genesis of the "OED"', *Modern Philology*, 90:1 (August 1992), pp. 1–45.

Mill, J. S., 'Coleridge', *Utilitarianism and Other Essays*, ed. Alan Ryan (Harmondsworth: Penguin, 1987), pp. 177–227.

Newlyn, Lucy, ed., *The Cambridge Companion to Coleridge*, ed. Lucy Newlyn (Cambridge: Cambridge University Press, 2002).

Pater, Walter, 'Coleridge', in *Appreciations, with an Essay on Style* (London: Macmillan, 1910), 65–104.

Seamus Perry, *Coleridge and the Uses of Division* (Oxford: Oxford University Press, 1999).

——, ed., *S. T. Coleridge: Interviews and Recollections* (Basingstoke: Palgrave, 2000).

Poe, Edgar Allen, review of *Letters, Conversations and Recollections of S. T. Coleridge*, in *Essays and Reviews*, ed. G. R. Thompson (New York: Viking, 1984), 181–8, p. 181; first published in the *Southern Literary Messenger*, June 1836.

Pratt, Lynda, 'The media of friends or foes? Unpublished letters from Joseph Cottle to Robert Southey, 1834–1837', *Modern Language Review*, 98 (2003), 545–62.

Prickett, Stephen, *Romanticism and Religion: The Tradition of Coleridge and Wordsworth in the Victorian Church* (Cambridge: Cambridge University Press, 1976).

Richards, I. A., *Coleridge on Imagination*, ed. by John Constable, *I. A. Richards Selected Works 1919–1938*, VI (London: Routledge, 2001; first published, 1934).

Sattelmeyer, Robert, and Richard A. Hocks, 'Thoreau and Coleridge's *Theory of Life*,' *Studies in the American Renaissance*, ed. Joel Myerson (Charlottesville: University of Virginia Press, 1985), 269–84.

Snyder, Alice D., 'American Comments on Coleridge a Century Ago', in *Coleridge: Studies by Several Hands*, 201–21, pp. 214–21.

——, ed., *Coleridge on Logic and Learning* (New Haven: Yale University Press, 1929).

St. Clair, William, *The Reading Nation in the Romantic Period* (Cambridge: Cambridge University Press, 2004).

Leslie Stephen, 'Coleridge' (1888), in *Hours in a Library*, 3 vols (London: Smith, Elder & Co., 1892), 3, pp. 317–43.

Stewart, Herbert L., 'The Place of Coleridge in English Theology', *Harvard Theological Review* 11 (1918), 1–31.

Stirling, James Hutchison, 'De Quincey and Coleridge Upon Kant', in *Jerrold, Tennyson and Macaulay, with other Critical Essays* (Edinburgh: Edmonston & Douglas, 1868), 172–224.

Symons, Arthur, *The Romantic Movement in English Poetry* (London: Archibald Constable, 1909).

Wellek, René, 'Coleridge', in *A History of Modern Criticism: 1750–1950*, 8 vols (Cambridge: Cambridge University Press, 1981; first published, 1955), II, 151–87.

Wood, Barry, 'The Growth of the Soul: Coleridge's Dialectical Method and the Strategy of Emerson's *Nature*,' in *Emerson's Nature: Origin, Growth, Meaning*, ed. Merton M. Sealts, Jr., and Alfred R. Ferguson, 2nd edn (Carbondale: Southern Illinois University Press, 1979).

Woof, Robert, and Stephen Hebron, *The Rime of the Ancient Mariner* (Grasmere: Wordsworth Trust, 1997).

Index

Abrams, M. H.   220, 225
Ackroyd, Peter   150
Aesthetics   58, 105–6, 150–167,
    171–185, 200–1, 211, 213,
    220–1, 257; *see also* autonomy,
    aesthetic; *see also* Aestheticism
Aestheticism   77, 167(n.5), 168(n.8),
    201, 217, 247(n.24), 257
Alderman, David   169(n.41, 51)
Alderson, David   67, 69
Alexis, Willibald   46
allegory   90, 99, 193, 195, 206, 242;
    see also symbol
Allsop, Thomas   7
Anderson, Benedict   107
Anglicanism   57, 59, 68–70
Apostles, Cambridge   68
Arabian Nights   37, 132, 147(n.12)
Aravamudan, Srinivas   106,
    111(n.34)
Aristotle   182, 217, 233
Arnold, Matthew   ix–xi, 69, 74–5,
    102–4, 157, 159, 163, 174, 197,
    227, 229, 257
Arnold, Thomas   68, 69, 257
Ashe, Thomas   8, 10
Ashton, Rosemary   21, 173, 241–2
Asiatic Society of Bengal   87, 97
Athenaeum (English)   25
Athenaeum (German)   59
Austen, Jane   139, 226
autonomy, aesthetic   151, 156, 181,
    195, 244, 257; *see also* poetry as
    poetry; *see also* Aestheticism

Babbitt, Irving   225
Bacon, Sir Francis   113, 119, 200, 205
ballad   129, 130, 132, 167(n.2);
    see also *Lyrical Ballads*
Bankim Chandra Chattopadhyay   86,
    91, 93–94, 101–7, 108–9(n.2),
    110(n.20), 111(n.32, 33), 254
    Dharmatattva   93, 94, 101–3, 105–6

Barbauld, Anna Laetitia   147(n.12),
    164, 165–6
Barbeau, Jeffrey W.   16(n.2)
Barfield, Owen   127(n.22)
Barnes, Thomas   176
Bateson, F. W.   234, 247(n.18),
    249(n.40)
Baulch, David M.   186(n.6)
Baumgarten, Alexander   220
Bayley, John   237–8, 241
Beach, Joseph Warren   127(n.23)
beauty   157–8, 162–3, 214–5, 218,
    233
Beckett, Samuel   245; *Not I*   136–8
Beddoes, Thomas   28
Beer, John   viii, 247(n.24), 249(n.41),
    251(n.79)
Bell, Clive   233
Bentham, Jeremy   71, 72, 92, 95,
    102, 221, 254; *see also*
    Utilitarianism
Betham, Matilda   79
Blackwood's Magazine   36–9
Bloom, Harold   239
Blunt, Anthony   214
Boehme, Jakob   195
Boening, John   173–4
Brewster, Sir David   48, 49
British Critic   70, 176
British Magazine   39
Brocken   48–49, 51, 53(n.32), 253
Brontë, Charlotte   59, 64(n.5)
Brooke, Stopford   13
Browning, Robert   139, 141–2
Burke, Edmund   57, 69
Burwick, Frederick   5, 253
Butler, Judith   82(n.4)
Byron, George Gordon   9, 92, 201,
    257

Caine, Hall   77, 166, 258
Cameron, Kenneth Walter   125(n.2),
    126(n.19)